A SPARK IN THE SMOKESTACKS

A Spark in the Smokestacks

ENVIRONMENTAL ORGANIZING IN BEIJING
MIDDLE-CLASS COMMUNITIES

Jean Yen-chun Lin

Columbia University Press
Publishers Since 1893
New York   Chichester, West Sussex
cup.columbia.edu

Copyright © 2023 Columbia University Press
All rights reserved

Library of Congress Cataloging-in-Publication Data
Names: Lin, Jean Yen-chun, author.
Title: A spark in the smokestacks : environmental organizing in Beijing middle-class communities / Jean Yen-chun Lin, California State University, East Bay.
Description: [New York] : [Columbia University Press], [2023] | Includes bibliographical references and index.
Identifiers: LCCN 2022060739 | ISBN 9780231194501 (hardback) | ISBN 9780231194518 (trade paperback) | ISBN 9780231550864 (ebook)
Subjects: LCSH: Middle class—China—Beijing. | Neighborhoods—China—Beijing. | Housing—China—Beijing. | Beijing (China)—Economic conditions.
Classification: LCC HT690.C55 L539 2023 | DDC 305.5/50951—dc23/eng/20230109
LC record available at https://lccn.loc.gov/2022060739

Cover design: Noah Arlow
Cover image: Shutterstock

For Tarak and Killua

CONTENTS

PREFACE ix

Introduction 1

Chapter One
A Stench on Success: Urban Middle-Class Homeowners
and Rising Environmental Challenges 27

Chapter Two
Gated Communities as Schools of Democracy 48

Chapter Three
Making Sense of External Threats: Individual, Collective,
and Representative Responses 85

Chapter Four
Mobilizing and Organizing for Environmental Collective Action 123

Chapter Five
Trajectories of Citizen Science 163

Chapter Six
Consequences of Community Environmental Organizing 208

Conclusion 253

NOTES 271

BIBLIOGRAPHY 301

INDEX 313

PREFACE

I spent the first few years of my life in Taipei. As a child, I remember my dad working two jobs—an assistant at a research center during the day and an editor at a newspaper agency overnight. After he would leave for work in the evenings, my mom and I strolled in the alleyways, always greeting the noodle shop owner next door, and sometimes stopping to watch the traditional glove puppetry shows hosted by the community temple. On hot nights, neighbors in the same alley would be sitting on their stoops, or on little stools, fanning their straw fans, conversing with their family members. One year, during a massive flood after a typhoon, I had no recollection of emergency personnel showing up. Instead, what I remember was that the neighbors we sometimes casually greeted all came out to help, clearing mud and branches from clogged gutters.

When I was six years old, my family immigrated to a small town two hours outside of Chicago, Illinois. A family car was a necessity for the first time, as no amenities were within walking distance. There were no roadside vendors, only super stores with humongous parking lots. We rarely saw neighbors, except for occasional block parties, where we learned the meaning of "communal potluck." Without even knowing the English alphabet, I was sent to a public elementary school, where I was the only kid of Asian descent. Three years of social studies and civics classes later, I started my first petition at the age of nine, protesting changes that had been made to a schoolwide writing competition, convincing classmates to sign it on the playground. Despite my efforts, no rule changes were made. The following year, my classmates and I were visited by education officials from Ukraine. Upon hearing the under-resourced school environments experienced by Ukrainian kids, I stayed after school—going from classroom to classroom—asking each teacher to donate school supplies, which I collected in a shoebox. Looking back, even as a kid, I believed in the power of many to achieve change.

At the age of fifteen, I became a "reverse immigrant," returning to Taiwan, just in time to prepare for high school entrance exams in a language (Mandarin) that I only had a conversational grasp of. Immersed in a public junior high school, I learned reading and writing almost from scratch. We moved back into our old home, in the same alleyway—the noodle vendor was now a much larger shop, and a new flower shop had opened in the alley. Nevertheless, I could still recognize most of our immediate neighbors. However, I suddenly became uncomfortably aware that we were always walking in the middle of roads with no sidewalks, squeezing by cars and motorized scooters. The small-town space I had grown accustomed to in Illinois was a thing of the past.

These foundational early life events informed my research in many ways: I began comparing the residential and public spaces, and how people interacted differently because of these spatial setups. I went out of my way to observe interactions between neighbors when a shared challenge emerged. I carefully reflected on my own participation in community affairs. Additionally, these cross-cultural experiences, though challenging growing up, led me to be fully bilingual (English and Mandarin) in reading, writing, and speaking, picking up linguistic cultural nuances along the way. I was not just learning a language—I needed it to *participate in* and understand the environment around me.

Two entrance exams later, I was accepted into National Taiwan University in Taipei. At the time, my dream job was to become a simultaneous interpreter and work for the United Nations (UN) in areas of humanitarian aid and disaster relief. Due to the diplomatic situation of Taiwan (not a UN member), I eventually went down a different path for graduate school, studying International Relations and Sociology, further developing my interests in the provision of community relief and services, as well as the building of community capacity and resiliency. Particularly, I wanted to know how community-building efforts might vary in countries with drastically different regime types. How might participation in this process differ for citizen groups under unique political circumstances? My curiosities led me to Beijing, where this project began.

Still, my simultaneous interpreting experiences and translation training in college remained relevant, having taught me the importance of upholding cultural context as a translator. To show respect to the participants whose quotes I used for this book, I made every effort to translate in a way that preserves and showcases culture-specific meanings, humor, and emotions. Even though I must preserve their anonymity, I am truly grateful for their contributions to this book, and for entrusting me with telling their story.

This project could not have been accomplished without the help and support of many individuals and institutions. I would say that my research journey truly started at the University of Chicago. There, I was lucky to have Professor Dingxin Zhao as my mentor. He not only introduced me to Sociology as a field, but also how to navigate field work in China, providing me with connections in local academia and in government. I also express my gratitude to my other dissertation committee members, Dan Slater and Terry Clark, who provided helpful suggestions since the very beginning of the project. I also received support from Cheol-sung Lee, who offered me feedback throughout the research process.

I am so appreciative of the support I received at the Stanford Center on Philanthropy and Civil Society (PACS), where I did my postdoctoral fellowship. As my mentor, Woody Powell played a pivotal role during my time at Stanford, helping me develop a sense of myself as a researcher and as who I wanted to be as a scholar. I would not be where I am today without his guidance and friendship. I also am grateful for all the long discussions with coauthor, friend, and writing buddy Aaron Horvath that pushed me to strive for research that could reach audiences beyond academia. Kim Meredith, who was the Executive Director of Stanford PACS at the time, not only cultivated a supportive postdoc environment, but also encouraged me every step of the way. I also want to thank my colleague Valerie Dao, who supported me as a friend and as a scholar. Val helped organize the book conference at which an early draft of the manuscript was presented. I benefited immensely from the book conference, where Andy Walder,

Sarah Soule, Ed Walker, Woody Powell, Aaron Horvath, and Christof Brandtner offered invaluable input that shaped the trajectory of this book. I am so thankful to have had that opportunity. Other friends and colleagues at Stanford played a role in the book-writing process: I especially thank everyone from the Stanford PACS Workshop (where we conceived the name of this book) and the Networks and Organizations Workshop who read and commented on chapter drafts during the book development process. I am also thankful to Ada Zhou, for her diligent research assistance and computer science expertise.

This project received financial support from the Department of Sociology at the University of Chicago, the Center on East Asian Studies at the University of Chicago, the American Journal of Sociology Graduate Student Fund, as well as the Stanford Center on Philanthropy and Society.

I feel privileged to work as a faculty member in the Department of Sociology at Cal State East Bay, where I receive support from the department, all my colleagues, and the students. My students at this public institution, the majority of whom are first-generation college students, truly push me to think about how this book, even though situated in urban Beijing, connects in many ways to our local communities here in California, whether on issues of housing, of community empowerment, or grassroots leadership.

I am also indebted to the remarkable editors who helped me reach the finish line with the book. I am extremely grateful for Elisabeth Andrews, who read closely read the chapters and commented on them. I also want to thank my Columbia University Press editor, Eric Schwartz, who believed in my vision for the book since the very first time we spoke. He understood that it was important to me that the writing style of the book remain approachable to a wide range of readers, even though the style is somewhat unconventional.

In closing, I dedicate this book to my family. To my dad, a.k.a. my favorite political scientist and the reason I became interested in the role of civil society in China. To my mom, who nurtured my bilingual abilities and helped me relearn Mandarin. And to my brother, Clement, who kept me sane throughout my academic journey, whether it was through fantasy basketball or online gaming. We always loved city-building and simulation games, which in many ways, captured my interests in how cities function.

PREFACE

Most importantly, I thank my partner for life, Tarak Trivedi, a die-hard Detroiter, whom I met in graduate school at the University of Chicago—an Obama–Romney debate dorm party to be precise. We grew together as researchers over the years, albeit in very different fields—him in Emergency Medicine and me in Sociology. But one thing that ties us together is our belief in the public system, working within it in hopes of improving access to healthcare services, access to education, and access to information. When we travel, we share a love for cities, learning everything we can about their histories, cultures, peoples, and public space designs. I see the reflections of so many of our conversations throughout this book, especially around people and their relationships to urban spaces. Last but not least, I dedicate this book to Killua, the best academic support dog. He has loyally sat at my side during all-day and all-night writing sessions, reminding me to step outside and enjoy the sunshine. Without the support of everyone here, this book could not have happened.

A SPARK IN THE SMOKESTACKS

Introduction

Neighborhood organizations have long been understood as sites of collective action in democratic contexts. But what happens when middle-class home ownership springs up for the first time in an authoritarian setting? What does associational life rooted in new middle-class housing communities look like? Can urban homeownership cultivate civic skills and capacity for organizing under authoritarian rule? In what ways and to what extent does the state shape homeowners' sense of civic responsibility?

Centering on three newly constructed gated homeowners' communities in Beijing—which I refer to pseudonymously as Community Meadow, Community Rose, and Community Marigold—this book tells a story of associational life among the emerging middle class in urban China. By delving into these housing communities' histories and conversations, and following the grassroots development of their respective movements, this investigation reveals how Chinese housing communities can act as "schools of democracy," cultivating civic skills among homeowners and building civic capacity in communities through informal civic life. As a result, middle-class communities have become wellsprings for collective organizing in this most unlikely of places.

The premise for this book arose from observing these three gated housing communities, located in different parts of Beijing, facing similar situations during the five-year span from 2006 to 2011. Communities Meadow,

INTRODUCTION

Rose, and Marigold were each located near a landfill reaching maximum capacity, with an incinerator slated to be built to manage the trash problem. In all three cases, community organizations formed and mobilized in opposition to the incinerator projects. How these organizations came into being—and what made some of their efforts more successful and more durable than others—are questions I hoped to answer when I first headed to Beijing in 2009.

A COMMUNITY TOUR

The first time I visited Community Meadow, on the west side of Beijing, it was a very cold day in the dead of winter. It was my first venture into one of the middle-class homeowners' gated communities that are now common throughout Chinese cities, a historical trend described in chapter 1. Because middle-class gated communities in China are referred to as "communities" in conventional literature,[1] I use the word "community" when describing these housing complexes. This concept is similar, in the physical sense, to the idea of a "tertiary-street community": residential units organized in aggregations of low-traffic intersections and street blocks that are accessible by pedestrians without requiring them to cross a major road.[2] In this setting, several gated communities make up what I refer to as a "neighborhood": a larger area in which several gated communities are situated, incorporating local amenities, schools, parks . . . and landfills.[3]

I arranged for the visit after learning that Community Meadow homeowners had organized to protest against incinerator construction, which led the government to postpone the project until further environmental evaluations were made. At the time of our meeting, the homeowners were still anxiously waiting to hear back from municipal agencies. I was fortunate to be able to access this community through a personal connection with a staff member of an environmental nonprofit organization. Had it not been for his work with homeowners on trash separation that year, I—a California resident with roots in Taiwan—would have been unlikely to establish contact with local residents. The trip gave me the opportunity to understand the newly formed associational relationships through the eyes of homeowners, to learn how they made sense of their surroundings, including shared spaces in the gated community, the local restaurant and event space, the polluting brick factory nearby, and the landfill.

INTRODUCTION

The gated community was different from what I had pictured when imagining housing for thousands of people adjacent to a landfill. I expected to find a run-down, underdeveloped area, but the surroundings were spacious, with blocks of attractive, newly constructed buildings. Beyond the concrete walls that enclosed the community, the residential buildings were each around eight stories high, with dozens of buildings arranged in clustered complexes spanning the equivalent of several city blocks. The buildings were bright and colorful—orange and yellow—juxtaposing the gray sky.

I approached a security guard at one of the entrances to the community. He directed me to a clipboard on which all visitors were required to sign in, reflecting surveillance that would only intensify in the years to come. Walking through the complex, I passed by community courtyards in which a handful of older residents walked with their grandchildren, all wearing winter coats and face masks. A community pond was surrounded by small stone stools. The landscaping was meticulous and beautiful, despite the freezing temperatures, and I was in awe of the vastness of the grounds and the abundance of shared communal spaces. In Beijing—a city known for its congested sidewalks, streets, traffic, and public transportation—it is uncommon to experience such spaciousness. While there are sizable city parks, I had never before seen such large *residential community* spaces (figure 0.1).

Although I was beginning to understand how the space fostered interaction among residents, it was hard for me to imagine that an environmental resistance movement had emerged in this quiet community. I was still more surprised after meeting the movement's unlikely leader, Huang *laoshi* ("teacher"), profiled in chapter 3 and 4. Huang *laoshi*, then seventy years old, had a stern demeanor, walking and talking briskly.[4] He told me that, like many of the other community homeowners, he had saved money to buy one of the newly built commodity apartments (*shangping fang*) in preparation for retirement. He had moved in less than five years before my visit and lived with his wife, daughter, son-in-law, and a grandson, whom he cared for during the day. Family life seemed to keep him occupied, yet he had somehow found time to organize for collective action.

I encountered the first of many seeming contradictions in the community's approach to waste management when we passed by a long row of trash and recycling bins near one of the community entrances. The Beijing municipal government was promoting trash separation—a policy that

FIGURE 0.1. Community Meadow, a typical middle-class gated community in urban China.
Source: Photos provided by homeowners.

INTRODUCTION

started around the time of the 2008 Olympics, when an influx of international visitors overwhelmed Beijing landfills—encouraging urban residents to recycle to alleviate the growing urban waste problem. Curious about the success of this effort, I lifted a few of the lids and saw trash in every bin, regardless of whether it was labeled as trash or recycling. It was striking that a community that would protest the city's plans to deal with excess trash through incineration was slow to participate in this individual-level effort to reduce the volume of its trash. Later, as explained in chapters 3 and 4, I came to better understand how little information many of the residents had acquired and how difficult it was for them to assemble effective, coherent, and consistent environmental proposals.

Exiting the gates of Community Meadow, we crossed the street to a restaurant, where we met with two of Huang *loashi*'s friends, Ms. Yu and Mr. Wu. While Ms. Yu was also a resident of Community Meadow, Mr. Wu lived in a gated community across the street, Community Pine. Although each community contained around two thousand households, Ms. Yu, who was in her late forties and employed as a university administrator, seemed to know people throughout the larger neighborhood area encompassing several gated communities, including Community Pine and nearby Community Willow. "She's like the auntie of the neighborhood," Huang *laoshi* told me, indicating the trust she had earned throughout the adjacent gated communities. The two homeowners had initially met on the online forum of Community Meadow, which Ms. Yu had joined to meet other homeowners and organize bulk purchases of home improvement items among residents. This strategy of connecting residents beyond community gates, further explored in chapter 3, turned out to be a powerful tool for amplifying resistance efforts.

Ms. Yu was the first to describe the landfill, located less than a mile away, to me. "You know, you don't smell the stench now," she told me, referring to the winter months, "but I sleep with a wet towel on my face in the summer, and the windows have to be closed. I consistently have nightmares about porta potties!" I tried to imagine this all-pervasive odor, but nothing at the time seemed particularly amiss about this neighborhood, which reminded me of my own California home with its walkability and the residents' easy familiarity with one another and with the restaurant owners and staff.

After our meal, Ms. Yu spoke with the servers about holding an event in the restaurant's upstairs space, exhibiting her networking skills as the unofficial neighborhood event planner and liaison. I left with Mr. Wu, the third homeowner at the table, a Beijinger in his late seventies with a thick local accent. He took me for a drive around the neighborhood in his clunky car, which seemed out of place among the sleek new residential buildings. Mr. Wu spoke passionately, arms waving, as he cruised down the middle of the quiet street with little regard to traffic lanes or signs.

Just beyond the neighborhood, he pointed out a crumbling brick building, telling me it was an old Japanese-era brick factory that currently emitted a lot of pollution.[5] It was evident that he viewed local air quality with great concern. He told me that he was excited that his forty-year-old son, who lived with him in Community Pine, was also starting to become interested in environmental issues. He asked if I had any articles on incinerators in the United States that I could share with his son, demonstrating an understanding that these issues were frequently discussed outside China. I was impressed with his expansive view of the topic.

Upon arriving at the landfill, we parked on the side of the street, next to a row of small, gray, single-story concrete houses. Mr. Wu explained that landfill workers lived in these tiny dwellings, which contrasted sharply with the bright and modern buildings of the gated communities. The air was thick with woodsmoke from their chimneys, though I noticed that Mr. Wu did not comment on this form of air pollution. Despite the freezing temperature, some of the workers had their doors open, which, from the smoke coming out of them, I perceived to be a measure to reduce the toxicity of the indoor air.

As we walked past these homes, Mr. Wu spoke expertly on seasonal wind directions and nearby weather stations that tracked meteorological data. Around us, plastic bags were strewn everywhere. They littered the hill we trekked up to view the landfill and were speared on the twigs of barren shrubs. It was the first time I had seen a landfill up close. It was more a large pit than a mound, and some of the trash was covered with tarps (figure 0.2). Everything seemed to be frozen. Although I understood that the landfill's proximity was worrisome for residents, I couldn't entirely understand why there had been such an uproar.

It was only on my second visit that I truly comprehended how the presence of the landfill affected homeowners. When I stepped off the bus in the heat of July the following year, I was immediately met with a wall of humidity infused with the pungent stench of rotting trash. I saw the landfill

FIGURE 0.2. A landfill in winter.

in the winter, but I most certainly smelled the landfill in the summer. The odor permeated every corner of Community Meadow. It was unbearable to walk around without a face mask, and even then, it was as if the putrid air was stuck within the mask, endlessly recycled.

Encountering the stench in the summer made the descriptions provided by the three activists much more vivid for me. For the first time I came to understand the significance of the fact that Community Meadow, Pine, and Willow homeowners had purchased their properties *without knowing that the landfill was there*. As described in chapter 2, purchasing one of these homes at the time did not necessarily involve visiting the site, because many gated communities were still under construction. Aside from confirming that the school district was good and hearing from the developers that the area had "good winds, good water," the homeowners with whom I spoke had learned very little about the area before moving in. Having purchased their homes in the early 2000s, they had not benefited from the now-widespread prevalence of online mapping. Even when I began fieldwork in Beijing in 2009, neither Google Maps (not blocked in China at the time) nor the local Baidu Maps was reliable. Buildings and residential complexes were mushrooming so quickly across the city in the early 2000s that mapping technology was struggling to catch up.

THE SPECIAL CASE OF ENVIRONMENTAL PROTEST

Community Meadow residents and their Pine and Willow neighbors were not the only homeowners to encounter a smelly landfill surprise followed by unannounced incinerator construction in the mid-2000s. Community Marigold (toward the northwest of the city) and Community Rose (in the east) encountered the same problem. As discussed in chapter 1, such environmental threats were stains on the rising trends of middle-class accomplishment, wealth accumulation, and improved quality of life. Despite the considerable achievement of homeowner status, newly middle-class residents could not escape landfills and incinerators in their backyards. Urban trash problems were so ubiquitous that one homeowner described the situation to me as "not even being able to move elsewhere in the city, because incinerators were following us everywhere."

The incinerator protests in these communities reflect a larger trend of environmental resistance in China coinciding with rapid urbanization across cities. Of all the mass protests that mobilized ten thousand or more participants in China between 2000 and 2013, more than half were documented as environmental incidents.[6] According to another estimate, protests against environmental pollution in the early 2000s increased at an annual rate of 29 percent.[7] Most environmental incidents involve only crowds of a few dozen or brief demonstrations that are quickly dispersed, but a few evolve into larger-scale mobilizations.

Based on my estimates, at least two dozen specifically *middle-class* protests against factory pollution or construction projects involving more than several hundred people were documented by the Chinese media between 2006 and 2014. A prominent case was the anti-paraxylene protest in Xiamen (in southern China) in 2007, where construction for a chemical plant had started without local residents being notified. City officials claimed that environmental evaluations by an expert panel had been completed before the project was green-lighted. Large-scale protests primarily comprising urban middle-class residents and "white-collar workers" were reported by various media outlets. Over the next eight years, similar anti-paraxylene protests erupted in the cities of Dalian, Kunming, Chengdu, Ningbo, and Maoming.

Although mass collective action on environmental issues is still rare in China, it has the distinctive feature of being generally tolerated by the state. Environmental grievances are among the more permissible issues for collective action in the view of the Chinese government, as opposed to protests against human rights violations or religious demonstrations, which are perceived as problematically political.[8] While environmental collective action can also be political in nature, the state is rarely its direct target. Environmental protesters are more likely to focus on construction companies, management companies, or lower levels of government than on central authorities.

Because of this relative tolerance, in contrast to other types of protests that are denied media coverage, environmental protest events sometimes escape censorship. In China, where the state controls the media, government officials dictate what type of coverage and narrative framing are allowed. Articles covering protest events are often published online, then quickly taken down. Because of these government–press dynamics, journalists use different strategies for different types of activism in response to varying degrees of state control. For example, to bypass censorship, local journalists may cover events occurring far away in other towns. Local media, on the other hand, self-censor or hide information about protests happening in their vicinity. It is not uncommon for the local press to report local protest stories only after they have been extensively covered by more remote publications.[9]

This delayed and circuitous reporting pattern is reflected in the experiences of Beijing homeowners in the three communities discussed in this book. Even when their anti-incinerator organizing timelines overlapped, they did not hear about one another's struggles until after the events had ended. There was some limited local press coverage of each organizing effort, but the focus of such stories was often the engineering problem of urban trash, rather than the social and political organizing efforts of the homeowners.

The trash problem is one of many environmental issues China has begun to confront over the past three decades. Because the central government has focused its environmental efforts on problems arising with rapid urbanization, citizen protests can at times align with the government's environmental initiatives.[10] As a result, despite official reluctance to recognize protests in the media, environmental organizing provides a unique opportunity for Chinese citizens not only to form associational bonds but also to mobilize for collective action with less likelihood of state interference than with other types of protests.

The Beijing anti-incinerator protests discussed in this book are a special case within this special case, reflecting the confluence of homeowner identity and environmental awareness. The Xiamen anti-paraxylene protests did not originate in residential communities; rather, information was circulated predominantly by opinion leaders, scientists, and public intellectuals.[11] In Maoming, anti-paraxylene protesters were from backgrounds of lower socioeconomic status, including rural farmers, unemployed youths, and shop workers.[12] The three anti-incinerator protests, in contrast, shared features with NIMBY ("not in my back yard") movements in the United States, in which homeowners resist land development or construction projects in their neighborhoods. On the surface, it might seem that the primary motivation of these Beijing homeowners to oppose incinerator construction was to protect their property values. However, if this was the entirety of the explanation, then the landfill stench that had been plaguing residents since they moved in would also have triggered substantial NIMBY resistance, but it did not. Environmental health concerns and perceptions of collective responsibility appear to have been the homeowners' motivation.

This book's deep dive into the experiences of three gated communities reveals that a sense of collective identity was a precondition for environmental action. It is important to note that NIMBY protests are not only location based—they are also made possible by strong place-based identities.[13] The experiences of these communities offer a glimpse into the process of place-based identity formation, or what I refer to as "becoming homeowners and neighbors." When faced with the landfill stench in their first year living in their new communities, homeowners did not yet have the civic capacity to mobilize for collective action. Three years later, however, owing to the connections established and skills developed in these communities, organizing had become a possibility, even though state responses (including soft or hard repression) shaped both the durability of community organizing and homeowners' sense of civic duty beyond their gates.

BECOMING A MIDDLE-CLASS HOMEOWNER IN CHINA

The mid-2000s is a unique time period to observe in urban China because of the massive wave of housing commercialization, described in more detail in chapter 1. The scope of this urban transformation in Beijing is staggering: thousands of new homeowners moved into hundreds of new gated communities in the same city at around the same time. Cities across China began implementing housing reforms in the 1980s, profoundly restructuring the known way of life for urban residents. Prior to the reforms, urban housing was provided mainly by the "work unit" (*danwei*) or, simply put, the workplace. Urban residents rarely encountered neighborhood amenities or conceived of social responsibilities outside the *danwei*. Their sense of belonging was centered on the work unit, rather than on their homes or neighborhood.[14] After all, they did not own their housing. Residents were organized by occupation, living in spaces regulated by state-owned enterprises and local governments. Health care, education, and employment were all provided by the workplace. Work-unit residents had little control over the quality of their housing, and homeownership was not possible as an ordinary citizen under the *danwei* system.[15] Urban lives looked similar for most—differences in social class based on housing or lifestyle were hardly discernible.

Housing reforms led to the abolition of the work-unit housing system in 1998, bringing about two significant changes: (1) the sale of work-unit housing (often referred to as "old neighborhoods") at discounted prices to existing residents, and (2) housing privatization and the construction of new commercial housing complexes ("new neighborhoods").[16] With rapid economic development in the 1990s, a "well-off" or "affluent" stratum of society gradually emerged,[17] which many China scholars refer to as the "middle class," broadly defined. Urban residents suddenly had increasing purchasing power, the ability to acquire and accumulate wealth, and the possibility of affording housing in the new neighborhoods mushrooming across Chinese cities.[18] For the first time since 1949, a significant segment of the urban population became homeowners—reaching 65 percent in 2001, 74 percent in 2003, and 82 percent in 2006.[19] And, for the first time, many people were moving into communities as strangers with no work affiliations, with housing and social services no longer provided for them. These economic and urbanization developments resulted not only in shifts in housing but also a drastic change in people's way of life. Property ownership placed agency into the hands of urban residents—housing matters and everyday needs were now in their control, rather than that of the government.

INFORMAL ASSOCIATIONS AND THE CIVIC CAPACITY OF URBAN GATED COMMUNITIES

Gated housing communities in China created unique spatial arrangements in urban areas—middle-class spaces—in which homeowners could foster a sense of collective identity tied to these spaces. A broad array of literature in urban housing and planning studies describe "gatedness" as connoting security and privacy.[20] In the American Southwest, gated communities protected the middle-class privileges of residents by excluding outside citizens, reinforcing notions of security and forging a sense of community among similar neighbors.[21] In Shanghai, communities are often planned in a way that displays a "distinct form of class territoriality with clearly marked out spatial boundaries and zones that are zealously guarded and fortified by high walls, fences, and surveillance technologies and private guards."[22]

In Beijing, however, although guard stations are present in virtually every gated community, security was not the main priority for the residents of the gated communities I studied. More important for these homeowners was the way in which the walling off of space reinforced a sense of place and an associated collective identity. What I observed was not a "retreat" of the middle class into "fortified enclaves,"[23] nor a desire for privacy within these walls,[24] but rather an active cultivation of community life, social capital, and civic engagement, as well as a desire to take on issues beyond the community as part of the homeowners' civic duty.

Within these new residential communities, middle-class residents in urban Beijing had the new experience of forming social associations such as soccer leagues, karaoke groups, and bird-watching clubs. The civic infrastructure within these communities—the constellation of informal associations, shared spaces, and the communal life and social bonds that weave through them—provided more than recreation. Participating in a soccer team, for example, also offers a free space in which neighborly camaraderie can develop, ideas can be discussed, shared interests can flourish, and a foundation upon which social cohesion can be built. Seemingly mundane group events like a bake sale or a group hike might later gain movement-style political claims. A bake sale can raise funds for a social cause; a group hike can be combined with raising awareness of the importance of protecting the natural environment. This type of "blended social action" is rooted in everyday civic life and informal associations.[25]

The idea that civic associations and shared communal spaces are essential to higher-level societal functions is exemplified in Alexis de Tocqueville's maxim that associations are "schools of democracy." Similarly, Putnam argues that diminishing opportunities for community involvement and person-to-person interaction portended the collapse of American community—and therefore democratic ideals—in the 1990s.[26] This notion was further explored in Small's study of New York City childcare centers, in which he observed that the social benefits of community organizations are often incidental to the purpose or mission of the organization.[27] The collective benefit is not necessarily the specific end product of participating in a specific activity—be it scoring in a bowling league, learning drills on a basketball team, or even improving local policies through a neighborhood environmental committee—as much as it is the effect of how participation occurs. Group purchases, message-board debates, after-work karaoke, or a trip to a scenic area after a community meeting all create feelings of connectedness, belonging, and shared roots.[28] For Small, overburdened mothers in the New York community he observed were certainly relieved by childcare services, but it was in the parking lot—where mothers dropped off and picked up their children—that they found unexpected forms of material, social, and emotional support. By convening regularly, dense networks of caring are forged, and people meet others to whom they can turn in times of need.

The same concept applies to environmental threats, whether for Chicago neighborhood residents battling a heat wave or Beijing homeowners organizing against landfills and incinerators. Communities with tight-knit support networks are likely to fare better in terms of health outcomes[29] and the success of collective action than those that are less well connected. Further, when groups of individuals—be they mothers or homeowners—share the belief that they can and are willing to overcome challenges and create change, they are more effective. This concept of "collective efficacy" is best observed under conditions of challenge, reflecting the notion that overcoming conflict and threat is an important part of civic engagement.[30] By this measure, the Beijing housing communities were well positioned for cohesion because of their proximity to sites of environmental concern.

In discussing the more abstract idea of civil society engagement, social scientists tend to focus on *formal* organizations: nonprofit or social movement organizations. While such forms are easier to observe than those that are informal, formal associations are often only the "peaks above the waterline, as opposed to the iceberg of citizen action underneath."[31] Citizen action is often organized less formally by grassroots groups and characterized by various types of informal gatherings.[32] The middle-class homeowners' communities featured in this book provide a glimpse of the full iceberg: stable spaces that foster various associations and collective action—formal and informal, mundane and claim oriented, successful and failed—that have become important components of Chinese civil society.

By interacting through informal civic associations, homeowners fostered not only social capital and trust but also civic skills and responsibilities previously unfamiliar to them under a socialist housing system. With these new skills, homeowners built civic capacity within their communities, establishing civic information infrastructures and cultivating community leaders through everyday participation. In Communities Meadow, Rose, and Marigold, this longer-term capacity-building allowed homeowners to organize when incinerator construction plans were revealed.

STATE SHAPING OF CIVIC RESPONSIBILITY

As an authoritarian regime, China is generally known for its repressive responses to collective action. Discussions of civic participation and the skills gained through participation have always centered on democratic rather than authoritarian contexts. So how, and why, is vibrant associational life able to be fostered in such an unlikely place? In addition to the special case of environmental protest, new housing communities offer a unique context for the growth of associational life. Verba, Scholzman, and Brady demonstrate that involvement with a wide variety of civic organizations—service oriented, associational, and advocacy focused—can equip participants with basic political skills such as speech-making, letter-writing, and meeting planning.[33] In middle-class communities in Beijing, homeowners learned how to write letters to property management to air housing-related grievances and demand homeowners' rights, conduct preparatory meetings to form homeowners' associations, and plan meetings and activities around community issues.

Community leadership is also nurtured through participation. When the environmental threat of incinerator construction loomed over homeowners' communities, the same skills developed in establishing social ties in the community were used in change-oriented forms of engagement incorporating claims-making. In the process of acquiring civic skills through informal associations in the community, homeowners built civic capacity that prepared them to organize politically when the time came. Further, preexisting attempts at collective action within homeowners' communities, especially around developer and property-management conflicts, offered a repertoire of organizing strategies that could be used against incinerator construction—similar to what McAdam and Boudet found with communities that were more likely to mobilize around risky energy projects (e.g., liquefied natural gas terminals).[34] Participation in a wide range of associations can thus be seen as a wellspring for political activism.[35]

However, not all middle-class gated communities mobilize in China. A perennial question in social movement studies is why mobilization for social movements does not occur more often.[36] Particularly in an authoritarian setting, an insufficient density or depth of informal associations (i.e., a lack of an organizational "ecosystem") leaves citizens more vulnerable to repression. As Edwards contends, if only one informal organization exists in an autocratic regime, the government can easily quell dissent.[37] However, if thirty informal associations are present, some will survive. He argues that often-overlooked informal groups such as youth clubs and temple societies are decisively important in struggles against authoritarian rule. Therefore, examining informal associational life rooted in middle-class gated communities can shed light on what these groups are able to contribute to larger organizing efforts.

Homeowners in an authoritarian setting inevitably face higher barriers to convening publicly than those living in a democracy, especially once engagement becomes directed more toward advocacy or change. To effectively mobilize and organize homeowners for collective action, whether internally against property management or externally against government agencies, Beijing residents in the three housing communities I studied found that convening was best accomplished via the internet, on online homeowners' forums. The internet as an effective mobilization tool has been covered by scholars such as Earl and Tufekci, who explored how the internet is used in social movements to mobilize activists who struggle to meet in person.[38] The unique role of homeowners' forums has also been discussed by scholars who study the mobilization of homeowners across urban China.[39]

What has been missing from these discussions, however, is how and why these specific online forums are effective. The success of an online community space is made possible not only by the platform but also by the social capital and civic infrastructure that are created and reinforced off-line—that is, in the community. Tufekci has described the short-lived nature of many online movements: with the success of certain online mobilizations, leaderless mass movements have started to emerge more frequently, but such movements are hard to sustain once the initial wave of organizing ends.[40] Without the trust and reciprocity established in physical spaces and the physical presence of community leaders, the virtual space lacks effectiveness.

To understand what made the organizing efforts of Communities Meadow, Rose, and Marigold possible, it was also important to investigate communities that were impacted by the same landfills and incinerators but were unsuccessful in collective organizing. To assess this, I observed the online homeowners' forums of housing complexes clustered in the same vicinities. In a process described in more detail in later chapters,

INTRODUCTION

homeowners in the nonmobilizing communities at times expressed similar concerns about the forthcoming incinerators, but their discussions were much less interactive. I found that simply airing grievances was insufficient for mobilization; success began with the *exchange of ideas for action*, which led to the ability to plan. As a result, many residents in the nonmobilizing communities with a strong interest in resistance crossed the virtual gates of the online forums to join the organizing efforts of Community Meadow and, to some extent, Community Marigold. In particular, residents of Communities Pine and Willow joined forces with the more robust association of Community Meadow, leading to a multicommunity effort that had greater success than its single-community counterparts.

As resistance against incinerator construction escalated in each location, homeowners also moved beyond the physical walls of their communities, organizing for collective action against the municipal environmental bureau, the central environmental ministry, and various local government agencies. At this point, government intervention became part of the story, as homeowners and community leaders sought access to legal institutional channels (i.e., they sought to engage in the political process) and ways to address environmental grievances publicly. The legitimacy of homeowners and their claims is shaped by the state, as is their degree of engagement.

Ultimately, when urban residents are prevented from engaging in the political process—regardless of how useful the political skills cultivated in their communities may be—their sense of civic duty is truncated by the state. Civic responsibility is fostered through associational life; a resident's sense of personal responsibility becomes integrated into their community. However, in an authoritarian setting, that integration can be severed or conditioned by state repression. The inability to affect the local community leads to disassociation with its collective identity. Therefore, although gated housing communities have the potential to foster civic capacity and create political change, this process depends heavily on the state. Once collective organizing goes public, the state has a strong influence on whether communities can organize in a durable manner.

The three communities featured in this book achieved larger-scale organizing to differing degrees. Community Meadow—along with Communities Willow and Pine—and Community Marigold were able to organize more durably than Community Rose. Meadow, Willow, and Pine homeowners' sense of civic responsibility went beyond their gates to incorporate environmental concerns in the larger neighborhood and even at the city level. Community Meadow's environmental organizing was tolerated by central-government officials, whereas Community Rose homeowners faced harsh repression, and Community Marigold's leader was first repressed and then co-opted by city-level officials. While associational life within all three communities' walls was vibrant, once issues and grievances went beyond the community, the state determined whether homeowners could be deeply engaged in political processes and, consequently, influenced their sense and scope of civic responsibility.

Many scholars have argued that, in a democratic setting, civic action fosters the development and cultivation of political skills that facilitate and safeguard citizenship and democracy.[41] Somers furthered the idea that citizenship can be defined as a process rather than a status: the development of citizenship rights depends on legal infrastructure and community capacities for associational participation.[42] Research on citizenship, she argues, should incorporate the sociological relationship "among public spheres, community associational life, and patterns of political culture."[43] This process is exemplified by middle-class homeowners in China: the patterns of associational life in housing communities and the relationship homeowners have with government officials during environmental organizing help homeowners make sense of what it means to be an urban citizen—specifically the public and political dimensions of being a citizen—and shape how residents interpret their civic responsibilities. In China, urban middle-class citizenship is a learned process, shaped not only by associational life and civic capacity but also by the political response to citizens' collective actions.

While this book does tell the story of a social movement, the focus is middle-class associational life. The environmental outcomes are of interest, but the heart of the story is the development of shared identity, community, and capacity, which proved resilient in the face of failure. When I visited the three communities following the protests, homeowners recounted experiences of both successful and failed organizing with equal enthusiasm, casting nearly all their attempts in a positive light. The tone of pride was not what I had expected to hear in homeowners' reactions to being arrested, detained, and repressed. It became clear that what the homeowners had been through was not just about anti-incinerator protests, or even the state's response, but rather the experience of organizing together as a community and developing civic skills. Homeowners were proud of these skills, which enabled them to establish durable community-based initiatives. For example, an outcome in one community was the establishment of a trash-separation company to increase recycling rates, while another saw the formation of an environmental group that tackled pollution problems in their neighborhood. Moreover, although none of the environmental organizing efforts achieved policy breakthroughs, in all three communities, homeowners ultimately incorporated their voices into various environmental nonprofits and therefore enriched the larger environmental civil society.

Physical spaces matter for collective action. The movement ecologist Dingxin Zhao found student dormitories and campus spaces to be the center of mobilization for the 1989 Tiananmen student movement.[44] In his study of the Paris Commune, Gould observed that what tied workers together were the social bonds they created as neighbors.[45] In both cases, individuals relied not only on the spatial settings of their communities to mobilize but also on the feeling of togetherness experienced because of the social ties nurtured in those spaces. In the same way, middle-class gated housing communities in authoritarian China have, through informal associational life and the building of civic capacity, become sources of collective action.

DATA

This book draws on data collected through online and off-line research. I used various sources, including interviews, off-line participant observation, online ethnography, media reports, official documents, government databases, and citizen-collected data.

In 2009, I began conducting fieldwork in Beijing with environmental nonprofits (or "social organizations," as they are broadly termed) ranging from government-organized nongovernmental organizations (GONGOs) to grassroots registered nongovernmental organizations (NGOs).[46] I was interested in how nonprofit organizations were part of the associational life that shaped environmental civil society in China. GONGOs, interestingly, were often the quickest to accept my request to visit. At the time, the key issue discussed across GONGOs was trash separation, or recycling. Every GONGO I visited would provide me with stacks of government-issued pamphlets and booklets on environmental topics.

With grassroots environmental NGOs, I embedded myself in their activities and campaigns, spent time in their libraries, and perused their documents, newsletters, and case-study collections to identify key environmental debates. Once again, the issue that surfaced was the urban waste problem. While GONGOs served as promoters of governmental environmental initiatives, grassroots NGOs seemed to focus their efforts on policy research work and short-term community environmental campaigns (e.g., teaching urban residents how to sort trash). Unlike what one would expect in a democratic setting, civic engagement and building connections with urban communities were not the focus of these NGOs; direct contact with residents occurred primarily through program delivery. However, from these organizations, I learned that several homeowners' communities in Beijing had been affected by landfills and that the city planned to address the problem by building incinerators.

To select cases, I used various NGO newsletters and case studies, as well as media reports when available, as sources of information on instances of struggles against incinerator construction in the country in the early to mid-2000s—there were roughly eleven. During that time, three were located in Beijing. I selected Beijing as the city of focus for the case studies based on the similarities in spatial setup, social class, and mobilizing potential of the three communities involved in resistance, as well as the varying consequences of their protests (table 0.1). Notably, the three instances of anti-incinerator organizing targeted three *separate* incinerator construction projects, further highlighting the ubiquitous issue of urban trash in Beijing.

In an authoritarian context, community-level social movement data are extremely hard to come by. Compared with the United States, where movement data can be collected via newspaper coverage or through reaching out to activists with publicly searchable contact information, in China, news coverage of such events is either purposefully vague or censored, with community leaders often staying under the radar. For this reason, I spent considerable time networking and establishing relationships with local grassroots groups to build trust and gain access to the communities I had chosen to study. My connections with grassroots environmental NGOs in Beijing allowed me to reach middle-class homeowners from five residential communities who had been involved in environmental resistance between 2006 and 2011 (the five communities I refer to pseudonymously

INTRODUCTION

TABLE 0.1
Summary of case selection and setup

	Meadow, Willow, Pine	Rose	Marigold
Spatial setup	Gated communities	Gated community	Gated community
Social class	Middle class	Middle class	Middle and upper-middle class
Mobilizing potential	Active associational life, collective environmental grievances, leadership group	Active associational life, individual environmental grievances, individual leader	Moderately active associational life, individual environmental grievances, individual leader
Consequences of organizing	Government acceptance, incinerator relocation, durable community organizing expanding to other environmental issues	Government repression, incinerator construction, short-lived environmental organizing	Government co-optation, incinerator construction, durable but individual-oriented environmental organizing

as Meadow, Willow, Pine, Rose, and Marigold). Because my fieldwork in Beijing ranged from 2009 to 2013, I was simultaneously reconstructing trajectories of organizing, experiencing new events as they unraveled, and awaiting the consequences of earlier events.

Through introductions from nonprofit staff members, I was able to enter these communities and meet homeowners who had participated in the environmental organizing. I recruited most of my informants using a snowball approach: the homeowners introduced me to other homeowners, who offered stories of both collective action and their broader community lives. Some were more willing to talk than others, and most information was shared through casual conversations in community spaces or local restaurants over several months, rather than through formal sit-down interviews.[47] When possible, I sat in on in-person homeowners' meetings to observe their discussions of local environmental problems.

To gauge state response, I interviewed any government official from the district, municipal, or central level who was willing to talk with me about urban trash issues or incinerators. Most were environmental or Urban Administrative and Law Enforcement Bureau officials (*chengguan*) who were aware of homeowners' organizing activities but were not charged with responding directly to their environmental grievances. Some officials were reluctant to share what they knew about the protests, but what they chose to talk about instead—such as the environmental education of citizens and their understanding of incineration—yielded interesting observations about the relationship between different levels of the government and middle-class residents in Beijing.

With press coverage and social media posts about collective action prone to swift removal by the Public Security Bureau (a.k.a. the internet police) and information about environmental impact difficult to obtain through official or online channels, homeowners relied on their own data collection to document their protests. This process involved assembling careful news reports and files related to their collective action, including taking photographs and video recordings of conflicts. Homeowners also created and distributed materials such as booklets about the protection of environmental rights, posters, petitions, self-administered surveys, transcripts of lawsuits, and documentation and recordings of complaints filed with various government branches. These archives were key data sources for me, as they provided me with a deep understanding of how the homeowners framed and interpreted the incinerator issue, their collective action, and the risks associated with their collective action.

Another source of data was the online homeowners' forums (*yezhu luntan*) that residents used daily. Such forums, similar to message boards, are typically created by homeowners on a host web platform, free of cost.[48] Each forum I studied was organized by a single residential community, and all forums were hosted on the same platform. One homeowner usually becomes the forum administrator for a community, serving as moderator. Strikingly, many forums date back to before the homeowners had moved into their new housing complexes. Often, the forums were where homeowners "met" for the first time. The forums were so frequently used and so central to community identity formation that the homeowners often referred to one another by their forum usernames rather than by their given names. The online forums also allowed me to track nearby communities where environmental mobilizing was not happening even though these communities were impacted by the same landfills and incinerator construction plans as Communities Meadow, Rose, or Marigold.

Through in-depth online ethnographic work, which involved the long-term observation of these forums (and the forums of nearby communities), I was able to observe rich real-time accounts of how homeowners met

INTRODUCTION

for the first time, homeowners' association preparatory meetings (as well as meeting minutes), and, later, documentation of decision-making during environmental organizing against incinerator construction, as well as the eventual consequences experienced by these communities in the wake of collective action. This approach is similar to what Yang, one of the first scholars to study the making of cultural spaces on the Chinese internet, advocates: to move around flexibly across online networks, explore links, take notes, download information (since censorship is always a consideration), and return to sites for deeper exploration.[49] On the forums, I was able to observe homeowners experiencing and processing dissonance, forming collective identities, building community capacity, and coming to consensus or entering into conflict, as well as government intervention and censorship once incinerator resistance commenced. Online forum activities were reinforced by social capital and trust cultivated concurrently in the physical spaces of homeowners' communities and therefore were a valuable source of data for understanding community formation and community capacity.

I was referred to the content of these forums by nonprofit staff members and homeowners alike. The website that hosted the forums I observed was free and accessible, meaning that user activities were essentially in the public domain. None of the forums required a membership to view posts. In addition, the real names of homeowners were never revealed; forum users were identified only by their usernames. I knew the real-life identities of homeowners only when they chose to tell me their usernames. To my knowledge, this is accepted practice in the field. However, to further protect all homeowners, I use only pseudonyms in the book.

Finally, to better understand associational life at the city level, I scraped the Beijing government's registry of social and community-based organizations for 2017 and 2018.[50] This endeavor helped to situate homeowners' collective actions in the larger context of urban associational life. Combined with my ethnographic work in the communities, these big-picture data (discussed in the conclusion) allowed me to reflect on sociological ideas of organizational density, civic infrastructure, and civic participation. Though these ideas are traditionally explored in democratic settings, this book and its case studies demonstrate the shortcomings of focusing exclusively on formal (i.e., registered) associations without considering the potential of informal community associational life and how it contributes to the building of civic capacity and the creation of durable community organizations.

CHAPTER ORGANIZATION

Chapter 1 contextualizes middle-class homeownership in China through discussions of housing data, ideas of the new rising middle class, and the implications of homeownership and property rights. It then lays out the key environmental challenges brought about by rapid urbanization and the state governance of these problems. With the spatial distribution of the urban population changing dramatically as socialist work-unit housing came to an end during the housing reforms of the 1990s, increasing numbers of urban middle-class residents and the continuous construction of commodity housing in cities led to an increase in collective action by homeowners. Pollution problems threatening housing communities led to middle-class environmental participation and resistance, with divergent outcomes.

Chapter 2 reveals how homeowners initially demonstrated commitment to their communities. Homeowners' interactions illustrate a process of becoming neighbors: from early community activity participation to place-based collective identity formation to the attempted formation of homeowners' associations. While the three communities featured in this book exhibited various styles and degrees of engagement, the formation of homeowners' information networks (i.e., civic infrastructure), the cultivation of community identity, and the skills developed through everyday informal participation were the starting point of civic capacity-building for all of them. For example, residents engaged in organizing group purchases, documenting homeowners' meeting minutes, and drafting letters of complaint to property management. Through these activities, these new residential communities became schools of democracy in an authoritarian system, cultivating middle-class citizens' sense of civic responsibility and building capacity for later environmental organizing against municipal incinerator projects.

Chapter 3 demonstrates how homeowners in these middle-class spaces engaged in collective sensemaking and learning when encountering and processing new challenges and uncertainties. Residents of Meadow (and relatedly Willow and Pine), Rose, and Marigold transitioned from addressing internal issues to investigating external concerns through the leadership of community representatives. The chapter focuses on how homeowners began to discover and engage with issues outside their communities, specifically environmental threats. Although the issues were similar across sites, community responses differed. In response to landfill stench, some

INTRODUCTION

communities were able to collectively make sense of the problem because of key representatives who were able to connect resident dialogue across the larger neighborhood, articulating the issue for all homeowners as discussions unraveled. In facilitating this sensemaking process, homeowners came to view addressing the landfill problem as a collective responsibility and to hold one another accountable when mobilizing to take action. Other communities were not able to achieve this collective endeavor, even though individual residents complained about the stench both in person and online. Although key figureheads emerged in all communities, only in Meadow, Willow, and Pine did they facilitate cohesion by moderating the sharing and interpretation of common grievances around external threats.

Chapter 4 discusses how and to what extent these community leaders shaped the mobilizing and organizing that occurred. In some communities, an earlier emergence of representation helped homeowners organize for collective action with concrete plans and coherent rhetoric drawing on community volunteers and expertise. In other communities, leaders either had yet to drive the anti-incinerator conversation in the community or failed to fully leverage community capacity to organize stable planning committees or encourage community engagement in deciding on initial moves to protest the incinerator. Because of differences in how leaders leveraged capacity, initial protest actions varied, with some communities using preexisting resident mobilizing networks to hit the streets or stage public demonstrations and others engaging volunteers in drafting petitions and letters to air grievances via legal institutional channels with multiple government agencies. These tactical variations met with varying degrees of repression and intervention: institutional communications were acknowledged by authorities, whereas disruptive protests led to monitoring, arrest, and even detainment for some homeowners.

Chapter 5 focuses on how homeowners pivoted their anti-incinerator resistance toward data collection and research on environmental and health impacts as a way to more effectively pressure the government to halt incinerator construction. Citizen science became a middle-class alternative to disruptive protesting, and homeowners used their expertise, professional connections, and fundraising capabilities to produce environmental reports and analyses. This approach boosted the legitimacy of homeowner initiatives when they took further protest actions through legal institutional channels (such as filing lawsuits and petitioning), as they were able to supplement their arguments with data. Although homeowners' citizen science varied in both information type and accuracy, its use allowed residents to comprehend the incineration issue more deeply, to better understand environmental laws and case studies, and to produce and present scientific evidence to government officials and environmental nonprofits.

Chapter 6 focuses on the consequences of organizing for Meadow, Willow, Pine, Rose, and Marigold homeowners. Community leaders perceived that their organizing efforts had made a difference, regardless of the outcomes for incinerator construction. Their organizing showed that urban middle-class residents had the ability to bring environmental issues to government attention through dialogue with municipal agencies and officials. Perhaps more striking is that, even though organizing durability varied across communities, homeowners were universally able to cultivate an increased environmental consciousness and a deeper understanding of environmental rights and laws. They also enhanced their knowledge of and interactions with the government system, using newly learned civic skills such as petitioning and letter-writing. Further, citizen science expanded not only middle-class environmental participation, requiring homeowners to research and interpret complex environmental information, but also a sense of civic duty that extended beyond community boundaries.

In contrast to a shrinking middle class in the United States, new middle classes are rising and expanding in urban centers across developing nations. The "middle class" is not just a socioeconomic status, however. It is also a collective identity shaped by urban residents experiencing associational life, learning what homeownership means, and defining themselves as both members of their communities and as citizens of a larger society. In Beijing, the associational life of the expanding middle class in their new urban dwellings is transforming the social fabric of a rapidly developing city and paving the way for broader civic engagement.

Particularly in a nondemocratic context—where we might expect citizens to avoid activities that could attract government attention—it is valuable to understand how active civic life is fostered. This book traces the development of informal and formal associational life for urban middle-class homeowners in China who have access to social connections and professional resources. When leveraged effectively, these advantages allow homeowners to engage in organizing for collective action, which in turn cultivates the capacity to form durable organizations that have the potential to address broader social and environmental problems.

Chapter One

A STENCH ON SUCCESS

Urban Middle-Class Homeowners and Rising Environmental Challenges

To explain the context in which environmental community organizing arose among the Chinese urban middle class in the early 2000s, this chapter provides an overview of housing reforms in China, the emergence of private ownership of newly constructed homes, and the broader demographic trends influencing these changes. With rising urban homeownership in Beijing, the number of established community organizations also grew as residents began to form associations to confront issues affecting their quality of life as homeowners. Because a rapidly increasing urban population was also leading to pressing environmental threats, including air pollution and trash problems, both government officials and urban residents were scrambling to comprehend and respond to escalating environmental issues.

The breadth and intensity of collective action described in this chapter and throughout the book may seem surprising given China's authoritarian governance. Authoritarian settings impose stringent barriers to collective action because the state views social unrest as a threat to the maintenance of social order. However, in China, both central and local officials have shown greater willingness to tolerate collective action against environmental degradation than in response to other issues. Environmental pollution threatens all citizens—even government officials—and government plans to alleviate pollution problems have been consistently high on the national agenda for the past twenty years. Additionally, urban environmental resistance typically involves an educated class of resourceful professionals—the "middle class"—with significant consumption power and social connections. In other words, these citizens can leverage available resources and gain access to channels through which they can voice their concerns. Further, an educated and upwardly mobile citizenry is a demonstration of state power to the outside world; thus, the repression of middle-class voices is disadvantageous for foreign relations. As a result, middle-class protesters in China have succeeded in engaging in dialogue with both local and central officials, even achieving outcomes such as the relocation or shutdown of polluting factories and the fining of corporate polluters.

As Chinese middle-class citizens began to cluster in urban gated communities in the early 2000s, associational life within those new spaces gradually took shape. First-time homeowners learned to mobilize for collective action as a group—initially within the residential gates, addressing issues with property management and real estate developers and forming homeowners' associations (HOAs). In this process, homeowners cultivated a sense of collective identity as members of the same community through both informal group activities and more formal organizing. Moreover, they developed civic skills, such as petitioning and letter writing, that they could later apply to causes beyond their gates. These middle-class homeowners, in their new shared spaces with newfound collective identities—arrangements and conditions that had not been possible before housing reforms—became socially engaged citizens. These critical junctures of urban development, discussed here with reference to Beijing but also occurring elsewhere in China and the world, provide an opportunity to reflect on how citizens react to, adapt to, and participate in shaping social changes.

A BRIEF HISTORY OF CHINESE HOUSING POLICY

Before 1978, private housing, homeownership, and associated property rights were virtually nonexistent. Since 1949, the Chinese government had nationalized land ownership and monopolized all land transactions. The production, distribution, and management of urban housing was controlled directly by the government; the state served as both landlord and developer.

During this period, Chinese society was organized under the "work unit" (*danwei*) system. Everything from housing distribution to medical care, education, and employment was tied to the work unit.[1] The unit determined not only individuals' work status but also their communal lives, with social connections centering on the *danwei*.[2] Public housing was allocated by the state to the *danwei* and then distributed to individual households. Housing allocation was based on seniority, performance, and the needs of employees, and rents were heavily subsidized.

Although the *danwei* was designed to meet housing needs, the allocation system was fraught with problems. Low rents and reliance on government subsidies meant that the *danwei* had little capacity to manage the overall maintenance of public housing. The cost of upkeep often fell to individual families, many of whom were either unable to afford the costs or unwilling to spend their money on housing they might lose to reassignment. Living conditions were generally poor, and as the pace of urban growth picked up, housing shortages became commonplace.[3] For example, it was not uncommon for a family of three generations to be living in one room of a house in Beijing. Additionally, unequal and corrupt housing allocations often occurred.[4] Work units with stronger government backing and greater resources were able to provide vastly better housing for employees than those without such backing and resources. Within units, job position and length of time with the unit also determined the type of housing given to a family.[5] Though the work unit was originally intended to be a system of equality, glaring inequalities were generated among and within work units.

Aware of these issues, government leaders worried that the housing shortage and poor maintenance of urban housing would lead to mass grievances and social instability.[6] In the late 1970s and early 1980s, the state began investing in housing construction to alleviate the problem. Some work units were able to construct large apartment buildings, but in bigger cities like Beijing, the situation was slow to improve. Consequently, the government decided to transition to privatized housing: in 1980, Deng Xiaoping, the leader of China's economic reforms, determined that urban residents should be allowed to purchase housing or build their own. Following that decision, the first legal protection allowing private households to own, purchase, sell, and rent private homes in urban areas was officially established in 1983. Finally, in 1987, the government acknowledged that the housing allocation system was placing a heavy burden on the state and not truly resolving urban housing issues. With that declaration, housing privatization became an important part of China's economic reform goals.

With the housing reforms, the Chinese government first made moves to privatize existing public housing by giving *danwei* residents the chance to obtain full or partial property rights through purchases at market or cheaper prices, followed by plans to commercialize the entire real estate market.[7] In the late 1980s, there was a push for the gradual sale of work unit–controlled housing to existing tenants. Families in unit housing were encouraged to buy their apartments from employers at discounted prices; households that did not want or could not afford to purchase their unit homes were forced to pay much higher rents. During this transition period, in the 1980s and 1990s, new housing was also constructed by municipal governments and sold to private citizens. For this publicly constructed housing, work units subsidized some of the housing costs for their employees, having quickly discovered that most families could not afford housing at full price.[8] However, this type of urban housing, while an upgrade from the earlier *danwei* housing, was often still of poor construction quality.

In the mid-1990s, the new housing market began to take shape, with the second stage of housing reforms emphasizing the commodification of housing, in which private businesses (rather than the state) developed new homes. In 1998, Chinese cities were urged to speed up the reform toward housing monetization. The state encouraged urban residents to "discard their old socialist welfare mentality and to embrace private home ownership."[9] A new state slogan captured the shift succinctly: "Housing is no longer a welfare item; it is now a commodity!"[10] At that time, urban residents were encouraged to buy affordable housing with prices coordinated by their work units or other commodity housing on the market.[11] As the allocation system came to an end, commercialized housing real estate emerged, officially detaching housing from the work unit. From the late 1990s onward, new commodity housing catered to middle- and upper-middle-income families, primarily taking the form of gated enclave communities.[12] In the early 2000s, after thirty years of housing-related reforms, an urban housing market was at last established in all Chinese cities. The majority of urban residents now obtained their housing on the private market rather than from the government or their employers.

A STENCH ON SUCCESS

LARGE-SCALE RESIDENTIAL DATA

A marked trait of China's development as a country is its speed of urban growth. In 1978, at the start of China's economic reforms, only about 18 percent of the total population was living in urban areas.[13] By 2012, more than 50 percent of the total population lived in cities.[14] A steady uptrend was seen in urban population growth compared to that of the overall population, with a notable uptick after 2000 (figure 1.1). These data indicate that within China the population is becoming more concentrated in cities. The sudden increase in urban population growth aligned with the establishment of the new urban housing market in China and the associated explosion of new housing construction (figure 1.2). In a similar uptrend, the disposable incomes of urban households have also increased dramatically nationwide since 2000 (figure 1.3).[15] In Beijing, available data show that the disposable income and annual expenditures on housing of urban households have both grown rather steadily in a span of twelve years (figure 1.4).[16] This information indicates that families were likely using existing savings for housing expenses, such as rent. Taken together, the data paint a portrait of urban China at the turn of the millennium, one characterized by growing city populations, the establishment and growth of middle and upper-middle

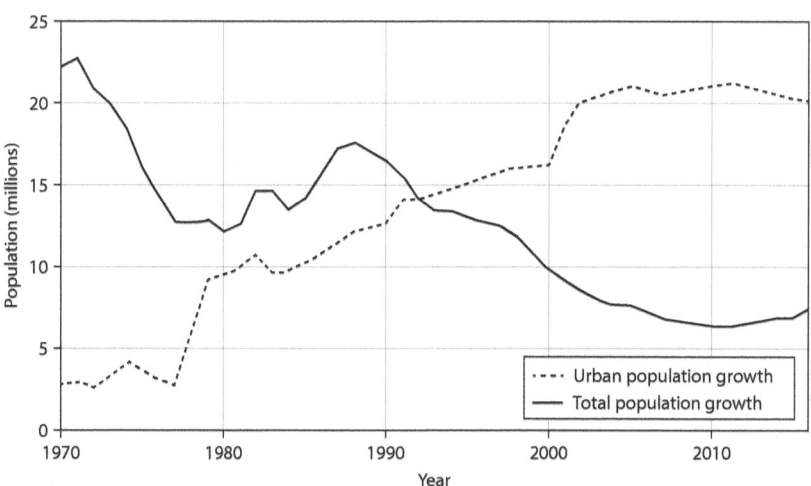

FIGURE 1.1. The urbanization of China, 1970 to 2016.
Source: World Bank, "World Urbanization Prospects: 2018 Revision," World Bank Open Data, 2018.

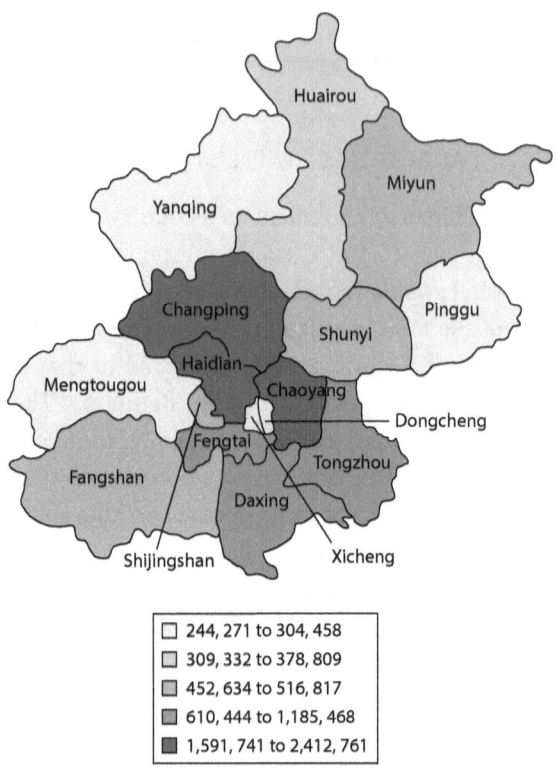

244, 271 to 304, 458
309, 332 to 378, 809
452, 634 to 516, 817
610, 444 to 1,185, 468
1,591, 741 to 2,412, 761

FIGURE 1.2. Total area (in square meters) of Beijing homes built after 2000.
Source: National Bureau of Statistics of China, *China 2010 County Population Census Data* (Beijing: China Statistics, 2011).

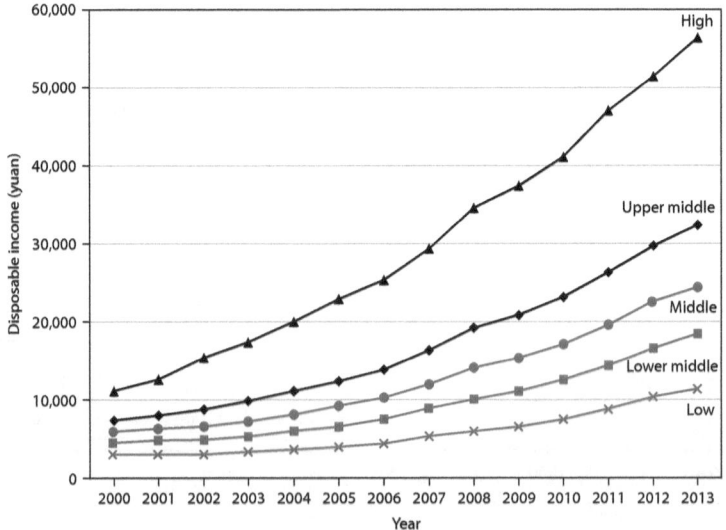

FIGURE 1.3. Disposable income of urban households by income category, 2000 to 2013.
Source: National Bureau of Statistics of China, *China Statistical Yearbooks*, 2000 to 2013 (Beijing: China Statistics).
Values have been adjusted for inflation using the 1996 Consumer Price Index.

A STENCH ON SUCCESS

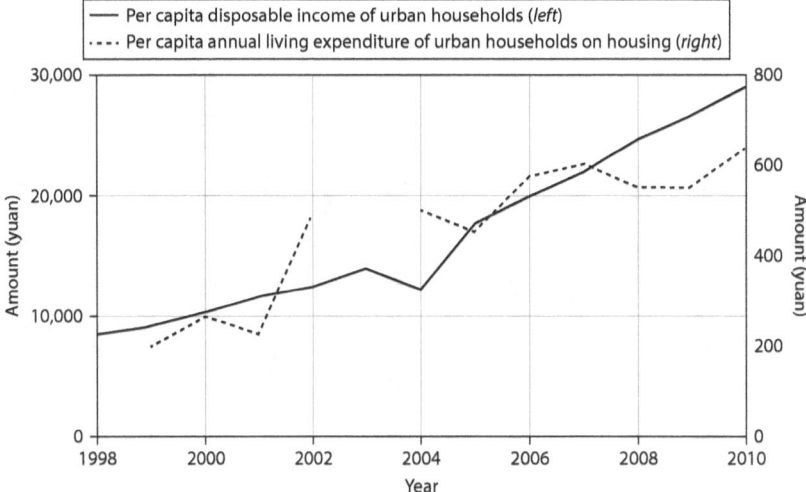

FIGURE 1.4. Disposable income and annual housing expenditure of urban Beijing households, 1998 to 2010.
Note: 1998 and 2003 data unavailable for annual living expenditure
Source: National Bureau of Statistics of China, *China Statistical Yearbooks*, 1998 to 2010 (Beijing: China Statistics).

classes with increasing consumption power, and citizens' willingness to spend on housing.

In addition to the increased spending power of urban residents, housing reforms made homeownership more accessible by the early 2000s—the period during which the homeowners featured in this book purchased their first homes. In less than two decades, China shifted from being a country with predominantly public housing to one with the highest rate of private homeownership in the world.[17]

Available data for Beijing reflect patterns of growth in home ownership similar to those seen at the national level. Since 2003, the proportion of people who rent their homes has generally decreased, whereas homeownership has increased (with the exception of 2013 and 2014, likely because of deteriorating housing affordability; figure 1.5).[18] During this period, even though homeownership was increasing, newly built commercial housing was costly, and it was common for multigenerational families to purchase a home together. Figure 1.6 shows housing prices for commercial residences nationwide from 2007 to 2016; note that the country's average housing price was much lower than that of Beijing (as well as Shanghai and the rising Chinese "Silicon Valley" of Shenzhen).

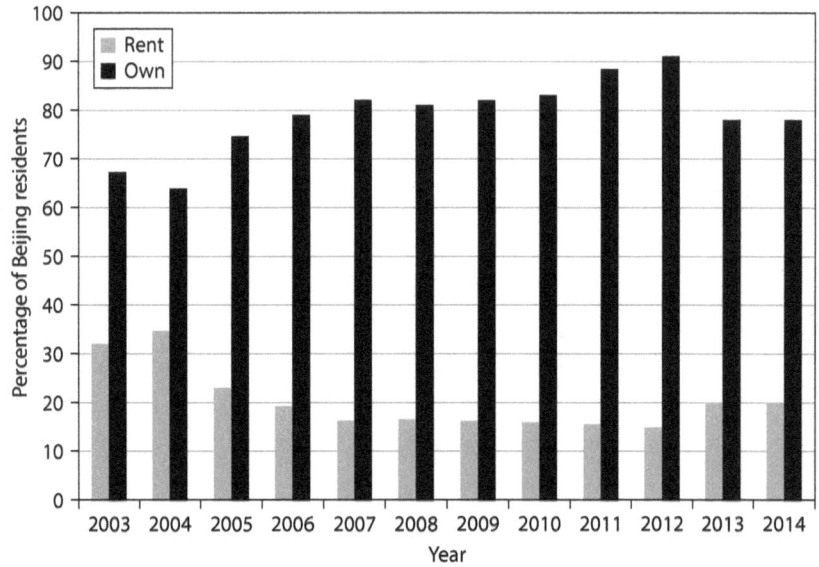

FIGURE 1.5. Percentage of tenants versus homeowners in urban Beijing, 2003 to 2014.
Source: National Bureau of Statistics of China, Beijing Statistical Yearbooks, 2003 to 2014 (Beijing: China Statistics).

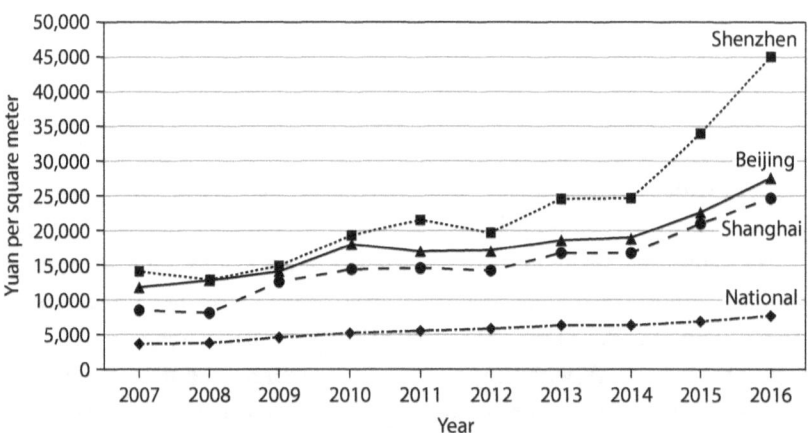

FIGURE 1.6. Average prices of privately owned commodity residences across China, 2007 to 2016.
Source: Wan fang shu ju (Firm). China Real Estate Statistics, 2007 to 2016, EPS shu ju ping tai [EPS China Data Platform], accessed 2016 to 2018, http://www.epschinadata.com/index.html.

Extrapolating from the data, in 2016, the average price of a 100-square-meter home (about 1,076 square feet) outside these three cities was around 747,600 yuan, or about $115,794 in U.S. dollars. Meanwhile, a home in Beijing of the same size would have cost around 2.75 million yuan, or $420,000 in U.S. dollars—roughly 3.5 times the cost of a home outside these three major urban areas. Apartments or villas that were marketed as "luxury" dwellings were even more expensive, priced at almost twice the cost per square meter of an average commodity residence in the same city.

EVOLVING CONCEPTS OF PROPERTY RIGHTS

Because of the steep cost of housing, new homeowners were careful to monitor the building of their homes, many of which were still under construction at the time of purchase. Through this vigilance, homeowners aimed to ensure real estate developers upheld promises made in purchasing contracts, such as the use of a certain quality of building materials or even specific brands of materials. Once in their new homes, residents then carefully monitored property-management companies responsible for the upkeep of their gated communities. These self-advocacy activities, in which middle-class Chinese homeowners have been engaged since the early 2000s, can be characterized as *weiquan* ("rights-protection") activities and viewed as part of a larger emergence of rights-protection consciousness in China during this period.

The term *weiquan* came into use in the 1990s along with early consumer-rights movements. Frequently used to describe contemporary protesting, it places emphasis on dissenters "protecting their legal rights" rather than disrupting the social order. Definitionally, citizens pursuing *weiquan* are engaging in a form of "rightful resistance," creatively invoking laws and policies rather than simply "resisting" government authorities.[19] The idea of "rights defense" has become more prevalent in recent years, applying not only to government targets but also to businesses such as property developers and property-management companies. By characterizing protests as *weiquan*, citizens avoid the appearance of challenging the state; rather, they call on the principles established by the state to protect citizens.

Before 2007, however, no formal legal system had been enacted to protect private property rights. As homeownership boomed, including in the Beijing communities featured in this book, tensions arose between homeowners, as yet unprotected by law, and property developers and managers.[20] For example, developers and property-management companies often engaged in commercial pursuits that conflicted with the interests of homeowners, such as selling neighborhood parking lots to outsiders, using common areas for commercial activities, and even reselling community spaces.[21] Struggles with property developers over construction shortcomings and with property management over the use of community spaces have been the topics of several studies.[22]

The Property Rights Law, enacted in 2007 after nearly a decade of discussion, for the first time specified the rights and responsibilities of all parties involved in the housing market, including real estate developers, property-management offices, and homeowners. This law also described the steps homeowners could take to address disputes with property management.[23] However, this law was enacted only after the homeowners discussed in this book had purchased their homes in Beijing.

A RISING "MIDDLE CLASS"

With the introduction of commodity or private residences, urban landscapes have also transformed. In city centers across China, most old *danwei* neighborhoods have been redeveloped, with residents of lower socioeconomic status being relocated to peripheral urban areas. Because of urban sprawl, what used to be rural land has turned into priority development zones, technological parks, large shopping centers, and private housing developments. Urban centers now include semigated and gated residential communities in which middle- and upper-middle-class homeowners reside.[24] Gated commercial housing communities, in particular, house a large number of middle- and upper-middle-income homeowners and have become sites of middle-class identity formation.[25]

The gated and therefore segregated nature of these communities has been a subject of much interest.[26] Studies of gated communities in North America illustrate that the desire of middle-class individuals to cultivate a secure and distinct lifestyle motivates the gating of residential communities, particularly in the suburbs.[27] In recent years, the movement of middle-income citizens to inner cities from suburban areas and "revamping" neighborhoods to suit and preserve their lifestyles and preferences has contributed to gentrification in the United States.[28] Similarly, urban gated communities in China cultivate and preserve emerging middle-class identities while middle-class residents strengthen their connections to the spaces they occupy to preserve their living standards and property rights.

This rise of a white-collar stratum of society in Asia has been widely discussed over the past three decades and has been attributed to Asia's "miraculous" economic development (e.g., in Taiwan, South Korea, Hong Kong, and Singapore) and remarkable gross domestic product (GDP) growth in China, Nepal, and India.[29] Aside from adding to the economic development of the region, the rising and upwardly mobile middle class has cultivated a distinct form of social life and culture. While it is difficult to pinpoint exactly who belongs to the middle class, many conceptualizations point to certain occupational and educational statuses in an urbanized and industrialized society (e.g., Vogel's study of Japan's emerging middle class).[30] Historically in the United States, new middle classes were shaped by the growth of corporations, with white-collar workers representative of a distinct and expanding social stratum.[31] However, there is still much ongoing debate over how to define the middle class in China.[32]

Some scholars describe the Chinese middle class as consumers with purchasing power who either play a role in demanding political rights or are afraid of upsetting the state to protect their newfound wealth.[33] Others focus on the "multiplicity" of this social group,[34] expanding the meaning of "being in the middle" in urban China to broadly comprise living a relatively affluent life, obtaining formal education, and being well informed about current events and social issues.[35] Zhang found that in South Korea, China, and India, the "new middle class" is a "complex and unstable social formation" of people with diverse occupations and social backgrounds.[36] What links them is not social position but rather a similar lifestyle orientation expressed through homeownership, consumerism, and economic liberalism.[37] The latter definition best characterizes the Beijing homeowners featured in this book, whose lifestyle orientation is expressed through gated community life and homeownership. As later chapters will discuss, this orientation has been learned and constructed together by these homeowners in the context of residing in their new community spaces.

This new middle class in urban China—characterized by homeownership, upward mobility, and consumption power—has brought about new ways of living in cities. It has been a central force in the formation of new urban communities in which civic skills and ideas of citizenship are cultivated.

Shared community spaces and the quality and comfort of life these residential spaces offer reinforce the homeowner identity and its associated middle-class status. Under these conditions, place and class have become intricately linked, as new homeowners develop a sense of communal responsibility within their gates, as well as a broader sense of civic responsibility through collective action and engagement with environmental issues reaching beyond their immediate communities.

Because the Beijing homeowners I studied fit the broad concept of the "middle class" in terms of homeownership, occupation, education, and lifestyle (and living in a rapidly urbanizing and developing city), I will refer to them as such in this book. However, it is uncommon for these or similar homeowners in China to use the term "middle class" in reference to themselves. They are more likely to think of themselves as homeowners, neighbors, or Beijing citizens than as members of a particular social class.[38] According to Zhang, an identifying question that people under the former *danwei* housing system would have asked one another was, "What work unit do you belong to?" She explains that the equivalent contemporary inquiry is, "What residential community do you live in?"[39] This shift indicates that urban residents are now increasingly identified—especially socioeconomically—in relation to the spaces in which they reside.

HOMEOWNERS' FORMAL ASSOCIATIONAL LIFE

The management of residential spaces has also shifted over time. Residents' committees (RCs) were originally created in 1954 to ensure local neighborhood monitoring. At the time, they were composed of "activist" residents who were not members of the Communist Party but supported the maintenance of political order in their neighborhoods.[40] However, urban neighborhood management largely remained the responsibility of the governmental *danwei*. Following the economic and housing reforms of the 1980s and 1990s, RCs came to be managed by state administrative staff rather than residents and gradually took on more community responsibilities, providing both administrative and welfare services to neighborhoods.[41] As housing privatization accelerated, real estate developers, property-management companies, homeowners, and HOAs all took on aspects of influence and oversight. At the neighborhood level, RCs represent the state; developers and property managers represent market forces; and homeowners represent social forces. While developers often hire property managers to maintain good relations with local governments,[42] homeowners and HOAs may struggle against these other actors.

Unlike HOAs in the United States, which primarily make and enforce inwardly directed rules for community residents and their properties, Chinese HOAs generally focus their work outward on relations with other parties, helping and mobilizing residents to solve neighborhood problems by circulating petitions, organizing demonstrations, or filing lawsuits against developers.[43] Additionally, whereas American HOAs often have formal funding structures that incorporate property-management costs, homeowners of new residential complexes in China pay monthly fees directly to property-management companies, with independently organized HOAs left to fund themselves through homeowner donations.[44]

While HOAs in China have been permitted by law since the 2003 Regulations on Real Property Management, in reality the rules and conditions for their establishment remain prohibitively stringent.[45] For example, an association must elect a steering committee with the approval of at least half the homeowners in a given residential community. Any major HOA decision related to changes in community structure or facilities requires the approval of at least two-thirds of the homeowners. Conducting such elections and obtaining such approvals require a significant amount of time, to which many homeowners are reluctant to commit. Moreover, even with unlimited time, it would be a tremendous challenge to mobilize even half the homeowners in a gated community of ten thousand residents.[46] In newly built communities where homeowners do not yet know their neighbors well or have their contact information, self-organizing is a struggle. As a result, most housing communities have yet to form official associations[47]—and many try and fail, as the examples in this book show.[48]

Importantly, HOAs are the first true autonomous organizations in China to be run by homeowners and to represent homeowners' interests. However, the formation and operation of an HOA, especially at the preparatory stage, can be subject to interference by the RC, such as through involvement with the HOA preparatory committee or the nomination of homeowner representatives.[49] While residents of the communities featured in this book rarely mentioned RCs, when they did, they complained that RCs did not protect residents' interests. Some homeowners also said that they did not know who was involved in their RC, despite the RC serving as the most local level of government and presumably including resident representatives (though not necessarily from their own gated communities).

OTHER FORMS OF HOMEOWNER SELF-ORGANIZING

In addition to formal HOAs, homeowners around the world engage in many other forms of self-organizing to protect their property, community, and lifestyle. Residential gates themselves are understood as a form of middle-class organizing to defend lifestyle through spatial and social exclusion.[50] Residents in the northeastern United States were also involved in years of NIMBY ("not in my backyard") struggles against proposed incinerator sites.[51] In China, homeowners' movements were virtually absent under the *danwei* system but have emerged in recent years along with private homeownership.[52]

One of the few well-documented studies of movements by Chinese homeowners examined the case of a protest in the southern Chinese city of Guangzhou in the early 2000s in which middle- and high-income homeowners resisted a road construction project.[53] The homeowners learned about a large road that was to be constructed running directly through their quiet neighborhood and attempted to file lawsuits, petition, and organize protests. However, after much back-and-forth among the local government, the construction company, and homeowners, the road was constructed. Nevertheless, the residents persisted in protesting, employing tactics to discourage new homebuyers from purchasing apartments in the area. Their actions brought the construction company to the negotiation table, where it was agreed that the construction company would beautify the road and limit the level of noise if the residents would stop their disruptive activities.

Such resistance has become more prevalent as residents in urban areas of China have become more affluent.[54] These cases of self-organizing and resistance by homeowners are significant, regardless of their failure or success in achieving their intended outcomes. The ability to organize within a residential community paves the way for other forms of collective action and to address issues other than property rights.

Since 2006, the term "community social organization" (*shequ shehui zuzhi*) has come into common use, in alignment with the growth of privately owned residential communities.[55] According to China's civil affairs bureau (the government agency in charge of regulating social organizations), community organizations are defined as organizations "in a limited geographic area (community), that satisfy the different demands of community residents, that conduct activities which are legally permitted." The term "community" (*shequ*) is administratively defined as either a subdistrict or several residential neighborhoods within a subdistrict. However, community organizations vary across provinces, and what constitutes a community organization can be locally specific. For example, in the southern province of Yunnan, community organizations must be nonprofit, charitable, and focus on social service (similar to the concept of charitable organizations in the West). However, in other Chinese provinces and in Beijing, there are no such requirements. Based on registration data, most community organizations are actually established by residential housing communities, much like the ones featured in this book, and the names of specific housing communities are attached to their records.[56]

As community-based organizations became more prevalent, the government became keen to regulate them. In 2009, a community social organization registration (reporting) system was established. "Community Organization Reporting Trial Regulations" were announced in Beijing and several other cities, stipulating that after authorization from a local government RC, a community organization must file a report with a local government supervisory unit and then contact local civil affairs agencies to formally register.[57] Registered organizations range from community security patrol associations to sports clubs and environmental cleanup squads.

The stories in this book, however, focus on informal rather than formal associations. While community organization definitions and a registration system are telling of a larger trend toward self-organizing among citizens, an exclusive focus on formally registered groups overlooks a significant portion of urban community life and environmental organizing. The following chapters reveal how active community associational life in new housing communities occurs primarily through informal groups, none of which is initially registered with the government. For example, in Community Meadow, where a community environmental organization was officially registered in late 2010, residents had been engaged in environmental organizing work since 2005.

Middle-class homeowners are a growing urban group, deeply tied to their communities with respect to space, as an outcome of structural forces such as housing reforms and urban design, and with respect to identity, as a consequence of being homeowners in a shared space. The actions they take to protect their property rights and quality of life become stepping stones for environmental organizing when communities find themselves faced with common external grievances. Their experiences participating in both formal and informal associational life create repertoires from which they can draw when they begin to tackle environmental threats such as landfill stench or incinerator construction. In the early 2000s, as urban environmental problems plagued new homeowners and threatened their quality of life, environmental resistance against municipal projects gained momentum. Some of this activity has been researched by studying protests, yet documented protest events represent only a small proportion of homeowners' actual collective action. As residential housing complexes mushroom in cities, collective action within communities—likely unrecorded in any official manner—is bound to occur more often. This book goes inside these unofficial conversations to examine how urban residential collective action takes shape behind the scenes.

ENVIRONMENTAL DEGRADATION

Along with increased homeownership and economic development in urban areas have come a surge in construction projects and increases in factory emissions and the number of cars on the road. Pollution has impacted everyday quality of life in China, taking a particular toll on urban residents. More than a decade before the global COVID-19 pandemic, Beijing residents were rarely seen outside without face masks. Rather than the weather, people made small talk about air pollution. However, no citywide protests over air pollution have been recorded—urban residents seem to have normalized smog and face masks.

Although air pollution remains an issue common to all urban residents, hyper-localized issues appear to have more salience. Polluting factories and construction projects next to residential communities have triggered a level of resistance unseen in response to citywide problems. As local sources of pollution were perceived as a direct threat to their middle-class way of life, homeowners began to play a larger role in environmental organizing in the early 2000s. Often dissatisfied with government responses to their grievances and with a distrust of government-produced environmental impact reports, homeowners looked for other ways to address the problem, including through citizen science and community data collection (chapter 5).

A STENCH ON SUCCESS

STATE GOVERNANCE OF ENVIRONMENTAL PROBLEMS

With urban expansion occurring so rapidly, the government of China had little time to predict or mitigate the resulting environmental degradation, and environmental issues did not become a key concern for the government until the early 2000s. In 2004, economic losses as a result of environmental pollution amounted to 3 percent of annual GDP.[58] Air pollution has been the biggest (and most visible) challenge for the national government as it tries to balance environmental protection with urban development.[59] The issue of air quality became particularly salient before the Beijing Olympics in 2008, as the government attempted to improve air quality in anticipation of the surge in tourism and media coverage. This effort included a program to limit traffic and reduce emissions by implementing strict restrictions on vehicles, construction, and factories and spraying roads with water to reduce dust. Some of these controls were relaxed after the Olympics, but measures such as traffic control remained in place in Beijing.[60] Nonetheless, Beijing's air quality remains among the worst in the nation.[61]

Given the severity of the country's environmental problems, the state's handling of these issues has become critical to both its governmental legitimacy and the stability of the nation. Environmental degradation triggers dissent, which poses a direct threat to social stability. With respect to the government's official stance toward environmental protection, China has some of the world's most comprehensive environmental laws and regulations. However, many challenges are faced in the implementation of these laws at the local level. Local governments are incentivized to skimp on regulatory implementation and enforcement. Pursuing polluting practices to achieve higher GDP growth and strengthen local development remains a priority for many localities. A "pollute first, mitigate later" attitude is readily found among many local leaders.[62]

Overall, administrative and legal systems for enforcing environmental laws are weak. Central environmental officials have expressed frustration with provincial and local officials, complaining that "as soon as their backs are turned, local officials return to pollution, reopen illegal mines, or resume timber-cutting even if there is a logging ban."[63] Central officials supervise environmental protection bureaus (EPBs) and offices at the provincial, county, and township levels, but they cannot issue binding orders to provincial governments. Local governments still make decisions for local

EPBs in terms of budgets, personnel, and the closure of polluting plants.[64] Therefore, the deeper problem of environmental stewardship in China lies not in the lack of environmental regulations or the laws themselves but in the disincentives to enact them at the local level and the lack of public confidence in the equal application of laws. Rules are often broken and sometimes unclear, and many environmental legal provisions in China are vaguely worded, with no enforcement mechanisms specified.[65] Officials and businesspeople find ways around regulations, and few polluters are prosecuted even if they are issued warnings.[66]

Some of these tensions become evident in the plights of the communities described in this book, as homeowners begin to interact with both local and central officials over environmental complaints. Such homeowners are a potential rising force for change. Urban citizens now demand government accountability as environmental problems grow more severe. Several institutional channels exist through which citizens can voice their environmental complaints, including the petitioning (*xinfang*) system. This system is part of traditional mass-line politics and provides nonbinding political consultation for the masses. To avoid overwhelming central-government agencies, local consultation agencies are designed to take on most of the work.

This structure is still in place today, and a large number of petitions are received annually in the "social disputes" category (20.6 percent of all petitions), which includes environmental and property rights grievances.[67] In Beijing alone, 26,103 such petitions were received in 2006 (the most recent year for which data are available).[68] Although petitioning is an accessible institutional channel, the associated complaint letters are often "absorbed" locally, and few reach the central government. However, homeowners located in Beijing have the advantage of accessibility as they live in proximity of both central and local government agencies and can therefore deliver letters directly to central agencies.

In addition to petitioning, environmental complaint hotlines are available to the public. These hotlines, which connect citizens with government staff, provide an outlet for individuals to express their environmental concerns. However, as with many institutional channels for expressing grievances, many Chinese citizens were not fully aware of this option until a documentary was released online in 2015 (later removed by officials). Following its release, there was a surge in hotline complaints. Later chapters will explore how homeowners in one of the featured communities attempted to use such a hotline in the early 2000s—to little effect.

THE URBAN TRASH PROBLEM

Because of the crowding of cities, urban trash became a pressing issue in China in the early 2000s. The government scrambled to respond to the problem without any effective waste management systems having been in place before the surge in urban growth. Most of the landfills in Beijing were built in the 1990s on what were then the outskirts of the city. But given the continued construction of new housing, these areas are no longer the outskirts but rather part of the expanding urban center. With landfills quickly reaching capacity, the central government made plans to construct a dozen waste incinerators nationally within a period of ten years.

Estimates for the time period featured in this book indicate that China created more than 360 million tons of domestic waste each year—160 million tons in cities alone (equivalent to about 18 billion bags of garbage)—with the quantity growing at a rate of 8 percent each year.[69] In Beijing, 18,000 tons of garbage were generated *per day*, but the city was able to process only 11,000 tons daily.[70] This shortfall posed a challenge for all levels of government. Around 50 percent of the garbage was placed in landfill, 12 percent was burned, a little under 10 percent was used for fertilizer, and the rest was left untreated, according to a 2012 report by China Dialogue.[71] From the perspective of the state, incinerators offered a quick fix: they would solve odor problems and resolve space issues, and some would be able to generate electricity. Many of the municipal officials I interviewed viewed incineration as an "unavoidable option" as land space available in the city to bury trash was running out.

With the municipal landfills built in the late 1990s filled beyond capacity, incinerators were planned to be located adjacent to the landfills. Some were meant to gradually replace the landfills in the ensuing decade, but in the latter half of the first decade of the 2000s, most landfills and incinerators were slated to coexist. Two problems erupted at that point. First, the landfills had been taking on increasing trash over the previous five years but had not until then reached the level of methane gas production to cause a noticeable stench. Second, many new residential communities were built in the early 2000s, and new homeowners were unknowingly moving into areas of Beijing where the landfills were located. As more and more people moved into their new homes, the landfills were reaching maximum capacity and beginning to emit a rotting stench.

The stench started to trigger concerns among Beijing homeowners in residential communities by about the middle of the first decade of the 2000s. Despite their discomfort, many homeowners tolerated the landfill stench for several years after moving in. Some reasoned that because the landfills had been there before them, there was little they could do. A turning point in homeowner attitudes occurred when incinerator construction projects were planned without clear communication or discussion with the homeowner communities. The following chapters will illustrate how, having had time to interact with one another as neighbors, establish trust and associational networks, and experience some forms of collective action against property management, homeowners in some communities were able to participate in collective sensemaking around the issues of landfill stench and incinerator construction by sharing and discussing information on their online homeowners' forums and in person.

INCOME FIRST, IDENTITY LATER

In the early 2000s, middle-class residents in Beijing mostly worked in white-collar jobs—for example, in banking, finance, accounting, or information technology—and saved up income to purchase a home, often with the help of their multigenerational families. However, their *identities* as homeowners were forged not in the act of purchasing a home but rather in community experiences with other homeowner residents later on. While social protests are not a new phenomenon in China, what makes this book's case studies unique is how these middle-class homeowners were able to create capacity to mobilize for collection action in their communities through informal activities such as sports clubs and through formal organizations such as HOAs (or at least preparatory HOA committees). They cultivated community networks and homeowner leadership, which enabled them to mobilize and organize against landfill stench and incinerator construction. These efforts included educating their communities about the issue of incineration, engaging with representatives of various levels of government, and injecting citizen-science data and voices into their discussions with government agencies, environmental experts, and environmental nonprofit organizations. Their collective actions went beyond one-time events, counteracting the descriptive statistics that suggest that organized protest is isolated to mass incidents.

If the efforts of the communities featured in this book were considered only in terms of single events such as protests against incinerator construction, then the rich stories of how middle-class residential communities cultivate homeowners' identities and how residents experience associational life would be lost. Further, community environmental resistance not only points to a larger process of middle-class voices being incorporated into policy considerations but also vividly demonstrates how urban middle-class residents form ideas of civic responsibility through engagement within their communities and in the public sphere beyond their gates. Gated communities, newly constructed in the early 2000s, became a wellspring for collective action and a school of democracy for homeowners in an unlikely place: under the authoritarian Chinese state.

The following chapter explores how associational life, both informal and formal, is cultivated within homeowners' communities. Facilitated by shared space, homeowners in gated residential areas together learn the meaning of being a homeowner, coming to understand and define themselves as part of their respective residential communities.

Chapter Two

GATED COMMUNITIES AS SCHOOLS OF DEMOCRACY

Voluntary association, viewed as the foundation of a healthy participatory democracy, is most frequently conceptualized as arising within democratic settings. However, informal associational life also exists under authoritarianism and within autocracies. Despite the difficulty of tracking informal associations, particularly in such contexts, examining their influence is vital to understanding how and when citizens mobilize in opposition to governmental power. A lack of such organization in an authoritarian setting leaves citizens vulnerable to repression,[1] as an oppressive government can swiftly quell uncoordinated dissent. But when many informal organizations exist, they represent collective voices that can overcome the silencing effects of autocracy.

This chapter examines how such associations have begun to form in China's new urban middle-class housing communities, shedding light on what these groups can achieve inside their gates and what they may bring to larger organizing efforts. Gated housing communities in China are unique spatial arrangements in urban areas—middle-class spaces—in which homeowners can foster a sense of collective identity that is tied to these places. The "gatedness" reinforces identity formation and facilitates associational life; the gates themselves provide a clear-cut boundary, not only for assembly but also for mobilization.

In Communities Meadow, Rose, and Marigold, even before moving in, many prospective homeowners attempted to connect with one another on an online homeowners' forum run by the internet company Sohu. There, they expressed their excitement at becoming homeowners for the first time, exchanged tips on things to watch out for during the closing process, and shared advice on dealing with real estate developers and property-management companies. In some communities, in-person meetings took place before homeowners moved in; dozens of soon-to-be residents of a community traveled across Beijing to meet and talk about housing-related concerns. For many, the process of becoming a homeowner—defining a collective identity, learning about property rights, and bonding with new neighbors—began before the sales of their homes closed.

This chapter begins by describing the physical layouts of gated communities and the characteristics of their residents, then discusses how online forums helped residents begin to develop the collective identity of "homeowner" and how they framed their commitments to their new living spaces as "community identity." The process of becoming neighbors is examined, revealing variations in how informal associational life took shape in these communities online and off-line, and how such actions fostered networks of trust and helped residents develop the civic skill of organizing. Because this chapter focuses on homeowner activity oriented *within* their housing communities, in contrast to chapter 4's focus on actions that look *outward* toward government systems, this chapter also describes homeowners' early efforts of collective action against property management. An important lesson homeowners learned from interacting with property management is that a collective voice is more powerful and effective in exerting pressure than are individual voices. The final section of the chapter recounts residents' successful and failed attempts to amplify their collective voice by organizing homeowners' associations (HOAs).

Though circumscribed by the community gates, all the actions taken to develop networks and assert homeowner rights contribute to homeowners' civic education. While the communities in the three locations exhibited varying styles and degrees of engagement, forming homeowners' information infrastructures (i.e., active use of the online homeowners' forum for many purposes), cultivating community identity, and developing skills allowed communities to build capacity for later collective organizing. Civic education begins in these middle-class spaces, allowing individuals to engage in collective decision-making when encountering and processing new challenges.

Although gates can be seen as representing a middle-class retreat into a life of comfort, safety, and privacy,[2] this chapter shows that vibrant associational life exists within many gated communities in Beijing, fostering social capital online and off-line and shaping the desire and the needed skill sets to take on issues beyond the gates. The imagined boundary of the gates was eventually erased in some communities (though not in others). Some homeowners learned to define their roles and responsibilities as part of a larger community, whereas others remain gated in identity and in action (discussed further in chapters 3 and 4).

SPACE AS COMMUNITY

Most new middle-class residential complexes in China are gated, with groundskeeping, facility maintenance, sanitation services, and security supplied by property-management companies (*wuyei* or *wuguan*). These complexes and their condominium-like arrangements are not unlike some urban condominium communities in the United States, though much larger in scale. Gated residential communities in China span the equivalent of several city blocks and can house hundreds, thousands, or even tens of thousands of households in multifamily apartment-style complexes or single-family townhouses or villas (figure 2.1). Although gated communities

FIGURE 2.1. The layout of a typical middle-class gated community in urban Beijing.
Source: Photo provided by a Community Rose homeowner.

GATED COMMUNITIES AS SCHOOLS OF DEMOCRACY

vary in the degree to which they emphasize status or luxury, nearly all feature convenience provided through amenities such as supermarkets, day cares, playgrounds, and scenic areas within the gates.[3]

The three gated community sites that are the focus of this book were established at roughly the same time: Community Meadow's two phases of construction were completed in 2005; Rose's four phases were completed between 2004 and 2008; and Marigold was completed in 2005. Whereas Rose is organized as blocks of high-rises and Meadow is a mix of high-rises and townhouses, Community Marigold stands out with its all-villa layout, touting a more luxurious and exclusive style of middle-class living.

Community Meadow and Neighboring Communities Willow and Pine

Community Meadow is located in one of the more populated districts on the western side of Beijing. A small river runs close by one side of the community, with mountains serving as the neighborhood's backdrop. A guard station stands at the entrance with an automated gate for cars to pass through and a small side gate for pedestrians. Across the street are several commercial establishments including a restaurant and supermarket. At the entrance to Community Meadow, a bulletin board features property-management announcements and updates on new government initiatives related to the community (e.g., trash-separation guidelines). Within the gates, the community houses 2,202 households in a brightly colored mix of modern townhouses and high-rises of four stories or more, occupying 78.3 acres in building area. To accommodate these residents, more than 2,600 parking spots are available in the community, some at street level and some underground. (Even so, it is not uncommon for drivers to try to squeeze additional vehicles into illegal parking spots or to park on the grass.)

Shared community spaces are provided as courtyards, pavilions, and a pond shaded by newly planted trees. Many of the courtyards are circular, with benches along the periphery facing inward. Here older residents can be seen taking walks and saying hello to one another, often stopping for a leisurely chat. A few pieces of children's playground equipment are arranged in a circle, with benches all around on which parents and grandparents can sit while children play. Meadow homeowners are of all ages, mostly ranging from their thirties to their seventies. Most have jobs in the technology and finance sectors or hold administrative positions in government-related institutes (common middle-class occupations in urban China), while some older retired residents live in the community with their extended families.

Two gated communities are located near Community Meadow: Willow and Pine, each accommodating more than 1,200 households. When residents began moving into Meadow and Willow in 2005, Pine was already an "older" gated community, having been completed in 1998. Initially, these gated communities sat separately with few connections among them, but as landfill problems and incinerator construction threats unraveled in the larger neighborhood, the three massive middle-class spaces mobilized for action, led by residents of Meadow. Chapter 4 details the mobilization process; the physical setting description provided here demonstrates that upward of 5,300 households from these three gated communities had the potential to mobilize.[4]

Community Rose

The second site, Community Rose, is also located in a highly desirable district of Beijing with convenient transportation and amenities. Whereas Meadow is to the west of central Beijing, Rose sits to the east. Community Rose is much larger than Meadow, Willow, and Pine, with 150 acres of building area and 6,901 households by the end of four phases of construction.[5] Composed entirely of high-rises, its tower blocks range from eight to thirteen stories tall. Similar to urban condominium complexes in the United States, but unlike the other communities studied, in Community Rose the outer edges of the community house several small businesses, including a dry cleaner, a small supermarket, and a hair salon. While the buildings are less colorful than those of Meadow, lavish European-style sculptures line the main driveway leading into the community, which looms beyond twelve grandiose Greek columns. Underneath this entrance is a guard station, with a nearby bulletin board much like Meadow's.

In juxtaposition to the ornateness of the main entrance area, a small children's playground with just a few pieces of equipment is tucked away in a corner of the community, as though an afterthought. In contrast to Meadow, there are fewer benches and common areas for Rose homeowners to gather, but well-trimmed hedges and neat cobblestone paths lead up to each building entrance. The main gathering place is located beyond the community walls: a nearby soccer field and a basketball court frequently used by Rose's notably younger homeowners. Primarily in their thirties and forties, these homeowners work in technology, finance, or creative-industry jobs. As in Meadow, some older residents live with their extended families. Although other similar gated communities are situated near Community Rose, none joined in the later organizing efforts against incinerator construction (chapter 4).

Community Marigold

The third community site, northwest of central Beijing, has a layout distinct from Meadow, Pine, Willow, and Rose. Community Marigold, with 610 villas and townhouses and occupying a whopping 197 acres, is the most sparsely populated by far. A river runs along one side of the community, which boasts a three-acre mega conference center, a two-acre artificial lake, six parks, and numerous botanical gardens. With its single-family homes and sprawling grounds, this community is most similar to gated communities in U.S. suburbs; its website promises "North American style with French baroque architecture."

A guard station allows only authorized vehicles through the gates. Compared to Rose and Meadow, Marigold is a much quieter community, with fewer people walking around outside. Instead of a communal parking lot, homeowners have their own garages, sharing only a mailbox area. Because each home is separate, homeowners run into each other in person less frequently than in the other communities. Marigold homeowners range in age from their thirties to their seventies, holding white-collar jobs in tech, banking or finance, and legal firms. Many spoke of having busy professional lives and traveling frequently for work; some worked elsewhere in the country during the week and came home only on weekends.

Although Marigold presents itself as a more luxurious community, and medium-sized Marigold villas are twice the size of Meadow's three-bedroom condominiums, the cost per square meter is lower than that of Communities Meadow and Rose because of Marigold's farther-flung location. In other words, although Community Marigold exhibits a much more extravagant ambience, it is still in the affordable price range for a middle-class person in Beijing. However, it is a community that is marketed as upscale, and based on my observations, it is populated almost exclusively by nuclear-family households (rather than the multigenerational households seen at sites like Meadow, Willow, and Pine). It could therefore be the case that white-collar Marigold residents were able to afford homes on their own, rather than needing additional financial support from extended families, and chose a community in which this arrangement was typical. As associational life developed—largely online rather than in person because of the community's dispersed layout—Marigold residents formed a strong "wealthier-homeowner" identity (as they described it to me), differentiating themselves from "other types of gated communities" in which residents are more tightly packed.

Table 2.1 shows that while communities varied slightly in terms of building types, most consist of high-rises or a combination of high-rises

TABLE 2.1
Gated community sites

	Meadow	Willow	Pine	Rose	Marigold
Housing design	21 low- and high-rises, 4 stories or higher	24 high-rises, 6 stories or higher	30 high-rises, all 6 stories; 300 villas and townhouses	51 high-rises, ranging from 8 to 13 stories	610 villas and townhouses
Year constructed	2005	2004	2001	2004 (phases 1 and 2), 2007 (phase 3), 2008 (phase 4)	2005
Area of residential space (in acres)[a]	78.3	39.5	123	150[b]	49[c]
Number of households	2,202 (1,490 at phase 1, 712 at phase 2)	1,454	1,884	6,901 (1,312 at phase 1; 2,935 at phase 2; 1,520 at phase 3; 1,134 at phase 4)	610
Percentage of green space[d]	34%	58%	38%	33%	64%
Number of parking spots	2,600	500	200	2,500	610 (individual garages)

Source: All information drawn from the real estate websites Anjuke (https://beijing.anjuke.com) and Fang (https://fang.com/), accessed 2018

[a] Real estate websites provided the approximate acreage of the land upon which homes were situated but did not always provide the acreage of the entire community.

[b] 150 acres at the completion of four phases. During the anti-incineration mobilization, only two phases had been completed; thus, at that time, the community was about 75 acres, half its completed size.

[c] Including the river walk, artificial lake, and park, Community Marigold is situated on 197 acres, with 49 acres devoted to housing. With fewer households and more land, Marigold has a larger proportion of green space than the other communities.

[d] The percentage of green space is the total amount of land allotted for green space in the community.

and townhomes. Limited information was available on total acreage, but available data on the area allotted for residences show that these communities are expansive. For example, the total area taken up by residences in Community Rose (150 acres) is approximately 1.5 times the size of the Mall of America or the Disneyland theme park. More than half of Willow's and Marigold's community areas are allocated as green space, demonstrating purposeful environmental considerations in the design of new housing construction. Parking was a problem for everybody—even in Community Meadow, where the number of parking spaces exceeds the number of households, residents described problems of parking overflow to me. Although there are variations in the physical layouts of the communities, with Meadow (and neighboring Willow and Pine), Rose, and Marigold located in separate areas of Beijing, all were adjacent to existing landfills—even Marigold, with its wealthier homeowners and reputation as a luxury community.

COMMUNITY AS VIRTUAL SPACE: ONLINE HOMEOWNERS' FORUMS

One key barrier to organizing for homeowners in an authoritarian setting, in contrast to those in democratic settings, is the difficulty of convening publicly in large groups. Whenever eight or more homeowners gather together in China, for example, they are required to ask property management for permission to convene. When homeowners meet to discuss issues that are grievance or advocacy oriented, property management sometimes refuses to let residents use community spaces to congregate. Because of this restriction, homeowners either relocate meetings to the privacy of their homes or move online to virtual homeowners' forums.

In China, where freedom of speech is limited, online spaces have become important places to share information and public opinion. In mobilizing and organizing homeowners for collective action, whether internally against property management or externally against government agencies, recruitment and discussions often take place online. This remote gathering takes place on blogs or microblogs (*buoke*), discussion forums, and bulletin board systems (abbreviated as "bbs" and popular among college students). Most forums used by homeowners in the early 2000s were hosted on a platform run by the private internet company Sohu.[6] Visually, homeowners' forums are organized as discussion threads, comparable to other common internet forums. The platform also offers a chat function, which homeowners referred to as "small windows" (*xiaochuang*).

Starting in the early 2000s, online homeowners' forums increased in popularity among residents of gated communities, and a number of scholars have documented the role of these forums in homeowners' mobilizations.[7] During the periods of collective action described in this book, posts about mobilization were frequently removed by the host company's platform administrators after pressure from the Public Security Bureau (a.k.a. the internet police) or by local officials, and homeowners' accounts would occasionally be suspended. When suspension occurred, residents often used the chat function to convey sensitive information, but chats could also be blocked (chapter 4). Although it was possible to pay for a hidden homeowners' forum, homeowners' discussions indicate that the price was considered high, and, despite the censorship, most homeowners viewed the public forums as a more accessible source of information than private forums, even in periods of collective action that attracted government scrutiny.

In addition to providing a virtual community space for homeowners, forums serve as infrastructures of community information. Some serve the function of a community newsletter, with homeowners regularly posting community-related information or updates.[8] Forums also act as sources of local news for homeowners in a context in which the mainstream media face censorship, amplifying news from outside the community gates that might be relevant to homeowners but not featured prominently in official sources of news. Forums are also places where networks of caring and support are forged, where mobilizing and organizing occur, and where collective sensemaking happens when homeowners are faced with a new challenge or threat in the community (as demonstrated in the antiincinerator mobilization process described in chapter 3).

The homeowners' forums used in Communities Meadow, Rose, and Marigold were all structured according to content categories common across the forums of gated communities in China:

1. General information provision or sharing (e.g., recipes, recommendations for tiles or appliances, news of a new restaurant opening)
2. Informal posts about associational life (e.g., forming a soccer club, meeting for badminton, planning a group outing, coordinating a group purchase)

3. Nascent efforts of collective action (e.g., airing and discussing grievances that lead to attempts at collective action, such as jointly filing a complaint against property management; discussions about organizing and establishing homeowners' associations)
4. Concrete calls for mobilization and organizing for issues outside the community (e.g., against road or incinerator construction)

In reality, the content areas frequently blend together;[9] a post about playing basketball on a Saturday could evolve into something like "Let's play basketball despite this landfill stench we should do something about."

Although younger and middle-aged homeowners tend to be the main participants on the forums, many older residents told me that they had forum accounts and read posts or asked younger family members to relay information from the forums to them. Older homeowners who organized off-line activities would usually have information about the activities posted online, typically with the help of younger family members or neighbors. The number of views of forum posts from Communities Meadow (and relatedly Willow), Rose, and Marigold generally ranged from a few hundred for a basic information post to a few thousand for posts related to a landfill or incinerator issue. The potential scale of viewership is evident from the most viewed and longest-lasting post, on Community Willow's forum (the most active online community). It concerned landfill stench and attracted more than 83,000 views and more than 550 responses (with around 50 percent of recurring users posting multiple comments) over a span of six years, with Meadow and Pine homeowners participating as well.[10]

The size of the communities poses challenges to facilitating joint efforts with nearby communities, but as the popular Willow forum post suggests, the forums helped overcome some of these obstacles. These online relationships also fostered off-line connections, and vice versa. For example, Meadow residents were able to quickly connect *online* with residents of other communities located in close *physical proximity* (Willow and Pine). As discussed later in this chapter, Willow maintained an active informal associational life and various forms of collective action but fostered stronger relationships virtually rather than in person, whereas Meadow homeowners were active both in face-to-face and online settings. Meadow and Willow residents began to refer to each other on virtual forums, cross-posting content, and eventually connecting in person. On the other hand, some residents of Community Pine, not as active within its own gates or online, chose to work with Meadow and Willow residents when the time came to protest incinerator construction. Community Pine's Mr. Wu (who took me on the neighborhood tour described in the introduction) emerged as a prominent leader of citizen science (chapter 5).[11] When Willow homeowners interacted online but had trouble mobilizing off-line participation in their community, they were able to interact with organizers from Meadow, which provided them with more off-line opportunities to meet.

Online community spaces are made meaningful only when understood in relation to the social capital created and reinforced in off-line spaces—in this case, the physical spaces of homeowners' communities. As Tufekci observed, with quick and massive (and often leaderless) online mobilizations on social media, movements become difficult to sustain once the initial wave of organizing ends.[12] Virtual spaces require the trust and reciprocity rooted in off-line physical spaces or the presence of community leaders to be effective, all of which are present in China's middle-class gated communities. In short, in-person interactions reinforced online trust and deepened virtual connections; online exchanges expanded participation and community networks.

COMMUNITY AS IDENTITY: HOMEOWNERS AND THE BIRTH OF ASSOCIATIONAL LIFE

Compared with renting, homeownership grants citizens a heightened sense of belonging and greater interest in participating in neighborhood associations.[13] However, homeownership is a *learned process*. Regardless of the type of housing—whether a brand-new condominium in a gated community, a suburban home, or an urban townhouse—each new homeowner goes through a process of making sense of what it means to be a homeowner through learning about their rights, a process shaped by their neighbors and surroundings.

Homeowners learn to interpret their property rights from what they read, what their friends say, and what their new neighbors tell them. These rights—to having contractual obligations met by developers, to timely responses from property management, to being treated as homeowners as soon as down payments are made, and to form HOAs to make collective demands—strengthen both residents' understanding of what

GATED COMMUNITIES AS SCHOOLS OF DEMOCRACY

homeownership means and their identity as homeowners. In this process, the *community* dimension of homeowner identity emerges. Homeowner identity is very much tied to *place*—gated communities and the people within them—and what it means to be a homeowner is collectively defined through interactions and actions taken with other homeowners. This sense of community, or community identity, cannot be understood separately from homeowner identity. Although variations exist in how passionately homeowners framed their commitment to their communities, their living space remained a key component of their identity as a homeowner.

What stands out for first-time homeowners in China—in contrast to those in the United States, for example—is not only the amount of attention placed on properties under construction but also the eagerness of soon-to-be residents to meet and discuss homeownership with their new neighbors before moving in. The construction of their identity as homeowners begins in the process of seeking information from one another before moving in. Upon moving in, homeowners learn to be neighbors by sharing a physical space and by interacting with one another in informal and formal associations. In Communities Meadow and Rose, the ideas of "community responsibility" and being a "good neighbor" were raised on the online forums, whereas for residents of Marigold, attachment to their "wealthier community" was evident in online posts, but homeowners did not go out of their way to organize group activities.

Preparing to Be Homeowners

In the early 2000s, when a large number of middle-class homeowners first purchased homes in areas under construction in China, most were unable to see the finished product until a year or two after their purchase. Homeowners often paid a large portion of the cost as a down payment (or even the full cost of the home) to secure a discounted price. As property developers (*kaifashang*) used some of this money to finish construction, many homeowners watched the developers closely to ensure they upheld building standards. By this time, cases had been documented of homeowners being taken advantage of by developers who had used materials or appliances of poor quality, violating their contractual agreements. Another source of contention was the service fees charged by property-management companies.[14]

The homeowners' forums of Community Meadow and neighboring Willow were active even before construction had finished. A common focus of discussions online was concern over real estate developers using cheaper construction materials than agreed upon. In Meadow, months before residents moved in, some homeowners traveled to assess the site and then posted photos of the construction progress to their forum. These photos depicted buildings nearing completion, surrounded by large piles of bricks that would eventually become the walls surrounding the community. The photos also capture an architectural model of the community, next to which a row of four plaques praises the project with pronouncements like "Beijing's outstanding real estate" and "Outstanding energy-saving design."[15]

While homeowners thanked the photographers for providing a view of the building process, one forum user (from neighboring Community Willow) cautioned everyone not to be too gleeful about the plaques. "There are too many outstanding appraisals these days," he wrote. Other homeowners noticed that the buildings in the model looked different from those at the construction site and urged one another to "save all the photos as evidence." One resident mentioned that she had heard stories of developers scamming homeowners, cautioning, "Whoever believes developers is a foolish home buyer." Online, homeowners asked one another about housing contracts, sought recommendations for lawyers who could review contracts for them, and posted hundreds of messages detailing their worries of being shortchanged by property developers. As homeowners sought advice and resolutions to their concerns, they also demonstrated their middle-class ties; for example, by writing about a friend who had also bought a home or sharing contact information for a lawyer.

Online discussions also moved off-line. Shortly before closing on their homes, Meadow homeowners arranged a hot-pot gathering at a restaurant close to their new community.[16] A group photo shared online shows residents at several tables brimming with hot-pot ingredients. Another photograph shows makeshift signs taped to the restaurant window spelling out "Community Meadow." Forty homeowners attended (including "two underaged and one unborn child") and got to know one another and exchange tips on interior finishes and home closing procedures. Ms. Yu (mentioned in the introduction), the organizer of the event, carefully documented, "Spent a total of 1,057 yuan [$155 in U.S. dollars], averaging

28.75 yuan/person, collecting 30 yuan/person × 37 people = 1,110 yuan, with 53 yuan left. The leftover money will be used for future hot-pot events. End of report!"

This post demonstrates the nascence of community gatherings at Meadow, with their exchanges of experience and advice, as well as an astounding accountability to one another and the expectation for future events.

One homeowner reflected afterward, "Thanks, everyone, for your kind hearts. The gathering was so joyful today . . . met many new people who I have only chatted online with like 'old friends.' So happy." Similarly, another responded, "Next time, I'll treat all our old friends to Peking duck." These messages show that when they finally met in person, some Community Meadow residents already felt like old friends from having interacted so frequently on their forum. The excitement and uncertainties of becoming first-time homeowners led them to actively seek connections both online and off-line, solidifying the shared sentiment of "We're in this together," as several homeowners wrote.

When Meadow homeowners prepared to close on their homes, they received advice from residents of neighboring Willow, whose homeowners had completed their closing procedures a few months before. To better prepare for closing, Meadow homeowners organized two in-person meetings. At the first, homeowners discussed writing a joint letter to property management addressing some of their move-in concerns, such as final inspections before closing, and clarifying procedures for addressing contractual obligations for interior finishes that had not been fulfilled (e.g., the wrong or a cheaper brand of sliding doors or the wrong window-siding material being used). The second meeting was carefully documented, as it involved a homeowner-organized workshop featuring information on the closing process (provided by a construction supervision company using the meeting as an opportunity to sell their products) and an in-person signing of the joint letter that had been composed during the first meeting.[17] The organizer of the meeting wrote, "When I was on the [rented] shuttle, I saw only twenty or so homeowners and was disappointed. But when I got there, I saw a lot of homeowners who went in their own cars—felt so much better. After a quick count, I saw more than seventy people. It's hard to organize an activity. Of course I hope many people attend. Besides, we had to collectively sign the letter—the more people, the more effective!"

Residents of thirty-nine households signed the letter at the event. Some homeowners fretted that the letter had too few signatures to have an impact with property management. "Please contact me proactively, and come sign the letter," the organizer urged online, providing both his home and office addresses. The degree of effort to form a united front before the closing process was substantial, given that for many households it required hours of travel each way through traffic-congested Beijing.

In neighboring Community Willow, which was the most active online early on, the forum provided a play-by-play of community happenings. While initial organizational efforts were remarkable—five in-person homeowners' meetings occurred *before* moving in, homeowners regularly reinforced their commitment to helping one another, established a collective decision-making (polling) process, and signed a joint letter addressed to property management—online interactions ultimately culminated in a failed organizing effort for a large group of fifty to one hundred homeowners to close on their homes collectively.[18]

Early on, Community Willow's Mr. Zhao, in his late thirties and working at a tech company, asked on the forum about potential interest in an in-person homeowners' meeting: "People who want to meet up, respond to this post!" he exhorted. Around twenty people responded, and Mr. Zhao followed up by posting a poll for a convenient meeting location, providing five options:

> The poll is anonymous. Friends who are voting, please send me your email [and] your name or forum username. My email is [redacted]. Some people did not leave me their numbers, and there may be limitations in how many texts you can send [depending on phone plan]. I think the best way to communicate is through email, especially as forum users increase. This is the first time we're getting people together, so it's a bit rushed. Therefore, the voting period [for location selection] is less than a day. That way I'll have half a day to notify everyone. You may select multiple locations. This poll is anonymous!

This simple post to plan a meeting is a striking example of participatory democracy at the community level and contrary to what one would expect in an authoritarian setting. This level of detail and an effort to establish transparency in community decision-making and processes of providing input were already apparent before residents moved into their new homes. While democratic participation in China may not mean voting on ballot measures or running for office, forum polls like this one that gather community opinions and frequently appear online demonstrate a key democratic principle of decision-making by majority. This type of polling would also be used during the homeowners' resistance movement against incinerator construction.

Mr. Zhao soon released the results of his poll. For meeting location, he presented the two cafés that had scored the highest as options and provided information on their average prices for coffee and tea and their parking options. He wrote, "For the first meeting, there's no specific agenda; people can talk about whatever they want. I will document important issues that people have in common and allow those to become later meeting topics and further discussions."

Eighteen people attended at the first meeting, which was meticulously documented in a forum post, serving as both community newsletter and meeting minutes. After each person introduced themselves and shared their experiences and reflections regarding purchasing their homes, broader issues were discussed, specifically around dealing with developers. The post documented that "so far, everyone came to a basic consensus on how to be unified to protect homeowners' rights." The homeowners in attendance called the gathering a "historic meeting." Actionable items were identified, in particular "getting developers to provide details on 'decorations and equipment standards,' in accordance with appendix 3 of the housing purchase contract." At a single meeting that took place more than a year before construction was complete, new homeowners shared stories of home buying, learned to interpret their contracts together, gave one another advice, and arrived at a consensus about what to demand of the developers.

Willow residents were also beginning to demonstrate a commitment to their community during this time. A homeowner who had signed up to attend the first meeting was involved in a scooter accident on the way to the meeting. Addressing this resident, Mr. Zhao wrote on the forum, "Be careful when riding next time. You know, you are not only representing yourself; you are now representing all of Community Willow as well. (Next time I will drive you. I have not been on a scooter in ages!)" The homeowner responded jovially, "Hi leader, I'm the one who got into the accident, feeling bad about it. You should be consoling me! But the scooter has been fixed!" Though Mr. Zhao's post features some light ribbing, it also reflects how some homeowners were starting to think of themselves as "representing all of Community Willow." This feeling of pride and representation forged strong identities as not only homeowners but specifically Willow homeowners.

A second homeowners' meeting was organized a few weeks later, with more than thirty people in attendance. There, the residents drafted an open letter to property management detailing problems in the community, particularly related to equipment and appliances installed in their homes. The letter addressed issues homeowners had raised on their forum and during in-person meetings and included signatures from forty-seven households.[19] Online, Mr. Zhao further encouraged homeowners to "come together [and] work hard for others and themselves to attain a quality living environment." These group actions reflect how the need to collectively protect homeowners' rights had become clearer as more resident gatherings and discussions took place. As residents settled into their new identity as homeowners, they were learning to support one another to resolve shared problems in the community.

By the fourth meeting, in early 2005, Willow homeowners had established three small groups, each consisting of three to five people: the window-screen, parking, and balcony working committees. Homeowners were urged to contact group members with issues or suggestions. Those who missed the fourth meeting were also encouraged to reach out to committee heads if they wished to join a committee. Homeowners were starting to exhibit strong organizational skills and the ability to organize themselves into small task forces with divisions of labor. Regardless of whether actual change would be achieved through interactions with property management, these new skills and abilities helped build community capacity and would later prove useful when homeowners organized to resist incinerator construction (chapters 4 and 5).

In their forum responses, residents who did not attend meetings demonstrated just as much passion as those who did. One homeowner explained that she had not been able to attend because she worked in the suburbs, in state-owned telecommunications. However, to contribute, she offered to type and print a directory of homeowners' addresses and phone numbers. She also volunteered to conduct outreach for the next homeowners' activity.

Another homeowner, who shared that he had a background in architecture, said that he would report back after checking out the community's ongoing construction. "I'll try my best to serve neighbors," he said.

These responses do not accord with Zhang's description of middle-class homeowners shying away from public participation in the private setting of gated communities.[20] Although, of course, many homeowners did not participate in these forums or activities, a large number showed their eagerness to contribute to the community and help out in some way. Leaders like Mr. Zhao further exemplify this community spirit: for each homeowner who created an account for the Community Willow homeowners' forum, Mr. Zhao posted an individualized welcome message.

In online preparations for the final homeowners' meeting before moving in, Mr. Zhao addressed the group by calling on a strong collective identity. He counseled soon-to-be Willow residents that "we homeowners, as a group, are more vulnerable" than property management and stressed how important it was to "come together to protect our rights before moving in." The last meeting was set up to organize homeowners to "collectively close on homes." To ensure that Willow homeowners would stay unified in the process, Mr. Zhao drafted a closing guideline for homeowners that he described as emphasizing "a promise to work together" and addressing property management in a "legal and rational" way. More than two thousand people read the post, and fifty-seven responded, asking to join the collective closing. Some homeowners who traveled outside Beijing for work even wrote that they would send family members to attend.

Despite this strong interest, the collective closing did not actually occur. Through a forum poll, fewer than ten people indicated they would attend, so Mr. Zhao called off the event. When receiving an individual closing notice from developers a few weeks later, he completed the closing process on his own with his lawyer. Although the event was not a success, Mr. Zhao was undeterred from his mission of strengthening the homeowners' position relative to that of the developers. After his closing, he provided a detailed account of suggestions from his lawyer, mostly regarding which developer's fees were appropriate and which would be prepaid but should be reimbursed later on. Mr. Zhao thanked the homeowners who had called to check on him throughout the closing process and noted that he had run into a few homeowners in the community who stopped to chat with him in a friendly way.[21]

These pleasant exchanges, however, did not portend in-person involvement in organizing efforts at Community Willow. While Willow residents were active online before moving in, off-line interactions did not seem to translate to the same type of engagement. Homeowners possessed some skills to organize themselves, but the absence of more active in-person and informal activities of associational life (e.g., hangouts, group outings, sports clubs) remained an obstacle to effective organizing. Therefore, moving in became an opportunity to bolster online interactions among homeowners who had already begun forming their sense of community and making sense of communal challenges together.

On the other side of Beijing, this process was slow to begin in Community Rose. While there was a smattering of welcome messages on the Community Rose forum when new homeowners joined, it had nowhere near the volume of Willow's forum activity. A homeowner named Ms. Hua, an industrial designer in her early thirties who would later emerge as a leader in organizing against the landfill and incinerator, made a down payment in December 2002 for a two-bedroom home and reached out online to her soon-to-be neighbors. Before moving in, very few homeowners used the Rose forum, so Ms. Hua frequented the forums of other communities built by the same property developer. She met a few Rose homeowners virtually and recommended one to serve as the forum moderator (though she received no reply). Determined to find pertinent housing information, Ms. Hua sought information on other community forums regarding signing contracts with developers, and she contributed information on various forums, reminding new homeowners to pay attention to certain details when finalizing their housing contracts. Though the new homeowners of Community Rose did not meet in person before moving in, Ms. Hua and some other Rose residents were already starting to learn about exercising their rights and were eager to share their knowledge with others.

The third community site, Community Marigold, shared with Meadow and Willow its homeowners' interest in connecting online prior to moving in (around mid-2005). Unlike the Rose forum, the Marigold forum was established before homeowners closed on their homes; similar to Meadow and Willow, homeowners logged on to ask about construction and renovations, share advice on furniture (sometimes knowing enough about one another's design preferences to say, "It's not your style!"), post updates on construction, express worries about contracts with developers, and list issues to be aware of when inspecting their homes before closing.

Some posts demonstrated how homeowners were beginning to feel a sense of pride in being part of the Marigold community. Several months before moving in, the Sohu platform hosted a vote for the "best gated community." Marigold homeowners encouraged one another to vote ("Our community is ranking is so low right now; are people not noticing the poll?"); guided other homeowners to the location of the poll, specifying, "You can vote only once a day per person; we need more popularity!"; and asserted, "We must rank in the top one hundred." (Three days later, Marigold ranked within the top two hundred participating residential communities in China but ultimately did not make the top one hundred.)[22]

Much like those of Meadow and Willow, Marigold homeowners began to make plans for gatherings prior to moving in and even asked whether it was possible for developers to create a "relatively private space" within the community for future HOA activities. "We really have a need for this," one Marigold homeowner wrote. The move-in process was more drawn out for Marigold homeowners, spanning a period of six months compared to a few weeks in other communities. One in-person homeowners' gathering was organized before anyone had officially moved in. Details of the meeting were not available online or provided to me, but a post that followed shows how homeowners sought to share information with one another, share their excitement about moving in, and provide input into communal affairs:

> It was a beautiful day today, and we were all in good spirits. I happened to run into the development manager near the conference center [after the meeting], learned some things, and wanted to share with everyone: (1) by the end of the year, there will be more than two hundred households moving in; (2) the [redacted] road in front of the community will also be expanded to become a six-lane two-way road; (3) second-phase home prices have evidently increased; (4) the conference center will hopefully open up this year; it is worth looking forward to the facility and service; (5) the developer is adding extra beautifications to the community; (6) there is a plan to open up a south gate; (7) regarding yard renovations, we can all try to negotiate with the landscaping company recommended by the developer; (8) a bigger supermarket will be built near [redacted] (this counts as good news as well); (9) regarding a shuttle bus in the future, they need us homeowners to

raise demands; the developer's attitude [toward this] is positive, so we should reinforce communication with them and raise our suggestions. I ran into some homeowners today who were in the process of moving in; they seem satisfied. We didn't make the wrong decision.

This post illustrates how the relationships of Marigold homeowners with developers and property management seemed to be more positive than those of other communities, at least initially. To uphold the reputation of a luxury community with good property management and services, the Marigold developers seemed to show more willingness to engage with homeowners, as exemplified here.

These examples of online and in-person discussion and coordination across communities illustrate how first-time homeowners in Beijing were preparing themselves to be homeowners, seeking support and solidarity and encouraging one another to stick together and voice their concerns collectively. While in-person gatherings remained informal for Meadow and Marigold before residents moved in and Community Rose was comparatively quiet, even online, Willow homeowners were already setting up committees, taking meeting minutes, and trying to engage in collective closing. To varying degrees, yet at all sites, the homeowner identity was beginning to be shaped collectively through online networks of engaged homeowners. This identity was very much connected to the gated community itself: in each location, homeowners represented their community, taking pride in being part of the community, and wanting their community to be seen as desirable.

As homeowners moved into their communities, informal associational life took shape, and efforts of collective action were fostered. Because of the physical layout of the communities, Meadow, Willow, and Rose homeowners began to see and interact with one another once they were living in their new homes. In Marigold, it was rarer for residents to physically cross paths, which made in-person gatherings more limited than in the other communities.

Informal Associational Life and the Fostering of Neighborliness and Trust

As homeowners took up residence inside their gates, informal associational life began to take shape through sports leagues, group purchases, sharing information of all sorts, and teaching and learning from one another. By interacting through informal civic associations, homeowners fostered not only social capital and trust but also civic skills and responsibilities previously unfamiliar to them. In participating in Ping-Pong practice or making group arrangements to purchase luxury tiles at a discount, friendships develop, ideas are discussed, shared interests are cultivated, the foundation for social cohesion is established, and skills for civic capacity are developed. In convening regularly, homeowners build trust in one another and establish networks of caring and sharing to which they can turn when collectively faced with a threat. The informal associational activities in which homeowners take part represent participation in the general sense of voluntary community involvement rather than actions that can lead directly to political or policy change.[23] However, a discussion about the pros and cons of balcony styles—a mundane activity—can gain movement-style claims when homeowners collectively pressure property management to uphold promises made to allow for balcony remodels or petition to be permitted to hang laundry on their balconies.[24] In collectively writing and filing a complaint or learning how to write and frame a petition, homeowners gain civic skills that can become useful in later political participation.[25]

In Community Meadow, homeowners were especially active in organizing group purchases, such as tiles, appliances, and space heaters. Ms. Yu and Ms. Ding, both middle-aged homeowners who had met on Meadow's online forum before moving in, spearheaded these activities. Initially, the two women got to know each other by exchanging tips and deals on materials for renovations, and when they finally moved in and met in person, a sense of immediate "trust and connection" was felt, as they recounted during our interviews. One homeowner told me, "If you can trust someone in a group purchase, you can trust them in most aspects of life!" Another homeowner explained, "Trust [is built] through group purchasing. You can tell if someone does something for the greater good [of the community]. If you're selfish, people would have scolded you and 'run you out' in two days. Who would want to do group purchasing with you if you're only in it for yourself?" In addition to demonstrating the effort and organizational skills of the coordinators, group purchasing engaged a large network of homeowners, fostered meaningful connections, and strengthened trust among homeowners who participated.

Residents also got together for shared meals. Hot-pot lunch gatherings continued to be organized in Community Meadow by Ms. Yu, who also invited prospective homeowners from the second phase of Meadow construction. On average, these meetups would receive more than one hundred RSVPs. One homeowner attempted to mobilize others on the forum: "Let's aim to reserve the entire restaurant; we need a hundred people!" Another expressed hope that homeowners would participate "with the goal of getting to know one another, understanding one another, and communicating with one another." Ms. Yu emphasized to me that these gatherings were activities "among Meadow homeowners only, without any external people." A homeowner shared her thoughts online after a get-together: "It was all about sharing, exchanging. Before we knew it, it was 3 P.M., and we still felt like we didn't want to leave each other. But this is the start of our new life; we have a long and plentiful days ahead of us, right? We can get together anytime. [I'm] so happy to have such good neighbors. A lot of neighbors couldn't make it today for various reasons. We are all looking forward to seeing you, seeing your beautiful homes—and our happy days together."

The term "long-term neighbors" was often used among homeowners in Meadow. As they began claiming their homeowner identities, they envisioned a long, happy community life together.

In nearby Willow, Mr. Zhao continued to lead organizing efforts after residents moved in. In keeping with the precise and practical tone he had set, initial posts on sports groups, group purchases, and group outings carried only pertinent information, in contrast to the warmth and neighborliness expressed on the Community Meadow forum. For example, a month after residents began moving in, Mr. Zhao posted a long list of potential sports and leisurely weekend activities residents could take part in, such as shopping excursions, games like badminton or chess, and day trips out of the city to visit a dam or pick fruit. Responses established an early pattern of detailed planning among Willow residents, but the events themselves often went unrealized. Mr. Zhao mused online that perhaps the low participation was a reflection of homeowners still busy getting settled in. He recommended the forum as a place to "look for neighbors who had the same dreams and ambitions" and encouraged suggestions for activities and invitations for events.

When sports clubs were established in Willow, associational life picked up. Four sports clubs—badminton, basketball, soccer, and Ping-Pong—began meeting weekly. Club members worked together to find a time and location for games. The badminton club, for example, ran a community poll to decide when and where to meet after several homeowners had scouted out potential badminton courts. Notably, the function of these sports clubs was not solely participation in the sports themselves, or even health and fitness. These clubs became sites where homeowners gathered to talk about shared challenges in the community. For example, in a recruitment post for the badminton club, the organizer wrote, "Dear neighbors, after a summer of hard work building our nests, we've finally moved into our beautiful homes. Even though we're still fighting for a lot of things, such as [reducing] noise in the neighborhood . . . in this cool autumn weather, please don't forget to strengthen our physiques. As a saying goes, 'The body is the essence of revolution.'"[26]

The post goes on to list the reasons homeowners should consider joining the badminton club. In addition to the benefits of health and enjoyment, the organizer wrote that participation

> increases relationships. . . . "It takes a hundred years of cultivation for two people to ride on the same boat." It is fate that brought us to settle in the same community. We're normally busy individually, and it might be hard to see each other every week, every two weeks; if we don't even know each other, how [will] we realize the idea that "distant relatives are not as good as close neighbors"?[27] After playing badminton, we can get to know each other, share a meal at a good restaurant; we can sit on the floor, converse with our legs crossed, talk about life, talk about the future. In strengthening our bodies, we can also enhance the relationship between neighbors.

Once more, homeowners demonstrated the desire to get to know one another and build a communal life. They imagined a future as homeowners casually sharing meals and intimate conversation. Informal associational life strengthened bonds between homeowners, fostered camaraderie, and provided a support network.

Across the city in Community Rose, online activity picked up substantially after residents moved in, reflecting the influence of being together in person in the dense housing arrangement. As with Meadow, a neighborly sentiment was evident in homeowners' posts on the Rose forum. Posts discussed many aspects of homeowners' daily lives. In addition to serving as a source of information and a hub for organizing group purchases, the Rose forum was used as a daily chat thread of sorts, often featuring posts that were casual and conversational. For example, posts about working overtime were common, as were responses from homeowners empathizing and offering encouragement. Homeowners wrote about their pets, in one instance asking for advice on an ailing Brazilian turtle. The forum was also a successful vehicle for organizing frequent in-person gatherings, such as meals, karaoke outings, yoga, salsa dancing, and belly-dancing classes, and for sharing photographs of gatherings.

Rose homeowners also formed a community basketball squad and a soccer team—complete with uniforms—that practiced every weekend. Team leaders organized tournaments with other residents of other gated communities, during which Rose's (nonacrobatic) cheerleading squad tried its best to "show community spirit." Within a year of moving in, homeowners were attending one another's weddings, throwing birthday parties for one another, and spending New Year's Eve together. Ms. Hua wrote,

> Everyone comes from everywhere; we hold different positions at work; this little town [community] in the big city has shrunken the space between us, shortening the distance between us. Ever since moving in, we all are neighbors. As the traditional [sayings go], "Distant relatives are not as good as close neighbors," [and] "Water from afar cannot quench close thirst." The family clans of the past have gone away; the contemporary [gated] community as a group has gradually matured; everyone walks together; we are a group. There are older people with abundant experiences, [and] there are fledgling youths; there are bosses and employees; there are officials [and] civil servants. Overall there are experts of all sorts. If there are problems, we all help each other; if there are challenges, we all come up with methods [solutions]. We only need everyone to be twisted together as a rope; there would not be a knot we cannot undo, no difficulty we cannot overcome. When good things happen, we don't forget each other; when we have happiness, everyone shares it. We all work in different places, [so] it's hard to always get together, but internet technology has shrunken our time differences, [so] we can leave messages online, wish each other happy holidays, [and] everyone can see it. Not seeing each other doesn't mean we don't know each other; not getting together does not mean we don't know each other well. We live in this group as big modern family members.

GATED COMMUNITIES AS SCHOOLS OF DEMOCRACY

Ms. Hua, whose online efforts had persisted through the initially cool period of online activity, had very much become the center of the forum. More than two thousand homeowners read each of her posts, even when she was just complaining about working late. They also messaged each other in the forum chat and went on to install the instant-messaging application MSN Messenger to further support their interconnections. In our interview, Ms. Hua gleefully recalled adding 118 community friends to her contact list within days. Online, Rose's young homeowners described how they viewed themselves as "family." One homeowner wrote, "Not so sure about the physical aspects of our community [buildings]; the neighbors are what makes this community great!"

Meanwhile, in Marigold's villas, in-person interactions among homeowners were more limited. The only regular meeting was the "homeowners' club," which gathered in the conference center every two to three months. Homeowners waiting to move in also attended these meetings and would tour the homes of current residents. In some of these meetings, homeowners would encourage one another to seize opportunities to provide input to property management or developers. The second Marigold homeowners' meeting, which occurred while new residents were moving in, included only about a dozen homeowners. Nonetheless, the organizer remarked online that she "really felt the growth of the team." Photos of the meeting show homeowners sitting around a conference-room table, with some appearing to take notes. Records shared online show that attendees spoke of transportation safety within the community (e.g., adding speed bumps and warning signs), the size of trash cans in homeowners' yards ("small ones are better"), and issues related to pets (reminders to "make sure large dogs are secured before going to communal areas" and to pick up after pets). Community rules were being set by this homeowners' club, which later set the stage for the formation of the Marigold HOA.

Outside these formal meetings, a small number of homeowners (those who were active in the homeowners' club) began to organize outings, and a few small picnics were held by the community's lake. Online discussions show the difficulty of mobilizing homeowners in Marigold for outings (many traveled for work) and the lack of organic opportunities to run into one another physically, thus making homeowner interactions more formal (i.e., limited to establishing rules together at club meetings).

Online, Marigold homeowners connected by asking about home appliances and furniture, sharing humorous articles, and searching for golf buddies. Notably absent from Marigold's forum, in contrast to those of the other communities, was the organizing of group purchases; the "wealthier-homeowner" identity likely made this type of activity seem undesirable or unneeded. Instead, with respect to homeowners' design and furniture preferences, more expensive foreign brands were frequently referenced. This aura of exclusivity was reflected in comments about upholding high standards for home quality: "Our community might not be the most expensive, but it has the highest value, and we need to make sure it's a place that everyone yearns for."

Even though in-person interactions were infrequent, Marigold homeowners gradually cultivated relationships as neighbors online. When one homeowner was in critical care after a second liver transplant, a neighbor posted, "Regardless of whether it's real or false [news], as neighbors, let's pray for Brother B! He's always supported the work of our homeowners' club and would often tell me he wanted to join our activities in the future!" Another responded, "Even though I don't see him often, I feel close to him still. Maybe it's the effect of his personality on the screen [online forum]; he is so outgoing and kind. May the heavens protect his safe return!"

Shared tragedies or challenges experienced as a community often bring homeowners closer. Soon after that homeowner's medical crisis, Marigold homeowners collectively experienced a tragedy within the community that inspired them to start pushing back against property developers. That incident is explored in the next section alongside other efforts of collective action across the communities.

Efforts of Collective Action and HOAs: Gated Communities as Schools of Democracy

Commonly, efforts of collective action in gated communities revolved around addressing grievances against property management: complaints that these companies were not doing a good job of maintaining the environment of the community, were not being responsive to homeowners' demands, or were trying to enforce rules that homeowners did not support. To make demands to property management, homeowners had to learn how to write letters of complaint, frame problems in petitions, and mobilize enough residents to collectively sign a letter or show up at the on-site property-management office as a collective.

At first, homeowners would copy strategies they had heard or read about from other communities that had successfully pressured property management to make changes. Typically, a homeowner would share a story on the community's forum about "a friend they know" who successfully participated in collective action, inspiring other residents to follow that example. In framing demand letters, gathering community feedback, and mobilizing residents, middle-class homeowners moved from a personal understanding of individual grievances to a collective understanding of common grievances and learned how to take concrete action. The networks that homeowners formed through informal associational activities played an important role in mobilization; for example, residents might be asked sign a demand letter when registering for a group purchase, or a group of residents might play basketball together, discussing how to frame a grievance while they play. In addition, the repertoire of protest strategies (e.g., letter-writing, petitioning) established through struggles with property management gave homeowners tactics to draw on later when faced with environmental threats (chapter 4). These skills, collectively learned in the community from other homeowners (even if only through hearsay), helped communities build the civic capacity needed to solve shared problems and develop leadership, a voice, and a sense of belonging. In this process, homeowners also become more civic-minded and willing to take responsibility for their community.

Only a few months after moving in, Community Meadow residents began experiencing problems with remodeling enclosed balconies. Meadow homes came with open balconies, but most homeowners disliked this design given the horrible air quality in Beijing, occasional dust storms and sandstorms, and prohibitions against line-drying clothes on open balconies. Initially, homeowners tried writing a series of request letters to property management, collectively signed. Several letters later, property management responded, stating that the request for the construction of enclosed balconies was "unreasonable." This response angered many residents, including some who preferred the open balconies, as they felt homeowners should have the freedom to choose the style they wanted. One homeowner suggested that the community collectively demand that property management offer plans for specifications, styles, and colors for both open and closed balconies or guide a few homeowners in designing model balconies so others could replicate the design. Homeowners who agreed to these specifications could then sign construction agreements to enclose their balconies. Making specific demands, wrote that homeowner, would reduce contradictions among homeowners and help them maintain solidarity on other issues.

These efforts were slow to coalesce, and the issue dragged on. After a month of back-and-forth with property management, the Meadow residents rallied collectively, as one online post captured: "Let's gather on Sunday at 1 P.M. in front of the property-management customer-service door. We will collectively discuss the problem regarding enclosing our balconies with them and raise concrete solutions to the problem. Please follow this post; we'll communicate more about this. Let's all go, united, on the same day. Let's avoid going with only a few people each time." Homeowners were eager to protect their rights together, as exemplified by one homeowner's post: "I live on the first floor! I'm signing up to participate! I am also going to bring my kid and let her learn, from a young age, how to protect our own legitimate and legal rights [*weiquan*]!"[28]

This effort of collective action was partially successful in that it led property management to state that they would authorize construction but only if more than 80 percent of homeowners agreed to enclose their balconies. Because coordinating more than 1,700 households was beyond the organizers' capacity, this obstacle forced homeowners to seek other methods of redress, and calls for an HOA emerged. This rallying cry signified the shift from informal efforts of collective action to a formal organization that could serve as a legitimate and unified voice for homeowners.

As discussed in chapter 1, HOAs in China reflect the complex power relationships among developers, property-management companies, and homeowners.[29] In November 2006, only a few months after residents had moved in, Meadow homeowners attempted to establish the preparatory committee for an HOA that would, as one post stated, "represent homeowners' rights [and] help communicate, facilitate, and organize various affairs." One homeowner advocating for an HOA wrote, "We support the formation of the HOA preparatory committee and hope that everyone can actively support this! We should do this now, not later . . . because there are a lot of things to communicate with property management." The post generated more than 2,400 views and forty-two responses from neighbors pledging support. Some volunteered to help and listed their qualifications or reasons for backing the initiative. A few examples illustrate the enthusiasm expressed by homeowners:

"I strongly request to participate! I'm an engineer after all!" (stated in relation to balcony construction problems)

"I very much support this! I hope someone in the community who has a law degree can join this preparatory committee!! [Another community] who just won a lawsuit [against property management] won because they had two lawyers in their HOA!!!!"

"When can we sign [up] for this? I heard that if 80 percent of homeowners agree, then an HOA can be formed."

"Perhaps each complex should select one HOA representative and then pick leaders for each building. This way it's more convenient for them to contact homeowners and easier for organizers, too."

"Great timing with this advocacy [for an HOA]; I strongly support this! Property management is largely ineffective, [and] developers don't do anything. A lot of things require us to be in solidarity, acting together."

"I support this! I'll join. Does building 23 have a representative?"

At the time, landfill stench was worsening for Meadow (and for nearby Willow and Pine). Ultimately, the urgency of addressing the landfill problem and then learning of municipal plans to build an incinerator eclipsed the HOA organizing effort, which was delayed until 2008—more than two years after residents moved in. However, their initial preparations for an HOA helped Meadow homeowners understand the potential mobilizing structures of the community. For their mobilization against incinerator construction, homeowners organized similarly—by residential building—to encourage participation (chapter 4). Although their efforts to have enclosed balconies allowed and to form an HOA were stalled, the organizing involved in those activities built the civic capacity of Meadow's residents, with networks established and civic skills learned by participating in informal associational activities and taking collective action.

Similarly, in nearby Community Willow, efforts were increasing to engage more homeowners in community decision-making processes. For example, as a means of communicating more effectively with property management, Mr. Zhao encouraged homeowners to bring their complaints collectively instead of individually. He ran several community polls to receive input. In one, he circulated a short survey titled "Problems in Our Community," which included a list of issues for homeowners to vote on and rank in terms of importance:

> This survey was created to clarify the issues everyone cares about [and] to provide a direction and goal for collectively resolving these problems. Please fill in what you feel is important and hard to resolve as an individual. The voting procedure is not anonymous! I will post the results openly:
>
> 1. Enclosed balcony problem
> 2. Surface parking problem
> 3. Window-screen quality problem
> 4. Window and door quality problem
> 5. Other (please specify)

Only four people responded, but the post was viewed 570 times. As Mr. Zhao continued to post surveys (on topics such as construction materials needed to enclose balconies), more people began to respond. In Community Willow, seemingly every gathering and homeowners' meeting was preceded by a poll administered and tallied by Mr. Zhao. Off-line, he continued his organizing role, talking to older residents who were only observers on the forum to ensure they also had a say in community issues. A few older residents told me that Mr. Zhao was always eager to help his neighbors. When calls for an HOA became stronger, it was Mr. Zhao who leaped into action.

Community Willow's effort to establish an HOA paralleled that of Meadow: although its progress was slowed when attention was diverted to the landfill and incinerator problems, the preliminary HOA organizing efforts helped to boost collective response to these issues. Mr. Zhao's posts about forming an HOA demonstrate the community's increasing understanding of collective organizing: "A letter of intent must be sent to the *jiedao* ["street-level" subdistrict office] to form the HOA preparatory committee; therefore, I have already prepared the letter and required forms. Now we just need volunteers to be responsible for collecting signatures from homeowners. I'm thinking we could get one or two volunteers per building (if a lot of people sign up, then we could have one person per unit block, too). The main job of the volunteer is to solicit and gather signatures and feedback from homeowners in each building." Homeowners responded, agreeing with the plans, emphasizing that the HOA should address communication issues with property management, and reiterating the importance of homeowners having community interests "at heart."

Over in Community Rose, while informal associational life had grown more vibrant, fewer collective efforts were being made to address property management with a unified voice. Although Rose experienced the same issues with property management as other communities—such as the use of low-quality building materials and a lack of response to questions about security—residents did not appear inclined to coordinate their efforts. To address this lack of collective action, Ms. Hua stepped in to take the initiative in preparing for an HOA. Along with several young homeowners, she attended a homeowners' workshop in central Beijing on how to form this type of organization. Immediately after attending, these homeowners posted what they had learned on the Community Rose forum, including the various procedures and steps involved in forming an HOA, as well as the related challenges (e.g., getting enough participation).

Soon after the workshop, Ms. Hua announced online that after two weeks of active planning among homeowners, the HOA preparatory committee for Rose had been formed. In particular, she thanked older residents who had volunteered, listing their names in a forum post and acknowledging those who had agreed to print and distribute materials on organizing an HOA. She wrote, "Because there are more young people in the community, most people are working folks [*shangbanzu*]![30] Usually we have fast-paced lives, and stressful work, so this time around, buildings 10 and 11 played key roles in organizing the preparatory committee, with mostly older participants. They understand that young people are busy—and for our housing situation to improve, they courageously, actively, and optimistically stepped up. I hope that everyone will proactively support their work! We younger folks [on the team] will also continue supporting their work online."[31]

The issues that the Rose HOA preparatory committee focused on included fees for property management, parking, and heating, as well as community greening issues. Initially the issue of community shuttles was on the agenda, but, as Ms. Hua wrote, "Given the age of the HOA members, we can pick only the four most urgent problems to negotiate with property management. . . . Even though there are a lot of problems, we need to tackle them one by one. Everyone must be patient. Don't treat these cute old people like a complaint box or let them [get] too tired; they are old, and some even have heart disease. Please be understanding!"

This commentary captures how older homeowners took responsibility for official committee roles, while younger homeowners drove the direction of online discussions and recruitment because of their ability to spread information and mobilize quickly online. Ms. Hua, in particular, led online recruitment:

> In the meantime, to avoid being ignored by property management, I suggest that during this period of time, if they come to your door or call you to collect certain fees, please politely tell their employees to contact the Rose HOA preparatory committee. This way, property management will actively coordinate with the committee to do further work instead of ignoring them. . . . Each building in the community may be facing different problems, so we suggest that homeowners actively share information with one another; then we can continue to have volunteers to be committee members, committee heads, and more participants!!! Homeowners who actively want to join the preparatory committee, please send me a chat and leave me your contact method!

Although the preparatory committee was formed quickly, formation of the HOA itself failed because of the regulatory barriers requiring a high number of homeowner votes. Later in the year, another homeowner tried to organize a "virtual HOA" on the forum, but the idea was quickly shot down by others for not following the regulations for establishing an HOA. Much later, in 2009 (after anti-incinerator protests had occurred), Ms. Hua reversed her earlier position on the HOA, commenting that she believed it was better not to have an HOA: "Don't say I'm rebelling," she wrote. "I have my reasons and plenty of evidence, not to be discussed here."[32] Nonetheless, in the process of recruiting for an HOA, homeowners gradually developed skills that carried over to organizing for collective action against incinerator construction. Ms. Hua, for example, followed up her HOA workshop by attending workshops on environmental topics. The younger Rose homeowners maintained a robust online network and recruited quickly and effectively during anti-incinerator mobilization. Some older homeowners, meanwhile, remained integrated with the process off-line, maintaining relationships with other residents in their buildings and helping spread awareness of the landfill issues.

GATED COMMUNITIES AS SCHOOLS OF DEMOCRACY

Community Marigold did not follow this pattern of transitioning from organizing in opposition to property management to attempting to form an HOA. Initially, there was very little contention among homeowners, developers, and property management. Although a small number of homeowners met once every few months to discuss community issues, the rest of the community showed no signs of becoming unified, which may have been because of a lack of shared challenges. Nevertheless, residents were able to form an official HOA, given the lower number of households in Marigold at the time, thereby requiring fewer votes.[33] An announcement was posted on the forum congratulating homeowners on forming an HOA, but many residents had no idea who its members were. Some requested that information about the HOA members be made public: "Can you tell us who was selected for the HOA and what their backgrounds are? Shouldn't they also publicize their contact information and carry out community polls?" Without receiving a response, the same homeowner followed up with a second post: "Selected HOA representatives should have 'community and public spirit'; this should be a priority. They should definitely not treat the position as power or a title; this is an opportunity to serve everyone. I've heard of communities where people in HOAs used their positions to pursue personal gains; this type of person should never become a representative."

Although this HOA took shape in 2006, its members made no concrete efforts to mobilize their neighbors by encouraging more homeowners to participate. The association did not appear to serve the purpose of engaging homeowners, nor did homeowners who were not on the committee feel that their voices were represented by the association.

Although homeowners expressed pride in being part of Marigold—for example, "Let Marigold be the best community there is!"—they did not exhibit a felt sense of responsibility for the community. This apathy remained for several years after the initial wave of residents (about half the community) moved in in late 2005.[34] However, in 2009, three problems occurred almost simultaneously that inspired solidarity in the community: news of road construction near the community (chapter 3), news of landfill expansion and incinerator construction nearby (chapter 4), and the tragic death of a community toddler crushed by marble that fell from a fireplace. Although the child's mother did not publicize information related to the accident on the forum until three months after it had occurred, the belated news of the death, caused by shoddy construction work, led to a wave of outrage, quickly uniting shocked and angry homeowners.

That the news of such a tragic accident did not spread earlier, even offline, demonstrates the lack of homeowner networks at the time in Marigold. However, once the incident was known, many homeowners took part in describing the tragedy in detail on the forum: the marble panels on the wall above a fireplace became detached and fell on a little girl playing in her living room. Homeowners quickly dubbed the tragedy "Glue Gate" (because the developers had used cheap glue to fasten the marble pieces to the wall), and posts on the topic flooded the forum, at times outnumbering and therefore burying conversations about the road and incinerator construction. Most posts were similar to one another and often titled "Glue Gate." These were shared and reshared over several months, as were satirical commentaries on the "developers' advanced glue technology."[35] However, despite the devastating nature of this tragedy, responses never reached the point of unified collective action; only individual complaints were written to the developers.

In contrast to experiences at Meadow, Willow, and Rose, the lack of in-person interactions in Marigold stunted efforts for collective action. Early on, the community's forum came to serve as a central information infrastructure amplifying local news (e.g., on road expansions and construction) but failed as a vehicle for collective action. Later on, however, a small-scale collective mobilization was launched against road construction, as described in chapter 3. Although this effort was short lived, it led some homeowners to communicate with one another more frequently off-line despite their busy schedules, which facilitated their later efforts of collective action.

With the exception of the "wealthier" Community Marigold, within the gated community walls, we see nascent efforts of collective organizing against property-management companies that often ignore homeowners' demands or take little action to resolve community problems. This organizing reflects the concept of "collective efficacy" in which individuals come to believe that they can and are willing to work together to produce results. According to Sampson et al., collective efficacy is best observed under conditions of challenge, indicating that overcoming conflict and threat is an important part of civic engagement.[36] Yet even when homeowners come together in this way, obstacles abound. Property management responds more readily to groups of homeowners than to individuals—but not to their satisfaction. As a result, homeowners turn to other methods of collective action, forming HOAs to amplify and codify their collective voice.

GATED COMMUNITIES AS SCHOOLS OF DEMOCRACY

Because of China's complex government registration procedures (discussed in chapter 1), many efforts to form HOAs fail. However, in the attempt, homeowners learn how to plan and conduct preparatory committee meetings, write bylaws, mobilize homeowner participants, and seek equal or specialized participation (e.g., "one from each building" or "make sure there's a lawyer"). The civic skills learned in these Tocquevillian "schools of democracy"—middle-class housing communities in the heart of authoritarian China—help build capacity and prepare homeowners for collective organizing against government officials.

COMMUNITY CIVIC CAPACITY

Civic education for China's middle class arises in gated community spaces. Meet-and-greet gatherings, activities of informal and formal associational life, and efforts of collective action all contribute to the development of civic skills. These skills, such as communication, organization, and collective decision-making, are needed for homeowners to participate meaningfully in civic and (later) in political life as urban citizens. In democratic settings, such skills have been defined as writing letters, filing complaints, communicating persuasively, continually monitoring public issues, planning strategies, organizing and attending meetings, participating in decision-making, and collaborating in a team.[37] Despite the unlikely sociopolitical context, homeowners in Communities Meadow, Willow, Rose, and Marigold learned these skills. They also became motivated and interested in learning about issues that affected their environment, cultivated a collective homeowner identity tied to their sense of community, and strengthened ties to existing networks of engaged homeowners.

Several conditions served to reinforce this process. With the exception of Marigold, the physical layout of these communities facilitated frequent face-to-face interactions. Additionally, across all locations, the waves of homeowners moving in at about the same time created a natural time for making introductions and forming connections. Further, most residents were first-time home buyers, which allowed for a collective homeowner identity to emerge as they learned from one another how to interpret property rights, deal with developers and property management, and turn to one another for information and support.

Associational activities of all sorts provided spaces not only to discuss community grievances but also to nurture trust among neighbors. The lack of informal aspects of associational life in Community Marigold hindered efforts of collective action, but its online information infrastructure, like those of the other communities, helped homeowners forge connections over time. When faced with challenges, communities built further solidarity. More complex challenges—dealing with the landfill and incinerator plans at each location—would eventually push these Beijing homeowners into organizing large-scale collective actions. These activities required the use of their information infrastructure, community networks, and civic skills (chapters 4 and 5). In the context of a social movement, the tactical repertoires established by some communities through early efforts of collective action helped homeowners navigate the process of organizing once they went beyond their community walls to face government opponents.

Chinese middle-class homeowners in gated communities build their capacity to organize in various ways, first within their communities and later beyond their gates. This reorientation outward requires homeowners to start claiming external issues as their own, expanding their sense of civic duty. When this sense of duty is contained within the gates of homeowners' communities, it can mean mending a window screen for a neighbor, resolving a problem in a shared parking lot, or dealing with community trash. As their civic engagement expands to take collective action against the construction of a road, subway line, or incinerator, homeowners must take the skills they have learned within their communities and apply them to navigating the more complex system of government agencies. In doing so, they face new questions. When a letter or petition addresses not property management but government, which agencies should they contact? When making their case, who and what else can they point to as being affected by the problem? Ultimately, whose duty is it to make things right?

As homeowners' shared issues expand out of their gates into the city, voices representing community interests emerge. These community leaders arise in each community featured in this book, though emerging at different stages in the process of organizing and taking on different responsibilities. The following chapter highlights the key roles leaders play in identifying, framing, and making sense of grievances for other homeowners and how they push the boundaries of community issues to become more outward facing. Whether a community leader is able to achieve inclusivity or facilitate collaboration across communities influences the durability of homeowners' organizing efforts.

Chapter Three

MAKING SENSE OF EXTERNAL THREATS
Individual, Collective, and Representative Responses

For Communities Meadow, Willow, and Rose, early shared grievances were internal, involving property management or developers and issues immediately related to housing. As time went on, however, their concerns began to expand beyond the community gates. Will a bus line be established near the community? Who is responsible for making the nighttime construction noise? And, most importantly, what is causing that rotten stench?

Uncertainty lies at the heart of many crises, whether an environmental threat or a pandemic emergency. When people are faced with a threat that they cannot understand from their own experiences, they look for information to help them make sense of the situation. They may be able to learn from others' interpretations of the problem, reshaping their own interpretations and creating a new understanding of the problem through collective sensemaking.[1] External challenges also create conditions for community representatives to emerge. These representatives are able not only to guide conversation internally—helping to make sense of uncertainties that a community faces as a collective—but also to articulate the issues affecting them, linking their community to the larger society.[2] In the context of middle-class residential communities in contemporary Beijing, in which communities are faced with new challenges or external threats, some community members become information providers, delivering news to and sharing knowledge with other homeowners online and in person. Other community members become mobilizers, encouraging and inspiring people to do something about the problem they commonly face. And some step up as organizers, planning and strategizing, leading the dialogue, and coordinating efforts among information providers, mobilizers, and other organizers.

This chapter is organized by community, demonstrating how Meadow (and relatedly Willow and Pine), Rose, and Marigold transitioned from addressing internal issues to investigating external concerns through the leadership of community representatives. The chapter focuses on how homeowners began to discover and engage with issues outside their communities, specifically the environmental threats of road construction, noise and air pollution, landfill stench, and planned incinerator construction. Although the issues were similar across sites, communities' responses varied. In Rose, homeowners tried to make sense of environmental threats on their own and took action as individuals, whereas Meadow provided an opportunity for collective sensemaking through sharing experiences. In Meadow and neighboring Willow, representatives emerged early on to guide this sensemaking process—organizing and summarizing complex information, soliciting community input, and narrowing down and synthesizing interpretations of a problem. In Marigold, however, community leaders did not emerge until the situation became more pressing. The unique features of each community, and the ways in which their associational lives developed (described in chapter 2), influenced their varied strategies for confronting external issues.

The emergence of these communities provided an opportunity for leadership to be cultivated internally, by arranging group purchases or activities, establishing homeowners' associations (HOAs), and planning collective action against property management (chapter 2). Such leaders, who are embedded in the institutional contexts of a community, share both space and an identity with their fellow community members (e.g., as homeowners, as Meadow homeowners, or as neighbors). Community leaders understand the rituals that produce commitment and solidarity among homeowners. They also benefit from the trust that permeates their community's social networks and enjoy legitimacy in their community. When external threats arise, the need for representation and authoritative voices increases, as homeowners turn to one another for guidance to interpret and navigate the uncertainties.

MAKING SENSE OF EXTERNAL THREATS

MEADOW, WILLOW, AND PINE

Chapter 2 revealed how homeowners in Community Meadow and nearby Community Willow were active online and off-line in organizing informal community activities, from sports clubs to dinners to group purchases of interior-design materials. Community Willow was the most active online, but several Meadow residents also coordinated large group purchases, which connected homeowners virtually and in person, creating a robust network of trust, caring, and support. Both communities were proactive in their efforts of collective action directed toward property management whenever housing-related grievances arose. These attempts were largely unsuccessful, however; property management often ignored homeowners' collective demands and letters of complaint. To find alternative ways to pressure property management, homeowners in Meadow and Willow prepared to organize HOAs, which would provide each of their communities a more formal and unified voice. However, this process of organizing was paused when landfill and incinerator problems emerged.

In the organization of both informal and formal associations after moving in, Communities Meadow and Willow were led by emerging representatives who were able to engage many homeowners in making communal decisions through polls or direct requests for input. The skills learned, networks built, and modes of communication established through these efforts also proved helpful in mobilizing homeowners to address common concerns or threats outside their community walls, from public-transportation planning to landfill stench. The representatives organizing group purchases and community outings became the leaders to whom neighbors turned in times of uncertainty to make sense of new problems.

Although Pine's online forum was largely silent (because the community had been built before its online platform was created), as common issues in the larger neighborhood loomed, Meadow and Willow homeowners communicated with other nearby middle-class communities, incorporating Pine homeowners into discussions of transportation lines and landfill stench. The ability of these three communities to connect with others beyond their gates allowed them to think about the incinerator as a collective issue facing the larger, multicommunity neighborhood.

A First Look Beyond the Gates

A little more than a year after moving in, Meadow and Willow homeowners started to discuss transportation projects near their communities. Meadow homeowners were excited to learn that a subway line was being extended into their area. In Willow, homeowners were researching bus lines and beginning to advocate for changes that would benefit not just the community but also the larger neighborhood.

An older resident of Willow, Mr. Ru, sought information about two bus lines that ran in the area and talked with staff members at the bus station about moving the routes closer to the community. Mr. Zhao, a younger Willow resident and his community's forum moderator, helped Mr. Ru post his suggestions to the bus company online, adding a Google Earth map marked with suggestions for the routes. Mr. Zhao wrote on the forum,

> Mr. Ru invited me today to speak with the bus station manager, Ma, and another person in charge (sorry, I forgot his last name; I deserve a slap). We met face to face and exchanged ideas, [and] we also scouted the potential [new] route. To explain this more clearly, I couldn't find a more detailed map of the areas surrounding the community, so I grabbed a Google Earth screenshot. Because it was free, the map is not the newest, but the roads are on there and can provide a decent explanation. I will provide descriptions along with the photo for everyone below. Mr. Ru wrote an appeal letter addressed to the bus company to push this issue forward. If you feel that this is beneficial for our travels [transportation], please continue to pay attention to announcements on the forum. We will publicly post the suggestion letter and openly collect people's signatures. We look forward to your support.

This forum update raised awareness of neighborhood transportation plans and prepared neighbors to mobilize, in the form of providing their signatures for Mr. Ru's letter of appeal. While Mr. Ru contacted the bus station, Mr. Zhao helped facilitate, leverage, and guide the transportation conversation in the community. In a separate post, Mr. Zhao shared Mr. Ru's draft letter to the bus company, urging, "Please provide your input, everyone!"[3] The letter requested several changes to the two existing bus lines, explaining that these modifications would ensure better transportation for *all* communities in the area, including nearby Community Meadow. One of the requests read,

Even though [Meadow] is only four kilometers away from the closest subway station, there is no bus line running [there], so a lot of residents have to take illegal unlicensed taxis to the station. The current trend of the government is to crack down on illegal taxis, but there are still a lot of unlicensed taxis out there. It is clear that riders still have a pressing need for them and . . . have no other options. . . . If bus route [redacted] could be changed in response to public demand and instead pass through [redacted] locations, we homeowners and families of Willow would be very happy, and [we] eagerly look forward to possible changes. We hope that the company could authorize this to relieve the transportation challenges of citizens in this area.

Mr. Ru's letter strategically linked the community transportation issue to a government concern, demonstrating that homeowners' lives intersected and aligned with local efforts to combat illegal taxis. In addition, mentioning a community other than his own shows that homeowners were starting to understand that the problems they faced were also experienced by those in other communities. Homeowners from both Meadow and Willow responded eagerly to this post, some providing suggestions to strengthen Mr. Ru's argument:

"I support this! It [would be] even more persuasive to add the total number of households of Willow and Meadow and the surrounding areas [in the document], [which] would amount to four thousand household residents."

"Mr. Ru, thank you for working so hard on this! I want to pay respect to you! In addition, I also agree with what another homeowner said: if you can add the numbers of households in the communities around this area, it would be persuasive!"

"I am embarrassed to say we at Meadow have had some internal disagreements recently, [and] a lot of energy has been spent taking care of those disagreements.[4] Therefore, we haven't made very much effort regarding the overall environmental development of the whole [neighborhood] area. Thank you, Willow, for walking ahead of us."

These responses indicate that homeowners from both communities believed that including quantitative data would strengthen their appeal and illustrate that Willow homeowners knew enough about neighboring Meadow to have an accurate count of its households. Homeowners in both communities were connecting more frequently on the Willow forum and, now that they were settled, looking outward at issues impacting the larger neighborhood.[5] The comment from the Meadow homeowner, particularly their expression of shame over failing to pay enough attention to the issue, suggests that some community members felt they had a responsibility to work toward improving conditions for the larger neighborhood.

Collective Sensemaking of Landfill Stench and Incinerator Construction

Soon after the bus-line discussion, in August 2005, Meadow and Willow residents began discussing the worsening landfill stench, posting regular updates with increasing urgency. Many posts started out as individual complaints from homeowners describing their discoveries of the landfill or how they experienced the stench. For example,

> Yesterday in Meadow, around midnight, I caught a strong whiff of trash, [and] it spread into the home. It was like this again today. I drove around in my car . . . the smell was emanating from the mythical landfill everyone's been talking about. It was around 1 A.M. I found the person on duty [at the] the property-management office, described the situation to them, and walked with him around the community. . . . Building 32 still had smells, but around buildings 33 and 34, the stench worsened. We ran into a construction [worker] and the community security guard. They both admitted that the smell was really strong . . . I couldn't even keep the windows open in my house. . . . Behind the community, there was a police car parked there, so the property manager [and I] went to ask the police; we got some evidence. The smell is indeed coming from the landfill. The landfill, to save money, directly emits smells; if they burned methane, then it wouldn't create a stench. A Willow homeowner filed a complaint (with no results) . . . the property manager also looked helpless when hearing this. Tomorrow I plan on going to ask developers at the housing-sales office to see if they have any answers . . . feeling dismayed.

This post indicates that even property management was initially unsure where the stench was coming from. Engaging with the local police was the homeowners' first step in turning their attention outward to try to understand and obtain narrative "evidence" of the stench. A Willow homeowner posted a similar comment, documenting attempts to determine the source of the nightly stench:

MAKING SENSE OF EXTERNAL THREATS

Tonight, I was walking around in the community, [and] I discovered a potential reason for the trash smell in the community. [As] I passed the northwest corner of the community, a strong and rancid smell floated to my nose, [and] it turned out that it was the community trash area. A few workers were putting trash into the trash truck; the smell was from that. I originally thought that the landfill smell was coming from the nearby landfill, but this stench is the same as what we smell every night. I asked the security guard if the trash stench was coming from the landfill or the community trash area. He said [the] trash area (but I'm not sure if he understood what I meant ... maybe he understood it based on where I was standing today when I asked the question: next to the trash area). Dear homeowners, if the smell is truly from the community trash area (I'm not completely sure), I would [be] happy and worried ... happy because the landfill isn't impacting us and that we can deal with it as a community, make changes (give pressure to property management to improve trash-collection procedures), and possibly resolve the smell. The worry would be [that], after such a long time, property management [would] not treat this as an issue!!! Even if the nightly stench might not be from the community, it still shouldn't be that smelly during trash collection. They should improve the procedures and think of ways to keep the community trash area clean. What does everyone think? I just discovered this reason; I don't know if it's correct. I think we should ask property management.

This post conveys the confusion felt by many community residents. The stench was experienced daily, but they had yet to pinpoint its source. Property management did not address the issue to their satisfaction, and this homeowner went online to seek out the opinions of other residents. A homeowner from Pine, also confused about the landfill stench, crossed platforms to post the following on Meadow's forum:

Recently, I've been seeing a lot of posts regarding the landfill near Meadow. Some people are saying there is stench; some are saying there isn't—is there or isn't there? On a bright and sunny day, I wanted to make sure how severely the landfill was impacting us. (1) I found the landfill. I arrived at Meadow around 10 A.M., to observe more easily. I parked my car and switched to my folding bike. At the time, the temperature was around thirty degrees [86°F], with level 2 to 3 wind. [Against] blue skies [and] green mountains, Meadow's colorful buildings stand out. I walked around Meadow and didn't really smell anything, but I did smell summer flowers. At the time there happened to be an older man walking his dog by the construction site, so I walked up to him asking where the landfill was and whether there was a smell nearby. The older guy was very direct: "The landfill is to the northwest; the smell is strong here." I asked him, "Why can't I smell it?" He said, "The smell is only at night; it's very smelly."[6]

This Pine homeowner was beginning to reach out to Meadow homeowners to make sense of the stench, even visiting the community in person, noting its colorful buildings and flowers. This homeowner went on to conduct a "smell test" at different times of day, documenting her observations on the forum. Although she reported that the smell was not evident during the day or in the evening, she acknowledged what other homeowners had stated: that the stench got stronger later at night and that it could continue to worsen. She wrote, "If the temperature were to be a little higher, the wind a little stronger, the night a little later, the trash a little more filled, then Meadow would find the situation hard to escape. . . . This is no longer about whether it's easy or not to reside there; it's a problem with the large living environment now."

Such posts—and there were many similar examples—demonstrate several trends: (1) Many homeowners had never actually seen the landfill before. Even though it was only five kilometers away (the same distance from Marigold to its landfill), it was "mythical"; (2) individuals tried to make sense of the problem on their own, often using imprecise and confusing technical details; and (3) homeowners shared their discoveries with the larger community, asking for thoughts, ideas, and feedback on their proposed solutions. They tried to understand the issue from the standpoint of their own gated communities first but, lacking answers, expanded outward to investigate: What is the landfill? Why is there a stench? Who can resolve the problem?

Emerging Community Representatives

As homeowners turned to one another to make sense of the looming landfill problem, several representative homeowners emerged to lead and guide the conversation. In Willow, this was Mr. Zhao. He was the homeowners' forum moderator and was well known in the community for holding homeowners' meetings, encouraging group activities, and planning collective action against property management (chapter 2). Mr. Zhao was a young businessperson in the technology industry, in his late thirties at the time ("unmarried," I was told), who enjoyed collecting information of all sorts—about public transportation, the landfill, and later the incinerator—and sharing it with other homeowners in the community. He frequently made appearances on the Meadow and Pine homeowners' forums to post news that concerned all three communities. Although Pine never achieved the same level of online participation as Meadow and Willow, the homeowners from Pine who later joined the mobilization against the incinerator knew Mr. Zhao well, describing him to me as the "bearer of information" and the "connector." When I asked about Mr. Zhao, one Willow resident told me, "If there [are] conflicts between the residents and property management, Zhao is usually the first to argue with [property management]." When in need, community members in all three communities turned to Mr. Zhao.[7]

While the online forums were benefiting from Mr. Zhao's work to bridge conversations across middle-class communities in the area, landfill discussions taking place in physical spaces were particularly encouraged by two other community representatives: Ms. Yu and Ms. Ding from Community Meadow. The two women, who were actively involved in organizing group purchases, repurposed their networking abilities to inform homeowners of the landfill and its associated problems.

Ms. Yu, in her fifties at the time, was retired from the Chinese Academy of Social Sciences (a government institution), where she had performed administrative work until she fell sick with a respiratory illness that ended her career. Often hosting Meadow homeowners' meetings in her home, she, like Mr. Zhao, was her community's forum administrator. Many homeowners referred to her as the "auntie" (*dama*) of the community. Ms. Ding was younger, a mother in her thirties at the time, with family in the United States (as she would always remind me when we spoke). Ms. Yu and Ms. Ding worked together often, distributing flyers in the community announcing homeowners' meetings and later distributing pamphlets related to landfill concerns and incineration planning. Homeowners described both women to me as "really engaged in the public affairs of the community," "extra passionate," and "busybodies, managing resident affairs, public affairs, things that are tiring and a lot of work."

The Meadow representatives also collaborated with Willow's leader: Ms. Yu often reposted Mr. Zhao's announcements, making sure that Meadow homeowners received the information he had shared with the Willow community about subway construction, changes to bus stops, and updates on the landfill. In these communities, Ms. Yu and Ms. Ding played mobilizing roles, and Mr. Zhao played an organizing role. Mobilizers increase the number of people taking collective action or help with coordination, whereas organizers mobilize and motivate homeowners to care about issues, provide technical information and support, and help make sense of a problem as a collective.[8] Ms. Yu and Ms. Ding were effective distributors of information, using their preexisting group-purchase networks to spread important messages both online and off-line. Ms. Yu, the auntie of the community, would stop to chat with everyone she crossed paths with about community affairs and kept them updated on actions they needed to take, in coordination with Mr. Zhao's strategies. Mr. Zhao played a role in interpreting and organizing community information, which he relied on mobilizers like Ms. Yu and Ms. Ding to convey to others.

At the end of August 2006, homeowners across Meadow, Willow, and Pine came together on Willow's forum to keep a running record of issues related to the landfill stench. Improving upon the previously scattered posts on the topic, they began a central thread for observations. The progress of this thread, which homeowners regularly updated, best demonstrates the communities' collective sensemaking of the landfill stench. Mr. Zhao began,

> According to homeowners' suggestions, I established this post, specifically used to record landfill stench. No matter what time the stench strikes, keep replying to this post, and record the situation. When posting, please pay attention to the following points: (1) please describe the time the stench hits and the weather conditions at the time (e.g., sunny day, cloudy day, if there is wind, wind direction, etc.). If possible, note the time you experienced it; (2) if someone already posted around the same time frame and has similar recorded descriptions as you, please reply to their post to reinforce proof. To make it more convenient for everyone to record, I will pin this post to the top [of the forum].

As individual posts around the stench increased, Mr. Zhao organized the observations into a central thread to which all Meadow, Willow, and Pine

MAKING SENSE OF EXTERNAL THREATS

homeowners could contribute. The centralization of this discussion helped homeowners make sense of their experiences with the landfill stench collectively. And in encouraging residents to reply to one another to "reinforce proof," Mr. Zhao created a neighborly dialogue that engaged many community members who would otherwise have been posting personal complaints on the forum. Highlights of the discussion in the first month of the thread demonstrate how the discussion evolved from sharing personal experiences to offering increasingly scientific explanations of landfill pollution (though not always accurate), suggesting ways to take action, and finally offering potential solutions.

Initial posts focused on complaints:

[August 29] "Have a home but hard to go home, have a home but hard to live in; this is the situation now. Seeing this place with such a beautiful environment, I often think she's an angel, heaven, in the morning, but at night, she becomes a devil, becomes hell."

[August 29] "At 8:35 A.M. today, the stench filled the sky; weather: cloudy, no wind."

[August 30] "In Pine last year, around the bus stop, the smell was already strong [and] wouldn't stop day to night . . . the smell of the landfill is because it is discharging methane, so if we want changes soon, we need to have the landfill quickly build a biogas collection and treatment system."

Within the first week, the discussion began to turn toward solutions:

[August 31, from Mr. Zhao to a Pine homeowner] "Thank you for providing evidence. Welcome, you and your neighbors. Please frequent our community forum. Everyone can work hard together and resolve the trash problem plaguing citizens."

[August 31] "Yes, while everyone is complaining about the stench, why not exchange self-help methods to suppress the stench?"

[August 31] "Ha ha, you all are always complaining. Why don't we ask the [real estate] developers to resolve the problem? Everyone, stand together!!"

Going into September, suggestions became increasingly concrete and pointed toward potential resources:

[September 1] "I got brothers and sisters at a powerful agency [friends in the government] to inspect this. This type of stench in the air means that it contains highly toxic gases such as hydrogen sulfide, sulfur dioxide, [chloramine],[9] and dioxins, which cause severe damage to the respiratory tract and nervous system!!!!!!!"

[September 1, Mr. Zhao in response] "Is this inspection report effective? If yes, then we can take it to the health and disease control department.[10] Because it [the landfill] is no longer just smelly; it is truly threatening the bodily health of the people."

[September 16] "Whenever someone sees them [workers at the landfill], they directly burn the trash! No wonder the trash always smells like it's burnt. Everyone, please hurry and call the *chengguang* [Urban Administrative and Law Enforcement Bureau] complaint hotline."

[September 22] "I've been thinking of designing a stench time chart [with] every fifteen minutes as a unit and one sheet a day [and] giving it to the security guard on duty at the gate; they can record for us. I feel that it is unrealistic to only document times on the forum. Even if we gave it to bullshit government officials, it wouldn't be persuasive. I'm currently in a master's program at school, a major related to sociology, [and] I want to put some of my efforts in. I don't really know where Willow security guards are; where do I go to talk to them about this? Now, Meadow across the street has more homeowners moving in [during later phases of construction], so I want to also talk to Meadow security guards. This way, we can have a more comprehensive record (if with some simple training the gate security guards can carefully record). If any hero on here can guide me, I'll go communicate with the security team. In addition, I hope to talk to higher-ups in the environmental field, hoping that when we submit a report to the government, we can make a report that is academically persuasive. This type of concerted effort along with scientific evidence would yield better results. My email is [redacted]."

[September 23, Mr. Zhao in response] "[Using] this multipronged approach, [working] hard together, the results will definitely be good. Property management manages the security team, so if you are able to get an OK from the property manager, you can realize this plan. However, the security [team] is often in flux; this [will be] inconvenient for cross-examination [of proof] later on."

Although very few homeowners followed Mr. Zhao's suggested recording format (to include "weather, time, and date"), the progress of the exchanges shows that homeowners ventured into the unknown to try to make sense of new information and understand what was occurring in their surroundings. In sharing experiences, responding, adjusting, and reinterpreting, homeowners attempted to decrease their confusion around the landfill stench and, later, emerging information on incinerator construction. With the facilitation and guidance of a community representative, Mr. Zhao, homeowners began to develop interpretations of the landfill problem, narrow down those interpretations, and search for solutions as a group. In the sensemaking process, individuals integrate multiple sources of information and synthesize the information they receive over time.[11]

Instead of shutting down conflicting or confusing information (e.g., an inspection report of unclear origins), Mr. Zhao facilitated the conversation, offering guidance and input and connecting the dots for homeowners trying to make sense of the landfill situation. He often took complex information from environmental reports and tried to present it in a more accessible way. When he learned of the incinerator plans, he shared them on the forum, indicating both the potential benefits and the health threat: "I hear it will become an incinerator, which will stop the stench [and] even generate electricity. But it would create dioxins—a globally recognized toxic substance." Having a joint thread to share their landfill experiences publicly, homeowners were able to learn from and support one another through the process of sensemaking.

In neighboring Meadow, Ms. Yu was inspired by Mr. Zhao's commitment. In our interview, she recalled becoming increasingly concerned with the landfill and alarmed by the news of plans for incinerator construction. Like most local homeowners, she had not known about the landfill before moving into Community Meadow in 2005. She told me,

> We were delayed in realizing this . . . it wasn't until we smelled the stench. Then we found out mid-2006 that they were going to construct an incinerator here . . . we realized the problem was severe. Some dogs in Meadow got sick. I was talking to a young couple about problems with toxins in the air, like dioxins. A lot of homeowners, you know, many, just had an "it is what it is" attitude initially. Because the landfill was already there when we moved in . . . we just kind of accepted it as fate. But the incinerator, it came afterward . . . to construct something now, we are not going to stand for this. I felt tired, too, but I saw [Mr. Zhao] work tirelessly in spreading this information, so I didn't give up on telling people to care.

Ms. Yu described homeowners as experiencing a shift in attitude: they had originally viewed the landfill as a fixture in their lives with which they were stuck. Even in the forum discussions featured earlier, most homeowners focused on finding ways to alleviate the stench, rather than shutting down or relocating the landfill. However, homeowners perceived news of plans for a *new* incinerator as a chance to take a stand and were particularly moved by Mr. Zhao's active organizing efforts. As homeowners got to know one another within their communities and across neighboring complexes, other residents' work on behalf of the communities motivated more homeowners to participate in activism.

On the Meadow homeowners' forum, news of the incinerator surfaced in August 2006. Another Meadow homeowner and later a community leader, Huang *laoshi* (mentioned in the introduction), described homeowners' shocked dismay about the incinerator when I spoke with him: "Nobody had known that the incinerator was going to be constructed until a homeowner from Meadow visited an urban-planning fair exhibiting all the planned projects in Beijing and discovered that the incinerator was slated to be constructed near the landfill that had been plaguing us. We were so shocked—what... aside from a landfill, there will be an incinerator now? Only when we went to ask [local district officials] did they share the information on the incinerator."

The landfill stench had already been plaguing the community, so an unannounced and secretive plan to build an incinerator added insult to injury, inspiring outrage across Meadow, Willow, and Pine. Ms. Yu described to me how the community reacted to the discovery of plans for incinerator construction, after their initial burst of anger:

> We then went to learn about dioxins, incinerator pollutants, from homeowners in the community who had chemistry backgrounds and others; there were hundreds of people who were very proactive [about taking action]. We were all concerned because we had spent a lot of money buying these homes. If they were really going to build an incinerator, we *could* quickly sell and move away, but then we thought, "*Or* we could try to fix it, through our own efforts, [and] see if there can be change."[12] The motive was as simple as that [to see if the homeowners could effect change]. We had more meetings about this and saw one another a lot.

Homeowners in these communities felt a sense of investment in their homes—both financially and emotionally. This emotional investment inspired a sense of responsibility not to sell their property and abandon the community but to trust their community's collective efficacy to effect change. Mr. Wu, the elderly Community Pine homeowner who took me on the neighborhood tour and later became essential to the anti-incinerator organizing effort,[13] put it well: "We all participated because we saw other neighbors participating."

Community Inclusiveness and Collective Responsibility

These online and in-person dialogues culminated in mobilizing for collective action in the form of a letter signed by Willow and Meadow residents in December 2006. The letter was drafted by Mr. Zhao and other homeowners (including Ms. Yu and Ms. Ding), who referred to themselves as the "mobilizing committee." They posted the letter to the forum and called Meadow and Willow residents to action.[14] The letter described the problem of the landfill and incinerator in the context of the communities, outlined plans for action, and encouraged people to participate, framing the problem as a "collective responsibility." In crafting the letter, a unifying interpretation of the problem was put forth publicly across communities after months of exchanges and sensemaking among homeowners.

The letter opened by addressing the residents of Meadow and Willow as "neighbors" (Pine was not addressed, as it had no representatives on the mobilizing committee) and providing a description of the landfill and its stench:

> Dear neighbors of Willow and Meadow,
> Hello, everyone. The landfill problem has become a serious issue in many of the communities in the area and [for] those who live around the landfill.... The [landfill] equipment is starting to age, [and] the fluids produced by the trash are not being properly treated and [are] severely threatening the safety of nearby canals. The gas emitted by [the landfill] has a high concentration of hydrogen sulfide, methane, and other smelly toxic gases that damage the health of surrounding residents. Especially since 2005, as people started moving to our two communities [Meadow and Willow],

everyone has personally experienced this problem. At the same time, people have also used various channels, bringing up this issue to several government agencies—how the landfill has affected our lives and bothered us. . . . The problem of the landfill, especially the stench plaguing the residents . . . has in fact gotten worse. Before, when it was only in the summer that the stench bothered people, it was all right. This year, not only did the stench increase in the summer (the number of times we smelled it) [but] even in the winter, the stench was still there. When [it was] bad, it would even be a few days in a row.

In this first section of the mobilizing letter, the committee provided a coherent definition of the landfill problem—no longer just mere speculations. Mr. Zhao was able not only to use information provided by homeowners—some scouring the internet for general information on the landfill, some speaking with friends who worked in engineering or chemistry or who had government jobs—but also to organize the information to generate a clear interpretation of the problem for all Meadow, Willow, and Pine homeowners. Next, the letter provided an interpretation for homeowners of the threat of the incinerator:

Recently, we learned from some media reports that there were geographical observations conducted to plan for a new waste incinerator. Environmental evaluations have been completed, and a project development committee has been established. . . . If we don't take any actions, the construction for this incinerator [will] start in March next year [2007] . . . and it [will] start functioning by the end of 2008. Once the incinerator starts functioning . . . although the stench that bothers us will be alleviated, the incinerator [will] create a byproduct of dioxins, which is internationally considered a toxic substance. Its effect on the environment and people's bodies is lethal . . . this is very concerning to us. It feels like we're . . . leaving the wolf's den but immediately entering the tiger's cave. . . . We understand that under current technological conditions, even countries that implement trash separation well do not have a good way of managing this [incineration]. . . . We have urban trash, medical waste, plastics/toxic trash mostly, [and] the heat of combustion is low, so it doesn't even make sense to incinerate.[15] Also . . . the U.S., Europe, and Japan, even countries that had tried taking the trash-incineration path early on, have started heavily restricting the continued development of trash incinerators. According to Jiusan Society[16] reports, domestically in Beijing, Shanghai, and Shenzhen, constructed incinerators are not functioning normally; a lot of emission levels do not adhere to environmental requirements. Despite all of this, we're [China] still trying to import and use such a method to manage our trash; this is so hard to understand. Even if related agencies believe the conditions are different internationally, then why aren't we taking lessons from other Chinese cities?

This segment of the letter articulated that although landfill stench could be alleviated via incineration, the pollution associated with the incinerator would pose a further threat. This interpretation of the problem illustrates that homeowners' collaborative efforts had resulted in piecing together information about the implications of incinerator construction. What started as frantic posts and hearsay about chemicals had progressed to increasingly scientific presentations of information and case studies. On the forum and in person, community homeowners read and learned about incineration in other cities and countries, attaining and sharing knowledge together.[17] In this letter, it is evident that these efforts led to the collective conclusion that the incinerator was unacceptable.

The letter then put forth a call for collective action, indicating the coming together of middle-class homeowners in the area to address the issue:

> For ourselves, our families, and this land we once wanted to live on, generation after generation, we need to take concrete action.... Let related governmental agencies know that we are not satisfied with the delay in improving the issue of the landfill stench; [let us] be clear in stating that we are against the waste incineration project, that we are worried about the environment around the landfill and the destruction of the harmonic, healthy development of surrounding areas.

Given the committee's awareness that mobilizing for collective action can be risky in an authoritarian context, they worded this segment of the letter carefully. Rather than demonstrating anger with government agencies (which was evident in some forum posts), the committee used more restrained language, stating that homeowners were "not satisfied with the delay [in response]." This phrase was followed by the term "harmonic," often employed by the central government to describe developmental projects.

By borrowing this term, the committee signaled that homeowners were keeping in line with government ideals.[18]

The letter ends with an emphasis on following legal procedures and highlights the theme of collective responsibility:

> In conclusion, our communities will together launch a collective-action event. In carrying out this action, we will strictly follow legal procedures. However, before we can take action, we need enough people to participate [and] enough resources to have influence and achieve what we hope for. If you support this action and would like to participate, please respond below to show support, and use email as a method to send your name, contact method, and name of community to us. Also let us know if you want to participate in organizing via email. So far, the concrete method and time of action still need to be decided in accordance with everyone's suggestions and objective conditions. However, we must further emphasize that in taking this action, we need people to wave flags and yell,[19] but we also need those who can actually carry out the tasks. To avoid any superficialness that may lead to the aborting of this critical event, after we take action, we will publicize the names of everyone who signed up but did not show up at the protest and their respective reasons. We hope that everyone thinks about this carefully, and please express yourselves carefully. If you give us your name and contact method, then it is a promise to everyone. Please be responsible for yourself, and be responsible for others.
>
> Email: [redacted] (please do not put sensitive words in the subject and content of the email to avoid being blocked).[20]

Ending the letter on the theme of collective responsibility established the importance of being accountable to one's neighbors. The committee stated its intention to publicly post the names of people who committed to attend the event but did not, as well as their reasons for not attending. This reporting did not actually occur, but choosing to state such an intention heightened homeowners' consciousness of accountability in participation, which is often a barrier to online activism efforts.

This letter serves as a reflection of Meadow and Willow as homeowners' communities. It shows the work of community representatives who stepped up to help homeowners understand new challenges—in this case, external threats to the community as a whole that are characterized by uncertainties.

The letter also illustrates Meadow and Willow residents' ability to come together as neighbors, view an issue as a collective problem, and participate to resolve that problem. Through their community representatives, homeowners voiced the belief that together they could change the situation—demonstrating collective efficacy—even if they had not yet concretized what that change might look like.

Homeowners generally showed support for this messaging in their responses to the letter, with one even urging neighbors from her community (Meadow) to "step up and not lose to Willow [homeowners]." The comment was intended to encourage healthy competition, with Meadow acknowledging that Willow homeowners were doing an exceptional job at mobilizing. There was also a relatively small amount of pushback against how the letter was worded. In particular, two homeowners commented that the language and tone of the letter were "too soft" and that a more forceful tone should "eventually be taken" to effectively convey their message to the government. However, community representatives did not try to quell dissent in this case. Instead, they tried to facilitate dialogue, encourage the sharing of information and ideas, highlight certain interpretations of grievances, and craft messaging that made sense for the larger community. Leaders who do this well—who promote dialogue and collective learning—are able to organize durably and sustain participation among community members.

When leaders are ineffective in soliciting and distilling community input—or when a community lacks a central representative at the time of mobilization—collective action becomes more challenging given the lack of coherent central messaging around the grievance. Although some leaders in Meadow, Willow, and Pine had yet to emerge at the time the letter was drafted, the development of leadership in these close-knit communities was well beyond that of Rose and Marigold at their equivalent stages of incinerator resistance.

ROSE

As described in chapter 2, Rose homeowners, much like those in Meadow and Willow, maintained an active communal life, as evidenced by frequent forum interactions and in-person events and outings. Young homeowners populated Rose's virtual space and were effective in spreading information and keeping in touch with one another. When homeowners came together to form an HOA, younger residents, led by the forum administrator, Ms. Hua, recruited homeowners to participate via the forum, assisted by older homeowners who spread the word off-line.

In contrast to Meadow and Willow, however, the forum was rarely used to collect input on communal problems. Although Rose also experienced problems with property management, unlike Willow homeowners, who frequently wrote joint letters of complaint, Rose homeowners organized far fewer efforts to address property management as a collective. Individual complaints about property-management shortcomings were shared online daily, but rarely did residents attempt to coordinate group action.

When concerns around a local construction site and landfill stench surfaced, a similar pattern was evident. Individual complaints were frequent, but no central representative emerged to interpret what the problems meant for the community as a whole. Homeowners were encouraged to complain via government hotlines, but the assumption was that they would do so on their own, without a representative offering a single collective interpretation. This lack of representation early on to coordinate understandings of the landfill stench, for example, meant that many uncertainties went unaddressed. Instead of focusing on determining the source of the stench, homeowners targeted blame at government agencies and officials. It was not until one homeowner, Ms. Hua, personally investigated the landfill that other residents began looking to her to lead the community's response to the trash problem.

A First Look Beyond the Gates

In May 2006, less than two years after the first residents moved in, homeowners encountered noise pollution from a nearby construction site. One homeowner raised the problem in a post that launched important discussions:

> Some time ago, some homeowners tried to communicate with the developer and construction company but did not receive a good answer for the nighttime construction problem. As tolerant and kindhearted homeowners, everyone slowly accepted how the noise was bothering people. However, recently, [with] the shameless developers and construction company, [we]

MAKING SENSE OF EXTERNAL THREATS

gave them an inch, and they took a mile. Not only do they do construction through the night during our hours of rest, [but] they also make piercing noises. It really is hard to bear . . . blindly tolerating does not yield good results. We should stand together [to] protect our legal rights. Even though they used some type of method to get authorization for nighttime construction, this cannot be their get-out-of-jail-free card—just like if a mentally ill person kills someone, they will not be dealt with as a normal person, but they definitely cannot be allowed to get away with it.[21]

This post reflects a problem outside the community that had been bothering some residents who had individually brought up the problem with the developers and construction company, without satisfactory results. For a while, much like Meadow, Willow, and Pine's tolerance of landfill stench, Rose homeowners also put up with the nighttime construction noise. However, when the noise got worse, the author of this post used mobilizing language to encourage homeowners to protect their rights, because silently tolerating the problem was certainly not alleviating the noise. The author provided a list of phone numbers the end of the post, including the developer's customer-service number and the hotline for the Urban Administrative and Law Enforcement Bureau (*chengguan*). And they encouraged homeowners to call government agencies to complain:

> Please stand together, homeowners. Use your own power, [and] file complaints through any channel possible. . . . This is the only way they [will] know that people are mad. . . . We are quality homeowners. Because of different situations, we're unable to stop their construction, but moving the construction to daytime is not just possible, it is their responsibility [to do so].[22] Therefore, again, hoping that you all do not just observe. Only through taking action can [your] own interests be protected. Additionally, I'm looking for the phone number for the township government, hoping homeowners who know could contact them or even call related district government agencies [to] give them pressure. Thank you, everyone!!!!!!!!!!

In contrast to Meadow and Willow posts emphasizing "collective responsibility" and taking action as a unified group, this post serves as an example of many Rose posts that emphasized taking action "on one's own," including mobilizing individual homeowners to call hotlines to address the problem.

The wording of the post also demonstrates the contrast between the unifying language common to the Willow and Meadow forums, such as "stand *together*" and "protect *our* legal rights," and the individualized language of the Rose forum, urging homeowners to "use *your* own power" and emphasizing the need to "protect one's *own* interests." While Rose homeowners did identify as part of a larger network of "Rose homeowners," when it came to collective action, the rhetoric seemed to be anchored in individual actions and personal definitions of problems. Similarly, posts encouraging people to file complaints offered little guidance on how to interpret the problem or frame the issue when filing those complaints. Many posts provided only phone numbers to call, of hotlines at first and then media outlets to seek publicity for the problem.[23]

Rose homeowners, on average younger than those of Meadow and Willow, also tended to self-censor less on their forum; for example, "It's 1:08, [and] I just called. The *chengguan* hotline said, "We don't care about this because they applied for nighttime construction authorization! Seriously, tmd [popular Internet expletive]!" Referring to government officials and construction companies as "shameless," "stupid," or "liars" was also common across complaints posted to the Rose forum, and such anger was reflected in the framing later used in the community's anti-incinerator mobilization (chapter 4). While angry rhetoric was an effective mobilizing strategy among younger Rose homeowners—getting people to hit the streets when it came to mobilizing against the incinerator—homeowners' emotions, in the absence of concrete plans for engagement and a coherent collective message crafted by key representatives, were insufficient for sustained organizing.

Making Sense and Taking Action as Individuals

Although the community's mobilization around external issues focused on individual actions, Rose homeowners still benefited from strong community networks because of their active associational life. As the issues of trash stench and pollution from a nearby pharmaceutical factory surfaced in July 2008, homeowners mobilized to make calls to government agencies and documented and shared the responses they received on their forum. Initially, many of these posts were unclear about whether homeowners attributed stench to the landfill or to the pharmaceutical factory's emissions.

MAKING SENSE OF EXTERNAL THREATS

This confusion perpetuated homeowners' uncertainty regarding the source of the problem. In documenting their experiences, Rose homeowners also focused more on airing grievances than on pinpointing the source of the problem, in contrast to the investigative work done by Meadow, Willow, and Pine homeowners. One Rose homeowner wrote, "Why is the stench so severe in Rose? [I] can't stand it. I suggest that everyone call the mayoral hotline to reflect this problem. The number is [redacted]. Let's strive to alleviate or get attention for this problem! It's popular to talk about environmental protection right now, but people's lives are still in dire straits!"[24]

The post called for individual homeowners to call a hotline, rather than take collective action together (e.g., by signing a collective letter or even drafting a template for people to use when calling a hotline). Responses to such posts were typically brief:

"Strongly agree to file complaints!"

"I think I smelled it yesterday but was too sleepy, so I smelled it half asleep, half awake! That felt bad! It's scary thinking about it! If it's some type of toxic gas, [I] wouldn't even know how I [would] die."

"Can someone think of a solution? Let's organize everyone to file a complaint together. There are so many young homeowners; what if they have kids in the future?"

"The stench smells like when farms dry-stack manure."

"There's a strong smell of chemicals, very concentrated. Even if you close your window it doesn't go away easily—it's all times of the day, sometimes at 11 P.M., after midnight, sometimes close to dawn—unrelated to wind direction—or weather—I feel like it's controlled by someone! Every time we mention this online, the smell goes away (for example, there's no smell today!!!)"

These responses indicate that homeowners reacted to and interpreted the stench in different ways and that no one stepped in to guide or facilitate the discussion. One response did suggest that Rose homeowners should "organize everyone to file a complaint together," but there appears to have been no follow-up or offer to lead such an effort. In the days following the introduction of the topic of the trash stench to the forum, a flood of posts appeared with titles such as "Hurry, everyone call hotline [redacted]!" and links to file complaints online.[25] Ms. Hua, the forum moderator (and an active organizer of group activities and the HOA preparatory committee, as discussed in chapter 2), received requests to pin posts with hotline numbers to the top of the forum. She was also actively involved in discussions of the stench, sharing her experiences and encouraging people to make complaint phone calls. Unlike Willow's Mr. Zhao, however, she did not help to interpret the situation or link various conversations together. An example of some of her comments in relation to those of other community members helps to illustrate her approach:

[Ms. Hua] "The stench wakes me up every night! This type of irresponsible discharge [while] surrounding residents have increased in numbers! This is unscrupulous! The numbness of the government makes us feel helpless. . . . I even called the cops once, and they came over to tell me that it's because I smoke too much and that they can't smell anything!"

"I'm letting my husband call, too! Let's all do this!"

[Ms. Hua] "I pray that this phone number works. Neighbors who experience the stench like I do, let's pick up the phone and reflect this issue [and] stop coming online to complain. The more people who call in, the more powerful it is! It's not enough to rely on someone to organize something! Call every day, reflect every day! I don't believe this can't be fixed! Call!"

"I hope neighbors who are able to print conveniently can print out this number and post it in the elevators. This way, neighbors who cannot go online can also know the phone number. Let's act together!"

[Ms. Hua] "I received a phone call back from the [district] environmental protection bureau today, [and they] said it [the stench] was [caused by] the landfill [and] that they were actively taking care of the problem. Using some type of high-tech method, they can get rid of the stench in two to three months."

Although Ms. Hua exhorted homeowners to follow her example of moving beyond complaining to taking individual action—"Let's pick up the phone and reflect this issue [and] stop coming online to complain"—she appeared to be casting doubt on the efficacy of collective action, insisting, "It's not enough to rely on someone to organize something!" Other homeowners tried to spread awareness in the community by posting the hotline numbers in physical locations, yet this activity, too, served to facilitate individual rather than collective action. Additionally, while Ms. Hua seemed to have received answers from a district environmental official, when I later spoke with her, she expressed doubt that the agency was telling the truth. The government officials with whom she interacted often lied to quell her complaints, she told me.

Even though some homeowners obtained some government responses from their hotline calls—learning that the stench was coming from the landfill and being told that district agencies were addressing the situation—much anger continued to be directed at government officials. Compared to Meadow and Willow, there was also less sharing of scientific data and information in Rose. In Meadow and Willow, Mr. Zhao and other homeowners engaged in a substantial amount of reading and research to try to understand what was causing the smell (e.g., how the landfill gas purification system worked). Although some of the information they shared was inaccurate, Meadow and Willow were establishing greater clarity around the issue. In contrast, when Rose homeowners shared responses from government agencies, the details were often vague—"some type of high-tech method"—and responses centered not on tracking down additional information but on complaining about government agencies or the incompetence of government officials. For example,

"I support taking action to protect our rights. These people eat, drink, and take from the people; why can't they be responsible, steadfast, and work hard for the people??? These people are more fit to raise pigs than to be civil servants."
"We need to storm government agencies, make a mess of things; [I] believe that would be a little more effective!"
"Some civil servants and police are even fit to be called hooligans. Just because they come from good backgrounds, they get to sit in that position, doing nothing, staying there, and hurting people."[26]

Homeowners were clearly frustrated with government officials, likely in response to perceived inaction regarding the stench and perhaps also to frustrations with the hotlines. Residents seemed to feed off the energy of one another's forum posts, fanning the flames of anger. This reinforced attitude of anger likely increased people's distrust in the responses officials provided. Even though Rose homeowners were told that the landfill was the cause of the smell, widely differing opinions on the source of the stench persisted. One homeowner described to me her frustration upon learning about the landfill after moving in, whereas another insisted on the forum that the pharmaceutical factory was the problem:

"Why didn't the government tell the real estate people or tell whatever property-management company was selling the apartments that there was a landfill nearby? We had no idea! We moved here without knowing. And why were housing complexes authorized to be built nearby if the landfill was already there? There were definitely personal interests involved!"

"The stench near us is the pharma factory, pharma factory, pharma factory, pharma factory!!! Pharma factory! Everyone, emphasize this when you call! This morning at 9:30 A.M. when I passed the pharma factory, it was so smelly! Everyone, stop being confused by these people [government agency personnel]!"

The Rose homeowners' attitude of distrust is reflected both in the accusation of "personal interests" and the exhortation to "stop being confused by these people." Regardless of the actual source of the stench, homeowners seemed to agree that government officials were to be blamed and that government shortcomings led to the environmental problems they were experiencing.

As the Olympics rolled around in early August 2008, however, posts on the Rose forum quieted down on the stench issue. When I spoke to Ms. Hua in 2009, she had several theories about the silence: (1) she suspected that the pharmaceutical factory may have been shut down during the Olympics; (2) posts may have been monitored and blocked by the internet police more frequently during this time; and (3) homeowners, including Ms. Hua herself, "knew better than to cause a ruckus during an important national event." Even though young homeowners were openly critical of government agencies in July, they were well aware of the risks of taking action during the Olympics—they explained that the government would try to maintain "social order" more strictly for reputational purposes. However, Ms. Hua recalled hearing garbage trucks going in and out of the landfill area during the Olympics, and the smell of trash remained potent.

A Risky Encounter Produces a Community Representative

Ms. Hua, who was thirty-four years old when the landfill issues arose, was a freelance industrial designer. She was well known in the community for raising indoor plants, belly dancing, and her skill in crafting dance costumes. She had more than one hundred Rose homeowners as friends on her chat program (MSN Messenger), and she was in frequent contact with

MAKING SENSE OF EXTERNAL THREATS

most of them. On the day of the Olympics closing ceremony, she could no longer stand the mysterious smell or the uncertainty around its source. This, she told me, is how it all started: how she discovered that an incinerator was being constructed 1.5 kilometers away.

On that day, Ms. Hua left Community Rose in the morning and drove her car to the landfill to investigate. She said she had refrained from going earlier as she had not wanted to cause trouble during the Olympics. "I felt like I already gave face [respect] to the government. I've put up with this for so long, [but] the biggest event of the country [is] ending, so now I'm going to expose you [the government]," she told me.

She recalled the experience of seeing the landfill as follows:

Nobody stopped me [from going inside]. I dressed professionally and entered what looked like a construction site. I thought that if anyone questioned me, I would say that I was there for a meeting. So I came up with this lie, and I drove my car in. After I drove in, I got out and walked around the landfill. When you drive in the dirt is dry, but after you walk around, you'll see water oozing out. The ground was wet; I stepped in it, and my foot sunk in—the devices were not working, the big rusty bolts were falling off of them—I realized a lot of things were not being used and looked like they were in violation [of environmental standards]. . . . All the temporary [dispatched] laborers were sleeping in this little house on the side. The landfill trash was there; the wind was blowing trash around, everywhere; nobody was working; the trash trucks were driving in and out. A lot of trash was scattered about, [and] I was standing in the midst of all that. I felt the methane in the air, and I couldn't even open my eyes. It was that smelly!

By nightfall, the stench was stronger. Ms. Hua decided to take two friends—the Yangs, a young couple who were also Rose homeowners—with her to the landfill and sneak in to obtain photographic evidence. She recalled that, even at night, she saw smoke pouring out of the pharmaceutical factory near the landfill. Within minutes of pulling up, they were stopped by a man dressed in dark clothes who "looked like he was conducting inspections on the landfill" and "being sneaky." A verbal confrontation ensued between Ms. Hua and the man, as Ms. Hua was trespassing and trying to take photos of him without permission. The incident ended with the man running off and calling the police. Insistent on getting photos,

MAKING SENSE OF EXTERNAL THREATS

Ms. Hua stayed to take pictures, particularly of the equipment that the man had left behind (a tripod and a laser level for measuring terrain), but the police soon arrived. According to Ms. Hua, the two police officers wanted to document the reported incident and took down her personal information. They did not give her trouble for trespassing but asked about the scuffle. After leaving the area, Ms. Hua's anger was "uncontainable," and she made up her mind to "expose information" about the landfill to other homeowners: "People need to find out we've been lied to for four or five years!" In her eyes, the landfill was mismanaged; in her photos, the landfill facilities and equipment looked rusted and decrepit. To Ms. Hua, both aspects represented the dishonesty of government officials, especially after representatives had responded on the hotline that officials were addressing the stench problem.

Ms. Hua promptly posted all the pictures she had taken to the forum, along with more than sixty thousand words of text, describing her run-in with the police and what she had witnessed. However, each photo and description that she tried to upload was "instantaneously and continuously deleted by the web platform." Ultimately it took three hours to upload her post successfully. Around midday the following day, she recalled, she woke up to see that dozens of homeowners were waiting for her on the forum chat, frantically pinging her with messages. "Weirdly, it was quiet outside," she remembered. "I couldn't hear any trash trucks and didn't see any smoke outside of the window. I sensed something was wrong."

Although Ms. Hua had always been a central figure in the community, especially on the forum and in organizing community events, it was not until her risky encounter with the police at the landfill and her long forum exposé that homeowners begin to gravitate toward her as a representative and an authoritative voice on what the community was experiencing. In producing a detailed report and obtaining what homeowners viewed as photographic evidence of landfill mismanagement, Ms. Hua made more progress on the issue in one day than had all the calls made to hotlines. Homeowners now turned to her for information on the landfill (mostly her photographic evidence) and were soon mobilized to protest publicly.

In the days following the "nighttime fight incident" at the landfill, as she called it, Ms. Hua and her friend Ms. Yang tried to find out as much about the landfill as they could. After considerable effort, Ms. Hua tracked down the phone number of a person in charge of the landfill facility. She called to obtain information about the landfill but instead was told about plans for a new waste incinerator. Panicked and angered, Ms. Hua and Ms. Yang went straight to the municipal planning office. As Ms. Hua recalled, "They didn't want to give us anything [information], so we kept asking and forced them to say something about the new incinerator plans. This is how I found out about this. . . . I'm just so curious; I just want to know all their [the government's] secrets. I was curious; that's why I went to the landfill. Maybe I'm too curious!"

Ms. Hua seemed proud that she was able to extract information about the secretive incinerator plans but acknowledged that her curiosity sometimes meant trouble (referring to what happened to her after Rose's anti-incinerator protests, discussed in chapter 4). Much like in Meadow, Willow, and Pine, the government's plans for incinerator construction were not publicly known. Ms. Hua posted all the information she had gathered on the forum and asked all her MSN Messenger contacts to read her posts. From that point onward, Ms. Hua became a lead organizer of Community Rose, as homeowners geared up for anti-incinerator protests one week later (chapter 4). She was able to tap into her robust community networks to persuade neighbors to hit the streets in a short amount of time.

In contrast to residents in Meadow and Willow, Rose homeowners did not seem to have a common understanding of the stench. The information about the incinerator plans was unexpected, and before learning about it, residents disagreed about whether the stench was coming from the landfill or the pharmaceutical factory (or both). While some homeowners talked about what actions to take, mobilizing efforts centered on asking individual homeowners to call environmental or government hotlines to complain about the stench, each telling their own version of the story. There was no clear call for collective action as a *unified* group of homeowners, nor did Rose homeowners try to reach beyond their gates to collaborate with similar gated communities in the area. (There were two other gated communities nearby, but they remained relatively silent on the landfill issue.) Notably, although many Rose homeowners were clearly angry about the stench, no one but Ms. Hua traveled the mere 1.5 kilometers to investigate the landfill in person. As a result, Ms. Hua was the only person with firsthand knowledge of the problem (as demonstrated by her sixty-thousand-word post) and the sole interpreter of the grievance when it came time to engage in street protests. Without the *collective* sensemaking and learning process experienced by Meadow and Willow residents, the community leader Ms. Hua was never able to bring Rose homeowners together in a sustainable way (discussed further in chapters 4 and 5).

MARIGOLD

Because of the expansive layout of Community Marigold and the busier schedules of its upper-middle-class homeowners, residents of the all-villa community did not run into one another often. Accordingly, the informal associational life of Marigold was less pronounced than in the other featured communities; while some residents golfed or went for picnics together, few group activities took place. Unlike in Meadow and Rose, the creation of the Marigold HOA was neither an outcome of opposition against property management nor an attempt to address common grievances. Rather, it focused on providing guidelines for keeping the community clean and safe. Therefore, although Marigold did establish an HOA, few homeowners outside the small committee were actively encouraged to participate in community affairs.

Because engagement and representation were limited in both informal and formal associations in Marigold, efforts of collective action were stunted when external problems concerning the community as a whole emerged, including a new road being built, landfill expansion, and incinerator construction. These issues surfaced on Marigold's forum, but, much like those of Community Rose, the discussions lacked a facilitator and comprised only individual complaints placing blame on local officials. And Marigold had a further disadvantage in community organizing: while Rose had in Ms. Hua a clear representative in terms of informal associational life, and Meadow and Willow had the even more engaged representatives of Mr. Zhao, Ms. Yu, and Ms. Ding, Marigold had no such representation early on. However, the Marigold forum played a role in maintaining a loose network of homeowners, which was later activated to mobilize quickly against the landfill and incinerator. Only after this organizing began—and people became aware of the risks the community was facing—did a clear homeowner representative emerge to guide the community's anti-incinerator resistance.

MAKING SENSE OF EXTERNAL THREATS

A First Look Beyond the Gates

In Marigold, the news of a major road-construction project adjacent to the community occurred almost simultaneously with residents' discovery of the landfill expansion and incinerator construction project (in late July 2009). A Marigold homeowner came across an announcement posted on a bulletin board at a local government office regarding the construction of a new road. The announcement mentioned the results of a public-opinion poll concerning the project, but the homeowners with whom I spoke reported that if such a poll had been conducted, it never reached Marigold residents. According to the homeowner who saw the announcement, the new road would disturb their quiet community. He posted what he described as a "letter of complaint"[27] to the Marigold forum:

> What a strange construction project! Is it to benefit or to harm the people? . . . Why? For smoother traffic? There is already another road nearby that allows high speeds. And it was constructed just last year. Now they want a parallel street, only one kilometer apart; there is no need! That is redundant construction! . . . Residents on both sides of the road, we must be against this! Because it pollutes the environment, destroys ecology, creates noise, disturbs the peace and quiet in the area . . . we don't agree with this! Does the government have too much money to spend? The district official has a PhD and should be smarter than others . . . taxpayers' money is being spent[28] . . . the people trust the [Communist] Party! I suspect that someone has tricked our PARTY.[29] Because as residents along this road, nobody has told us about this; our right to know has been stripped away from us! Is it because someone told the Party that we wanted a road?? No!! . . . We will fight till the end; if we can't do it at the district level, we will go to the municipal level; if not, then to the central level.

Much like Community Rose homeowners, Marigold homeowners were angry and described the project as redundant and wasteful. However, in contrast to Rose homeowners, who placed blame for local disturbances on the incompetence of *all* government agencies and officials, this Marigold homeowner was more precise in assigning blame to individual *local* officials. He acknowledged that people trust the central government and indicated that the Communist Party probably did not play a role in making this particular decision. Later forum posts also mention the Party. In China, the distinction between local and central government is frequently used as a framing tactic; citizens often characterize a problem as being not with the party-state but with individual (sometimes corrupt) officials. For the homeowner who posted the letter of complaint, "fighting till the end" entailed starting from the lowest level of government and moving upward; this wording also demonstrates that the homeowner perceived the problem to be at the local level. As with early complaints on the Community Rose forum, this post lacked specific details and a call to action, despite its apparent intent to mobilize residents. A single homeowner responded to the online letter, stating, "Sounds reasonable, support," but the thread did not continue.

Several days later, another homeowner located the environmental impact assessment for the road-construction project and posted it in its entirety on the forum, inserting her own commentary and critique after each item evaluated. For example, she pointed out that "based on the conclusion of the report, the project after its completion would bring about traffic that would impact air quality, increasing noise. This project definitely would have a negative impact on the environment. [On] the existing [redacted] road, traffic runs smoothly; to construct another road truly would pose more harm than good."

This technical presentation of information was very different from the form of communication on the Meadow and Willow forums, where Mr. Zhao played a central role in making information within complex reports accessible to community members. However, the Marigold homeowner who posted the environmental impact assessment encouraged others to "find more information, do more research, raise more questions, and report this [research information and findings] to related agencies." As in Community Rose, the responsibility was placed upon individuals to take action, yet unlike on the Rose forum, no phone numbers were listed for homeowners to file complaints. Further, this post received only one response, which mentioned similar communities in the area that might also be impacted by the new road: "I very much agree with your analyses; however, why did the leader of the district make this decision? I support homeowners unifying: Community Marigold, Community Dandelion, and Community Daffodil[30] . . . let's come together! Would the district government allow this type of mass incident?[31] Only by coming together can we be successful."

MAKING SENSE OF EXTERNAL THREATS

Despite this post's call for cross-community unity, the online conversation did not continue, and no multicommunity effort was evident. However, about ten Marigold homeowners came together to sign a makeshift banner reading, "Strongly against construction of [redacted] road. Protect our quiet and peaceful home." The residents hung the banner by the road but within the community gates. Unfortunately, homeowners reported on the forum that the banner was "torn down violently and taken away by someone who claimed to be part of the township government." One homeowner questioned, "Who contacted the government during the weekend? The community is the yard of us homeowners; who can come in here and take our things? I believe this is definitely not anyone from the Communist Party!! With President Hu's leadership in the central party, proposing a wise and people-oriented direction of governance, why are there still government officials so brazenly and rashly handling people's complaints? The outcome will be severe! Let's get together and protect our home!"

Once again, this homeowner differentiated between the Party (i.e., the central government) and the local officials against whom residents were filing complaints. Many Marigold posts made this distinction between the Party, viewing it positively, and local officials, whose efforts they viewed as failures. This community sentiment resurfaced later on during anti-incinerator organizing and played a role in the eventual outcome of Marigold's protests.[32] Overall, Marigold homeowners' responses to the removal of the banner reflect dissatisfaction with the local government:

"I resent this. I don't know why these so-called [local] government officials won't let us ordinary folks say a single thing. What are they trying to force us to do?"
"Resentment! Strong resentment!! These people are not fit to be government officials. We should ask the township government (?) to hand over the banner!!!!!"[33]

These posts again demonstrate outrage directed at local officials, who were perceived as both repressive and incompetent. The open questioning of local authority also seems to have gone unchecked (similar to Rose homeowners' publicly observable contempt for local officials early on in the organizing process).[34] However, within two weeks of Marigold homeowners' discovery of the road-construction plans, the project was halted and soon canceled. Marigold resistance had not progressed beyond the banner and online commentary, but a nearby community appears to have more effectively mobilized against the project. A Marigold homeowner posted a news article reporting that five hundred older residents from a seniors' community had collectively petitioned for the cancelation of the project. In response, the article claimed, the township government sent representatives to meet with local residents and promised to "stop the construction" and "listen to the public." While homeowners were happy with the outcome, conversations around a lack of trust in local officials left lingering uncertainty among Marigold residents as news of incinerator construction surfaced.

An Unexpected Discovery and Spontaneous Protest

When the road-construction plans were discovered at the end of July 2009, news of landfill expansion and incinerator construction also surfaced when a Marigold homeowner happened upon the information in an administrative building. Marigold homeowners at first seemed more intent on addressing the road-construction problem: the road, at one kilometer away, would be closer than the incinerator (five kilometers away), and the issue of potential noise seemed more tangible than potential problems caused by the landfill or incinerator. I believe that a key explanation for this prioritization—though no homeowner ever said so to me—is that the landfill near Marigold did not cause a stench for the homeowners.[35]

As news spread that the road construction had been halted, however, posts on the forum started to turn to the topics of the landfill and incinerator. Typical statements included "Incinerator construction poses even more of a threat than road construction"; "Homeowners, can you tolerate the incinerator polluting our living environment?"; and "Looks like our home values are going to fall; landfill, road construction, what a pity."

Unlike Meadow, Willow, Pine, and Rose, which have extensive records of forum posts, for Marigold, it was difficult to trace how the landfill and incinerator came to be seen as problems on its forum. Comments were few and scattered, and discussions most often did not pick up where they had left off. No homeowner representative surfaced to moderate the posts or guide the dialogue. Because of the lack of leadership and ongoing forum discussion, very little collective sensemaking could be observed online.

MAKING SENSE OF EXTERNAL THREATS

While it is possible that dialogue and sharing experiences of external threats occurred off-line, the lack of online documentation (i.e., with the forum serving as an archive) meant that Marigold homeowners had no common space to learn about one another's experiences. Without documentation, ideas become more ephemeral and conflicts and contradictions more challenging to negotiate and resolve. Further, of all the communities, Marigold experienced its external threats least directly: the road had not yet been constructed, and the landfill did not cause a smell within the gates. In the absence of pressing threats, residents felt less of an urgent need for collective sensemaking.

To understand how Marigold homeowners came to perceive a threat from the landfill and the incinerator plans, I posed the question to Mr. Lu, a talkative contract lawyer who was forty-eight at the time of the discovery and who would later play a key leadership role during anti-incinerator protests. He described the discovery of the plans as a "coincidence." He recalled that Ms. Wang, a fellow homeowner, had gone to the township administrative building one day to run errands. By chance, she saw posted on the lobby bulletin board a government environmental evaluation announcement for an incinerator to be built next to the landfill. Upon returning home, posted to the online forum: "Does everyone know? The biggest incinerator in Asia is about to be built here!" The post received immediate attention across the community. Mr. Lu, who was on a golf trip abroad at the time, received a call from a Marigold neighbor the same day. "She told me that the government announced a plan to build a waste incinerator near our homes without soliciting public input," he remembered.

Receiving that phone call was the first step in Mr. Lu's trajectory toward becoming a community leader. He eventually became so well known that long before I met Mr. Lu, I had heard a great deal about him from environmental NGO staff members. They described him as "entertaining" and "flamboyant" and said that he "would talk your ear off." From his boldly colored clothing to his dynamic storytelling, Mr. Lu was known for enjoying attention. He was also described to me as someone whom homeowners would call if there was a problem. Although he was not active in organizing community activities (indeed, no one was in Marigold) or part of the original HOA, he eventually became the face of Marigold's anti-incinerator resistance after being detained for protesting (chapter 5).

The process that led to that detainment began soon after Ms. Wang's discovery of the bulletin board announcement. A post appeared on both the Marigold forum and that of another nearby villa community about holding a meeting "for those who wanted to be more proactive in resisting incinerator construction." Mr. Lu, who attended the meeting, recalled that halfway through, a homeowner slapped his hand on the table and yelled, "What meeting? Let's hit the streets!" Mr. Lu told me, "We got to the meeting and expressed our anger. We tried to talk about what to do . . . but we were so angry. . . . Then when a homeowner yelled, 'Let's march, let's drive,' . . . I was in. Some people were worried, but most of us—we were an emotional group; nobody could stop us. We immediately went to get our cars. There was no planning or preparation; it happened so suddenly."

Homeowners in more than sixty cars joined the "car march," some with paper signs on the windows reading "no incinerator." The procession attracted attention from the media and then from the government. The suddenness of the car march—taking place before homeowners fully understood the problem, either individually or as a group—led to some later challenges in collective organizing (discussed in chapter 4).

WHEN LEADERS REPRESENT COMMUNITIES

The trajectories of Communities Meadow, Rose, and Marigold show how, a year or more after moving in, homeowners began to engage in issues that situated them in the context of a larger neighborhood and required external engagements with actors outside their gates. Such external issues are often mired in uncertainty. When an issue is pressing and threatening to the community as a whole, homeowners need to make sense of the situation, individually or collectively.

In Meadow, Willow, and Pine, homeowners viewed themselves as good neighbors and were able to confront the incinerator threat collectively. Eventually, they embraced a simplified interpretation of the problem—the incinerator might alleviate landfill stench but would pose a health risk—despite initially contradictory opinions articulated on the forum. Community figureheads—Mr. Zhao, Ms. Yu, and Ms. Ding—were able to link online and in-person conversations, bridging Meadow and Willow and welcoming Pine homeowners into the dialogue. Mr. Zhao encouraged all neighbors, regardless of which community they called home, to share their experiences on the forum and provide input on plans for collective action. Because of his facilitation, homeowners were able to learn about the issues they were facing together in a collective process. By learning together, they came to view addressing the landfill and incinerator problems as a collective responsibility, agreeing that "participation is a promise to everyone." Additionally, leaders' efforts to be inclusive of the three communities, interpreting the incinerator as a "neighborhood" problem, not only allowed for sustainable participation over time among a large number of homeowners but also shaped how these communities monitored environmental problems in their neighborhood after their incinerator struggles ended (chapter 6).

Although Community Rose enjoyed a tight network of young homeowners who had gotten to know one another through community activities and forum exchanges, response to the stench problem centered on individual rather than collective action. Although posts urged homeowners to make calls to complaint hotlines, no coherent interpretation was provided to guide homeowners in framing their grievances. This lack of collective sensemaking, combined with uncertainties around the source of the stench, likely limited the impact of residents' calls. Surprisingly, although residents of Community Rose displayed the most uncertainty about the cause of its stench problem, they appeared to be the least active in gathering information. Meadow and Willow homeowners cited government reports or personally investigated the stench, and Marigold homeowners unearthed environmental impact assessments. Yet in Community Rose, Ms. Hua seems to have been the first to visit the landfill, only 1.5 kilometers away, even though the stench had been plaguing residents for more than a month. After her risky encounter at the landfill, community members began to view her as the sole representative of the issue. Because of this perception, in later protest events, Ms. Hua was very much the articulator, framer, and strategist in Rose's anti-incinerator struggles.

In Marigold, community networks were not as tight-knit as those of Meadow, Willow, or even Rose. Because of limited forum use and scarce in-person meetings, homeowners did not have a platform to share their common experiences of what they perceived as external threats to the community: a new road, landfill expansion, and incinerator construction. Marigold was also distinguished by a lack of reported landfill stench, which likely limited individuals' interest in and experience of the issue. Importantly, when homeowners learned about the plans for incinerator construction, no recognized community representative had emerged. A group of about ten people organized a small-scale action in response to an external threat—hanging a banner declaring the community's opposition to the construction of a new road—but it was not until the impromptu car march against incinerator construction that Marigold homeowners came together in any significant numbers.

Interestingly, despite their comparative lack of group cohesion, Rose and Marigold homeowners publicly protested incinerator construction much sooner than homeowners in Meadow, Willow, and Pine. However, this speed did not necessarily benefit their causes: Meadow, Willow, and Pine homeowners took longer to organize, but the extra time was spent on creating a coherent understanding of the issue internally and messaging about grievances. This deliberation proved to be beneficial later on, as homeowners were able to articulate a clear message to government officials and other external actors, select appropriate tactics, and frame their grievances in a way that allowed them to engage in sustained dialogue with government officials (chapters 4 and 5).[36]

In each community, conditions were present for leadership to emerge—a collective identity as homeowners, preexisting networks, associational activities that required representation, and community problems that needed to be resolved—but not all community leaders emerged on the same timeline or for the same reasons. Some leaders emerged early on through community events (Mr. Zhao, Ms. Yu, and Ms. Ding), whereas others appeared only later, in response to external pressures (Huang *laoshi* and Mr. Wu, discussed in chapters 4 and 5) or after taking risks or facing government repression (Ms. Hua and Mr. Lu). All these community leaders, however, share the common features of being cultivated by their communities and playing a role in bolstering community capacity.

As homeowners began to protest publicly, the timing and type of community representation became key factors in the progression of events. The characteristics of leaders also became important in shaping protest strategies and framing how community grievances and demands were presented externally, ultimately influencing how government officials responded. The next chapter shows that although all communities mobilized for collective action, some were better at organizing than others, depending on whether and to what extent leaders were able to represent their communities and build and leverage community capacity.

Chapter Four

MOBILIZING AND ORGANIZING FOR ENVIRONMENTAL COLLECTIVE ACTION

As homeowners in Meadow, Rose, and Marigold learned more about incinerator construction, they faced the question of how to take their grievances public. Because they could apply what they had learned through organizing informal activities in the community, drafting letters of complaint to property management, and mobilizing residents to collect signatures, homeowners across all three community sites were able to mobilize for collective action against their respective incinerator threats. Community representatives who emerged early on (chapter 3) helped articulate homeowners' collective issues to various actors beyond the gates. At this stage, some communities could already rely on their representatives to lead conversations about the problem, educate neighbors, and propose actions. Additionally, some homeowners were able to tap into their networks both within and outside their communities as they strategized, identifying experts and volunteers to guide the organizing process. In communities where representatives were slow to emerge, however, uncertainties around the trash problem persisted, and actions were undertaken by individuals rather than organized collectives, impeding early organizing efforts and tactics.

This chapter discusses how, although all communities *mobilized* for collective action, some did not succeed in *organizing* sustainably. While these two concepts are often conflated in literature, it is important to distinguish between them. According to Han, mobilizing is transactional, focusing on involving people with latent interest in an issue without developing their skills or motivations for action. Organizing, in contrast, is transformational. Organizers invest in developing the skills—and therefore the capacity—of participants to engage with one another to become activists and leaders themselves.[1]

In Communities Rose and Marigold, successful mobilizing took place; specifically, leaders focused on encouraging people to protest. Ms. Hua in Rose and Mr. Lu in Marigold served as mobilizers who prompted action among homeowners already concerned about the trash and incinerator issues. However, these leaders did not develop or even draw on existing community strengths. Leaders in Community Meadow and its neighbors went further, becoming organizers as well as mobilizers. Mr. Zhao in Willow and Ms. Yu in Meadow cultivated homeowners to become activists, creating the conditions for additional representative leaders to emerge within their neighborhood. Whereas Ms. Hua in Rose struggled with sustaining engagement among homeowners on the trash issue, and Mr. Lu in Marigold operated as an independent actor rather than supporting collective action, Mr. Zhao in Willow and Ms. Yu in Meadow steadily expanded the number of people involved in the anti-incinerator cause, allocating responsibilities, facilitating interactions, and building relationships.

In addition to their organizing efforts, leaders in Meadow and Willow were also more successful in their mobilizing efforts than those in Rose. The collaboration between the two communities aided in this effort, as did their connection with Community Pine and outreach to businesses in the area. Marigold's mobilizing also found more success than that of Rose because of its cross-community outreach. Marigold homeowners, located near several similar communities, used their personal connections to rally nearby residents to participate in a public demonstration. (However, Marigold's success was short lived, as government crackdowns soon followed.) In Rose, mobilizing was constrained by its exclusive focus on its own community. Although there were many other communities nearby, cross-community connections were not made.

This chapter also highlights the initial approaches to advocacy each community took toward collective action, largely guided by community representatives, who in each location emerged at different stages of the process. Some communities developed deliberate and even sophisticated strategies, whereas others lacked a coherent or organized planning process. However, establishing initial tactics was important across all communities, as doing so marked the first time homeowners as a group came to interact with government officials directly over the incinerator issue and set the stage for later interactions with government agencies. While the various actions taken in these initial phases were fairly common tactics among Chinese protesters, regardless of social class, what set these middle-class homeowners apart was their ability to draw from personal and professional networks, rely on their communities' preexisting capacity for action (i.e., civic skills and some community leadership), and, as discussed in chapter 5, a shift to a strategy of "citizen science" in later phases of the struggle.

Among these common tactics are letter-writing and petitioning, often used in both urban and rural protests in China.[2] These tactics, which involve the in-person delivery of a letter or petition to government agencies or officials, are commonly used because they follow the legal institutional channels established by the state and are therefore less likely to lead to repression.[3] In recent years, disruptive protests have increased, but aggrieved citizens still prefer to protest via institutional channels or to use a combination of both institutional and disruptive approaches.[4] For example, collective petitioning has become a popular tactic for citizens, as they can exert more pressure on government agencies by delivering a letter of complaint as a group than as a single individual. While collective petitioning can turn disruptive, for example when citizens block access to a government building,[5] it is rare for such public demonstrations to arise without an accompanying letter-writing campaign.[6]

When publicly disruptive protests occur, common tactics of repression include police harassment or visits (at home or in the workplace), censorship, and arrest or detention. Often, repression is not only physical but also psychological (e.g., emotional blackmail) and is often imposed directly by the government on the individual actor and through their networks.[7] Authorities may pressure family members in individuals' workplaces—particularly those who work in jobs in some way connected to government agencies or who receive government benefits—and expect those family members (or even friends) to exert pressure on the individual. While these are known tactics in China, none of the homeowners featured in this book appeared to have experienced repression from actors other than police and government officials; none reported that family members had been threatened; and there was no evidence of pressure from their workplaces.

While repression was limited to those who demonstrated, it was swift and strong in Communities Rose and Marigold, both of which took the unusual route of demonstrating disruptively without also taking the institutionally approved path of letter-writing. Meadow, together with Willow and Pine, began by pursuing legal institutional channels, a choice that ultimately contributed to their success when they hit the streets.

ANTI-INCINERATOR ACTION IN MEADOW, WILLOW, AND PINE

Clear plans, procedures, and assignments were in place at Meadow and Willow when these neighboring communities began organizing against incinerator construction. Homeowners from both communities formed a "core action committee" to address the trash and incinerator problems, assigning organizing tasks to smaller groups. This division of labor mirrored Mr. Zhao's early organizing efforts when residents first moved into Willow, in which various committees were responsible for addressing distinct issues concerning homeowners' interactions with property management and developers (chapter 2). Mr. Zhao's meticulousness, initially evident in his maintenance of transparent records on the homeowners' forum and his engagement homeowners in various decision-making activities, fostered a sense of trust and neighborliness as anti-incinerator action commenced. The group was also able to draw on its prior experience with writing letters of complaint and gathering signatures, which both Willow and Meadow had done in earlier efforts of collective action against property management.

In addition to distributing tasks among a large number of volunteers, Meadow and Willow's core action committee also sought to draw expertise from their community networks. Specifically, the committee looked for homeowners with legal expertise, whose counsel helped them decide that pursuing institutional channels would be the most appropriate course of action. However, homeowners soon discovered that although letter-writing yielded some dialogue with government officials, it remained ineffective in addressing the trash problem. Responses were often slow and dismissive.

A First Step in Organizing for Environmental Action

The day after calling for mobilization on the Willow forum (chapter 3), Mr. Zhao posted about setting up an in-person meeting that would bring Willow and Meadow homeowners together to plan for collective action. His post read,

> Hello, everyone:
>
> After speaking with Ms. Ding from Meadow, we have decided to hold a meeting on Saturday at 13:30 in the conference room of Willow to exchange ideas about the trash problem and actions [to take]. The meeting agenda is [to] (1) gather the intellect and ideas of everyone and confirm our method of action; [and] (2) establish an action preparatory committee, divide up responsibilities, [and] implement tasks for our next steps. Welcoming everyone to actively attend.

Mr. Zhao was diligent in detailing his expectations of participants:

> To ensure we hold a successful meeting, please pay attention to the following items, and prepare in advance:
>
> 1) Each community should have a person documenting meeting minutes. After the meeting, the minutes will be released together [with those of the other community]. If any homeowner has a recording pen [device], please also bring it along and temporarily let the minute taker use it. It will be returned to you after the meeting.
> 2) Every person who attends the meeting, please summarize and organize your viewpoints to avoid speaking haphazardly. This will allow the meeting to be productive.
> 3) To make use of every person's strength, the intention is to establish several task groups, such as a finance group (in charge of overall management of finances), [a] promotions group (in charge of external publicity and contacting media), [and a] legal group ([to] provide legal advice and support for related activities), etc. Welcoming everyone with related expertise to participate actively and bravely take on these burdens.

In this post, Mr. Zhao provided a clear meeting agenda and plan for taking meeting minutes (and making records transparent), as well as plans to move forward with task forces that would take on the various aspects of collective action. These plans demonstrated that Mr. Zhao and Ms. Ding were actively seeking and mobilizing a large group of volunteers and distributing specific responsibilities. The task forces enabled small groups of homeowners to manage various aspects of organizing independently, and their ability to work outside meetings of the larger group was key to scaling up Meadow and Willow's collective action. Mr. Zhao's post also made homeowners aware that the group needed resources—both financial and legal—to take their anti-incinerator protest outside the community gates. The organizers sought expertise within their own communities from homeowners who were accountants, lawyers, or communications experts. As one homeowner observed on the forum, "You've thought about this very thoroughly!"

More than 2,500 homeowners read the post. Several responded by encouraging people to spread the message off-line by printing and posting flyers. The speed of this response to mobilizing was astounding, demonstrating the well-established, tight-knit networks within Meadow and Willow. Within two hours of Mr. Zhao posting about the meeting, a Meadow homeowner had created and uploaded a template for a flyer announcing the meeting. Others volunteered to print and distribute the flyer, with one homeowner suggesting that everyone on the thread put flyers up in their buildings.

One unknown, however, was how property managers would respond to the flyers—or to the homeowners' attempt to organize around an environmental issue. Although property management likely hoped for a resolution to the trash problem, they had little incentive to encourage actions that would attract the attention of police and government officials. With respect to the flyers, one online respondent opined, "I think it should be OK if we clean [the flyers] up afterward," and another suggested using a glue stick rather than tape "for easier cleanup." The uncertainty about the attitudes of property management toward their organizing efforts led Mr. Zhao to schedule the meeting for a Saturday, when property management representatives would not be present in the community.

MOBILIZING AND ORGANIZING FOR ENVIRONMENTAL COLLECTIVE ACTION

These online and off-line communication efforts were successful in reaching interested homeowners from both communities. In the first official cross-community meeting, homeowners discussed strategic plans for organizing and formed the core action committee. This committee derived from and replaced Community Willow's earlier "mobilizing committee" (chapter 3), signifying a move from mobilizing to organizing for collective action. Dozens of homeowners self-organized into the task groups outlined in the meeting agenda. Participants were also eager to involve residents unable to attend the meeting. As one homeowner wrote on the forum, "In sociology, there is a term, 'the silent majority.' To be honest, this refers to those who are pissed off but yet don't say anything. This action [of creating task forces] will let us see how many of [the] 'silent majority' we can mobilize."

Mr. Zhao announced on the forum that by the following day, the finance group was already active:

> To resolve problems related to trash, the "trash problem action committee" needs funding and support in order to take action. Therefore, they are reaching out broadly to homeowners to raise funds. The money raised will be entirely used on activities related to resolving the trash problem. In addition, I want to especially note that since the money raised will be used on activities that would benefit all homeowners as a group, the action committee will request in our next meeting that all homeowners share these costs. The committee will manage the raised funds very strictly and use funds appropriately. Therefore, at our first meeting today (December 23), we chose two homeowners to be responsible managers of this money. For those who are interested in providing funding or support, please contact [username] from Meadow (via forum chat) and [username] from Willow (via phone [redacted]; suggest that you text to save costs).

Naming the issue the "trash problem"—a phrase that would be used continually to encompass both landfill and incinerator concerns—Mr. Zhao laid out a clear plan for mobilizing needed resources, organizing how the resources would be managed, and establishing protocols of transparency so that other community members could be involved. Homeowners embraced the idea of fundraising and, as always in Willow and Meadow, joined in the dialogue. They posted suggestions on the forum about who should donate and how much, and Mr. Zhao continually responded. For example,

"I think we should collect money from each household. We can talk to property management [and] have them collect money for us. Because this is an issue that concerns every household, money collection wouldn't be excessive."

"Administrator [Mr. Zhao], give us an amount. If it's too much, we can give the money back; if too little, we can give more. No matter what happens, we would have tried."

[Mr. Zhao in response]: "It should still be voluntary; it's not that apportioning [money] is impossible to achieve, it's just that it would be difficult to implement currently."

"Recommend that we collect 100 yuan [$15 in U.S. dollars] from each household. It's not realistic to collect money from every household, but of the 1,200 households, it would be best to collect from 1,000 households. This way, [those who are] giving money won't feel like they are being taken advantage of."

"Recommend getting signatures first. If we get 1,000 household signatures, then we can collect money."

"Recommend Administrator [Mr. Zhao] speak to Ms. Liao who organized [the] community water quality inspections from before. We could take the leftover money we donated to do water quality inspections and use it for funds to resolve the trash problem."[8]

[Mr. Zhao in response] "Ha ha, donations should follow voluntary principles. In addition, I believe that we should insist on the principle of one issue, one donation—no mixing together of issues. If you donated once to water quality inspections, you could contact Ms. Liao, get the leftover money back, then donate to this trash activity. This would be more appropriate."

Mr. Zhao continued to maintain transparency and dialogue throughout the fundraising discussion, always responding thoughtfully to homeowners' suggestions. The dialogue also indicated that this was not the first time Willow had organized fundraising in the community, previously having collected funds for water quality inspections quickly and transparently. The anticipated response of property management continued to be a topic of interest, in this case with one homeowner expecting not only that organizing efforts would be tolerated but also that property management would be willing to assist the effort by collecting funds. Other posters, however, were more cautious about attracting the attention of property managers, worried that they would try to curb mobilizing efforts.[9]

In response to homeowners' feedback, the finance task force quickly put forth a clear set of rules in a policy document. These rules specified how task force members would manage the money, including by providing receipts, creating a cash account, assigning a person to manage accounting, and publishing accounting records online every fifteen days. Rules for managing expenditures were also determined: four representatives from Meadow and Willow would be in charge of approving expenditures; if an amount for an activity was deemed too high, discussions with the core action committee would be required. In addition, any homeowner with a concern about how expenditures were being handled could request a review with the core action committee. Homeowners were also encouraged to provide additional suggestions for supervising the use of the money collected. The finance task force's detailed policy document demonstrated organizers' efforts to be transparent and to engage homeowners in the organizing process.

This policy document was just one example of the copious amount of documentation produced during Willow and Meadow's organizing meetings. Meeting minutes and other records were clearly time consuming to produce (and likely tedious to read), yet the preservation of such archives served several important functions. First, it allowed busy middle-class professionals who traveled for work to catch up on what they had missed. Many homeowners posted apologies for missing meetings and promised to read the records, talk with neighbors, and make donations. Second, documents were available for Willow, Meadow, and Pine homeowners to consult as they talked with one another about the issues, posted to the forum, and worked in task forces. Third, the archive served as a set of organizing resources, building both a playbook and a culture for organizing work in the three neighboring communities.

Initial Strategy for Advocacy

As the task groups were launched, another wave of recruitment occurred, with the leaders providing details about which areas of action required assistance from volunteers. Four days after the core action committee was formed, Ms. Ding of Community Meadow wrote a post titled "Recruiting relevant personnel—It's time for everyone to stand up!" Her post described plans for environmental organizing and explained what each task would entail:

1) Deliver letters of complaint to designated agencies showing opposition to construction of the [location redacted] waste incinerator.

Description of situation: . . . We have one homeowner who knows an employee at the National Environmental Inspection Office and can help introduce us to designated people in charge, allowing us to give them the complaint letter, thereby avoiding bureaucracy and saving time.[10] It might be the case that we would only find out in an impromptu way when the person in charge is present, so we need a person delivering the complaint letter to be someone who is ready to go at any time. Therefore, we need to recruit a few people who have time normally, homeowners who can leave at any time, representing all of us in giving the complaint letter to designated departments. Separately, if we need a bigger crowd to exert pressure on related authorities, we will need more people to take half a day off work (usually in the morning).

2) New Year's promotional work

Description of situation: According to [our] plan, during [Western] New Year's, we at Meadow and Willow will start the promotional work around the landfill; the poster boards and promotional flyers are currently being made. To prevent volunteers from being overworked, each community needs twenty to thirty volunteers, taking turns. Every shift should only be about two hours. . . .

3) Provide legal, policy, [and] regulation expertise, guidance, and advice.

Description of situation: With the activities carrying forward, we deeply feel that this activity involves many different aspects. To ensure that activities are carried out legally, professionally, and efficiently, we need to recruit experts or employees in related fields, so when we come across problems and questions during our activities, they can provide timely and accurate comments and suggestions.

If you are willing to participate in the above work, please use email, text, phone, or forum chat to contact us according to which community you are in. An able fellow needs the help of three other people[11]; the more people [who] collect wood, the higher the flame.[12] Your passionate participation will certainly add hope; your negligence and indifference equates to giving up. Hoping homeowners can make the right decisions at this important time point.

This recruitment post, with its specific requests and rationale, set a course for the initial advocacy strategy used in Meadow, Willow, and Pine. Homeowners would pursue legal institutional channels by delivering letters of complaint to various government agencies. They would draw from their own networks—for example, one homeowner had connections at a state-level environmental office, which allowed them to avoid having to jump through bureaucratic hoops. Additionally, homeowners sought out legal experts within their communities to guide them through the petitioning process. Although many members of the core action committee, like Mr. Zhao, had experience writing letters of complaint (such as those directed to property management), the procedure for delivering and filing a formal petition—as well as the process of determining to whom to address the letter—was more ambiguous to them.

A key first step for the core action committee and task forces was to develop a list of names and email addresses of government officials to whom to send the letter. The list included professors and researchers at local district universities who also held government positions, such as city planning and environmental bureau posts. In addition to researching institutional channels through which to lodge their complaints, organizers also planned promotional activities within their communities to educate homeowners on landfill and incinerator issues. At the time, many homeowners were unclear about how incineration worked. With the help of residents with backgrounds in chemistry, the core action committee put together a campaign to educate the community. Whereas collective learning around landfill stench had been more ad hoc through the online sharing of common experiences and information (chapter 3), during the time of anti-incinerator organizing, creating educational activities more intentionally and moving them off-line to physical spaces became priorities so that more homeowners could be reached (figure 4.1).

These educational campaigns helped engage more homeowners in the process of developing the petition. Letters of complaint, first drafted by Mr. Zhao and other members of the core action committee, went through several rounds of edits to incorporate homeowner suggestions. The letters focused on how community residents had found out about the trash issue, outlined why incineration would be harmful (based on information from two published articles),[13] and pleaded for government agencies to reconsider their decision to build the incinerator. Each letter was signed

FIGURE 4.1. Meadow homeowners reviewing educational poster boards created by fellow residents about the incinerator problem, January 2007. Many residents who passed by would stop to read and discuss the plans for incinerator construction.
Source: Photo provided by a Community Meadow homeowner.

by more than one hundred homeowners. Volunteers were then divided into groups to deliver the letters in person to the district government, the Beijing Municipal Administration Commission, the Beijing Environmental Protection Bureau (EPB), and the State Environmental Protection Administration.

A homeowner on one of the delivery teams recounted her experience online:

> At 8 A.M., I rode in Mr. Q.'s car. By 9 A.M., everyone [homeowners] was gathered there. They were busy at work but asked for time off to come; it was really something! The most moving part was old man Mr. Ru,[14] because it was so cold today. When we were dividing up where we each would go, I was supposed to go to the EPB, but I was wearing too few layers [and] was worried I'd be too cold, so I requested to go to the district government instead.

MOBILIZING AND ORGANIZING FOR ENVIRONMENTAL COLLECTIVE ACTION

When we were picking locations, Mr. Ru said, "You all choose first. I can go wherever." This old man, in such cold weather, was working so hard for the neighborhood; every compliment pales in comparison. When we arrived at the government building, I suddenly understood that this majestic district government [building was] built using people's money, [but] we can't even enter. We talked to the guard at the gate in the freezing winds for a long time, [but] the guard would just not let us [in] to see our parent officials.[15] In the past [historically], citizens could stand outside of the government [location] with drums making complaints, [and] parent officials had to receive cases in person. Now we are just reflecting a problem; [we] can't even enter the gate. You tell me how weird is this! [It] might be that I've been a housewife for too long [and have] stopped understanding how society works.

This passage exemplifies how homeowners from Meadow and Willow worked together, negotiating roles, getting to know one another better, and exhibiting neighborliness and kindness toward one another. As homeowners stepped beyond their community gates to address the trash issue, however, they faced a new barrier in the form of another set of gates: those of government agencies.

The homeowner continued her account of the encounter at the district government building:

With the help of one of the homeowners, we could only have two people enter [and] give the document to the district Political Consultative Conference representative. The representative, Mr. Z., said, "If you'd love to put this [document] here with me, then put it here. I can only follow the rules and send it along to Letters and Visits." I asked him, "Under what circumstances would you take on this case?" Mr. Z. said, "Go online to see who the representative is for your specific area [and] have him write a proposal. We can only accept proposals." Ms. H. from Meadow told me that she'll find a way for the document to get to the district head, [but] I feel that if we keep doing this, the letter will never get to the district head. The funny thing is the two young receptionists there spoke to us with such "bureaucratic tones"; it looked like they thought they're really somebody, working in the government. This post isn't intended to complain about our experience; it's to highlight how difficult it is to handle things in China. When [will] they [the government] truly serve the people?

The frustrated tone of the post illustrates that, although the homeowners had pursued established institutional channels, they were still faced with bureaucratic challenges. Homeowners were prevented from entering the government agency, prevented from delivering their letter to the person in charge, and instructed to follow additional bureaucratic procedures. Further, they felt disrespected by the agency receptionists—younger than themselves—who seemed unmoved by the homeowners' pleas. Because of this encounter, the homeowner who posted her account of her experience perceived that the government (as represented by Mr. Z and the receptionists) was not serving the people appropriately.

Rather than being discouraged by these obstacles, however, homeowners became more determined to organize effectively. Huang *laoshi* of Community Meadow emerged as an organizer at this time. As a volunteer delivering the letter, he was struck by the experience of arriving at the EPB office only to learn that five "official" signatures from homeowners were required to file the complaint collectively. Although more than one hundred homeowners had signed the letter, their signatures were not sufficient to identify them in the way that "official," identification-verified signatures would. Huang *laoshi* later recounted to me a standstill at the gates of the EPB with a small group of homeowners: "Which five people will step up? I was scared. Most people were scared and didn't really understand the petitioning procedure . . . but the clock was ticking. 'It [will be] sunset if we drag it out,' I thought. 'I need to step up.' If I didn't, who else would?"

Huang *laoshi* remembered that decision as the transformational moment in which he became deeply engaged in collective action. He would later become not only one of the community experts on the harms of incineration but also a speaker giving talks all over Beijing about the community's anti-incinerator resistance, despite having no scientific or environmental background (he was a retired administrator of a government institution). His example shows how, in addition to the homeowners who provided expertise as legal and scientific professionals, others, like Huang *laoshi*, provided valuable contributions by becoming self-taught experts in both petitioning and incineration.

Not only did the challenges encountered at government agencies ultimately have a positive effect on the homeowners in terms of strengthening their capabilities and their commitment to organizing, but they also appeared to cause a stir among officials. Within a week, homeowners heard that their first set of letters of complaint were gaining government attention. One homeowner posted "unofficial" information she had obtained from a fellow resident on the Willow forum: "According to a homeowner whose name I do not want to reveal, the anti-incinerator construction actions of the two communities [Meadow and Willow] have been acknowledged by related leaders within the district government. Apparently their attitude toward the incinerator construction is not as determined as we had thought; there is some pushback from other PCC[16] representatives. . . . Therefore, we should see some hope. . . . Let's continue our actions, continue gathering signatures, promote the issue, [and] actively participate in the New Year [incinerator education] activities in the community."

In the absence of official responses to their letters, homeowners used their networks to obtain "unofficial information" and gain insights into government discussions. They learned of representatives in the Political Consultative Conference who apparently shared the homeowners' opposition to construction of an incinerator at the designated location. This encouraging news provided additional momentum to the communities in their ongoing organizing efforts.

A second round of letters was drafted and delivered to additional agencies: the State Bureau for Letters and Visits, the municipal government, the water bureau, the municipal development commission, the district development commission, and the housing development commission—any agency residents could imagine having a connection to the incinerator decision. As the petition circulated more widely, "unofficial" hearsay gave way to actual exchanges and meetings between government agencies and homeowners.

A post recounting a phone conversation between a homeowner and a Letters and Visits official indicated that the bureau had received the letter: "[Bureau officials] felt the district government did not handle the situation appropriately, that they should not have made plans to construct the incinerator in a windward location, in close proximity to residential communities." Although the response from Letters and Visits seemed promising, it also expressed that the case was not truly in that agency's hands. The official on the phone promised to "treat the case as a priority and contact designated government agencies to deliver the information, but related agencies central and local would be the ones to handle the case."

Following that call, several government agencies sent representatives to the subdistrict office that governed Meadow, Willow, and Pine to provide an explanation of the project for homeowners, calling this event a "symposium." The speakers were district urban management officials, incinerator experts,[17] and a representative from the landfill. Homeowners prepared documents in advance to present their stance against incinerator construction. Afterward, a homeowner wrote that the presentations from the speakers were impressive, reporting that they "followed logic, [were] powerful, [and were] backed by evidence," though this resident seemed to doubt the evidence offered. This homeowner argued that the incinerator experts were "misleading the government" with their supposed evidence that incineration was safe and beneficial and that the incinerator's location was appropriate, in that incineration would have a limited negative environmental impact on the local area. One of the members of the core action committee noted on the forum that the experts received a lot of pushback from homeowners: "They had come here expecting to promote their waste incinerator. They didn't expect this [from us]; it was an immediate blow to their authority as experts, [and] they couldn't even justify what they were saying."

During the meeting, the landfill representative explained that the landfill had already exceeded its capacity and was unable to process sewage and garbage in a timely manner. Building an incinerator was therefore a waste-management priority, he argued. Finally, the district representative promised additional symposia in the future and acknowledged that the district urban management officials had been late to communicate with homeowners, which had led to "strong dissatisfaction" among residents. Homeowners on the forum noted that the district representative apologized for the situation. However, they recounted that he had also explained that there was really no other location in the district suitable for the incinerator to be located. According to the homeowners, he promised to deliver their demands to the "district" (without specifying which agency) but evaded their requests for a public hearing on incinerator construction.

Reflecting on the symposium, Huang *laoshi* told me, "They [government officials] came to communicate with us. . . . Here [in the communities] there are a lot of professionals [and] homeowners coming back from [traveling] abroad, so they know that these things [incinerators] are really risky and controversial abroad. At the time, they [government officials] said really nice things, sugarcoating what they said. They kept saying if you burn the trash, it won't be smelly anymore."

MOBILIZING AND ORGANIZING FOR ENVIRONMENTAL COLLECTIVE ACTION

As Huang *loashi*'s "sugarcoating" comment suggests, homeowners were generally dissatisfied with the government response to their complaints.

At the end of January, homeowners held a second meeting to talk about the trash problem, with more than three hundred people in attendance. At the meeting, with guidance from community members with legal backgrounds, the core action committee decided to file for an administrative reconsideration (AR), a legal action taken by citizens to prompt a government agency to review and reconsider an administrative decision that may violate citizens' rights.[18] This more formal filing triggers a requirement for the government to review and respond. The push for filing an AR followed Meadow and Willow's general strategy toward advocacy: conducting all activities in a "legal, effective, and orderly manner."

A homeowner with a legal background recommended that the group file the AR with the Beijing EPB specifically with regard to the environmental impact assessment that had led to the incinerator construction being greenlighted.[19] During the drafting of the AR, the EPB published an abridged version of the environmental impact assessment online— "as a result of collective petitioning pressures," homeowners explained to me. Community members were also successful in obtaining documents from the landfill company. In formulating their arguments for the AR, the core action committee drew on data from the documents of both the government and the landfill company. For example, the AR cited the amount of trash the planned incinerator would be able to process—1,200 tons per day—and pointed out that the actual trash intake was already 1,800 tons per day, meaning that incineration would not resolve the trash problem.

The core action committee also set an action item to encourage Pine homeowners and nearby businesses to engage the larger neighborhood in signing the AR. However, as homeowners' participation grew across the neighborhood, promotional activities within their communities began to receive negative attention from local officials.

Early Soft Repression

Thus far, actions taken by homeowners in Meadow and Willow had involved only established institutional channels: letter-writing, petitioning, and preparing to file an AR. Homeowners had even been successful in bringing government officials into their subdistrict to discuss the trash problem. Nonetheless, dissatisfied with government responses, the core action committee pushed ahead with a new promotional activity in the communities. Whereas the earlier campaign of educational posters was kept within community gates, a new plan was established that would be outward facing: banners hung from balconies displaying slogans against incinerator construction.

Potential slogans were posted online for discussion, including the following:

"Against construction of trash incinerators here!"
"Don't want stench, don't want cancer!"
"Protect the air, the water, our home!"
"We don't want to breathe poisonous air!"
"To have health, then to have (social) harmony!"
"Landfill brings stench, incinerator brings cancer!"

The rhetoric remained unaggressive; even the concept of "social harmony" was used, a term often used by central state officials. The core action committee solicited volunteers from Meadow, Willow, and Pine living on the upper floors of buildings visible to main roads to hang banners off their balconies. The banners were bright red with white characters, hung vertically and spanning four stories (figure 4.2).

Just one day after the banners were unfurled, officials from the Urban Administrative and Law Enforcement Bureau (*chengguan*) appeared in the community. One homeowner in Meadow recounted the experience to me: "I remember—the wind was strong that day . . . the city management officials came [and] looked around the entire day. They told people that they should take down the banners—they went to the households on the top floors that were hanging banners [and said] that they would be penalized [fined] if they continued to display them."

When *chengguan* officers came to "look around" in the community, it made some homeowners nervous, as the officers were perceived as trouble.[20] Mr. Wu, from Pine, who had volunteered to hang a banner off his balcony, recalled that the officers came to his home and told him to take down the banner "because the banner had to do with the appearance of the city (*shirong*)." He said, "They [the *chengguan*] came, observed us for a day, and on the second day, they told us to take it down." Although

MOBILIZING AND ORGANIZING FOR ENVIRONMENTAL COLLECTIVE ACTION

FIGURE 4.2. Community Meadow's anti-incinerator banners. The closest one reads, "We do not want to breathe toxic air!"
Source: Photo provided by a Community Meadow homeowner.

Mr. Wu did not indicate that the officers used physical force or intimidation, the homeowners followed their instructions, likely acknowledging the reputation of the *chengguan* for escalation and the homeowners' wish to avoid potential fines.

Just as their banners were being challenged by the *chengguan*, homeowners discovered that some of their online forum posts were disappearing. Mr. Zhao, after calling and speaking with an employee of the homeowners' forum web platform, posted the following: "According to the employee, because the word 'incineration' (*fenshao*) is a censored term (to avoid being deleted, I used a homonym here for "shao" [to burn]), every post with the term will be deleted by the system. The ones we're seeing currently that still have the term were ones that we manually recovered [reposted]. But because we have limited people working on this, and the workload is heavy, we cannot recover all of the posts. Because of this, I recommend that when you post, use other terms as a substitute, such as [homonym]."²¹

This sudden removal of incinerator-themed posts was the homeowners' first encounter with censorship on the Meadow and Willow forums. Not once during their organizing and collective action against property management, complaining about the landfill, planning of large homeowners' meetings to discuss trash problems, or even sharing of negative experiences of delivering letters to government agencies did they find their posts censored before this point. However, it seemed that the *public* displays of the anti-incinerator banners worried local police (translated as "public security": *gongan*) and the *chengguan*, prompting closer scrutiny of the online forums. The banners, even with their nonaggressive slogans, were viewed as a potential threat that could lead to disorder, a common concern among local officials. But rather than convincing homeowners to shy away from the online forum, the censorship motivated them to keep posting. "This is normal," wrote one homeowner. "It's interference and an order from governmental agencies, obviously." Understanding censorship as "normal" led homeowners to simply use different words where necessary. They continued their online discussions and kept working on the AR.

By early February, after many rounds of feedback and revision, the final draft of the AR was complete. An event was planned for a Saturday on which homeowners were to meet outside Community Meadow to sign the AR. Now better informed about government processes, they knew they would need to bring copies of their personal identification cards. Doing so meant that homeowners' identities would be made known to government officials, which was a commitment beyond merely signing one's name to a letter of complaint. A group of homeowners would also be present to distribute anti-incinerator flyers to areas surrounding the communities.

The AR was officially submitted to the EPB on February 11, but it would be months before homeowners received a reply. At this point, homeowners were starting to realize that pursuing legal institutional channels, while mostly safe and somewhat useful in eliciting government responses, was not ultimately effective because complaints were easy for government officials to disregard. While waiting to hear back regarding the AR, homeowners resumed their anti-incinerator educational activities in the community. However, at the end of February, homeowners were once again visited by police and officials, who instructed them to cease all promotional activities within their communities, including distributing posters and flyers. While homeowners did not know what the consequences would be if they continued their educational activities, the pressure from these official visits was sufficient to curb their actions.

Although government repression was not severe for Meadow and Willow homeowners—mostly taking the form of in-person warnings and online censorship—it made many homeowners feel that they were losing the battle to stop the incinerator. So the core action committee began to consider additional strategic directions. Chapter 5 describes how, as homeowners studied the environmental impact assessment and learned more about incineration through community educational activities, they were able to pivot strategies. Their emerging approach of citizen science (i.e., public participation in scientific research) focused on critiquing the assessment, collecting information to conduct their own environmental evaluations, and running community surveys modeled on the assessment's public opinion surveys. This shift toward data collection, the use of survey methods, and presenting findings to government officials allowed the homeowners to prolong their dialogue with government decision-makers.

ANTI-INCINERATOR ACTION IN COMMUNITY ROSE

Chapter 3 described how Ms. Hua, Rose's community representative, snuck into the landfill and incinerator site near her community, initiating a confrontation with an inspector who reported her to the police. Because of her perceived willingness to take risks (as understood by homeowners who read her lengthy account of the encounter and saw police and government officials visit her home the next day), Rose residents embraced Ms. Hua as their representative in confronting the trash issue. In the weeks following her on-site investigation, Ms. Hua tracked down information on incinerator construction, becoming angrier the more she learned. Fueled by this emotion, she turned to mobilizing homeowners to hit the streets in a public demonstration.

In recounting the mobilizing process, Ms. Hua described carrying the workload on her own. She was a solo operator in her efforts to obtain information on the landfill and incinerator construction. Other homeowners continued to post reports about their conversations with government representatives on complaint hotlines, but, unlike in Meadow and Willow, no clear organizing process emerged to prepare homeowners for collective action. Anger toward government officials was palpable on the forum posts, but no plans were made and no tasks assigned. Even mobilizing for a public demonstration fell solely to Ms. Hua and a few others, conducted through texting and MSN Messenger. This effort exemplified another contrast with Meadow and Willow: rather than bureaucracy and banners, the Rose demonstration focused on disruptive action, blocking the main street that garbage trucks used to drive into the landfill. This public protest resulted in a government crackdown, followed by the repression of Rose homeowners both online and off-line.

Mobilizing but Not Organizing

One of the first things Ms. Hua (in her midthirties at the time) described to me was how many people of her generation were "angry youths" (*fenqing*). She explained that while anger might initially spur some action, people's motivation tended to burn out. "These types of young people . . . when they're mad, they're very powerful, very passionate, but if you let it drag on for too long, they can't do it, they can't do things sustainably," she told me. After encountering the police, even her friends the Yangs, the young couple who went to the landfill with her on the night that made her a community celebrity, "came back feeling disappointed, like they've taken big blows, feeling like they had no hope in the government." Ms. Hua felt that there was no one to whom she could really turn as an ongoing collaborator in community organizing.

The morning after Ms. Hua's landfill confrontation, after she posted her angry sixty-thousand-word exposé of what she had "uncovered" (chapter 3), she found that she had been contacted by a large number of neighbors on the forum chat. One homeowner had heard that "government officials had seen [Ms. Hua's] posts and were holding meetings." Another told her that "officials were looking for her through the information police had obtained from her the night before."[22]

Indeed, an official from the municipal planning office arrived later that morning in a black government Audi and knocked at her door, accompanied by several police officers. Apparently, they knew that she had snuck into the landfill, but at the time they did not know she was the author of the

MOBILIZING AND ORGANIZING FOR ENVIRONMENTAL COLLECTIVE ACTION

lengthy anti-incinerator post. She told me, "They started questioning me about me sneaking into the landfill and asked why. They didn't even know I was the person who posted the exposé at the time. . . . It wasn't until after they had more contact with me that they discovered my online username, and then they started listening to my phone calls and monitoring my online activity."

While Ms. Hua only suspected that her phone line had been tapped, she found evidence that the forum was being monitored: some of her comments were blocked from being posted, and some posts were mysteriously deleted. The police visit was upsetting not only to Ms. Hua but also to her neighbors. When nearby homeowners saw that the police were questioning her, they were livid, she recalled. Between Ms. Hua's online exposé and the swift interference by government officials, homeowners became irate.

Rose homeowners' next step was to try an institutional channel by calling hotlines (as discussed in chapter 3) to lodge complaints with government agencies. Unlike in Meadow and Willow, however, homeowners were encouraged on their forum to make calls as individuals rather than as a collective. These complaints did sometimes prompt government responses. For example, after lodging a complaint, one homeowner heard from the Beijing EPB and posted the following on the forum:

> I received a response from [the] EPB officially: "The landfill stench problem is not a problem that [the] EPB can resolve; it requires the coordination of multiple governmental departments. It will not relocate [the landfill]." Currently, an incinerator is being constructed. After burning, it will create carcinogens in the air. We will suffer from toxins for fifty years, [since] the landfill will be used for fifty years. If we don't ask for the stopping of construction now, we will be poisoned for the rest of our lives. The EPB even said that incineration "cannot resolve the stench issue." The stench will continue year after year because trash needs to release toxins when it's sitting there.[23] We've been asking daily about the methane. . . . We care about our health, our family's health. Hoping everyone stands up and takes responsibility for our own bodies.

Another homeowner responded: "Yes, I have called uncountable times. As soon as I call, they already know who I am. . . . I feel like [the] EPB doesn't care. They keep saying we'll bring this up, we'll bring this up—bring this up to [expletive] who? Nothing has actually been resolved."

These reports demonstrate how easily individual hotline complaints were dismissed or referred to other agencies (see chapter 5 for more on how complaints were pushed from one agency to the next). Despite continually hitting this bureaucratic wall, Rose homeowners remained focused on encouraging individual actions: making individual calls and taking responsibility "for our own bodies." Over several weeks, according to forum reports, the tone of the hotline calls escalated, and exchanges became increasingly combative. On the forum, young homeowners expressed that they had very little faith or trust in the system or in the competence of government officials. As a result, when Community Rose did turn toward collective action, Ms. Hua and others bypassed institutional channels in favor of disruptive tactics. "We were just so angry," Ms. Hua emphasized to me once again.

After two more weeks of online complaints and angry posts, a call for mobilization was briefly circulated online before being removed by censors.[24] This post, written by a lawyer in the community, took quite a different rhetorical approach from that used in Meadow and Willow's reasoned strategy. Appealing to Rose homeowners' emotions, it read like a poem:

> Tomorrow, let's go take a stroll!
> The stench, like a ghost, is hovering in the air.
> The victims in this area, north, east, south, west, are taking action,
> To protect their own health and survival, to protect their beautiful land,
> they will fight!
>
> To those who are building the facilities, fight them!
> To the managers and businesspeople carrying out the project, fight them!
> To all the agencies who allow this to happen, fight them!
>
> These years, we chose to wait kindly, patiently caring,
> Hoping one day, we would have fresh air to breathe,
> This is a baseline expectation . . .
>
> But as time goes by, the stench is increasing in frequency,
> All the agencies again and again make excuses and shirk responsibility;
> the situation is getting worse!

These days, the truth has been uncovered, the lies have been exposed.
With the stench bothering us,
We have discovered,
Our kindness has been taken advantage of, our patience seen as weakness,
The smell has gotten more concentrated!!

Maybe after a while, the stench will become poisonous gases,
They are insulting and trampling on our dignity!

So much anger!
No more patience!

We can no longer be quiet,

Today, we are forced, we choose to fight!

Don't back down; to allow the bad to happen is to bully the good!
Don't stand for this; to empathize with the bad is to attack the good!

Regardless of whether you're a government official, employee, or vagabond, you aren't free from this harm because of your position;
Regardless of whether you're a cop, a judge, or a security guard, you aren't free because of your uniform.

Tomorrow, let's go take a stroll![25]

Whereas Meadow and Willow's post calling for mobilization, crafted by the meticulous Mr. Zhao and the communities' core action committee, emphasized collective responsibility, orderliness, and cooperation with other communities in the neighborhood, this post primarily expressed rage and called for an end to "patience." The post emphasized that everyone in the community, regardless of their job or title, was negatively impacted by the trash problem.

The post also specifically targeted government agencies and those building the incinerator—"fight them!"—which is likely why it was quickly removed from the forum. However, the post survived via cut-and-paste in chats among homeowners. The community member who sent the post content in a chat to Ms. Hua told her that a high-ranking district official had been made aware of the post, possibly notified by lower-level officials monitoring the forum. With the district government on alert, any call for mobilization was likely to be monitored closely.

In describing the mobilizing process, however, Ms. Hua did not view the post as a contributing factor. She remembered the decision to protest beginning with "a bunch of neighbors talking downstairs in the community on a Saturday morning.... Suddenly more homeowners were starting to gather, getting angrier as we talked about the landfill, and then, swearing to 'fight until the end,' we hit the streets to block garbage trucks going into the landfill area."[26] No clear protest planning preceded the event, but Ms. Hua said that homeowners texted one another urgently to get as many people as possible to participate. The tight-knit social network among the homeowners in Rose facilitated a rapid mobilization. Residents quickly gathered outside the community gates, most wearing face masks with words written on them in magic marker. Protest photos saved by homeowners show that some masks read "anti-stench," and others displayed the word "toxins" crossed out (figure 4.3).

The police soon showed up in a large public security van, and government officials who had arrived in cars were "watching from the sidelines."[27]

FIGURE 4.3. Community Rose homeowners protesting on a main street and blocking garbage trucks from entering the landfill. The white van is a public security (police) van, which arrived to disperse the protesters, who were blocking traffic.
Source: Photo provided by a Community Rose homeowner.

MOBILIZING AND ORGANIZING FOR ENVIRONMENTAL COLLECTIVE ACTION

In photos provided by homeowners, police holding loudspeakers can be seen, as well as several officials holding up signs reading "Disruption of public order is prohibited. Immediately stop illegal behavior." Ms. Hua told me that a journalist from BBC China was also present, which she learned after the fact when the network's report was circulated among homeowners.[28] Although rain began to fall during the protest, people continued to block the streets so that, according to Ms. Hua, even buses could not pass. Protesters also used adhesive tape to stick pieces of paper reading "stink" onto police cars.

After some time, *chengguan* officials appeared and attempted to negotiate with Ms. Hua to disperse the crowd. Out of fear of being detained, she refused to give them information and denied any part in mobilizing the homeowners. "I was unwilling to say anything," she recalls. "I didn't ask anyone to protest; I just wanted to resolve the problem. I told the *chengguan* I wasn't the leader, but he thought people would listen to me because he had somehow found out I was the forum administrator. But I told him it's not like the people were my soldiers." The protesters were then disbanded, partly because a number of homeowners were taken away for questioning. Ms. Hua expressed a particular incredulousness over "entire families" and "doctors" being targets of this repression.

Although Ms. Hua was the main community representative for Rose in many ways—the organizer of informal activities and the homeowners' association preparatory committee, the forum administrator, and the researcher and distributor of information about the landfill and incinerator issues—she did not wish for this role to be acknowledged outside the community gates. Detainment or arrest for her role in disruptive protest could result in her husband or extended family members being monitored or, even worse, harassed at home or even at their jobs, a common tactic of repression used by the government. Her fear of detainment led her to actively deny her role in leading demonstrations and mobilizing protesters.

Government Repression

After the demonstration, Ms. Hua called for a second disruptive protest six days later. Photos of the event show a few grandparents wearing face masks, holding their grandchildren's hands while they march outside the community gates. Ms. Hua showed up wearing a hazmat suit, intended as a commentary on the toxic conditions of the landfill area. An official from the subdistrict office arrived after less than an hour to disband the protesters. Some were pulled aside and held at the site for questioning, but none was detained.[29] Recalling this protest, Ms. Hua focused on the dwindling number of protesters—very few participated, she told me. However, she took time to show me protest photos and posters featuring caricatures of government officials she had designed and privately circulated to neighbors via text or email. Although this protest was short lived, she used her hazmat suit and the posters to make the incinerator issue more tangible for community members.

This second public disruption triggered more overt repression both online and off-line. Comments and posts disappeared from the Rose forum as soon as they were posted. *Chengguan* and police officers started making frequent stops in the community, paying visits to the homeowners who were most active on the forum after having determined their usernames. However, as in Meadow and Willow, instead of shying away from the forum in response, young Rose homeowners were seemingly emboldened, continuing with their online public discussions about government officials. Although repression is often described as the shutting down of activity in an authoritarian regime, Rose homeowners continued on, openly sharing and thus normalizing their experiences of being visited by police as a means of ongoing resistance. These discussion threads made instances of repression experienced by homeowners more transparent, which seemed to help reduce uncertainties around repression and even to normalize repressive tactics. The posts also often incorporated a joking tone, using fear-free language to discuss state intervention. Comments on a forum exchange titled "The police did a home visit, talked about building the legal system!! Great intelligence work! Amazing!" were characterized by a light and often ironic tone:

"You've been exposed, too! Ha ha."
"Posting leads to home visits? Time to install a camera!"
"I'm guessing you've already been visited before—ha ha, from [your] IP address, they get your address, ha ha."
"Let us know a few methods of avoiding detection."
"I used to want to be a police officer when I was little—not anymore—but being a cop in our area means they're also smelling the stench every day, and they have to take care of our problems—we should understand that they can't do anything about this—support their work everyone; we're all suffering."

MOBILIZING AND ORGANIZING FOR ENVIRONMENTAL COLLECTIVE ACTION

"Home visits are normal. It's important to deeply discuss the stench [with police]."

"It's hard being JC [*jingcha*; "police"]; if we're not happy, they need to work overtime. The ones who came last time, most were pretty nice. Everybody chatted like brothers. Now when we see each other, it's quite refreshing."

"Me, too, I got a home visit. To be honest, it's nothing to worry about. Right now our legal rights are being violated. It's not like we did something wrong; we are just protecting our rights."

"Police being involved means our efforts are not in vain; that just means someone upstream is paying attention. Do not bow down to power; this is a milestone. The revolution is not successful yet. We need to not give up!"

In addition to making light of the situation, some homeowners showed sympathy toward the police. Others normalized the police visits—a common tactic of repression used by the government—even viewing the visits as a chance to discuss the trash problem with police and as an indication that government agencies were now listening to them. The comment referring to anti-incinerator resistance as a "revolution" showed one homeowner's willingness to continue organizing; this homeowner also viewed government attention as a positive sign.

It is also clear from these posts that residents knew their online activities were being monitored, yet they continued communicating in this way. Far from being dissuaded by the repression of their online activity, forum rhetoric took on a more defiant tone after a large number of posts were removed. To stake a claim to their online community space, dozens of homeowners directly challenged the officials monitoring the forum:

"Government leaders reading these posts, look over here!"

"Ban my username if you want!"

"Ha ha, they're mad at this. They don't really have this ability to ban us all! That's why we're still online every day!"

"You think that deleting posts is the way to get rid of dissent? The public's eyes are bright. With the technology now, deleting a few posts means achieving peace???? You're only deceiving yourself. Hilarious!!!!!!!"

These posts, none of which was written by Ms. Hua, reflected the same tone she used when recounting her experience of government censorship and repression to me: one of defiance and sometimes contempt. These comments also showed that no matter how many posts were removed or how many accounts blocked, these young, tech-savvy forum users were actively looking for alternative ways to post. Their continued online activity was also a method of resistance. Homeowners found workarounds to continue posting: signing up for new accounts with new usernames, signing into blocked accounts repeatedly to overcome the blocking, and avoiding sensitive phrases such as the name of the landfill and the characters for "incineration" (a similar phrasing strategy to avoid censorship was used in Meadow and Willow). This online defiance continued for weeks, as homeowners challenged officials with posts directed at those whom they suspected were monitoring the forum.

While many residents expressed defiance and some expressed fear, many also expressed disappointment in the government, encapsulated in comments such as "I feel like I love the Party, but the Party doesn't love me," which questions the Chinese Community Party principle of caring for and serving its people. Some of this frustration prompted talk of leaving China: "The police called me [and] said that my [online] speech was 'not good, not like a person who is contributing to Party and state building efforts.' . . . When I picked up the call, I was working, so I didn't have time to talk to them in detail. I just feel helpless. The earlier I can emigrate, the better!"

For the middle class, emigration was beginning to seem achievable, which it generally is for those who can save enough money and obtain a work or education visa. However, without providing concrete details, mentions of emigration mostly demonstrated the dismay some homeowners felt after interacting with a government that was not only ignoring their problems but also intervening in the private community spaces, both off-line and online, in which residents took pride. In response to this post, other homeowners echoed the desire to leave the country or at least the community, if and when they could afford it: "I used to judge people who emigrated; I felt our country was great. Emigrating means going to a place where I wouldn't know any person [or] place, [and] I would have language barriers and face discrimination. But I have changed my mind. . . . Hurry and make money to emigrate. Emigrating means I can breathe clean air abroad, [and I] don't need to be breathing in toxic gases here, slowly committing suicide."

Disappointment in government response to the incinerator issue served as the basis of such comments. In a new country, this homeowner imagined, new challenges would arise, but at least there would not be air pollution. This escapism also shows the weariness homeowners felt in dealing with constant government monitoring. The frequency of the monitoring was reflected in Ms. Hua's recollections of the period, during which she was visited by officials many times:

> They were trying to suppress protesting, our rights protection, our voices. . . . They used all kinds of despicable methods, like "fishing" . . . fishing is when they try to bait you to commit a crime . . . if you take the bait, you become a criminal. . . . They tried to make me sound like I was anti-Party and anti-state, but I was not.[30] I was trying to preserve my rights. . . . I wasn't falling into their baits. I would never fall for it. I understand their tactics, [and] I have been in contact with these tactics so many times [in this process]!

Ms. Hua made a clear distinction between protecting her rights as a homeowner—interpreted as "rightful resistance" (see chapter 2) and being "anti-Party" or "anti-state"—a criminal offense. While she continued to resist government pressures, she perceived that other homeowners were becoming worn down by the repression and losing enthusiasm for the fight. She complained to me, "I feel like a lot of neighbors were eating prepared meals [i.e., freeloading]. They didn't want to be threatened by the police, so they would push everything on to me, [as if saying,] 'You do it alone. We're all behind you reaping the benefits.' If you [were] mobilizing them to come participate in a meeting, they were not that passionate about it either. They're angry youths [*fenqing*]. Yes, they were angry at the time, but even the anger was not sustained.[31] This is a prevalent disease among our generation."

This commentary showed that Ms. Hua viewed her generation—those in their late twenties and early thirties at the time—as being only superficially engaged in civic issues. To her, young community members were eager to protest the first time but did not seem interested in longer-term organizing work involving planning and strategizing. Their anger mobilized them to participate early on, but Ms. Hua largely acted alone in organizing the homeowners' next steps following the street protests.

Chapter 5 discusses how, like Meadow, Willow, and Pine homeowners, Ms. Hua eventually tried a new strategy, turning to data collection.

While she and a few other homeowners continued protesting disruptively and experiencing government repression, she also began keeping photo documentation of smoke pollution, implementing surveys, and creating educational content based on her research on dioxins. Unexpectedly, her data collection caught the attention of an environmental lawyer, who then helped her file a lawsuit against the Beijing EPB.

Rose homeowners were able to mobilize but never made plans for organizing longer-term collective action. Ms. Hua, often acting and making decisions on her own, found it difficult to engage and motivate participants beyond forum posts, particularly in the face of government repression. The lack of longer-term organizing meant that Rose residents were unable to tap into their networks to find experts who could help resolve the incinerator problem. Collective learning, which played a key role in Meadow and Willow, did not occur in Rose because homeowners made complaints individually and had no central representative to create a coherent dialogue. While informal networks within Rose were tight knit, homeowners did not reach outward to their occupational connections to access resources or contacts who might have helped prompt a meaningful response from the government. Perhaps, as young homeowners starting out in their careers, they had not yet cultivated deeper professional connections. However, Rose was located near several similar communities. Engaging with others in the neighborhood (as Meadow had) would have broadened their networks, but Rose homeowners made no conscious effort to do so.

ANTI-INCINERATOR ACTION IN MARIGOLD

Of all the communities facing an incinerator issue, Marigold was the one with the least frequent interactions among homeowners. Because of its spacious, villa-style design and its smaller number of residents, who seemingly had busier work schedules than those in other communities, homeowners had very little unstructured contact. However, a confluence of two events brought homeowners into closer contact with one another: the short-lived road construction grievance and the car march following the discovery of plans for incinerator construction (chapter 3).

Like Rose, but in contrast to Meadow and Willow, Marigold's initial mobilizing tactic was a disruptive public demonstration. Following the spontaneous car march, a second demonstration occurred. Because this demonstration took place during a public event, it immediately led to a crackdown and the detainment of protesters. During the protest, Marigold homeowner Mr. Lu came to view himself as a representative of the community, enduring repression as a result. With the government crackdown on the demonstrators, mobilization halted, although a few homeowners turned to other methods of addressing their incinerator grievance. Mr. Lu became a leader acting alone in a community that was less engaged (but had the potential to mobilize because of preexisting networks), and he chose to stop trying to motivate homeowners to organize. Instead, Mr. Lu independently pursued actions he believed to be most effective in addressing the incinerator problem.

Rapid Mobilizing but Not Organizing

The "very unplanned" car march against incinerator construction (chapter 3) caught the attention of government officials. Although no cars were stopped during the protest, officials came to the community a few days later. According to Mr. Lu, they claimed to want to "negotiate" with homeowners, but he felt that this stated objective was insincere. The message he received from these officials was that "citizens should just bear with the incinerator."[32]

Despite these likely intimidating visits, homeowners continued to investigate the incinerator issue, posting a series of analyses on incineration that they had gathered from various media sources. Because Marigold was the last of the three featured communities to resist incinerator construction (in 2009), these homeowners were able to access articles discussing the pros and cons of incineration that had been written after the protests by Meadow, Willow, and Pine and by Rose. However, the articles posted to the Marigold forum were often extremely long, with no spacing or formatting, making them difficult to read. Thus, readership was low, with each article typically getting fewer than fifty views. Whereas incinerator posts in Meadow and Willow were almost always read by more than a thousand people and often inspired hundreds of comments, most Marigold forum posts received no responses. Moreover, because of the low engagement on Marigold's forum and the lack of a clear forum discussion leader, no one documented the mobilizing or planning process.[33] Much like homeowners' accounts of the car march having spontaneously emerged, it is likely that plans for the public demonstration were also made quickly.³⁴

Initial Tactics

Mr. Lu was a contract lawyer, but he explained to me that he disregarded any "rational thought process" in his angry response to the incinerator news. He told me that, despite his legal expertise, it did not occur to him to suggest that homeowners pursue institutional channels to attempt to resolve the problem. Instead, he joined in when a number of homeowners from Marigold and two other nearby communities discussed plans, informally by phone, to protest the incinerator construction at an environmental exhibition in downtown Beijing. Mr. Lu recalled,

> Those emotions . . . you wouldn't understand . . . that anger, it was uncontrollable. . . . Why construct near our homes? I resisted [at the car march] and said no already—why would you [the government] still do it [build the incinerator]? There weren't really channels for collective action for us at the time. . . . The people needed an outlet to vent, to get balance. . . . When you're angry and your rights have been violated, and you [have] no channels to address the problem . . . what do we do? We had to do something that was over the top [disruptive]. You must. I know it's wrong, [and] it's clearly dangerous, but I just had to. It was mainly emotions.³⁵

This comment, which describes protesting as "wrong" and "dangerous," foreshadowed the repression Mr. Lu faced after participating in disruptive protests. However, he also viewed the tactic as the only way to resolve homeowners' anger. Much as with Rose homeowners, emotion dictated Marigold's initial disruptive tactics. Meadow and Willow homeowners, who spent much longer planning and learning about the issue, and who had clear leadership to guide dialogue, had a more measured response. Whereas anger was the clear driver in both Rose and Marigold, the word "angry" rarely surfaced in the protest rhetoric or justifications of Meadow, Willow, and Pine homeowners. This key point of tactical divergence can also be seen in the attitude of Meadow and Willow homeowners toward expressive language: when drafts of letters of complaint became too "emotional," forum commenters consistently suggested edits to retain a neutral tone. No such direction emerged in Rose or Marigold.

When Marigold homeowners assembled at the environmental exhibition, it was raining, Mr. Lu remembered. He recalled almost one hundred homeowners attending, mostly from Marigold but also some from two other villa communities in the area: Dandelion and Daffodil.[36] One homeowner from Dandelion brought a horizontal banner that read, "Strongly resist the construction of the [location redacted] incinerator." Many of the homeowners were women, Mr. Lu told me, theorizing that "men have explosive power but bad endurance. Women can keep things going. . . . There were thirty-to-forty-year-old working mothers in the crowd—more than half [the protesters] were women—who were very determined, very courageous at the right time." The women in the community made banners, coordinated meeting times, and followed up on the issue after protesting.[37] Both Ms. Hua and Mr. Lu emphasized the need for endurance in protesting, which at times included planning meetings (Rose) and tasks such as making banners (Marigold).

Mr. Lu recalled that, during the protest, he became very energized and moved to the front of the pack, chanting "Anti-incineration." For him, this was the transformational moment in which he came to view himself as a community representative. Reflecting on his experience, he explained, "I wasn't intending to be a leader . . . everyone was just looking for guidance at the protest. I felt like a new army recruit, a soldier holding a flag. In the crowd, it was as if everyone was yelling, 'Charge! Charge!' And then I charged up the hill, but once I did, I realized I was the only one standing on top of the hill with the flag. I thought, 'OK, fine,' and I took on the leadership role."

While some leaders organize protests, others emerge only in moments of resistance. Like Huang *laoshi* in Meadow, who realized that he was his community's representative only once he was standing outside the Beijing EPB building attempting to find five homeowners brave enough to provide "official" signatures for their petition, Mr. Lu in Marigold stepped up in the midst of a protest to assume a new role. And, because he was "standing at the front of the pack," Mr. Lu told me that he was also the first to be taken away by police when they showed up shortly after homeowners began chanting. Seven people, Mr. Lu included, were detained for five days.[38]

Government Repression

While I was curious about how Mr. Lu and the other six homeowners endured their five days of being detained at the district detention center, few details were provided to me. Most residents seemed eager to move on from the incident and quickly distanced themselves from the idea of further protesting. Two homeowners were worried about their families' safety if repression were to continue. This distancing eventually led to Mr. Lu's decision to shift to an approach of citizen science (chapter 5).[39]

Initially, Mr. Lu felt wronged by the detainment: "What else could we have done in that moment of anger?" Reflecting on the events a year later, however, he took a more positive view of the situation: "I was just trying to do something good . . . but now I realize sometimes we fight with the government, like husbands and wives fight. You love each other, but if you do something wrong, you [will] fight a little bit, but you [will] make up at the end of the day." This unconventionally forgiving view, which contrasted with the frustration expressed by the other homeowners who were detained, reflected the uniquely positive progression of Mr. Lu's relationship with the government (examined in chapters 5 and 6).

More common among homeowners was a sense of anxiety. Many were worried about family members who had been arrested. A Dandelion homeowner, Ms. Meng, whose husband was detained, wrote the following on her community's forum:

> In my thirty-plus years of life this is the first time I experienced what being sleepless and having no appetite feels like. It's been three days; my husband has been taken by police for three days already. He's in the district detention center, facing administrative detention for five days. I don't know if he's eating enough, if he's wearing warm clothes. I am going crazy waiting at home. I cannot believe that someone [like him] who has never even said a curse word, that this would happen to him.
>
> I collected a big bag of supplies and wanted to take it to him—things to wash up with, clothes to change into, and his favorite fruit. I drove there, [and] the wind was cold and [the] rain was sad. I don't know if it's the rain or tears that blurred my vision. Someone told me before that the detention center would only allow delivery of money or items Monday through Friday, but I still went. I just wanted to let him know that I am especially worried about

him, I especially think of him, I especially miss him. . . . I am so sad. . . . I am still going to go tomorrow!

In this post, Ms. Meng revealed her anxiety about her husband's detainment, which she characterized as highly unexpected, both in terms of her husband's gentle personality and her limited knowledge of the detention center. She also posted the location and visiting hours of the detention center, apparently for the benefit of other homeowners with friends or family members who had been detained. Taken together, Ms. Meng's emotion and description of her experience show that the abrupt detainment of seven upper-middle-class homeowners was shocking to family members and neighbors. The very public nature of the protest—held during a large conference—led to the harshest repression experienced by any of the featured communities: extended detainment. Some Marigold homeowners also said their homes were vandalized—one homeowner had black paint thrown on her windows ("by a man dressed in black"), while another had her windows smashed—and suspected that they were targeted for having participated in the protest. The government also banned the media from reporting on the protest, Mr. Lu told me.

This extreme government response, combined with the lack of online communication among homeowners (communication that, for Rose, served to normalize the experience of repression), was effective in suppressing further collective action. Citing concerns of safety for themselves and their families, Marigold homeowners refused to continue protesting. The arrests and detainments seemed to shake them to the core, Mr. Lu recounted. He said, "At the time, we felt alone; there was no one to help us. . . . We had thought about the issue, we resisted . . . we resisted to the max, the police took action . . . so what is there left to do? What do we do now?"

According to Mr. Lu, most homeowners were ready to give up because they could not think of other ways to take action. As in Community Rose, the issue of emigration arose in the wake of repression. One detained homeowner began to make plans to move abroad with her husband and children. She sent a letter to Mr. Lu, telling him she felt embarrassed for leaving because she had fought alongside him and had been detained, but, as a family, they could no longer "withstand the pressure." She wrote, "We have lost faith and hope in the country. I am so sorry, but I support your determination and will follow your actions closely."

The sense of "lost faith and hope" was likely linked to the unusual severity of the repression Marigold homeowners experienced. Middle-class citizens in China are aware they may face repression for disruptive collective action, but the government response is more commonly limited to the censorship and police presence experienced by Meadow and Willow homeowners. Educated, upwardly mobile citizens expect a degree of respect from the government as a means of maintaining social order and stability.[40] The detainment of Marigold homeowners—villa residents with high-status jobs—was unexpected. As upper-middle-class families with resources and connections, emigration was a realistic alternative to continuing to confront both political and environmental threats.

Chapter 5 describes how, after his detainment, Mr. Lu reconsidered his approach and decided to express his frustration through scientific research and writing. "We stopped protesting and started using intellect, searching for other ways to rationally resolve problems," he explained. Like community leaders in Meadow, Willow, Pine, and Rose, Mr. Lu pivoted from an emotional response to one characterized by a technical understanding of the problem (in this case, incineration). He also began the work of organizing, gathering a small group of homeowners to form a research committee that eventually produced a report on the urban trash problem in Beijing and submitted it to the municipal government. After this pivot to participatory citizen science culminated in the report, mobilizing within Marigold came to a stop, but Mr. Lu continued to pursue the issue of incineration on his own.

THE IMPORTANCE OF COMMUNITY REPRESENTATION AND INITIAL TACTICS

How and when community representation was activated shaped how mobilizing and organizing occurred in Meadow, Rose, and Marigold. In Meadow and neighboring Willow, the emergence of key representatives early in the process helped homeowners organize for collective action with concrete plans informed by community relationships and expertise. Previous informal networks and deep trust within Meadow and Willow contributed to the success of Mr. Zhao, Ms. Ding, and the members of the core action committee not only in mobilizing homeowners but also in distributing responsibilities across various task forces. When the time came to act, Mr. Zhao was able to engage many homeowners in a range of tasks, allowing them to take ownership of their contributions (such as delivering letters of complaint to officials). Additionally, engaging in this process activated more leaders, such as Huang *laoshi*, who emerged as a community representative during the petitioning event.

Rose also had the advantage of a tight-knit community network. However, while Ms. Hua was an effective mobilizer and successfully motivated homeowners to demonstrate publicly, she found it difficult to sustain collective engagement, an important element of longer-term organizing. She attributed these challenges to the age and emotional state of Rose homeowners, whom she described as "angry youths." However, Rose did not leverage community capacity as Meadow and Willow did. Ms. Hua did not seek out experts within Rose to help with initial protest planning or cultivate committees and task forces to craft a course of action, nor did she access the networks of other nearby communities. Nonetheless, when Rose homeowners faced government repression in the form of online monitoring and home visits, their close networks provided community support.

Like Rose, leaderless Marigold planned a disruptive public protest. The absence of informal associational life in Marigold and the lack of experience addressing grievances against property management laid little groundwork for community organizing. However, loose friendship networks in the community were sufficient to mobilize homeowners for collective action against the incinerator. To the surprise of these upper-middle-class residents, the protest was quickly repressed, with numerous people detained. This experience inspired Mr. Lu to take on the role of community representative, yet his late arrival to the role likely made him more susceptible to government influence (chapter 5).

By pursuing institutional channels and collaborating across communities and with neighborhood businesses, Meadow and Willow achieved collective learning and dialogue with government officials. Dissatisfied with the speed at which the incinerator issue was being addressed, residents expanded their educational and legal efforts, increasing community members' knowledge of incineration, as well as their understanding of petitioning and AR laws. These community education activities attracted the attention of local police and led to soft repression—online censorship and pressure to remove banners—yet the strength of organizing among Meadow, Willow, and Pine enabled many community members to continue engaging in letter-writing efforts, delivering letters to relevant agencies, and maintaining active interactions and discussions online.

The next chapter examines a common pivot across all communities toward citizen science: participating in self-organized data collection regarding the landfill and planned incinerator near each community. Citizen science, combined with the continuation of other protest tactics such as formal filings and disruptive action, altered the outcomes of resistance for the communities. Chapter 5 discusses how the use of scientific knowledge to engage in dialogue with the government is a uniquely middle-class approach that shaped how homeowners perceived their civic responsibilities beyond their gates.

Chapter Five

TRAJECTORIES OF CITIZEN SCIENCE

The previous chapter described the various ways in which the featured community sites began mobilizing against local incinerator construction projects. Community Meadow homeowners, along with their neighbors in Willow and Pine, began organizing against the incinerator outside their gates through legal institutional channels. These communities were able to find volunteers and community professionals to prepare the complex paperwork involved in petitioning and writing letters to government agencies. While these communications were acknowledged by authorities and even prompted visits from officials who came to share information, homeowners felt that the responses were insufficient in addressing their concerns about incinerator construction. Communities Rose and Marigold, however, launched their incinerator resistance with publicly disruptive demonstrations, which an ability to mobilize but weaker planning and community engagement than in the other communities. The public nature of these disruptions led to government repression, resulting in the monitoring, arrest, and detainment of some homeowners.

As residents grappled with how to pressure the government more effectively to stop incinerator construction, each community turned to a new approach: data collection and research. This process, in which "nonexpert" citizens engage in scientific data collection and interpretation, is often referred to as "citizen science."[1] Citizen science not only asserts the power of citizens to dispute the authority of expert science (e.g., contesting data from an electric company or from a government environmental bureau) but also engages citizens in policy debates and the decision-making process for science-based policies.[2] This chapter explores why, in an authoritarian setting where dialogue with government officials is especially challenging, these communities adopted citizen science and the extent to which their engagement in scientific data collection shifted government responses to their resistance.

Although the government response to each community's presentation of information and data on incinerator pollution varied, the communities' experiences of engaging in collective citizen science shared some common features. In each community, scientific data offered a means for middle-class homeowners—the educated and professional class—to force some concessions of authority from local and central government agencies. In this way, citizen science served as a tool for homeowners to provide *democratic* feedback on government decisions in an authoritarian context.

Unlike some other forms of resistance that are categorically suppressed, citizen science tends to be well tolerated in China, where science is held in high esteem. Scientific rhetoric is frequently used within the government, which often equates science with informational correctness. The Chinese Communist Party, the ruling political party in China, closely ties science to economic and technological modernization as keys to a strong nation. By extension, scientific data enjoy a position of legitimacy in China and are generally regarded as an acceptable tool for expressing citizen concerns.[3] Citizen science also pairs well with middle-class status: with homeownership regarded as a sign of economic progress and upward mobility in China (chapter 1), the development of a highly educated middle-class citizenry also serves as an indication of China's strength. At the same time, the attainment of higher education empowers the middle class to understand, interpret, and sometimes dispute expert data provided by the government. Middle-class homeowners are therefore uniquely well positioned to become citizen scientists.

Another benefit of taking an approach of citizen science is that when citizens present scientific data to government officials, the focus on numbers and objective findings allows both citizens and officials to appeal to reason rather than emotion in their interactions. For protesters, a focus on rationality means curbing disruptive behavior; for officials, it supports the exchange of ideas with citizens rather than repression. However, while science is understood in China to be the search for universal patterns or truths, *citizen* science is characterized by knowledge in a particular area and experiences tied to addressing a local problem with unique local characteristics. In other words, claims based on citizen science are received by government authorities through the lens of any previous experience it has with the presenting community. Homeowners' prior legal claims, protest tactics they have used, and the style of their leadership can affect whether their claims based on citizen science are accepted, co-opted, or rejected by government authorities, regardless of the scientific merit of their findings.

Across the three community sites, homeowners experienced data collection as an empowering activity. Citizen-scientist homeowners gained a sense of authority they had been unable to access in their previous efforts of pursuing legal channels or taking part in marches and demonstrations. In seeking ways to collect data, citizens overcame conditions that kept information limited and opaque: despite laws requiring that certain information be made available to the general public, these homeowners experienced barriers to obtaining documents and information pertinent to their concerns. With institutional and legal channels seeming to lead only to bureaucratic absorption (chapter 4) and government responses sowing confusion and dissatisfaction, scientific data collection and analysis enabled homeowners to become their own experts when they ceased to trust government-appointed specialists.

A key reason that some communities were able to pivot successfully to scientific data collection was that they had the resources needed to take this approach: a high degree of educational attainment and professional connections. These homeowners were able to interpret complex technical documents and academic papers, sometimes in English. Additionally, the relationships fostered in their communities and their use of online homeowners' forums allowed residents to mobilize others to help with data collection, including for specialized projects such as administering community health surveys. Other forms of data collection ranged from groups conducting small-scale research (Marigold) to widespread evidence documentation and population surveys (Willow, Meadow, Pine, and Rose). Data collection also allowed alternative forms of resistance to emerge, such as lawsuits. Although Rose homeowners (known for their disruptive tactics) were unable to prompt a satisfactory government response to their environmental evidence, their data unexpectedly attracted the attention of lawyers following their cause.

Across all communities, the move to scientific data collection and presentation prolonged dialogue between homeowners and government officials. Homeowners began by drawing on rhetoric from regulatory documents and reports produced by government agencies, such as the environmental impact assessments (EIAs) for the planned incinerator projects. Next they innovated by conducting their own research, data collection, and interpretation and then presenting their findings to officials. In some cases, these efforts succeeded in winning government concessions.

CONTEXT: CHALLENGES TO ACCESSING ENVIRONMENTAL INFORMATION FROM THE GOVERNMENT

China's Environmental Impact Assessment Law, implemented in 2004, requires that EIAs be completed and public hearings be held before all large construction projects begin. The law specifies that "for a special plan, which may cause adverse effects on the environment and may have a direct bearing on the rights and interests of the public in respect of the environment, the authority that draws up the plan shall, before submitting the draft of the plan for examination and approval, hold demonstration meetings or hearings, or solicit in other forms the comments and suggestions from the relevant units, specialists and the public on the draft report on environmental effects, except where secrets need to be guarded as required by State regulations."[4]

In reality, the lack of stringent mechanisms to enforce EIAs has resulted in the construction of a significant number of projects beginning without EIAs having been completed.[5] Even with completed EIAs—which were on file for each incinerator project the communities were protesting—the required public hearings are not always held. Across all communities, no resident posting on a forum or with whom I spoke had heard of a public hearing on incinerator construction or been asked to provide feedback on the project in any other form.

Two regulations that helped homeowners in Meadow, Rose, and Marigold adopt an approach of scientific data collection are the Open Government Information Regulations Act and the Measures on Environmental Information Disclosure, both enacted in 2007. The measures state that local government agencies must make available information about "matters of particularly great interest to the public," including regulations, regulatory documents, and results of investigations related to environmental protection and public health.[6]

Citizens who have environmental grievances may, in theory, walk into a municipal environmental protection bureau (EPB) and request environmental information or request such information through the EPB's website.[7] However, in practice, homeowners found it challenging to obtain "open information." For example, Mr. Wu from Community Pine described his visit to the Beijing EPB to obtain environmental impact information, stating that he had been asked to provide not only his identification card but also a personal signature stamp, household registration, and marriage certificate—items citizens are unlikely to carry with them—creating an additional burden to obtaining information. The recording of these personal details also indicated to homeowners that government agencies wanted to keep tabs on people making requests: the price of information is surveillance. When I asked an environmental official from the central government about the function of open-information measures, he told me, "All 'open-information' documents are problematic. There should supposedly be information transparency—unless it's a matter of national 'secrets,' including the violation of military, business secrets, et cetera—but, interpretively, everything can be a 'secret.'"

The government's protection of information that the law designates public created significant challenges for homeowners in their anti-incinerator battles. When environmental information was not available from the government or appeared untrustworthy, the solution was to collect it themselves.

CITIZEN SCIENCE IN MEADOW, WILLOW, AND PINE

When I met Huang *laoshi*, Ms. Yu, and Mr. Wu in the restaurant across from Community Meadow in 2010, I was struck by the expertise they demonstrated in speaking about the landfill and incinerator. These homeowners described the wind direction (which affected how the landfill stench was, and how potential incinerator pollutants would be, distributed), the location of the weather station measuring the wind, types of toxins, and incinerator trash capacity, among many other scientific and technical details. Instead of protest tactics, they spoke of facts, specifically how "the government" was getting incinerator facts wrong; instead of the wording of their petition, they spoke of the result of their community health survey. They presented the numbers to me, citing them as evidence disproving the claims of government experts and EIA results.

Huang *laoshi* explained why incinerator pollutants would be bad for the neighborhood: "Smoke pollution, air or atmospheric pollutants, they descend. Pollutants are bad like that; they are all in the air, waiting to come down. The inversion layers trap in air pollution close to the ground." Mr. Wu interjected with a relevant global comparison—"It's like Los Angeles"—and Huang *laoshi* was quick to respond with further global knowledge: "Yes, like Los Angeles, London, [and] the U.S. East Coast."

How did Meadow, Willow, and Pine homeowners move from writing letters of complaint in 2007 to engaging in expert discussions of incinerator pollutants in 2010? Chapter 4 recounts how homeowners filed an administrative reconsideration (AR) with the Beijing EPB in February 2007. However, it eventually became clear that, despite their best efforts to understand the complex administrative system, they had sent the AR to the wrong administrative unit—it should have gone to the State Environmental Protection Administration (SEPA), the environmental agency that oversees the Beijing EPB. Although the AR was accepted by the EPB, it was not referred to SEPA until early April. As homeowners waited for a response to the AR, they became worried that incinerator construction would begin.[8]

Incorporating Science, Law, and Collective Action

As homeowners waited for a government response to their AR, Mr. Wu, a homeowner from Pine, emerged as a community representative, actively engaged in obtaining documents from government bureaus. He visited the Beijing EPB on many occasions to obtain EIAs, not only for the incinerator but also for other projects impacting the community, to demonstrate the area's environmental status. Mr. Wu brought his professional expertise to these efforts: an older homeowner, in his seventies at the time, he was also a retired administrator from the Chinese Academy of Sciences, a national scientific think tank and research institution. Though Mr. Wu emphasized that he was "just admin" and not an environmental science expert, because of his work experience, he had a firm grasp on how government agencies functioned.

Huang *laoshi* described Mr. Wu as very knowledgeable, particularly with respect to current events:

> Old Wu, his best quality, compared to us, is that he reads the Beijing news everyday: TV and newspapers. Every day. Central policies, central [government] spirit . . . he has a very good grasp on it. This is very important. In China, when you're doing these things [protesting], if you're removed from central politics or policies, you would be so lost, you would feel helpless, you would feel that you're not sure if you're doing it right. But since Wu often reads the news, he would know . . . the central government says it a certain way, then this is how we would do it. Right? Or else you would be removed from the "central spirit" . . . after all it has a "strong spirit"! . . . So this [understanding of central spirit] is a special characteristic of community participation in China.

In accordance with this understanding of "central spirit" (generally meaning adhering to Party spirit or ideology but in this context referring to Mr. Wu's knowledge of evolving government policies), Mr. Wu believed that obtaining EIAs would be both helpful and legal, because the government had produced these documents. If homeowners could better understand the content of EIAs, they could make more persuasive arguments against incinerator construction. This effort was not without obstacles, however, such as demands from EPB officials for irrelevant documentation (e.g., a marriage certificate).[9]

Homeowners did succeed in obtaining a copy of the EIA for the incinerator project, along with the questions from the public opinion survey that had been part of the evaluation process. The government's version of the survey results stated that 51 percent of 85 respondents (out of 100 surveys administered) were in support of the incinerator and waste facility construction—just enough support to advance the construction project. Huang *laoshi* and Mr. Wu regarded the "51 percent" as a critical piece of evidence that government officials had fudged the survey results. "Even they were too ashamed to make up a high percentage of supporters!" Mr. Wu remarked.

Targeting this piece of information, with no Meadow, Willow, or Pine homeowners on the forum stating that they recalled having participated in the survey, Mr. Zhao and other community representatives made their first major foray into citizen science by replicating the survey and gathering their own data. They distributed the survey to 400 homeowners and surrounding businesses in the area. Huang *laoshi* proudly pointed out to me the "close to 97 percent response rate," as 387 responses had been collected. None of the respondents agreed with incinerator construction, he told me.

On the forums, Mr. Zhao engaged other homeowners in reading the EIA, and several homeowners pointed out questionable aspects of the assessment after conducting their own online research. For example, they questioned the accuracy of the wind direction stated in the EIA—northeast—as this contradicted what was stated on the district government's website: northwest. Homeowners also pointed out that an important canal near the construction site (within 1,100 meters) was not listed in the EIA and that the number of residents in the vicinity of the incinerator was substantially underestimated. The potential relationship between the landfill and the incinerator was also unclear, homeowners found, as the EIA did not provide information on whether incineration would reduce the landfill's overflow or the pollution of nearby canals caused by the landfill. Another concern raised by homeowners was that the EIA failed to address the noise pollution that would be caused by incinerator machinery. One homeowner wrote on the forum, echoing a dominant sentiment, "The EIA only offers 'projected impact.' This type of projection is not founded on any truth."

Huang *laoshi* also recalled the community's frustration with the EIA's lack of acknowledgment of existing environmental problems in the area: "The other [concern] is [that] the environmental pollution situation in the larger [neighborhood] area must be described more accurately, but the EPB couldn't see the landfill here, couldn't see the brick factory or . . . the asphalt factory has a lot of pollution, too. In the EIA, this was not described at all. It was as if this was an 'environmentally pure place,' but in fact we already had a lot of pollution. In the report, there was nothing. They didn't even describe [the environmental] capacity [of the site]. None of this was in the report." For Huang *laoshi*, the neighborhood environment did not have the capacity to further absorb pollutants from a new incinerator, because other types of pollution already existed, even though the EIA did not acknowledge this.[10]

In April 2007, more than one hundred Meadow, Willow, and Pine homeowners gathered in front of the EPB to file a collective petition, which included a letter to the bureau with citizen scientists' own environmental impact findings. Protesters held up signs reflecting these findings, including the alliterative slogan of "*shangfeng, shangshui, shang* [district redacted]," which loosely translates to "wind and water flow from the direction of [the district]."[11] This slogan illustrates the increasing sophistication of the homeowners' campaign: not only representing the struggles of the homeowners of gated communities in the vicinity of the planned incinerator but also framing the issue in relation to the impact of the incinerator on a greater number of Beijing residents. Water and wind both flow away from the district of Meadow, Willow and Pine; thus, the incinerator and its pollution would affect Beijing citizens downwind and downstream.

According to Huang *laoshi*, homeowners gathered in front of the EPB, maintaining an "orderly protest." Several EPB officials came out to talk with the homeowners and received their petition. Homeowners spoke with the officials about the stalled response to their AR and their concerns about the EIA, including the error in reporting wind direction. They also mentioned that the report seemed to downplay the risks from dioxins: while it specified that pollution would be most concentrated about one thousand meters from the incinerator chimney, it neglected to mention that that area was in the vicinity of a lake and key water source. The officials present responded that they "had never said those things" (even though the statement in question was in the EIA) but promised to relay the information "to relevant agencies," Huang *laoshi* recalled.[12]

Although homeowners blocked the entrance to the EPB—a tactic that could have been viewed as disruptive—no confrontation ensued. The homeowners engaged in a calm dialogue with officials and departed without incident. This outcome contrasts with both the police crackdowns on the disruptive protests held by Rose and Marigold and the firm police response to the banners that had been hung by Meadow, Willow, and Pine homeowners (chapter 4). The legitimate action of collective petitioning, in conjunction with the formal filing of the AR and the scientific approach to challenging the findings of the EIA, seemed to shift government perceptions of these homeowners' protests away from questions of "disruptiveness" toward the legitimacy of the documentation they presented.

Soon after this collective action at the EPB, the environmental agency sent a letter to homeowners (whose contact information was included in the AR filing) addressing the issue of wind direction. According to Huang *laoshi*, the agency insisted that the direction noted in the EIA, northeast, was correct. Through further research, homeowners discovered that the weather station where wind direction data had been obtained was located not in the neighborhood but on the other side of a mountain. With this information in hand, Mr. Zhao and others prepared further communications to government agencies.

In May 2007, SEPA announced to homeowners that decisions regarding the AR would be postponed because of the "complex nature of the situation" and that the agency would not be able to respond to the request within the legally mandated time frame of thirty days. The response would be postponed another thirty days until June 12, 2007. Alarmed by this delay, homeowners assembled still more documentation of their recent findings, including information about wind direction, canal concerns, and the results of their public opinion survey. Many homeowners participated; although Mr. Wu was central in organizing the information, he relied on help from younger, more computer-savvy neighbors. Titling the document "Supplementary Suggestions for the AR," the committee sent its findings to SEPA within two weeks of notice of the delayed AR response.

Mr. Zhao and the mobilizing committee also decided to go ahead with a large-scale demonstration on World Environment Day in early June. More than one thousand homeowners from Meadow, Willow, and Pine gathered in front of the SEPA building that day holding signs and banners and wearing matching T-shirts with "Protect the environment" written on the front and "Against incinerator construction in [redacted location]" written on the back. As Community Rose did in the streets and Community Marigold did at the environmental exhibition (chapter 4), these homeowners gathered en masse to make a public statement. Yet, once more, rather than being met with repression as the other communities had been, Meadow, Willow, and Pine homeowners were acknowledged by government officials who listened to their demands.[13]

Far from inspiring a government crackdown, the homeowners' mass demonstration calling attention to their EIA-focused citizen science prompted a positive government response. Two days after the demonstration, the deputy director of SEPA publicly announced that the incinerator construction would be postponed until further environmental evaluations were made. A few days later, on June 12, the AR decision was officially published by SEPA: "The project construction should be postponed until further evidence is collected; the evidence evaluation process should be made public; the scope of public opinion should be expanded. The evidence and public opinion survey results need to be authorized by the Beijing EPB and publicly announced, then put on record at SEPA. The construction will not be allowed to start prior to public announcement or SEPA recording."

This response was a significant milestone, showing that SEPA had accepted many of the concerns raised by Meadow, Willow, and Pine homeowners regarding questionable content in the original EIA and a lack of public input in decision-making. However, homeowners on the forum perceived a need to continue pressuring the government:

"This phase was successful! But we cannot let our guards down."
"In the handling of this . . . the government's attitude is worthy of recognition, and thanks to SEPA, this has been dealt with fairly. We need to strengthen the communication with government departments, let more people [homeowners] participate, reflect their opinions, and finally usher in a decision to stop incinerator construction."
"One sentence—we need to fight sustainably! This is all that SEPA can do! The next step is up to us citizens!"
"This is great! I feel that the World Environment Day activity achieved its effectiveness. If they can really be transparent and open about their work, then it would certainly be the death of the incinerator! But to be sure, the trash problem has become more emergent. Maybe after a decade, the area surrounding Beijing will become a large landfill, [and] we [Beijing residents] won't be able to hide [from trash] anymore!"

These statements reflected an ongoing vigilance among the neighboring communities. After the announcement of postponed construction, homeowners in Meadow, Willow, and Pine carefully watched governmental websites for updates on incinerator construction. They read that the vice mayor of Beijing had said during a conference that officials would look into problems surrounding incinerator construction in the neighborhood but that an incinerator would still be built. With SEPA and the EPB speaking of "postponing," homeowners felt uncertain about how other agencies, such as the mayor's office, might influence the outcome.

Government Acceptance of Citizen Science

Huang *laoshi*, Mr. Wu, Mr. Zhao, Ms. Yu, and Mr. Ding continued to expand online discussions about the incinerator into off-line spaces: neighbors spoke in the parking lot after work, in the courtyard after dinner, and in the privacy of their homes. Homeowners became particularly focused on dioxins, a category of harmful pollutants present in emissions from trash incinerators. They researched and posted to the forum scholarly articles and news reports, including information on international cases. The international scale of research was new; though Mr. Zhao had used global examples in earlier posts (chapter 3), many homeowners were now posting, responding to, and engaging with information from incinerator case studies from other parts of the world.

With this growing international body of information on incineration outcomes came an interest in tracking pollution-related health effects in the homeowners' immediate area. Mr. Wu went door to door asking about "illnesses that could be potentially related to air, water, and soil pollution." The homeowners he surveyed candidly shared experiences of illness and deaths in their families. Mr. Wu concluded that the air pollution from an old brick factory nearby was "already causing upper-respiratory cancers in the community." The results of this poll, self-administered online in addition to the door-to-door efforts, found that "10 percent of total cancer deaths in the community were [caused by] upper-respiratory cancers in 2006." Mr. Wu kept a list of names of residents who had died of upper-respiratory cancers. "I list forty-seven people with cancer here," he explained. "Six to seven [residents] die per week [across all communities], so within these few months, one hundred people have died! Young ones, too—only fifty years old."[14] According to Mr. Wu, incinerator pollution would further exacerbate these health problems, resulting in even more deaths.

These health concerns were not reflected in the EIA, which focused only on environmental considerations. Community interest in gathering health data was a potent organizing mechanism, even if it was limited in its scientific rigor. Mr. Wu's survey methodology and statistical inferences were flawed, and many homeowners referred to the stench of the landfill as cancer causing or mistakenly spoke of incinerator "smells" caused by dioxins (which are odorless) as carcinogenic. Nonetheless, homeowners engaging in citizen science were proactive in seeking scientific "truths" to develop arguments that would facilitate dialogue with government officials. They discovered that presenting scientific information, including health information, was effective in engaging government officials and focusing these dialogues on objective data. Even though government officials sometimes disagreed with and challenged the homeowners' conclusions, dialogue was sustained over time.

This progress was paused during the Beijing Olympics in August 2008, however. Homeowners understood that it was not a good time to protest publicly—doing so would likely lead to harsh repression. Although several homeowners proposed collective petitioning in July, after an in-depth discussion, residents collectively agreed on the need for their strategy to acknowledge that the Olympics were a "critical event" in China. A community record explained: "Even though bringing up the incineration topic during this period of time may attract the attention of various agencies, it would be doing a disservice to our Olympics and bring shame on our Beijing. Because of this, we decided to not take any actions that may [have a negative] impact [on the Olympics]."[15]

Two months after the Olympics, a homeowner found out from a media article that the environmental reevaluations for the incinerator had been completed without residents being made aware. Incinerator construction was back on. The second wave of community organizing against the incinerator picked up within a week.

Ms. Yu recalled the process:

Within three days, we started a petition. Went door to door. Like canvassing in Taiwan, we visited residents one by one.[16] I tell them, "This is for us [the residents] and for the environment of Beijing." Sometimes it was hard to find a representative in a building to help—some of them aren't there in the mornings [because they are at work]. But I tell them, "Why don't you go home after work, and after dinner, drive over to my place [in the neighboring community], and visit people from 8:00 to 9:30 P.M. I'll even wait for you till midnight [to come back with signatures]." Some even agreed to do it without eating dinner first!

This round-the-clock commitment reflected the strong sentiment among homeowners learning of the renewed incinerator plans. Although collective action had slowed during the Olympic months, the necessary networks, strategies, and documents were in place for community representatives to quickly remobilize. In a matter of days, more than one thousand signatures opposing incinerator construction were gathered and sent to a number of government agencies, along with suggestions for alternatives to incineration.

In response, the district government sent representatives from the urban management bureau to speak with residents at a meeting held in Community Meadow in November. Homeowners again presented their scientific information and voiced their concerns. Yet, as the end of the year approached, media reports surfaced indicating that district officials were still adamant about proceeding with construction plans. Hoping to make an even stronger case, homeowners organized their collection of documents and signatures into a forty-nine-page booklet intended to "systematically communicate public opinion to the government," as the foreword explained.

This document, created in February 2009, was a synthesis of all the scientific research that homeowners had spent the past year compiling, reading, commenting on, and synthesizing. When I met with community representatives of the neighborhood in 2010, the booklet was the first thing they handed to me. Its table of contents reads as follows:[17]

1. Origins of the problem
2. Our basic stance
3. Need to directly address the existence and harm of incinerator pollutant "dioxins"
4. Constructing the incinerator near [redacted] area is the wrong location selection decision
5. Choosing to incinerate is an inappropriate choice of disposal technology
6. Citizens' voices
7. Attention and representative opinions from different fields
8. Suggestions for Beijing trash management measures
9. Conclusion and recommendations

The first section framed the origins of the incinerator issue using scientific concepts and language. Rather than reflecting the confusion-laden process homeowners actually underwent in experiencing landfill stench and discovering plans for incinerator construction (chapter 4), the opening paragraph suggested a degree of scientific proficiency:

> At the end of 2005, the district government announced an investment of 1 billion yuan[18] to construct an incinerator on the south side of the [redacted] landfill, with plans to start construction in March 2007. After the news spread, it immediately caused worry and faced opposition from those who care about district development . . . and those who reside in this area. The toxic gases produced in the process of incineration, smoke and dust, and particularly the production of carcinogenic dioxins, spread within human bodies, bodies of water, and soil sediments, unavoidably deeply impacting residents' health, severely polluting and influencing the water quality of water channels only a kilometer away, [and] severely influencing the safe quality of underground water sources that serve Beijing.

This paragraph set the tone for the document, which presented homeowners' scientific arguments and research supporting their contention that the incinerator project should not be postponed but rather completely abandoned. The booklet also pointed out that SEPA had failed to act on its decision to implement a transparent reevaluation of environmental impact in response to the communities' AR.

The booklet's appendixes featured numerous results of the homeowners' citizen science research:

1-1. Site selection map
1-2. Satellite image of surrounding areas of the incinerator (northeast)
1-3. Satellite image of surrounding areas of the incinerator (southeast)
2. Surrounding units and population at selected sites
3. Rights preservation activities
4. Plea of citizens (2009)
5. Attention and representative opinions from different fields
6. Incinerator bans in Japan, Europe, the U.S., and other countries plagued by dioxins
7. Suggested methods of trash handling

Demonstrating the citizen scientists' resourcefulness, the site selection map was based on a research institution's city planning map from the year 2000 that homeowners had found online. On the map, homeowners had marked the locations of residential communities, universities, and nearby villages and highlighted areas with designated uses, such as agricultural land, public green spaces, and water channels. The satellite images included in the appendix reflected homeowners' ability to leverage their earlier organizing experiences: they used images from Google Earth similar to those used to assess potential changes to bus routes in the neighborhood (chapter 3). Homeowners overlaid these images with red and yellow squares using Microsoft Paint to delineate residential areas and landfill and incinerator construction sites. Similarly, in the appendix 2 maps, the homeowners divided up areas around the incinerator according to research they had done on area size and impacted populations. This appendix included water sources, parks and preserves, residential communities, government units and schools, hospitals, science and research institutions, businesses and restaurants, factories, and other planned residential or commercial projects that homeowners calculated as totaling 3515.8 square meters and impacting 261,500 people.

In appendix 6, homeowners compiled case studies of trash processing from cities in Germany, Spain, and Portugal, presenting information on processing capacity, the years projects were commissioned, and the effectiveness of the technologies used by those countries. Homeowners explained to me that these case studies were intended to provide models for the Chinese government, but they also acknowledged the need to interpret these studies in light of local environmental considerations. Huang *laoshi* explained, "[China is] unlike Japan [where there are incinerators]... they're an island; the rain and wind take all of the pollution away. This area [we live in] is like a basin, so the pollution gets trapped in; that's why the smell is everywhere. EIAs have to take environmental capacity into consideration. They [the government] also need to understand geography and climate conditions. The pollution index is always higher in this area; it's like smoking in a house ... the smoke never leaves."

Demonstrating deep knowledge of international incinerator cases, Huang *laoshi* emphasized that it was important to understand these examples in terms of not only the engineering and technology of processing trash (which the government tended to focus on) but also local weather patterns and geographic features—to which the government had not been attentive, in his view.

TRAJECTORIES OF CITIZEN SCIENCE

The booklet's final paragraph reflected the homeowners' organizing journey—from early internal struggles with property management as first-time homeowners to mobilizing and organizing for collective action across communities and beyond their community walls: "We . . . as everyday Beijing citizens, [redacted] district residents, we yearn to have beautiful homes, [lives], and hopes. We represent our and your fathers, elderly [relatives], brothers, sisters, and children, we also represent our and your blue skies, grass, trees, and clear waters. . . . We sincerely plead [with] the government to not construct the incinerator here."

This closing paragraph reflected how these middle-class homeowners considered themselves not only residents of their respective communities—as they did when they moved in—but now also as residents of their district and citizens of Beijing. This transformation was observed throughout Meadow, Willow, and Pine's organizing process: first making sense of the issue within their own communities, then crossing community boundaries and engaging with others impacted by incinerator construction in the larger neighborhood. In effectively conducting citizen-science research, homeowners also came to understand the importance of their district as a key source of water and wind direction, reflected in the passage "we also represent our and your blue skies . . . and clear waters." Fighting for clean water and air free from pollution implied a fight for the well-being of not just themselves but all citizens of Beijing.

In March 2009, the booklet, signed by residents of and representatives of businesses in the area, was sent to SEPA, the State Bureau for Letters and Visits, the Beijing municipal government, and the local district government. Soon after, SEPA announced yet again that the construction of the incinerator would be postponed until further assessments were made. The decision came down, however, to the district government, which throughout 2009 appeared set on carrying through with construction plans.

Finally, in 2010, the district government relented. The Beijing municipal government announced that the incinerator was to be officially relocated after more than two years of public anti-incinerator struggles. Although there may have been other political reasons for the relocation, such as intergovernmental tensions or local government interests, the success of the homeowners' citizen-science strategies highlights the ability of middle-class citizens to insert themselves into government policy discussions and decision-making processes, even under authoritarian rule.

Citizen data collection allowed homeowners to thoroughly understand issues that affected them, discuss issues among themselves, and participate in bringing to light and presenting relevant information to government agencies. Because of their engagement in citizen science, many Meadow, Willow, and Pine homeowners felt involved in and informed about trash and anti-incineration debates in the public sphere, thereby developing a stronger sense of civic responsibility.[19] The problem of the incinerator concerned more than just their communities; it was also a larger pollution problem—related to water and wind—that would impact other residents of Beijing. And they believed that addressing it was the joint responsibility of homeowners and government actors.

Meadow, Willow, and Pine homeowners began their organizing efforts by pursuing institutional channels but found these efforts ineffective. Pivoting to citizen science, they conducted their own surveys, research, and risk assessments, which led to continued dialogue with officials from SEPA, the EPB, and the district government. This ongoing communication was made possible by homeowners' engagement with official rhetoric used in government-produced environmental documents such as the EIA of the incinerator, their use of scientific methods (considered apolitical) in collecting environmental data, and their compilation of scientific information, such as that from case studies, that was relevant to government decision-making processes. As Huang *laoshi* said of the citizen-science process, "Everyone's environmental consciousness increased in this process, including the government's, due to [our] frequent interactions with [officials]. They actually can listen. A lot of people within [the government] understood the information [we were providing them]." Citizen science not only educated and engaged the community members involved but also educated government officials, who in receiving the homeowners' reports also increased their awareness of environmental issues, according to Huang *laoshi*.

The strategies used by Meadow, Willow, and Pine homeowners together represent citizen science with local characteristics: while methods of data collection follow standard scientific principles, the sharing of scientific information can occur through myriad avenues, such as through institutional channels, public protests, and the presentation of detailed documents like the homeowners' booklet. In this case, because the communities' initial and central actions were legally and politically sanctioned, government officials were presumably less inclined to crack down when homeowners incorporated more disruptive forms of protesting in conjunction with their challenges to the conclusions of the EIA of the incinerator.

A clear contrast can be seen with Community Rose. While some of Rose's strategies of data collection were similar to those of Meadow, Willow, and Pine, Rose's divergent approach to community leadership meant that this community's efforts met with very different results in terms of government intervention. In line with their response to Rose's initially disruptive tactics, government officials continued to crack down on Ms. Hua's actions. As a result, Rose homeowners never developed the strong sense of civic responsibility seen among Meadow, Willow, and Pine homeowners, and they found themselves unable to participate in the political process.

CITIZEN SCIENCE IN COMMUNITY ROSE

When I met Ms. Hua in 2010, she handed me a small USB drive to plug into my laptop. "This is where I keep all the evidence," she told me. There were 159 items on the drive: photos, official documents, videos, transcripts, and notes. As she recounted her struggles, beginning with the nighttime incident at the landfill (chapter 3), she referred to certain files and instructed me to click through the relevant photos. In addition to sharing with me her anger toward government officials, her belief (and supporting photographic evidence) that the government had lied to Rose residents about when it was starting incinerator construction, and her detailed records of smoke emissions,[20] she also revealed that both she and her neighbor Ms. Yang were filing lawsuits over the construction of incinerators in the vicinity. "See, all this data," she said, gesturing at my screen. "A lawyer came across my photographs and records posted on our forum [in 2008] and was so impressed with how complete it was, he wanted to help me."

This shift from disruptive public demonstrations to scientific evidence collection and lawsuit filing occurred in the span of only a few months. Because of the shorter timeline of Rose's mobilizing, many events happened simultaneously. Unlike Meadow, Willow, and Pine homeowners, whose organizing activities were sustained over two years, Rose residents experienced their key events in rapid succession. As a result, homeowners

(Ms. Hua in particular) hurriedly swung between protesting publicly, pursuing institutional channels, and engaging in citizen science. This pace of activity meant that data collection occurred more quickly and involved only a handful of homeowners, with Ms. Hua organizing and presenting most of the information. When it became challenging to find an audience for the community's citizen-collected scientific information, Ms. Hua was the one to seek out other ways of using the data: through lawsuits and requests for assistance from environmental organizations.

Science and Disruption

After Community Rose's two public demonstrations at the end of August and in early September 2008, and in the midst of police intervention on their online forum and within the community space, a few individual residents faxed requests to the EPB for EIAs.[21] Heading into October, homeowners continued to pursue institutional channels, calling hotlines to press government officials for information. They also discovered that there was already a medical incinerator nearby, which had begun running in 2007.[22] Ms. Hua was livid. For her, the discovery of the medical incinerator was further confirmation that the government, broadly defined, had not communicated with Rose homeowners, who, in her view, should have been informed (as prospective homebuyers and community residents) about pollution from the nearby pharmaceutical factory (chapter 3), the landfill stench, planned incinerator construction, and the existing medical waste incinerator.

Hotline transcripts provided by Rose residents, who had begun recording some of their phone conversations with government officials, demonstrate several trends. Rose homeowners continued to experience frustration with institutional channels (chapter 4) after their public demonstrations. Additionally, rather than becoming clearer over time, homeowners' descriptions of the situation became more muddled with the broader range of polluting sources to address. Government responsibilities were another area of confusion: which government agency oversaw which project remained ambiguous to most residents. Because of this uncertainty, when attempting to file pollution complaints by phone—the method Rose homeowners continually used—they were bounced from agency to agency in search of the responsible party. The following phone conversation, recorded in

October 2008 between Ms. Hua and the environmental section chief in Rose's district management bureau, illustrates these trends:

MS. HUA: I'm from Community Rose. We've been troubled by the incinerator, the stench is horrible, and we were not able to sleep yesterday. I wanted to know what is going on with this.
DISTRICT OFFICIAL: What time yesterday?
MS. HUA: From around 11 P.M. last night, I started smelling the stench, even with the windows closed.
DISTRICT OFFICIAL: Really? You're from Community Rose?
Ms. Hua: Yes.
DISTRICT OFFICIAL: Hmmm, 11 P.M.
MS. HUA: I keep a diary. It documents the stench and the times, [and] it's gotten really bad . . .
DISTRICT OFFICIAL: Well, the incinerator, how should I say this, it's not our project. If you are talking about the nearby landfill being smelly, then [it is our jurisdiction] . . .
MS. HUA: We're talking about the [medical incinerator] smoke. There is smoke.
DISTRICT OFFICIAL: . . . You see smoke coming toward the community, yes?
MS. HUA: Yes, it's thick. I have photos. It's very, very concentrated. You can see it hovering during the night and during the day.[. . .]
DISTRICT OFFICIAL: It's not that type of stench from the landfill, right?
Ms. HUA: The landfill being smelly, it wouldn't reach beyond ten kilometers or five kilometers. We're about five kilometers away. . . . The smell will not drift that far, but this smoke feels like particles; you can feel the particles; it's very concentrated.
DISTRICT OFFICIAL: 11 P.M., you told me it was this time. Afterward I'll . . .
MS. HUA: I have detailed records here. Do you want to hear all the times [recorded]?
DISTRICT OFFICIAL: Is it mostly at night? This is recently?
MS. HUA: . . . Morning, all of October, we can smell it in the morning sometimes. Mostly it's at night more recently. The worst is during dinner time. [I] can't even eat; I would throw away food I made. It's so stinky, unbearably so. . . . Isn't there any regulation around incinerating?
DISTRICT OFFICIAL: No, this incineration . . . it . . . it will . . . um, it will completely be monitored. The entire city will be [monitored] . . .
MS. HUA: They haven't started monitoring. It's releasing toxins every day. The most harmful . . . toxin . . . [is] dioxins!

DISTRICT OFFICIAL: This is . . . very troubling.

MS. HUA: We're wasting money calling people about this. [With] every complaint we file by phone . . . our problems are not resolved. What is wrong? . . . And then one person says it's not their responsibility and pushes the case to another person, back and forth. It wasn't even easy finding this phone number I'm calling you on! From municipal management to district management, I had to ask a lot of people before obtaining your phone number.

DISTRICT OFFICIAL: (Laughs).[. . .]

DISTRICT OFFICIAL: Well . . . I . . . we will tell the city [the municipal government] about your situation.

MS. HUA: I hope they give me a response! . . . We called them last time, [and] they said we should be in contact with them over time. They said we would be able to go visit the site to see [the new] construction, but we have not heard from them since. They haven't contacted us; they have not even appeared once to check out the site. There has been nothing!

DISTRICT OFFICIAL: No, no, we won't do that [not get back to you]. That time [when you spoke to the municipal officials], I guess you were talking about the landfill, yes?

MS. HUA: No, the incinerator!

In this exchange, Ms. Hua tried to address smoke from the medical incinerator, but the conversation shifted to the unconstructed incinerator and the landfill. Like Rose's earlier struggles identifying the source of the landfill stench (chapter 3), homeowners continued to provide imprecise information concerning "stench," which now referred to both the landfill smell and the smoke from the medical incinerator. In the transcript, it is evident that the city management official was perplexed. He seemed to know of Community Rose's previous landfill complaints and believed Ms. Hua was speaking about the landfill, yet he also specified that incinerators were out of his jurisdiction.

Another hotline conversation recording, here between Rose homeowner Ms. Xi and an on-duty district government responder, reflected similar patterns. The responder knew about Rose's landfill issue yet referred the homeowner to a different governmental agency:

MS. XI: Hi, are you part of the [redacted] district government?

RESPONDER: Yes, hi.

MS. XI: This is Community Rose.

RESPONDER: OK, hi.

MS. XI: Is the district government's stench-management committee useless? Why is it smelly every day? I started coughing the moment I got home.

RESPONDER: OK, we can only help you by noting this; it will report the incident.

MS. XI: Who are you going to report this to? Why don't you care about anything?

RESPONDER: We can only record this and report. There is a stench problem in your area; it has been a long-term problem.

MS. XI: So, you admit that it has been a long-term problem.

RESPONDER: Yes. I suggest you call the municipal office. You can look at the sign there [at the incinerator site]. It says it is [under] municipal jurisdiction; it does not belong under the district.

MS. XI: The landfill, it is under the jurisdiction of the district though?

RESPONDER: Yes.

MS. XI: So, the incinerator is managed by the city? That's the problem. Don't you have a working committee that can resolve this problem? When we talk about the incinerator, you guys say that you can help resolve the landfill problem, but when we say we are addressing the incineration problem, then you tell us to call the city. Then we called the city, and they told us that you guys have a working committee that addresses [the incinerator]. We're being bounced around!

[...]

MS. XI: Who's your district chief?

RESPONDER: Yes, the district chief manages these things.

MS. XI: No, I'm asking, who is the district chief right now?

RESPONDER: I'm not sure who is in charge, but I'm sure there is a district chief.

[...]

RESPONDER: The district leader has been there [Community Rose]. He has described the situation to us. He deeply understands this, and he held a meeting there . . . ?

MS. XI: Which district leader came?

RESPONDER: I am not at liberty to reveal this, but he did have these descriptions. We're trying hard to take care of this.

MS. XI: What's your name?

RESPONDER: We normally don't give out our names . . .

This elusiveness, refusing to provide concrete information regarding responsible leaders or agencies, is common across many recorded conversations between homeowners and government officials—as is homeowners' frustration and outrage. Even after public demonstrations and several months of phone calls, homeowners could not pin down who was in charge. The phone conversations transcribed here show that homeowners were continually referred from district to municipal agencies and back again, from department to department, without receiving substantial information. Even once homeowners had established that the landfill was managed by the district government and the incinerator was managed by the municipal government, when calling these respective agencies, homeowners were often referred to yet another agency and phone number. Rose homeowners' lack of clarity on what they were requesting, reinforced by the revelations of additional sources of pollution, did little to aid their cause. Often, their calls focused on filing complaints, which were apparently recorded, but the exchanges did not appear to prompt government officials to provide the homeowners with information.

As Ms. Hua came to the realization that incinerator construction was starting—and that individual phone complaints were leading nowhere—she began to search for alternative ways to address the problem. What had started as a "stench" issue was now a combination of concerns about the landfill, pollution from the pharmaceutical factory, the planned incinerator, and the existing medical incinerator. Her pivot to citizen science began with keeping a diary of the date, time, and description of the stench (which she mentioned in her phone conversation with the government official). Soon after, she began adding daily photographic documentation of smoke emissions from the medical incinerator, noting the dates and times the photos were taken and publishing them on the Rose homeowners' forum (figure 5.1). Many of Ms. Hua's online posts were still being monitored and censored, but some photos survived censorship. She also circulated the photos to other Rose homeowners via MSN Messenger.

Soon, other residents began participating in this citizen-science effort by texting Ms. Hua with photos of their own, taken from various angles, from day to night. Ms. Hua organized all the photos herself. However, unlike leaders in Meadow, Willow, and Pine, who organized homeowners to prepare documents to send to a number of government agencies, Ms. Hua did not have a clear sense of how to use her evidence or where to send it. She attempted to tell government officials about it, but, as the transcript provided earlier indicates, this information had little impact over the phone.

FIGURE 5.1. A selection of Ms. Hua's photos documenting the smoke emissions from the pharmaceutical factory at dawn, during the day, at dusk, and at night, September to December 2008.
Source: Photos provided by Ms. Hua.

FIGURE 5.1. (Continued)

FIGURE 5.1. (*Continued*)

FIGURE 5.1. (*Continued*)

FIGURE 5.1. (Continued)

Ms. Hua also researched dioxins and became eager to share this information with other homeowners so they would understand the harms of the smoke they were documenting. After some online reading, she and a few homeowners created educational posters describing various pollutants and hazardous chemicals emitted by incinerators. Ms. Hua erected the posters in the Rose courtyard on the day of a community flea market in the hope of reaching many residents.

As dozens of homeowners gathered for the flea market and stopped to read and discuss the content of the posters with Ms. Hua, *chengguan* (Urban Administrative and Law Enforcement Bureau) officials showed up to patrol the event. Soon, a group of homeowners noticed some *chengguan* officials in uniform tearing down the posters. Many homeowners pulled out their cell phone cameras and began to take photos and record videos of the poster removal crackdown. Videos show residents yelling at officials to stop taking the posters down. After a few minutes, the police arrived, along with "a few officials dressed like civilians," according to the

Rose homeowners who witnessed the occurrence. Ms. Hua recounted this exchange as follows:

> One of the *chengguan* dressed as a civilian . . . he pretended to be a resident and told us that we were disturbing peace and harmony in the community, and then he pushed someone! We protesters started demanding to know who he was. Our group was small, around three to four people, but many passersby in the flea market area stopped to watch and pulled out their cell phone cameras to film what was happening. During the scuffle, one of the undercover *chengguan* dropped his phone, and people in the community took it [his phone] away. We knew they [those dressed in plain clothes] were part of the police and *chengguan* because we saw them being shuffled into police cars, protected by officers!

Here, Ms. Hua spoke of yet another incident of repression, even though her community's collective action was in the form of a display of educational posters, nothing disruptive. She seemed gleeful that some homeowners had gotten ahold of the official's cell phone, perceiving this action as an act of resistance. In the background of one video, homeowners can be heard chanting, "*Chengguan* officials are hitting us!" Police then shut down the flea market and warned residents that they would be detained if they did not disperse.

Because of the confrontation, this early attempt at collective action through citizen science was quickly terminated. Although the posters were not disruptive, the homeowners' interactions with the *chengguan* escalated into a disruptive public protest. With dwindling homeowner participation in anti-incinerator struggles, this third protest was by far the community's smallest with fewer than twenty people engaging with the police and *chengguan* officials.

Barriers to the Presentation of Citizen Science

The trajectory of Community Rose's citizen science shared some features with that of Meadow, Willow, and Pine, with institutional channels pursued alongside protests. However, the two groups varied significantly in their ability to engage government officials with their data and scientific rhetoric. Meadow, Willow, and Pine integrated science, law, and protest. In

Rose, these strategies were not well integrated early on: in their calls to hotlines, homeowners did not provide scientific evidence strategically, and their protest rhetoric did not reflect scientific findings.

The government response to Rose's attempts at citizen science must also be viewed in the context of the repression the community experienced in response to their earlier public demonstrations and online forum activity (chapter 4). Having established a repressive response to citizen uprisings in Community Rose, government officials were likely less willing to engage in further dialogue with the community regardless of the approach they took, even one based on citizen science. Government monitoring and forum censorship also inspired an emotional response from homeowners (chapter 4) that constrained their attempted pivot toward empirical technical and scientific discussions. As Ms. Hua expanded her data-collection efforts, other Rose homeowners did not similarly shift their focus to gathering objective data. Rather, their online communications continued to focus on anger and outrage.

One exception was Mr. Sui, who designed and carried out an online survey about homeowners' experiences of and attitudes toward the landfill stench. However, survey responses were collected in the form of replies to a forum post, which meant that everyone who responded was able to see the answers preceding their own. Unsurprisingly, given the lack of confidentiality, answers did not vary much. Further, only twenty-six residents responded. The results indicated that homeowners experienced "severe stench" in a frequent or continuous manner, that it had a substantial impact on their lives, and that they supported lawsuits as a potential solution.[23] All respondents said they (or their neighbors) had already contacted government agencies about the problem via online submissions, protests, or visits to landfill managers, but no progress had been made. I could find no record suggesting that the survey results were presented anywhere, and Ms. Hua (though the first to respond to the survey) never mentioned it to me in person. In contrast to the surveying done in Meadow, Willow, and Pine, which, while also methodologically flawed, reached hundreds of homeowners including those who did not participate online, Rose's attempt appeared not to add anything meaningful to its store of scientific evidence.

Recognizing that Community Rose was not making progress on its own, Ms. Hua reached out to professionals outside the community. She attempted to "sneak into" an environmental nonprofit organization conference in

Beijing intended for employees of these organizations. Believing that she would be able to convince an environmental expert there to help, Ms. Hua prepared several copies of a long letter she had written detailing the landfill and incinerator issues and providing information from her research on the harms of dioxins. She wore business attire (much like when she snuck into the landfill, as described in chapter 3), and, when asked about her organizational affiliation at the registration desk, she answered, "I am a concerned citizen who cares about the environment." She was allowed to enter after they took down her name and personal identification number. However, organizations seemed wary of her and refused to accept her letter when she approached them. She recalled, "Nobody dared to accept the letter. . . . Nobody contacted me even though I left my cell phone number. Nobody contacted me to give me advice."[24]

Although the conference did not produce any allies, Ms. Hua kept a list of environmental organizations that had attended the conference, later making calls to them along with her friend Ms. Yang. They eventually succeeded in reaching a person willing to provide "informational guidance" on incinerator technology, which helped them better understand the science behind incineration.

Toward the end of September, Ms. Hua fell sick with an upper-respiratory infection, which she defined as asthma and bronchitis. She showed me her chest x-ray (which showed the presence of an infection), a doctor's note, and photos of the medicines she was prescribed. Although her doctor's diagnosis did not specify the cause of infection, Ms. Hua attributed the illness to the smoke pollution affecting Community Rose. After she shared this belief online alongside her continuing data collection, a lawyer—"who paid close attention to environmental news," she said—took notice of her forum posts. Impressed by Ms. Hua's photographic evidence, the lawyer offered his assistance: they would sue the medical incinerator's management company and the site of the landfill and incinerator, run by Rose's district government, for causing the air pollution that had led to Ms. Hua's illness. They would demand reimbursement for the medical bill associated with the hospital visit, which amounted to around 200 yuan ($30 in U.S. dollars)—"a small amount," Ms. Hua said, "but this is not about the money; it's the principle!"

Months later, the court ruled that Ms. Hua had not provided concrete evidence of pollution and that there was no clear medical evidence that her respiratory infection was related to pollution. According to Ms. Hua, she was told that she had "the responsibility to tolerate the landfill and the incinerator," because the landfill "was there before you were." To her, it seemed that the ruling implied that she should have known the landfill was there before purchasing her home. Despite this unfavorable ruling, Ms. Hua (and later Ms. Yang) continued to file lawsuits as a means of deploying scientific data.

Rose homeowners also attempted to use the content of EIAs to engage with environmental agencies. Ms. Yang was one of the homeowners who had reached out to the EPB via fax to obtain the EIA for the incinerator project. She and Ms. Hua, along with a few other homeowners, read the EIA and conducted some related research, primarily online. Their plan was to file an AR after consulting with a lawyer, capitalizing on the experience they had gained speaking with lawyers following Ms. Hua's first lawsuit.

In contrast to the earlier hotline calling, which was neither collectively organized nor focused on scientific information, the AR campaign was Community Rose's first official interaction with a governmental agency (SEPA) in which the homeowners used data collected via citizen science. Among the scientific observations they integrated into the AR for the planned incinerator construction were the following: (1) the site selection for the incinerator was not appropriate—it did not consider changes in urban planning, such as the increase in nearby resident populations; (2) the results for the atmospheric evaluation for the area were incorrect, as they did not take into account pollution caused by dioxins or the environmental sensitivity of the area; (3) the wind direction stated in the EIA was unverifiable; and (4) the description of dioxins [atmospheric] levels in the report was unverifiable, as no testing had been done. On this last point, Ms. Hua and Ms. Yang also cited the standard safety distance from an incinerator to residential areas, which they had researched online.

Whereas the AR work done by Meadow, Willow, and Pine led to the postponement of construction until further evaluations were made, Rose homeowners received a response to their AR from SEPA that directly rejected the proposal to reconsider site relocation. The reply indicated that the project was not classified as "incineration in a highly concentrated population area," atmospheric inspections were conducted in the correct area and range, data on wind direction came from a district weather station (though which one was not specified) in 2002, and "adequate measures" were in place for the management and control of dioxin emissions.

Given that Rose provided arguments and information similar to what was provided by Meadow, Willow, and Pine, the differing outcomes likely had more to do with the communities' relationships with the government than with the scientific details in question. Although the scientific information provided by Meadow, Willow, and Pine was generally more detailed, a probable contributor to the success of their AR was their long-standing rapport and mutual dialogue with government officials. The residents of Rose, in contrast, were viewed as troublemakers. Ms. Hua and other Rose homeowners continually found themselves stonewalled in their attempts to engage with officials in more formal conversations despite having scientific evidence to support their arguments.

Following the AR decision, Ms. Yang and her lawyer decided to sue the EPB to obtain inspection information for the medical incinerator (this was essentially a request for data transparency). Her lawsuit stated that the emission inspections had not been conducted in accordance with environmental protection laws. In addition, Ms. Yang requested that inspection data and legal documents related to the authorization of the medical incinerator be made public or, if inspection data were unavailable, that the EPB provide a written document stating that the information did not exist. While the court specified that the EPB did need to provide the information that Ms. Yang had requested (but never received), abiding by the Open Government Information Regulations Act and the Measures on Environmental Information Disclosure, the ruling noted that the medical incinerator was built with sufficient distance from residential areas for safety and that the provision of inspection information was unrelated to "the [legal] rights of the plaintiff." Thus, the lawsuit was dismissed. Ms. Hua's and Ms. Yang's failed lawsuits demonstrated these homeowners' frustrated attempts to hold government agencies accountable for providing transparent information and for inspecting and regulating sources of pollution properly.

I asked Ms. Hua why homeowners had not filed a class-action lawsuit. She told me that she had tried to organize such an effort but that very few homeowners were willing to participate. Even those who were interested had vastly different goals in mind, reflecting the lack of clarity and cohesion in Rose residents' understanding of the issue and in their arguments against the incinerator. Ms. Hua explained, "Some wanted to tear down the incinerator and bring down the construction company; others wanted punishment for the company or better pollution control methods, et cetera.... It's hard to gather the thoughts of one thousand people ... a lawyer would be really tired. Everyone would need to provide their personal identification information; we all have jobs [and are] too [busy]."

Although these middle-class homeowners possessed the resources and capacity to organize their community, this lack of prioritization highlights a core challenge to collective action among working professionals. Homeowners not only held differing views on the ultimate goal of their anti-incinerator resistance but also were constrained by their busy working lives. Both factors prevented them from developing the coherent strategy necessary to mobilize a joint lawsuit.

Contrasting Meadow, Willow, and Pine with Rose shows that their similar methods of data collection and presentation—community surveys, posters, engaging with EIA content, and filing an AR—led to very different government responses. Instead of engaging in regular dialogue with Rose homeowners, government officials cracked down on their third protest (the poster display at the flea market) and rejected their AR, leading homeowners to seek another way to use their data (through lawsuits). Because government officials refused to consider the scientific information provided by Rose homeowners—likely because of their preexisting negative perception of these residents—Rose citizen scientists encountered one administrative blockade after another.

CITIZEN SCIENCE IN COMMUNITY MARIGOLD

In Marigold, as in Rose, homeowners began their collective action with two publicly disruptive protests—a car march followed by a demonstration at an environmental exhibition (chapter 4)—before pivoting to citizen science. Marigold's community leader, Mr. Lu, was able to shift his strategy to engaging with scientific content, much as the residents of Meadow, Willow, and Pine did. However, although Marigold's approach of citizen science enabled its leader to engage in dialogue with municipal government officials, this engagement was largely controlled by the government through co-optation, leading homeowners to abandon protesting.

When I met Mr. Lu in 2010, he had just come back from an "international incinerator tour" with the municipal government. In just one year, from 2009 to 2010, Mr. Lu went from detainee to media darling, becoming the "citizen representative for opposing trash incineration" who traveled around with government officials. Together, Mr. Lu and his former government adversaries visited incinerators and learned about the incineration technology used in other countries.

At the start of this journey, Mr. Lu experienced disillusionment. Reflecting on the September 2009 protest tactics that led to his detainment (chapter 4), Mr. Lu, who was a lawyer, said, "Legally speaking, we have freedom of speech, freedom of publication, and the freedom to hold marches. But can you actually march? No, because there's no actual procedure for you to achieve that. Legal rights in China are like a lot of nice apples in a tree, but they don't give you a ladder, so you'll never actually reach the apples."

Following his detainment, Mr. Lu understood that further disruptive protests were out of the question, so he began to consider other methods to convince the municipal government to relocate the incinerator. He recalled thinking, "Perhaps it's not through force, or even pressure; it should be done through debate. We should talk science, talk reason. Is the incineration plan made incorrectly? Or under what circumstances would incineration be feasible?" This change in strategy allowed Mr. Lu and some other Marigold homeowners to take part in citizen-science research on incinerator construction, though this work was achieved mostly through experiences cultivated by the municipal government, such as Mr. Lu's incinerator tour. As interactions between Mr. Lu and government officials improved drastically, his decision to become part of the government's public relations campaign marked the end of disruptive protests for Community Marigold.

Adopting "Expert" Citizen Science

After Mr. Lu and the other six homeowners were released from the detention center, a few Marigold homeowners came together to form a "research committee" that would dedicate itself to examining relevant environmental policies and collecting scientific information on incinerators, including international case studies. Mr. Lu said that he gave this strategy a lot of thought while in detainment and came to believe that a science-focused approach would be a more effective way to gain government attention and persuade officials to take homeowners seriously than would continuing with disruptive protests. Research tasks were split among committee members; however, the group was loosely organized and met only occasionally, connecting primarily via phone and doing research online. Among their outreach efforts was a campaign to contact trash experts abroad (demonstrating their ability to communicate in English), asking them to analyze the composition of Beijing trash so that the homeowners could better understand their situation and propose an alternative solution to incineration that would be feasible. They received responses and incorporated what they learned into a report.

Committee members compiled their findings in electronic documents, focusing on incineration technology and alternative methods for processing trash. The report of their collective findings underwent several rounds of revision, which involved ensuring calculations were correct, clarifying the text, and incorporating new data. Homeowners stressed that the economic calculations of trash processing were key to their argument. They hoped that by focusing on financial viability, they could make it clear that private companies that manage trash could continue to be profitable using other—nonpolluting—technologies. Many Marigold homeowners were businesspeople themselves and—unlike homeowners in Meadow, Willow, Pine, and Rose, who did not appear to consider economic factors—felt it was important to make an argument that emphasized continued economic growth.

The committee's final product was a forty-four-page report that was sent to the municipal government, which was in charge of waste incineration projects in their area. The report was titled "The Life-and-Death Decisions of China's Urban Environment: Waste Incineration Policy and Public Will." This title showed that Marigold homeowners had chosen to frame the trash issue from an urban environment and policy angle rather than focusing on the specific incinerator that would affect just their residential community (although a section of the report did address their struggles against local incinerator construction).

Highly technical content appears from the beginning of the report, as the following extract from the first page demonstrates: "We collected the opinions of the public and researched the experiences and lessons of international waste-processing and incineration technologies. Our suggestions are [that] Beijing, in regard to trash separation and recycling, should borrow from the Brazilian 'CEMPRE' model[25]; for waste material recovery, treatment, and reduction, we should learn and import developed-country processing technologies such as 'MBT + RDF.' "[26]

Examples of technologies from the United States, Australia, and New Zealand were also provided. The first page ended with the following sentence: "We hope that the suggestions [of technologies] in this report will be adopted by the government when making policy decisions." The report read like a formal policy proposal, complete with references including local and international academic articles, international government reports, and publications from environmental organization (as well as Wikipedia articles).

In the report, Marigold homeowners also questioned the rush to build the incinerator without first resolving existing trash problems, such as the lack of trash separation and recycling. Like homeowners in Meadow, Willow, Pine, and Rose, they pointed out concerns about dioxin emissions. However, Marigold's report incorporated more comparative data from academic articles. Unlike Meadow, Willow, and Pine, and despite the reference to "public will" in the report title, Marigold homeowners did not conduct community surveys to gauge the impact of pollution on local residential communities or residents' health. Had they done so, they might have benefited from the outcome seen in Meadow, Willow, and Pine following their survey, which generated discussion and brought people together in person and online to discuss their perspectives. In Marigold, only a small group of homeowners participated in preparing the report, and just a few residents shared articles on trash separation and case studies of incinerators on the community's forum. Overall, community engagement in Marigold remained low, much like their engagement with informal civic activities. Moreover, some homeowners did not agree with the citizen-science approach. Some indicated on the forum that, rather than focusing on research, they wanted to concentrate on one central point—"strongly against the construction of the [nearby] incinerator"—although they did not suggest an alternative means of stopping the construction.

At the end of 2009, Mr. Lu contacted a municipal urban management engineer, a government employee, who had spoken about incineration on a television talk show. Sensing an opportunity to gain a high-profile ally, Mr. Lu reached out to this engineer and shared the report with him. Mr. Lu mentioned no difficulty in contacting the engineer, which contrasts with the experience of the Rose homeowners who struggled to get the right person on the phone. Based on the ability of Marigold homeowners to contact experts who were in professionally powerful positions, I expect that he was able to make contact through his professional networks, rather than relying on online searches.[27] According to Mr. Lu, the report was quickly circulated within the municipal government after that exchange.[28] The product of Community Marigold's citizen science had officially reached the government.

Co-optation Through Citizen Science

Mr. Lu's transition from government agitator to government affiliate was swift. At the beginning of 2010, he was contacted by municipal officials and told that the construction of the incinerator had been temporarily suspended. Mr. Lu was then promptly invited on a government-sponsored tour of incinerators in Japan and Macau with urban management officials and other "trash management specialists" (i.e., government academics and researchers) as the "leader of the opposing party for trash incineration." He accepted just as promptly. When asked about the response of his fellow Marigold homeowners, who were not invited to join the tour, he told me, "Nah, they don't care. Everyone asks me about the motivation behind the government inviting me. But government motivation is unknown. . . . It's too early to assess results."[29]

Mr. Lu told me that the tour was intended to demonstrate how successfully incineration was being implemented in the two countries. At the beginning of the trip, he started a personal blog to record his experiences, starting with a few poems he wrote about his experience of collective action against the incinerator. He told me that he enjoyed writing and that the poems helped him express his emotions more vividly. He chose a blog over the homeowners' forum because a blog was more reflective and personal, he said. One poem captured his recent experience with citizen science:

> Starting tomorrow, I will be a melancholy person;
> Research trash, research the environment, research the future.
> Starting tomorrow, [I will] care about the air and pollution;
> I have a home; it faces the incinerator [area]; in warm spring the stench will come.[30]
> Starting tomorrow, I will be an angry person;
> Telling every friend the origins of my anger;
> Telling them the height of the chimney, the shape, and its harm.

In the poem, Mr. Lu mentioned his involvement in environmental research on air pollution caused by incinerators and his identity as a homeowner. Although he talked about his anger, this anger would be channeled into research activities, not disruptive protests. The day before Mr. Lu embarked on the tour, he posted on his blog that had been reading all he could about trash incineration: "This trip . . . I feel a lot of pressure, because on my shoulders, I carry the passionate hopes of our surrounding communities, and I feel the heaviness of this historic mission."

Although Marigold homeowners never created unity with other "surrounding communities" in their mobilizing or organizing, Mr. Lu viewed his trip as having the potential to help his neighborhood, all communities of which were threatened by the incinerator. The tour was the beginning of Mr. Lu's understanding of a larger purpose: he would be the community's representative and in this role would bring back information and engage with municipal officials—for the benefit of not only Marigold but also their neighboring communities.

Because the tour was organized by the government, it was covered closely by the media. While media outlets were largely barred from covering disruptive protests in their communities (some would try to, but online articles would quickly be removed), a number of outlets had been reporting more generally on the urban waste problem and the challenges of incineration. However, the government's involvement provided a green light for journalists to feature a "citizen against incineration"—Mr. Lu— free of censorship. Having been designated by the government as the "official opposition leader," reporters were encouraged to portray Mr. Lu as the oppositional voice—which would serve to demonstrate publicly that the government was listening to its citizens. Mr. Lu said that he received phone calls "hourly" from journalists wanting to conduct interviews with him. Reporters also followed his blog closely and quoted from it in their articles. On his blog, Mr. Lu reposted close to two hundred media articles about himself, complete with photos of him looking into recycling bins and walking alongside trash management specialists.

For the municipal government, Mr. Lu functioned as a well-educated and well-behaved anti-incineration poster child. Following this script, the media portrayed him as a wealthy homeowner and almost always mentioned that he was a lawyer by training, depicting him as a successful and educated citizen of Beijing who was amicably engaged in anti-incineration dialogue with government officials. In other words, the government's involvement with Mr. Lu appeared to be a masterful public relations maneuver. While this type of engagement is considered a form of co-optation, during the tour Mr. Lu did not seem to be hindered from pursuing his own goals of understanding the incinerator technology used in other countries, the waste policies of those countries, and alternatives to incineration. Moreover, the flurry of interviews and talk show invitations continued after Mr. Lu returned to China, and he greatly enjoyed these experiences, he told me. And environmental nonprofit organizations—some of the same organizations that had been reluctant to help Community Rose—asked him to give talks to their employees regarding his trip to Japan.

In our conversations, Mr. Lu interpreted the government's intentions, and his own actions, in a favorable light. "In China, it is rare that the government bow their heads to citizens . . . this was huge news," he said of the government's invitation to join the tour. Asked why he thought he had been chosen for this role, Mr. Lu said, "I believe they were touched that the people brought such a [scientific] report to them." These sentiments, however, appeared to reflect the cordial relationship he had come to enjoy with municipal officials during and after the tour, rather than his attitude toward the government at the time of the invitation, which may have been more measured following his recent detainment.

The international tour signaled to journalists and staff of environmental organizations (who are often wary of reporting on or incorporating citizens' anti-incineration stances into their work) that Mr. Lu had been "okayed" by the government and was therefore an appropriate person with whom to engage. As part of this constant media coverage, Marigold's citizen-science report was frequently referenced. Although the publicity did not yield concrete policy shifts, mentions of the report presented Marigold homeowners' engagement in environmental issues to a broader Beijing and even a national audience, implicitly endorsing the idea of homeowners taking part in collective action for environmental causes.

Though conducted through the mechanism of co-optation, the tour did engage Mr. Lu in discussions of incinerator technology and trash policy with officials. Later, Mr. Lu would be invited to sit in on government discussion panels reviewing trash policy. While this involvement was always filtered through the lens of government control, it is nonetheless an achievement for citizen input to be considered in the policy-making of an authoritarian government, even if it is only one individual participating in a circumscribed role (chapter 6). Mr. Lu's government involvement signified that Marigold's citizen-science efforts had been accepted by the government. At the same time, Mr. Lu was in a sense being exploited, in that officials also used their interactions with him as a chance to both quell disruptive dissent and generate positive public relations.

Later, Mr. Lu was able to point to new city regulations for trash management that he believed to be directly related to the Marigold homeowners' report (chapter 6). Far from feeling exploited by the government, Mr. Lu felt that he had participated in government policy-making through citizen science: "The problem with the government is that they don't know how to pick out a specialist from the crowd. They themselves don't understand [technical issues], and they also don't know who understands. So with divergent public opinions on trash management, the government needed to know what 'real professional opinion' is. They need specialists for each issue. It's a division of labor, and there will be better urban management that way."

Although Mr. Lu's view may be overly sympathetic, his assertion of the potential for government officials to partner with citizen scientists is not unfounded. Even within the context of co-optation, citizens and government officials do have the opportunity to exchange ideas. Regardless of whether these municipal officials set out to quell dissent, persuade citizens that incineration was "good," or pose as sympathetic listeners of public opinion, concrete conversations and dialogues were had in the process. Ultimately, these exchanges did not prevent incinerator construction at the Marigold site, but Mr. Lu continued to pursue the issue, changing career tracks to focus on urban trash management (chapter 6). Co-optation, it seems, might quell environmental contention but not environmental consciousness.

Because citizen science is shaped by local characteristics, Marigold homeowners' use of scientific content in their report leveraged the capacity of upper-middle-class professionals to understand academic papers, conduct cost calculations, reach out to global experts, and access appropriate government officials. Although both Marigold's and Meadow, Willow, and Pine's reports reflected scientific sophistication, Marigold and Rose shared a history of disruptive demonstrations followed by crackdowns and arrests, which likely influenced the government's inclination to control dissent in both cases. Rather than stonewalling as officials did with the combative

Ms. Hua, however, government officials saw an opportunity in the form of the charismatic Mr. Lu. This choice also had the effect of letting other Marigold homeowners' anti-incinerator voices fade into the background.

AN AUTHORITARIAN GOVERNMENT, THE MIDDLE CLASS, AND CITIZEN SCIENCE

Across the communities discussed in this book, citizen science surfaced as an alternative to disruptive protesting and a powerful boost to arguments made through legal institutional channels. Although citizen science manifested in different ways and with varying levels of accuracy, this approach allowed homeowners to better understand the issue of incineration, investigate environmental laws and case studies, and produce and present scientific evidence. Even Rose residents, whose data did not take them far in terms of local outcomes, saw their investigations influence environmental discussions more broadly, as Ms. Hua would later use the information when invited to workshops organized by environmental organizations (chapter 6).

Engaging with the content of government-produced EIAs and scientific rhetoric against incineration placed most homeowners in a safe space to press government officials to respond (with the exception of Rose's flea-market demonstration, which resulted in a crackdown portended by previous negative interactions between residents and officials). Ultimately, for Community Rose homeowners, their contentious relationship with government officials led them to seek other ways of presenting their data. Marigold homeowners were also involved in early incidents of disruptive protest, which likely influenced the government's move toward repression through co-optation in response to their technical report on alternatives to incineration. In contrast, Meadow, Willow, and Pine homeowners always chose institutional channels, frequently interacting with government officials and sustaining their citizen-science efforts over a longer period of time. When they eventually engaged in more publicly disruptive tactics, such as the World Earth Day march in front of the SEPA building, homeowners were careful to frame their protest slogans around scientific rhetoric and focus their demands only on the EIA and the AR ruling. These contrasting examples show that citizen science is generally acceptable as a means of collective action in China but that responses to citizen science are shaped by a community's previous actions and representatives' relationships with the government.

The observations of SEPA's response to *homeowners* are in line with previous cases in China in which SEPA was receptive to scientific data presented by *environmental organizations*. SEPA has a history of siding with environmental groups and holding sympathetic attitudes toward environmental issues more generally.[31] This sympathy appears to translate to an openness toward citizen science, as reflected in SEPA's decision to side with Meadow, Willow, Pine, and even with Rose in postponing incinerator construction until further environmental evaluations were made. However, SEPA did not rule in favor of Rose's AR, citing a lack of concrete evidence. Given that these similar communities were facing the same issue—and that Meadow, Willow, and Pine's AR should have set a precedent for Rose's, having occurred earlier—the explanation for the divergent outcomes seems to lie with the difference in the communities' relationships with the government.

Not all communities have the means to conduct citizen science. I met with a district city management official in 2011 about another incinerator being built in the city—this time more remotely, in an area where residents of lower socioeconomic status, farmers, lived. I had heard from an environmental organization that there had been some pushback from the farmers, some of whom were being relocated because of the planned construction, but that no collective action was occurring. Commenting on that incinerator, the official told me that he believed that the farmers were expressing dissent only because they lacked an understanding of the science behind incineration. If government agencies educated citizens more, he said, then residents would support incinerator plans. The commentary on social class stood out here: according to this official, farmers did not understand "science." Considering this comment in the context of the middle-class homeowners' resistance, it becomes clear that citizen science requires a certain standing in the eyes of decision-makers—in addition to time, professional connections, leadership, community mobilizing potential, and some formal understanding of how to present data in a way that adheres to government expectations. Attributes such as professional experience (e.g., Mr. Wu's work at a scientific think tank), knowledge of relevant experts to contact (e.g., Mr. Lu's instinct to call the city engineer), and the ability to gather community resources and volunteers to engage in citizen science are more prevalent among middle-class homeowners than individuals of a lower socioeconomic status. In this context, government officials also appear to be more receptive to arguments assembled by middle-class homeowners. In other words, citizen science is more likely to succeed as a middle- or upper-middle-class strategy.

In the process of protesting, pursuing institutional channels, bombarding government hotlines, and presenting scientific findings, homeowners came to better understand the structure and jurisdictions of government agencies over time, learned to prepare complex documents, and increased their knowledge of environmental issues—first with regard to landfills and incinerator pollutants, and later expanding into recycling and trash separation (chapter 6). Many of these lessons and experiences reached beyond community walls, fostering a sense of civic responsibility among many homeowners. As community residents concluded their diverging efforts of anti-incinerator resistance, the consequences of their collective action went beyond the government's decisions about constructing incinerators. Chapter 6 shows how the collective action of homeowners, even when "failing," played a role in fostering middle-class identities and a sense of civic responsibility, allowing them to build durable community organizations that would last beyond protesting. These organizations would go on to bring citizen voices into the discussions of the government and environmental organizations and tackle environmental challenges beyond incineration.

Chapter Six

CONSEQUENCES OF COMMUNITY ENVIRONMENTAL ORGANIZING

The previous chapters have shown how homeowners progressed from learning how to resolve housing issues within their communities to understanding how to collectively address environmental problems to others outside their gates. In this process, they expanded their spheres of responsibility from issues that concerned only themselves as homeowners to those that affected others in their larger neighborhoods. As a consequence of increasing their engagement in addressing collective grievances among residential communities—whether issues with property management, landfill stench, or the prospect of incinerator construction nearby—residents developed identities as individual homeowners, as members of collective communities, and as middle-class citizens of urban Beijing.

This chapter begins by exploring the government decisions that were ultimately made about each of the incinerator construction projects: one was relocated within the city, and two were later constructed at the originally designated sites. Those outcomes alone, however, fail to capture the full impact of the homeowners' environmental activism. Evaluations of the impact of social movements frequently focus on *immediate* outcomes related to movement claims (here, canceling incinerator construction), yet community organizing has consequences beyond a campaign's specific demands. To investigate these broader impacts, this chapter focuses on how middle-class identities were fostered as a result of anti-incinerator organizing. This identity formation is a combined product of engaging with citizen science; collaborating with other, similar middle-class communities; and, sometimes, denying or discounting the views of non-middle-class citizens experiencing similar struggles. In addition to the development of homeowners' identities as civically responsible middle-class citizens, some communities or representatives were able to build durable organizations that outlasted their efforts of collective action, organizations that continued to work on environmental issues such as trash separation and recycling regardless of the government's decision about incinerator construction.

Acknowledging that the consequences of activism are also related to self-perceptions, this chapter further describes how community representatives and other homeowners viewed their participation as contributing to social and political changes at various levels: environmental consciousness within themselves, environmental awareness in their communities, and the attitudes and policies of government. Even in a context of repression, homeowners observed positive changes brought about by their organizing efforts, even if it was simply to shed light on the issue of incineration. A narrower analytical focus on protest events or the outcomes of collective action against incinerator construction would miss these enduring shifts, which could be observed through the interactions between homeowners and government officials that continued long after protests had ended.[1]

Finally, an unexpected consequence of homeowners' organizing efforts was their newfound role in environmental education, exemplified by their participation in workshops and talks organized by environmental nonprofit organizations. Not only did the workshops bring homeowners from across three districts of Beijing together for the first time, but they also gave community representatives frequent opportunities to present their organizing experiences and citizen-science discoveries. This platform solidified their roles as citizen environmental specialists, playing a part in educating a larger urban population and incorporating their voices into Beijing's environmental civil society. Delivering environmental education reinforced community representatives' sense of civic duty.

Incinerator Construction Outcomes

In early 2010, after more than three years of homeowners' resistance, the Beijing municipal government officially announced that the incinerator planned for construction near Meadow, Willow, and Pine would be relocated. In a February 2010 news report, a Beijing Municipal and City Appearance Management Committee official cited the following reasons for the relocation: (1) the plans for processing water and gases generated by the adjacent landfill were not in place; (2) the location may become a core tech park development area; and (3) local citizens did not support the construction. Although technical and economic considerations were mentioned as reasons for relocation (as with most development projects), homeowners were officially cited as influencing the decision. To understand how and why these particular homeowners were able to sway authorities, I conducted formal and informal conversations with a number of government officials and environmental organization staff members.

In 2010, through personal connections, I was able to meet and interview a high-ranking official in the Environmental Impact Evaluation Department in the Ministry of Environmental Protection (MEP; formerly the State Environmental Protection Administration [SEPA]).[2] I first met Mr. Chen in Chicago, where I was attending graduate school. When I took him on a walking tour of my neighborhood, he stopped to pick up every piece of trash we came across, holding on to them until we found a bin for both garbage and recycling, then carefully separating out the plastics and placing them into the appropriate recycling compartment. I was surprised to see a bureaucrat actively practicing environmentalism—after all, I had spent years listening to Beijing homeowners describe how government officials did not care about the environment.

I asked Mr. Chen about his career as a central environmental official working in the area of environmental evaluations. He had managed environmental impact assessments (EIAs) for numerous projects, including the preservation of redwood trees in Shenzhen (in southern China), an underwater tunnel in Xiamen (also in southern China), a tunnel covering near Beijing to eliminate noise pollution, and Shanghai Disneyland, the assessment for which involved calculating the amount of trash that would be generated by visitors.[3] In short, Mr. Chen had ample experience evaluating large national government construction projects. Although he had not personally interacted with Meadow, Willow, or Pine homeowners, he was aware that they had protested in front of the SEPA building on World Environment Day. He explained that it was common for SEPA, as a central agency, to be unaware of local environmental grievances until issues "come knocking on our door" through such demonstrations.

CONSEQUENCES OF COMMUNITY ENVIRONMENTAL ORGANIZING

After learning about Meadow, Willow, and Pine homeowners' grievances in 2007, Mr. Chen traveled to the neighborhood's landfill and incinerator construction site to better understand the problem out of personal interest.[4] He did so on his own time one Sunday morning, he revealed. He wanted to learn more about the situation despite one of his friends who lived near the construction site insisting that there was no hope that incinerator construction would be canceled. When Mr. Chen approached the landfill, he was "chased away" by workers who wanted to keep him out of the area, he told me. Even as a high-ranking environmental official, his interactions with workers at the landfill did not seem much different from Ms. Hua's, in which an inspection agent called the police to report her sneaking into the landfill near Community Rose (chapter 3).

Because incinerator construction was locally managed, SEPA was not the primary agency overseeing the environmental evaluations for such projects. However, because Meadow, Willow, and Pine homeowners filed an administrative reconsideration (AR), which went to SEPA (the agency that oversaw the Beijing Environmental Protection Bureau [EPB]) and protested at the EPB's doors, the agency came into dialogue with the Beijing EPB, Mr. Chen explained. Commenting on the general relationship between local EPBs and the federal environmental authority (which by that time was the MEP), he said,

> It takes a while for the government to respond to protests in general. The key [holdup] is who will deal with it? [Local] EPBs do not have the best relations with the MEP sometimes because they feel that we take sides with residents, and it makes the bureau lose face. We [the MEP] only interfere, generally speaking, when things escalate. Local bureaus [EPBs] always try to suppress the issue at first. . . . Local interests are strong, [but] local EPBs don't care because after a few years, the officials won't be in that position anymore [because most rotate positions], and so it wouldn't be their problem. We [the MEP] have veto power: if we don't approve of a project after EIAs, the construction cannot continue. But, to be honest, many [MEP] officials are not really more environmentally conscious either.[5]

In Mr. Chen's experience, the tensions between local EPBs and central SEPA or MEP authorities were long-standing. When SEPA sided with local citizens, it was perceived as encroaching upon local EPB affairs. As a result, these environmental bureaus, naturally more entrenched in local interests and politics (e.g., because they have district agencies that manage landfills and incinerator construction) would feel pressured to permit local projects. Further, Mr. Chen noted that while it is EPBs who approve or reject plans for incinerators, it is city management officials who are in charge of their construction, management, and operation. These cleavages in responsibility among local agencies lead to conflicts in the interpretation of environmental regulations. While SEPA is generally careful not to intervene in local affairs, in the case of Meadow, Willow, and Pine, it was likely that the central agency's sympathy for the homeowners played a role in encouraging local agencies to reconsider the plan for incinerator construction and ultimately find a new location.

According to a staff member of an environmental nonprofit organization, Mr. Bo, who followed Meadow, Willow, and Pine's struggles closely and knew local government officials well, a key reason for the relocation of the incinerator was indeed "homeowner pressure."[6] "Meadow, Willow, and Pine were really successful," Mr. Bo told me, "but they were quiet about it. They treated the success in a very humble way because they [didn't] want the government to think that they were [causing dissent] by spreading the news of success around the city." He articulated the logic that even though protests and citizen-science efforts influenced a government concession in this instance, it was safer for homeowners not to frame this outcome as a "victory over government." Huang *laoshi*, from Meadow, reflected a similar sentiment: "The government is OK with us, because there is a lot of rational communication and frequent negotiation. They know that we won't cause problems for them."

While Meadow, Willow, and Pine homeowners quietly celebrated, the incinerator was relocated to a site in northwest Beijing, about ten kilometers away. Mr. Chen disclosed to me that another site had originally been chosen for relocation before the final spot was selected. This first option was near a Communist Party school, and the deputy principal of the school was openly against this relocation plan. Because of the school's political connections, the principal was able to interact directly with government officials regarding the plan, Mr. Chen told me. As a result, a new site was chosen, farther from Beijing's city center.

In its final location, nearby residents were poor farmers who lived in low-rent public housing. Mr. Chen drove me through the village during one of my visits to Beijing in 2011. The location was in a rural part of Beijing, and we drove past single-story abodes with concrete walls and battered wooden doors. Residents sat on stoops or stools in front of their homes, their hands busy shucking and organizing piles of vegetables. It was a sharp contrast to the modern urban scenery only ten kilometers away, where the middle-class homeowners of Meadow, Willow, and Pine had hung banners from their balconies and displayed educational posters in their spacious community courtyards during their organizing efforts against the incinerator. No protests were held in this rural community, Mr. Chen said. Many farmers were eventually relocated and given some monetary compensation from the government because the land was being used for construction. The success of the incinerator relocation, despite the presence of residents who would be affected, indicates that not all communities were able to resist (or even learn of plans for) incinerator construction. Being white-collar professionals or having connections with the Communist Party allowed middle-class stakeholders to develop a capacity to organize that was unavailable to working-class villagers.

Back in Meadow, Willow, and Pine, landfill stench remained a problem. Homeowners continued to complain about it regularly on the online forum. However, according to the community representatives, local officials promised that the landfill would "eventually" reach capacity and be shut down. Given their success with having the incinerator relocated, the homeowners were willing to wait it out.

However, not all middle-class communities were able to reverse incinerator decisions. In Community Rose, following Ms. Hua's and Ms. Yang's failed lawsuits, construction continued without delay. However, despite its crackdowns on protests and unwillingness to engage with homeowners' citizen-science data, the government did take some concessionary actions. First, government officials appear to have posted an "apology letter" on bulletin boards in the community. Ms. Hua told me that the letter was unsigned and had no official seal indicating which agency had issued it, but it was written from the perspective of the district government. The letter included a promise to alleviate the landfill stench but did not comment on the incinerator. From her standpoint, the unsigned letter indicated that the government was trying to show interest in the community's welfare but did not want to invite a response or be held accountable for any promises.

Second, in early 2010, a district government official contacted Ms. Hua and invited her and a few other Rose homeowners to tour the newly completed incinerator (figure 6.1). The landfill area into which she had initially

FIGURE 6.1. The park area outside the incinerator near Community Rose, with colorful flowers planted (top left and top right); the interior of the completed incinerator (bottom left); and the exterior of the incinerator with newly planted trees lining the road (bottom right).
Source: Photos provided by Ms. Hua, taken while on her tour of the incinerator.

FIGURE 6.1. (*Continued*)

snuck was now lined with newly planted trees and had a park with flowers ("lavender and carnations," she specified as a plant lover) and a sculpture. The newly paved roads outside the incinerator and landfill walls were now sprayed with "fragrant water," she told me, chuckling.[7] Ms. Hua also mentioned that the media had reported on these changes, calling the area a "dream park" for nearby residents.

Though much smaller in scale, this government-led tour is reminiscent of Marigold representative Mr. Lu's international incinerator tour, which also functioned as a government public relations effort. The district government's invitation to Ms. Hua demonstrated that even after repressive tactics had been used to suppress her forum posts and protest actions, officials reached out to her and sought to showcase their efforts to make the incinerator area attractive. Ultimately, it was important for the district to maintain harmonious relations with its citizens; the invitation thus served as an olive branch. Ms. Hua felt that the district had shown that improvements to the area had been made and that someone had been listening to the community's grievances about the stench.[8]

In 2010, on the other side of Beijing, Mr. Lu was awaiting the final decision on the construction of the incinerator near Community Marigold, which had been temporarily postponed. Mr. Lu seemed confident that the government would make regulatory changes on the issue of urban trash management, but he did not speculate on decisions about the incinerator. His thinking had progressed from opposing the incinerator to focusing on ways to manage urban waste, which he viewed as pertinent to reassessing incineration in the long run. Ultimately, although the incinerator project near Marigold was suspended for five years, in 2014 the municipal government announced that construction would move ahead as planned. According to a news article shared with me by an environmental nonprofit organization, a public hearing was held in early 2015 to address resident concerns before resuming the project. After homeowners expressed their dissent during the hearing, the presiding officials reportedly emphasized that mechanisms to monitor pollution would be strictly implemented. The construction was then promptly authorized by the Beijing EPB.

According to this news article, Marigold homeowners expressed varying opinions on this decision. One individual was quoted as stating that the government's decision to go forward with the controversial project would only decrease citizens' trust in the government. Another, however, said that holding the public hearing was a drastic improvement given the lack of transparency preceding the community's protests five years before. The article explained that those earlier anti-incinerator sentiments were less about waste incineration than about dissatisfaction with how the government was carrying out a public project (which would affect citizens' health) "behind the scenes," not taking public opinion into account. However, based on homeowners' forum data from 2008 and 2009 (when they mobilized for protests), it was apparent that Marigold homeowners were aggrieved about more than the veiled nature of government decision-making processes, citing concerns about health, pollution, and property values. The varying sentiments expressed in the article also indicated that Marigold homeowners had not come together to discuss a unifying agenda regarding the reinstatement of plans for incinerator construction.

Mr. Lu, also present at the hearing, was quoted in the article as saying, "The construction decision is set in stone now. Residents were putting too much hope into the public hearing." Mr. Lu also noted that he had become a "realist," believing that most anti-incinerator activists were too idealistic and that the public hearing itself had no substantial meaning. Mr. Lu's shift in attitude in 2015 reflects the experience he gained by establishing his own environmental trash-management company and his increased sympathy for the government stance on incineration following his 2010 tour. By that time, he had come to the belief that only through trash separation and trash management could the waste problem truly be solved; incinerator resistance was not going to resolve the issue. While Mr. Lu worked on building his trash-management company, the incinerator near Marigold was completed and officially activated in 2019.[9]

Despite the homeowners' environmental efforts, each planned incinerator was eventually constructed, although Meadow, Willow, and Pine succeeded in sparing their neighborhood from incinerator emissions. However, in each community, homeowners continued to interact with government officials after incinerator decisions had been made. Even in Rose and Marigold, where residents did not succeed in their efforts, community representatives perceived that they had still made a positive impact by raising government awareness of incineration issues. Further, many residents felt that they had moved into roles that allowed them to provide input into broader environmental policy-making.

Community-Government Relationships and Perceptions of Policy Impact

By organizing an anti-incinerator resistance and interacting with government officials, leaders from all three community sites cultivated relationships with central, municipal, and district agencies. These relationships shaped how community representatives perceived both the role of the government and their own impact on government decisions. While it is difficult to assess whether concrete regulatory changes directly resulted from homeowners' citizen-science efforts, homeowners did observe changes in government attitudes and behaviors toward environmental issues following their collective action. Regardless of whether their organizing efforts were repressed or tolerated, community leaders viewed the results of their struggles in a mostly positive light.

In Meadow, Willow, and Pine, where frequent dialogue between government and residents had taken place, community leaders often described the government as "serving the public." Commenting on the central government's role in serving its citizens, Huang *laoshi* said, "If most of the public don't agree with a development project, then it cannot become established as a project.... Anything that 'bothers citizens and hurts wealth' cannot be established as a project; the central government told me this. The central government supports citizens . . . you can't get away with doing local things like this. You can't say it's for local GDP, local interests, [or] development, so I'll harm the rights of the public. That is not allowed. The CCP [Chinese Communist Party] is here to serve people."

The trust Huang *laoshi* exhibited in describing the relationship between citizens and the central government reflects the successful outcome of incinerator relocation in his area; such overwhelming confidence in the central government was not evident among residents of Community Rose or Community Marigold. His statement also points to tensions between central and local government officials, similar to what Mr. Chen had described to me: the central government (SEPA or the MEP and the Communist Party) is viewed (or at least portrayed) as supporting citizens, whereas local agencies (EPBs or district agencies) are perceived as being at odds with citizens because of considerations of local economic and infrastructure development, often at the cost of public health. Based on forum posts in Rose and Marigold, it could also be the case that some middle- and upper-middle-class homeowners had a particular cultural disdain for local administrators. In forum posts, residents of these communities frequently referred to local officials as "dumb," "foolish," or "incompetent."

In addition to the willingness of the central government to help their cause, Meadow, Willow, and Pine homeowners also attributed their success to their knowledge of the political system. Not only did homeowners benefit from the presence of experienced community leaders such as Mr. Wu, who had worked as a government administrator (chapter 5), but most had also come to know local government officials by name during their efforts of collective action. Most homeowners with whom I spoke communicated a clear understanding of the municipal and district agencies responsible for the incinerator as a consequence of having participated in writing letters, editing and filing an AR, and sending these documents to long lists of relevant government departments (following an extended process of trial and error that began with sending letters to irrelevant departments).

Homeowners also perceived a shift in government attitude toward waste management following their citizen-science efforts. Huang *laoshi* commented, "I noticed that the government is changing. They are starting trash-separation efforts to cut down waste. They didn't think of this earlier [before the protests]; incinerators were the first thing they came up with. It's only a matter of time; it'll be like Taiwan, where none of the incinerators have much [trash] to burn [because trash is separated].[10] Some of the incinerators will eventually become defunct because they won't have a function. Burning trash is like thinking surgery is the answer to all diseases without knowing the root problem."

Huang *laoshi* believed that homeowners' collective citizen-science efforts had effectively introduced or reinforced an alternative idea (i.e., trash separation) for government officials to consider. Reflexively building incinerators—massive, costly, and risky endeavors he likened to surgical procedures—without knowing the origins of the trash problem could not be effective as a solution. Huang *laoshi*'s comments on government efforts accorded with my experience of visiting government officials at around the same time: urban waste and trash separation (recycling) were the focus of most conversations related to the environment, whereas these topics had not emerged as priorities in any earlier official policies or legislation.

Community leaders in Meadow, Willow, and Pine also believed that, since their collective action began, government officials had come far in recognizing the gravity of environmental problems. Community Pine's Mr. Wu explained that by continually visiting officials over several years, homeowners had persuaded the government to become more understanding and aware of citizens' concerns for the environment:

> For example, the incinerator is not here anymore, but they left two project plans in place here. One is a composting facility, and the other is a trash-sorting facility. They actually made public announcements for these though . . . now this is an improvement from the past. Before, with the incinerator, nobody even knew about it. . . . They announced [the plans] this time; it was published in the news and with phone numbers listed on the announcements [for addressing concerns]. We used to have to go beg for EIAs; now at least they are more sincere and transparent.

Mr. Wu's comment indicated not only that the government was seriously pursuing trash separation, planning for composting and trash-sorting facilities, but also that homeowners knew about these plans in advance via a transparent public announcement. He believed that officials had become more sincere in their environmental efforts, taking concrete steps toward solutions in dialogue with citizens. Overall, community representatives in Meadow, Willow, and Pine perceived meaningful progress in the transparency of government development projects, pointing to public announcements being made and information being more easily attainable.

Advancements in transparency also resulted in invitations for Meadow, Willow, and Pine homeowners to attend government policy meetings. Conversations among community leaders in 2011 indicated that they were sitting in on policy planning meetings and speaking of their attendance at these events in a normalized way. For example, Huang *laoshi* would offhandedly complain about what he disagreed with at the meetings: "I went to a legislation planning meeting the other day. The municipal government chief . . . he was explaining to me what was 'recyclable.' He defined it as 'things you can exchange for money.' . . . But glass . . . nobody collects glass now [for money].[11] Then [the chief] went on to redefine; he said ['recyclable' means] 'things that are reusable.' Those are all such narrow definitions." Not only did Huang *laoshi* frequently attend meetings but he was also engaged in discussions about trash separation and even criticized the government's definitions of environmental terms used in their regulations.

CONSEQUENCES OF COMMUNITY ENVIRONMENTAL ORGANIZING

In contrast, young homeowners in Community Rose who came into more direct conflict with government officials and police did not receive the same opportunities to participate in government policy-making processes after their struggles against incinerator construction. Homeowners in this community had pushed back against censorship, openly challenging government officials on their forum and yelling at *chengguan* (Urban Administrative and Law Enforcement Bureau) officers who came to the community to tear down their educational posters (chapter 4). Even in private chats and emails, Rose homeowners continued to deride government officials. Among the digital files Ms. Hua shared with me were photos of *chengguan* and other district officials whom she labeled as "traitors," "bandits," and "bastards." Frequently, Rose homeowners referred to government institutions as "incompetent" and their employees as "uncivilized" or "uneducated," even though the officials (including those from the *chengguan*) with whom they interacted had college or vocational college degrees, as required by state exams.[12] This rhetoric, alongside Rose homeowners' more aggressive public protest tactics—which they referred to as "fights"—did not cultivate agreeable relationships between officials and residents over time.

However, in 2010, when Ms. Hua reflected on her anti-incinerator resistance, including the failure of her lawsuits, she regarded her activism as "somewhat successful." Her negative but continual interactions with officials had led her to be invited on a tour of the newly completed incinerator and park, demonstrating the district's willingness to reach out even after repression had occurred. She believed that her scientific data collection and hotline complaints had led to small changes: "It made the government pay attention to the landfill and incinerator. They made efforts to clean up the area . . . even though some efforts might only be superficial." Though she viewed these government actions as potentially temporary and perfunctory, Ms. Hua appeared to take pride in inspiring some level of government response.

Meanwhile, on the Rose forum, discussions of the trash issue dwindled. One homeowner started a discussion thread asking others what waste-management advice they would give to the city of Beijing, but Ms. Hua was the only person who responded with substantial comments. She stated that the city needed to consider trash separation and composting (similar to the conclusions of Meadow, Willow, Pine, and Marigold homeowners). Although Rose homeowners' protests failed, and there was little engagement with this post, some homeowners were starting to think of trash as a city-level management challenge rather than myopically as an issue of stench and smoke plaguing just their community.

Emotions rose again, however, when homeowners heard about Ms. Hua's failed lawsuit regarding her medical bill. Several residents posted criticisms of the court with sentiments including "The people at the court should come live here [in the community]," and "Let the judges come experience this [at] midnight, when the stench [from the medical incinerator] is the worst." As the incinerator began operating in 2010, homeowners also complained about seeing smoke pouring out of the large chimney, alarmed at its proximity to their community. Despite this anger, however, homeowners did not appear to take any further action. This inertia reflected long-standing Rose attitudes: throughout the process of anti-incinerator resistance, most homeowners engaged in individual complaints rather than collective organizing.

Whereas Ms. Hua's distrust of the local government persisted following her tour of the new incinerator, Mr. Lu in Marigold had quite a positive view of the government after his tour with municipal officials. He felt strongly that he "got the government to listen and feel sympathetic." His description of government–community relations was best exemplified through his analogy of a blowout soccer game: "It's like us [the Chinese soccer team] playing the Brazilian team . . . we'll lose for sure, but we need to have good attitudes. We may be down 0–10, but maybe we can be 1–10 or 2–10 if we [try] hard. That's good enough. We wouldn't think we would win [against the government]; we would just think about how we [could] score a goal through teamwork, a beautiful goal so the audience and the nation would like it. The opposite team would be touched by our team spirit."

For Mr. Lu, citizen-science efforts were extremely important, even if their only outcome was to show the government that homeowners were trying to work with officials on the issue of incineration. He focused on the incremental changes he could make—equivalent to scoring one or two points against a team who could score many more—such as offering advice on waste management (e.g., establishing trash-separation procedures). In his view, it was unreasonable to evaluate achievements relative to the ultimate win, which would be the canceling of incinerator construction. These small acts of persistence, he believed, would gain admiration from government officials and allow some changes to be made. Mr. Lu's attitude shift from

CONSEQUENCES OF COMMUNITY ENVIRONMENTAL ORGANIZING

protesting against the government to embracing his own inferior position is an example of co-optation: the leader of a movement is absorbed into the government policy-making process (Mr. Lu was invited on a government-curated tour, deemed "citizen opposition leader of trash incineration," and invited to sit in on policy discussion panels), allowing the government to transform opposition into support.[13] However, in an authoritarian setting, it is a significant step for government officials to incorporate the voices of middle-class citizens into policy-making decisions, even in such a controlled manner, as opposed to involving only preselected experts.[14]

Further, although Marigold's open dissent was quelled, Mr. Lu believed that the municipal government had adopted ideas from the citizen-science report produced by their homeowner research committee, specifically the concrete changes related to government regulations of trash management and the establishment of trash-separation testing sites:

> Some people say their [the government's] goal is to buy you out. They [the government] want you to say incineration is good. But, they also feel that we should solve problems together. . . . This year, after I returned from [the incinerator tour of] Japan, my slogan was "No trash classification, no incineration; no trash legislation, no incineration." . . . Now what are the signals that the government has given me? First, they actually did pass a law. It's a draft . . . after receiving public suggestions, they passed the Beijing Municipal Waste Management Draft Regulations. Second, the city of Beijing started six hundred community testing sites [for trash separation]. The separation methods that the government issued were the ones I had suggested initially: wet and dry separation.[15]

Mr. Lu saw parallels between the citizen-science report produced by Community Marigold and the observable actions taken by the local government, specifically following his suggestions for trash separation. Also, much like Ms. Hua, who saw Rose's struggles as contributing to government awareness of the trash issue and triggering a citywide discussion, Mr. Lu perceived his efforts as influential in national discussions of trash policy, as a result of organizing and citizen science:

> Our organizing allowed people nationwide to be involved in the trash debate. I think this has historic significance. It's rare in China to have every citizen

and different levels of government agencies rationally discussing what is right, so I think this is something we're really proud of. We did not continue to intensify our protests . . . we transitioned, we used our intellect . . . we figured out what worked better in this Chinese system. We groped our way through, figuring out how to protest [using citizen science] but also figuring out a way to potentially affect government decision-making in a way that is rational and effective. So people [neighbors] tell me that we wrote history: rights preservation history. They say, "You pushed trash-separation [regulations], pushed for the establishment of environmental laws, pushed for the government's self-monitoring of administrative behavior [decision-making processes], and changing their perceptions." Regardless of what our ultimate outcome is [regarding incinerator construction], good or bad . . . Marigold citizens feel that we've already succeeded. We feel good about that.

Mr. Lu, speaking on behalf of his neighbors, felt positive about the changes they had helped bring about, believing that citizen science had led the government to shift its decision-making. He spoke more readily about the process of citizen science than about his early tactic of public protest and observed that the rational, scientific presentation of the incinerator issue allowed him to negotiate with the government and affect trash policy. Briefly addressing past protesting, he added, "Our actions pushed this [policy shift] to happen. . . . We know the government won't ever openly admit they listened to me and that my suggestions were reasonable and that it was wrong to arrest me at the time." While he seemed not to dwell on his time in detainment, it is unclear whether neighbors who were detained had similar feelings of understanding and eventual partnership with the government. The Marigold forum was quiet on these outcomes.

When I visited the three largest environmental government-organized nongovernmental organizations (GONGOs) in Beijing between 2010 and 2012, they were indeed heavily focused on promoting trash separation and recycling. As mentioned in the introduction, an environmental GONGO typically helps promote government environmental measures, usually through the distribution of pamphlets or educational booklets. The staff members I interviewed all spoke of trash-separation policies and were eager to provide me with stacks of print material on recycling. This focus indicated that the city was beginning to implement trash-separation regulations and promote education on recycling. Homeowners' push for trash separation helped introduce ideas of recycling and composting at the community level, evidenced by homeowners who were starting to talk about composting in person and online within their communities, recycling bins being placed within residential complexes, and environmental nonprofit organizations working on educational campaigns for trash separation in communities across Beijing.

Community leaders also viewed the role of government in policy *implementation* differently. Mr. Wu and Huang *laoshi*, for example, praised the role of "citizen specialists," such as community leaders, in policy implementation. They spoke of this untapped expertise—"We have so many specialists now, why can't the government use them to implement better trash management?"—and insisted that "new ideas from citizen specialists are needed." In contrast, even though Mr. Lu from Marigold believed that input from citizen science had clearly shaped government waste-management policies, he still believed that government-enforced trash separation would be more effective than community-led efforts. This attitude was likely shaped by his close relationships with government officials and the possibility that his company would eventually contract with the government: "I think [the implementation of] trash separation, whether it succeeds or not, is in the hands of the central government and whether they view this [issue] as important. . . . If they use their power, then our trash separation would for sure succeed. [A] top-down [approach] is the most effective."

What was common across all communities after their anti-incinerator struggles was a greatly improved understanding of how to navigate institutional channels. Homeowners reported that they now knew how to make complaints and provide feedback on policy decisions (even if doing so did not always yield concrete results). As Huang *laoshi* put it, a key lesson for homeowners was "learning how to interact with government agencies" through their experiences of organizing. As middle-class homeowners, they also had more leverage in negotiating with government agencies compared with other social groups because of their capacity to mobilize resources and connections. Homeowners often spoke of these connections casually but did not explicitly associate their professional networks with their class status.

A Rising Middle-Class Identity

In the process of organizing against the incinerator, some communities were able to effectively mobilize across similar middle-class communities and do so in ways that incorporated surrounding residents who were also affected by the landfill and incinerator issues. Meadow, Willow, and Pine not only successfully collaborated across their communities but also worked hard to mobilize and engage all residents in the larger area, regardless of their homeownership status. Early documents drafted by Mr. Zhao in Willow addressed the neighborhood beyond his community's gates. Representatives of the three communities eventually signed documents collectively with "residents of the area," which included working-class renters as well as businesses in the vicinity. This extensive collaboration helped Meadow, Willow, and Pine residents develop a deeper sense of civic responsibility, as they learned to think about themselves in relation to a larger, integrated neighborhood. Through their environmental organizing, homeowners learned about the people living in their larger neighborhood (chapter 3), educated themselves about government and policy-making processes (chapter 4), and developed the skills necessary to participate politically (chapter 5)—each step representing a dimension of civic responsibility. In learning about environmental challenges outside their communities, homeowners began to see themselves as part of their neighborhood and to believe that they had a responsibility to monitor and preserve the neighborhood's environmental conditions for the sake of the common good. Mr. Zhao exemplified this sense of civic responsibility in a forum post: "We need to continue what we're doing [and] actively pay attention to what is going on in the . . . neighborhood, using our specialties and privileges to take initiative, each and every one of us, [collecting] each bit of our power as a collective, together maintaining the fruits of our efforts by protecting our [environmental] rights."

Here, Mr. Zhao calls on Meadow, Willow, and Pine homeowners to stay informed about their neighborhood's environmental conditions. This passage also highlights homeowners' middle-class position: their ability to leverage specialized knowledge, social privileges such as professional networks, and access to resources. However, middle-class homeowners are identified in this passage not only by their socioeconomic status or professional networks but also by their civic-mindedness. They are citizens who care about environmental problems, and not only those in their immediate communities. Homeowners' sense of civic responsibility, cultivated through mobilizing, organizing, and collaborating, also became part of their middle-class identities.

CONSEQUENCES OF COMMUNITY ENVIRONMENTAL ORGANIZING

Like those of Meadow, Willow, and Pine, the residents of Community Rose were middle class, though they self-identified as "young homeowners." Rose homeowners also lived near several other middle-class gated homeowners' communities. However, unlike Mr. Zhao from Willow, who successfully connected people across communities, when Rose leaders organized for collective action, larger-scale neighborhood solidarity was never achieved. Rose's shorter organizing time frame may have limited the potential to foster such cross-community interactions, but few attempts to communicate beyond their gates were made, whether online or off-line. The style of activism in Rose remained individualistic, as evident in their lack of cohesive anti-incinerator messaging and their emphasis on individual actions when lodging complaints. Therefore, Rose homeowners' emerging middle-class identity was not shaped as a consequence of becoming part of a larger citizenry who cared about environmental issues. Instead, both Rose and Marigold residents defined their middle-class identity in juxtaposition to other social classes.

Near Community Rose, farmers lived in government-subsidized housing adjacent to the landfill. Ms. Hua often talked about these residents: "Nobody cares about them. . . . This government housing is for the poorest citizens of Beijing, right next to the landfill. They live closest to the pollution." Rather than describing the situation from the perspective of environmental justice—that it was the poorest people who were most likely to be unjustly situated near sources of pollution—Ms. Hua outlined the tension between middle-class homeowners and the farmers living next to the landfill:

> When we were protesting, [the farmers] were actually saying that we were jealous because they had the cheap housing. They were not even siding with us. . . . Now [the government agencies] are increasing the amount of trash being put into the landfill . . . so I don't really know what the attitudes of these poor citizens would be toward that. They may just receive compensation money; some others might just think, "Oh well, since I'm poor, I'll just bear with it." They don't know the consequences of these things . . . they could get really sick.

Comparable to the attitude of the municipal official who commented on farmers' lack of scientific knowledge (chapter 5), Ms. Hua believed that the peasant-and-farmer class did not understand the health consequences of pollution caused by trash (even though Rose homeowners also had to learn about this).

Ms. Hua also mentioned migrant workers at the landfill, whom she had seen when she snuck into the area (chapter 3):

> These workers don't have household registration, [and] nobody can prove whether they have illnesses or not, so when I later was complaining to the construction company about the incinerator, they accused me of lying: "You live several kilometers out and you're sick, but our workers are not even sick."[16] I can't see the health information of the workers, but I saw them all looking sluggish. They were emaciated and sleeping during the day! They're usually from Henan, Shandong, [and] Shaanxi provinces, with no insurance, no signed contract, no overtime pay. They have nothing; they are working hard without anything. They had a cafeteria there, too; it was so smelly, but they're eating in there! They slept during the day, in this little house without windows, on the floor.

Ms. Hua's account reflected my experience of seeing workers living in smoky conditions near the landfill by Communities Meadow, Willow, and Pine. However, her tone when describing the scene she witnessed (even more apparent in comments shared later in the chapter) emphasized concern about the problems emanating from the landfill, rather than concern for the plight of the migrant workers. Still, her account highlights the stark contrast between the upwardly mobile middle class and the lower-class migrant workers without household registration in China. Within a radius of a few kilometers, a glaring picture of inequality in housing and basic rights is observable to middle-class homeowners such as Ms. Hua (though this observation did not appear to generate an interest in advocacy or partnership; her focus remained on middle-class environmental rights).

When Mr. Wu from Community Pine took me on a tour to see the landfill in his neighborhood (described in the introduction), we passed similar farmers' housing. Unlike Ms. Hua, homeowners from Meadow, Willow, and Pine never mentioned different types of housing to me, but they did mark all housing clusters affected by incinerator construction on their citizen-science maps of the neighborhood. Their decision to acknowledge all residents showed that they were aware of variation in people's housing situation,

CONSEQUENCES OF COMMUNITY ENVIRONMENTAL ORGANIZING

including working-class residents living in government-subsidized housing and landfill workers living in dormitories. My interactions with Mr. Zhao and other community representatives also suggested that the homeowners in these communities made an effort to understand all the types of communities around them in their citizen-science research (e.g., calculating the number of people affected in each community, mapping the distance between their homes and the landfill), regardless of homeownership or social status—efforts that were not evident in Rose and Marigold.

Ms. Hua also spoke of another group of working-class residents living in the area, much closer to the incinerator construction site than Rose. They resided in older, formerly state-owned housing units that had been privatized and renovated. Although they were also homeowners, Ms. Hua never referred to them as such (even though she used the term to refer to herself and all Rose residents). In Ms. Hua's opinion, these residents purposefully ignored the landfill problem. She said that it was rumored that those residents had received government compensation and therefore did not complain about the incinerator construction. Aside from these comments, there was no evidence of Rose homeowners considering the experiences of the working-class homeowners who lived adjacent to the landfill when mobilizing for collective action.

This disregard of people of a lower socioeconomic status highlights an interesting issue: empirically, the collective idea of homeownership at the time seemed exclusively tied to middle-class distinctions or the middle-class way of life in the Chinese context. For example, online forum spaces—central to the everyday lives of middle-class communities and to their mobilization—did not include homeowners who were not residents of gated communities. Even though the platform was for *homeowners'* forums, these spaces seemed intended exclusively for the middle class. For instance, the home page leading to the forums was composed of commodity real estate advertisements and popular posts from various homeowners' forums, many of which included photos of upscale housing complexes. Accordingly, those using the platform were mainly residents of newly built gated residential complexes. The purpose of such forums was to enable homeowners to discuss renovations of upscale condominiums in massive, gated complexes, rather than renovations of small housing units located along the side of a street, and to offer help to homeowners within the gates, rather than to reach out to others living in the neighborhood.

This exclusivity was evident when Ms. Hua spoke of working-class residents. She identified them as a distinct social group even though, like her, they were definitionally homeowners. In discounting homeowners from a lower socioeconomic class, Ms. Hua adopted a tone of pride, contrasting how she and other Rose homeowners stood their ground in the anti-incinerator resistance with how working-class residents allegedly accepted government compensation rather than fighting back. This mode of distinction shows that while some ideas that reinforce middle-class identities are constructed in positive terms—for example, education, homeownership, and white-collar professions—middle-class status can also be distinguished by the negative process of exclusion.

Similar sentiments differentiating homeowners in gated communities from "others" also surfaced in Community Marigold. Frequent reference was made on their homeowners' forum to the idea that they were wealthier because they lived in villa housing (as opposed to condominiums). Notions of being wealthy and well connected also played a role in their citizen-science efforts, which drew upon professional networks and a sophisticated understanding of both scientific and political processes (chapter 5). Further, although the upper-middle-class Marigold homeowners initially chose a tactic of public and disruptive protesting, as had the Rose homeowners, Mr. Lu's retrospective account asserted that Marigold residents used "smarter" methods of protest. Mr. Lu opined that Marigold homeowners' negotiations with government via citizen science were superior to the tactics of other communities: "A lot of common citizens just go to the municipal government or the streets, causing traffic to be blocked, making a scene . . . it's illegal. I can see why people choose those actions . . . but our activities, why did they receive the attention of the entire country? We were also a rights-protection thing, but we went beyond this type of common citizen-rights preservation [tactic]. Through troublemaking we gained attention, gained the opportunity to negotiate with the government [through citizen science]."

Mr. Lu referred to other protesters as "common citizens"—an evident commentary on class—suggesting that Marigold homeowners had been able to transcend "common" protest tactics to gain leverage. This emphasis on being part of a wealthier group also appeared often in Mr. Lu's interpretations of government responses. For example, he described officials as being surprised that "wealthy citizens" would take the time to provide input on incinerator policy and evaluate the government's incineration plans, implying that wealthier citizens are not the "common citizens" typically expected to engage in rights protection in China.

Homeowners' ideas of middle-class status emerged even more prominently when they spoke of other environmental protests across China. Ms. Hua, from Rose, brought up the case of Panyu, a district of the city of Guangzhou in southern China. International media reports in 2009 described "propertied middle-class," "growing middle-class," or "burgeoning middle-class" protesters who had mobilized against incinerator construction plans in the city.[17] Before these protests, Panyu homeowners had visited a nearby incinerator in the village of Likeng, where poor farmers lived next to a functioning incinerator and had been protesting about high rates of cancer in the area since 2000.[18] Whereas Panyu's protests ended successfully in the relocation of the incinerator, the government provided no direct response to the plight of the Likeng villagers.

Ms. Hua equated the protesters from Panyu with Rose homeowners but described the protesters from Likeng in a different light: "Did you see? Panyu [incinerator] halted construction.... We [Rose] had proven you can do that—public protest. But in Likeng ... people are of lower quality ... they don't understand. They are pretty Mafia-like and mean. ... If that type of people start protesting ... how would you even negotiate with people like that? It's like 'playing lute to the cow'[19]: you can't talk sense into them."

This comment further demonstrated Ms. Hua's attitude toward groups of lower socioeconomic status, describing the farmers of Likeng as "lower-quality" people who are "Mafia-like and mean" and stating that they did not understand how to protest effectively. Considering that Rose's protest rhetoric had always been confrontational in their interactions with government officials, it is unlikely that Ms. Hua was differentiating Rose homeowners from the Likeng villagers on the basis of strategy. Rather, she seemed to point to implied differences in education (and therefore social class) and to perceived understandings of environmental issues—even though Rose homeowners had not always been able to establish the facts about the landfill or incinerator (chapter 3).

Ms. Hua's attitude toward the farmers living close to the landfill near Rose and her comments about the Likeng villagers echoed Mr. Lu's description of Marigold homeowners protesting "better" than others and with more "intellect," indicating shared sentiments toward those perceived as beneath their social class. Globally, environmental burdens are often shifted onto the poorest people.[20] While some middle- and upper-middle-class homeowners may believe they should be spared from pollution because of their higher status, this attitude did not deliver results for Rose and Marigold residents. In fact, anti-incinerator efforts were most successful in Meadow, Willow, and Pine, where homeowners incorporated a larger neighborhood into their environmental considerations and conducted research to learn more about communities of various socioeconomic statuses in the area. An inclusive effort led to the best outcomes.

In recent years, environmental organizing in China has been closely linked to the middle class and specifically to homeowners: the class of educated professionals with widespread personal connections. Stepping outside their gates to engage in problems more publicly, their middle-class identities are further solidified by acting as a group—beyond the identify of homeowner or of a single community—when they collaborate to resolve a problem that concerns people beyond their community or when they contrast themselves with others experiencing similar environmental challenges. When middle-class homeowners consider problems beyond their immediate identity as homeowners, they cultivate a sense of civic duty that allows them to move beyond single-issue organizing.

Civic Responsibility and Durable Organizing

Because representatives in Meadow, Willow, and Pine were able to mobilize volunteers across communities for organizing work, conduct surveys of residents in the area, and label maps of the neighborhood indicating people who would be affected by the incinerator, the homeowners in these communities became more acutely aware of the surroundings beyond their gates. What this awareness achieved, in addition to efficient organizing, was a cultivation of civic responsibility that extended beyond their communities. As Ms. Yu from Meadow put it, "We did this in the beginning for ourselves in the community and property values, but not anymore. It's about more than just us now; it's more than a single issue." After the decision about relocating the incinerator was made, homeowners, led by the core action committee, continued to tackle other environmental issues in the neighborhood.

CONSEQUENCES OF COMMUNITY ENVIRONMENTAL ORGANIZING

In Meadow, Willow, and Pine, leaders were able to form a durable community organization, which stayed active and met regularly over meals or tea in their homes, to discuss emerging environmental issues in the neighborhood. They also kept a watchful eye on existing pollution problems such as an old, polluting brick factory that was reportedly contaminating water sources. Having worked alongside one another for several years, the representatives naturally resumed their organizational roles. A clear division of labor could be observed: Mr. Wu was in charge of gathering environmental evaluations from government agencies. Huang *laoshi* gave talks to outside environmental organizations that were now eager to understand the communities' incinerator resistance as a successful case study (thereby earning the title of teacher, or *laoshi*). Ms. Yu organized meetings and meals, and Mr. Zhao and Ms. Ding gathered and posted environmental news and events on the online forum.

Although the neighborhood leaders were well organized, Ms. Yu told me that the community environmental organization they had formed at first remained unregistered with the government because the paperwork to become an official community organization was tedious, requiring a detailed reporting of members and meetings. However, in 2011 I found their community organization in city records, indicating that the Meadow, Willow, and Pine representatives had eventually gone ahead with official registration. The documentation-intensive process, reminiscent of filing ARs and collective complaints, would have felt familiar to these homeowners.

As part of the community organization's work at the time, Mr. Wu was advocating to shut down the polluting brick factory (which he showed me on the neighborhood tour, as described in the introduction). He told me about his progress:

> That brick factory, I went to check on them yesterday. They lied to the government that they had already updated their equipment [which filters smoke]. I then went to tell a subdistrict government official about it. I told him to go check. . . . Coals are cheaper to burn, [and] natural gas is more expensive, but [coal] pollutants are always over the limit. . . . The government actually issued an edict in 2000, saying that all such [old coal-burning] factories in Beijing should be torn down, but not all of them were. . . . This brick factory was built in 1951 . . . but is still burning coal to this day. This is bad for Beijing air pollution. They [the brick factory] are still denying it!

It appears that Mr. Wu confronted employees at the brick factory who denied that they were burning coal. Even though the government banned outdated coal-burning facilities in 2000, Mr. Wu suspected that the factory had escaped shutdown by lying about equipment updates. His decision to bring the issue to the attention of the subdistrict reflects his self-conception, cultivated through collective environmental action, as a neighbor who fulfills his civic duties. In addition to the detailed information on the brick factory's air pollution, Mr. Wu also cited figures about the factory's noise pollution based on data he had obtained from the EPB. Mr. Wu's experience organizing against the incinerator allowed him to continue research into other pollution sources in the neighborhood, bringing his findings back to Meadow, Willow, and Pine homeowners. His son was also helping him with research, he told me, indicating cross-generational involvement.

Concurrently, Mr. Zhao from Willow regrouped efforts to form a homeowners' association (HOA) (as described in chapter 2, the original attempt was cut short because of the emergence of the issue of landfill stench). This time around, homeowners' candidate profiles were posted online, listing their reasons for running. A common theme across the statements submitted by the ten candidates was an emphasis on "serving neighbors and community solidarity." The HOA—reflecting core community values of solidarity and neighborliness—was established successfully, with Mr. Zhao as a board member. In addition to the community environmental organization that the leadership group formed, Willow's HOA would also serve as a sustainable organization focused on resolving community issues.

Mr. Wu also described individual homeowners as becoming "professional petitioners" after anti-incinerator organizing. Many homeowners in the area were now well acquainted with filing letters of complaint and viewed it as their responsibility to the community to do so when a new problem materialized. He commented that the availability of the internet in the early 2000s had made information easier to access, allowing citizens to become informed and increase their environmental consciousness in ways not possible before then. In recounting these efforts, Mr. Wu was describing components of civic responsibility: homeowners engaging in active learning and participation, possessing the skills to do so, and believing they could make a difference.

Meadow, Willow, and Pine homeowners demonstrated in many ways that environmentalism and environmental awareness had become a key aspect of their lives as citizens. Ms. Yu explained to me, "We were not trash specialists, but we were forced to learn to be!" She was now composting at home to reduce waste, an action she had never taken before the anti-incinerator efforts. Meanwhile, Mr. Wu was pushing for property management in each community to implement recycling: "Homeowners' communities should do their own community management in terms of trash separation; we can cut our mixed waste in half. When I was young, there was actually a lot of metal recycling where I lived, [and] people would sell those metal scraps for money. There used to be those recycling stations, but nobody manages those now [in communities]."

Traditionally, recycling in China (and other East Asian countries) was facilitated by rubbish collectors who collected certain types of refuse (e.g., metal, aluminum, plastic, paper). Often older citizens using large hand-pushed carts or bicycles with wagons, these collectors would pass through small alleyways of neighborhoods to retrieve items and take them to recycling stations to sort and sell. As urbanization occurred, many rubbish collectors remained in older districts, but, as Mr. Wu described, newly developed residential areas did not seem to be cultivating this practice. Nonetheless, Huang *laoshi* often commented on new ways people were finding to reuse waste, citing the use of old plastic for building materials as an example.

Community Rose did not experience this type of lasting civic-mindedness. Ms. Hua often criticized homeowners in her community for not achieving more durable organizing. Describing her disappointment in fellow Rose homeowners for backing out of collective action, Ms. Hua stated, "Angry youths is a disease," complaining that young homeowners were not reliable participants in collective action. These sentiments contrasted starkly with her recollections of the early days of civic life at Rose, when homeowners organized sports teams and group outings and attended one another's weddings. Ms. Hua speculated that once the risks of collective action increased and the government and police became involved, residents' sense of responsibility toward the community faltered, regardless of the tight-knit friendships and neighborliness that had once been present.

Because of this flight from collective action, the work of organizing and citizen science fell to Ms. Hua as an individual, with some help from a small handful of other residents. A staff member of an environmental organization who met Ms. Hua at workshops told me that Ms. Hua experienced many challenges finding support in her community, indicating that she had spoken about her frustration with others. Community Rose never achieved the type of neighborhood integration seen with Meadow, Willow, and Pine. Factors contributing to the lack of durable environmental organizing in Rose include the demographics of their community, as many residents were young and individualistic and had busy schedules; having only a single representative in the community's organizing efforts; not engaging outside their gates; strong government intervention; and Ms. Hua's unfavorable views of working-class communities in the area.

Despite Ms. Hua's frustration with the lack of involvement among her neighbors, she was proud to recount her experience of organizing in Community Rose:

> My dad said that this was the most important thing I'd ever done in my entire life. My parents were scared for me . . . but you know, my dad was kind of like this when he was young. . . . He would see some injustice and report it . . . [and] he would write letters [of complaint]. . . . He once wrote an opinion piece on the railroad administration . . . they were illegally printing [inaccurate] train schedules. . . . It was published [in the] *People's Daily* back then, and he got 15 yuan in payment.[21] . . . I was ten years old when he did that.

This support from her family, even though they were fearful for her safety, was clearly a motivating factor for Ms. Hua. She considered her father to be an advocate against injustice (no matter how minor) and therefore believed that activism was also her duty. Although the broader community of homeowners did not develop a deeper sense of civic responsibility, Ms. Hua felt a transformation within herself with respect to environmental knowledge, making her an informed and engaged citizen:

> People call me "trash master" now, and to think I knew nothing about trash before this! I'm not really an expert; I mean, I do have professional knowledge—not of statistics—but I do know relevant information. . . . Even

though I know my protests failed ... [it is] one step at a time.... If because of my protests, I can stop other incinerators from being built [in other places], then it's also a success for me as a citizen. Getting people to pay attention to us, this is in itself a success, too. It wasn't that I needed the incinerator to be torn down to be successful. ... If they had torn it down, it would have just become a pile of metal waste ... that would become a bigger trash problem! ... All you can do is get government attention, let them know they need to do trash separation.... This is a success.

Ms. Hua's comment here captures her development of a broader sense of citizenship and civic responsibility. If, through her actions, she could make a difference in halting incinerator construction in other places, then she would view her efforts as a success and herself as an engaged citizen. Although she differentiated herself from a scholarly expert, she acknowledged that she had become something of a professional in terms of her trash-related environmental knowledge. In addition to pressuring the government to pay attention to issues of trash management, Ms. Hua felt that her civic duty entailed working to make government processes more transparent. She disclosed to me that she snuck a journalist friend into the courtroom during her lawsuits. "I wanted all the details to be publicly known!" she said (though what happened in the courtroom was never publicly reported).

A few years later, Ms. Hua sold her home in Community Rose, a decision that she said resulted from pollution-related health issues. She moved to another gated community across Beijing, away from the incinerator, to better recover from her respiratory problems. I spotted her posting on the homeowners' forum there, though she was not its administrator. The forum was less active than Rose's, but Ms. Hua continued to offer renovation advice and respond to posts regarding property-management fees.[22] One would expect that her civic skills would have carried over to her new community to be used when the need arose.

Similar to Ms. Hua in Rose, Mr. Lu in Marigold did not actively engage a wider array of homeowners in citizen-science efforts or in his interactions with government officials afterward. His relationship with municipal officials singled him out as a community representative without broader community agreement. Shaped by these dynamics, instead of forming a community-based organization as had been done in Meadow, Willow, and Pine, Mr. Lu decided to establish his own environmental company. The aim of his company, he told me, was to promote trash classification and separation, with a focus on processing kitchen waste in Beijing's residential communities. The company would help transform compost into fertilizer within communities (cutting transportation costs), fertilizer that Mr. Lu hoped could one day be sold for profit. After consulting with the municipal government regarding trial sites, Mr. Lu started by setting up small trash-separation sheds immediately outside a handful of residential communities across Beijing. Inside each shed were several bins for trash to be separated into, as well as simple trash-processing equipment, such as a food-waste dehydrator and a trash crusher. He hoped to run the trials for one month before working with the government to scale up his operations.[23] Mr. Lu explained his decision to register the organization as a business rather than a nonprofit:

> I believe that this has to be the business model . . . then trash separation [will] be done better. . . . It has a lot to do with different interests—government, citizens, waste collectors . . . so there needs to be a balance of these interests. Then it becomes scientific and sustainable. So, as a business, we will look for ways . . . I can't promise my way [will] succeed. But we are providing something for the government. . . . providing them with a debate, something to discuss, for them to see that we have passion and take concrete actions. We use our own money.[24] On our own, we look for ways to do this. . . . If we win, and these plans work, then the government should support this endeavor.

His statement reflected some aspects of Marigold's citizen-science report, particularly considerations of varying public and private interests (presented as cost–benefit calculations in the document). Mr. Lu also believed that the government was more likely to listen to businesses than to nonprofit organizations. Nonprofits, he said, lacked the professionalism and expertise of private companies. However, in a 2011 local news story covering his new company, it was reported that six environmental nonprofits had each offered two volunteers to help Mr. Lu run his trash-separation sheds and provide education on trash separation in the communities as he got the business up and running.

Mr. Lu registered his company in the same district as Community Marigold, and I asked him if he would try to encourage community homeowners to use his services. Although his first shed was set up outside Marigold, he emphasized that even though trash separation needs to start with individuals, it was ultimately up to the government to enforce the practice, rather than residential communities:

> Recycling has been done for decades in the U.S., [and] it has become a habit. . . . This is a hard project; we're starting from zero. [Chinese] citizens don't know how to separate trash; you have to teach them [and] give them information. Anything with education, it's going to be hard in the beginning. We can't go to every community, to each individual to give lectures. The government needs to do this. It's like the 2008 Olympics: it was great [governmental] promotion . . . so I believe that for trash problems, the government should promote it like the Olympics. Then, [trash] separation would be successful. Some government officials . . . they think that the quality or education of Chinese citizens isn't that high, so I think that's an excuse for them to do nothing. But if you do it like Olympics promotion . . . Chinese people listen. . . . In the U.S., they emphasize individuality, but here, if they [the government] say [to] support it, we support it. . . . We are responsive to the government.

This passage again demonstrates Mr. Lu's support for a strong governmental hand in implementing environmental measures. For him, trash management was a government, not a community, responsibility. This attitude contrasts with that of the Meadow, Willow, and Pine representatives, who took the reins in tackling new environmental challenges and viewed the job of monitoring pollution problems in the neighborhood as their own. Arguably, their locally powered approach may not have been as broadly effective as that of an environmental company working across many communities, but environmentalism became ingrained in the daily lives of Meadow, Willow, and Pine homeowners, enabling them to make significant positive changes in their neighborhood and inspiring other communities to take similar steps. Still, in establishing a trash-separation company, Mr. Lu exhibited his own sense of civic responsibility: staying informed about trash issues, finding solutions, and engaging in city-level government policy-making processes.

Business plans aside, at a personal level, Mr. Lu said he became more environmentally aware as a result of anti-incinerator organizing and the ease of accessing information:

> I'm more sensitive now.... Before I had little environmental awareness, but now I care about all environmental topics. It has to do with the internet, too, [and] easy information access. There is so much overlap in issues, regardless of what you majored in at school... environment, health, [the] future of the nation, all these things are tied together. Recently, I watched *An Inconvenient Truth*, the documentary by Al Gore, [and] I was so moved by it. It was the first time I realized that environmental protection isn't "Should I care?" It is "We must care." Because it's so related to our earth, our nation, and our fate.

Mr. Lu spoke of his personal investment in understanding environmental issues and recalled realizing that environmental protection is tied not only to the future of his community but also to that of the nation and the planet. Further inspired by his environmental organizing experiences, Mr. Lu ran for and was elected to an HOA board member position in Marigold in 2011. Chapter 2 described how Marigold initially formed an HOA, yet most homeowners neither knew about nor engaged with it. In his candidate election profile on the online forum, Mr. Lu promoted his company: "I designed [company name redacted] for the Beijing municipal government to set up a trash-separation system. It has been listed as a model project for the city of Beijing. The first community site has been opened and will start running soon. Through the company, I hope that I can help this community become the most famous trash-separation community in the nation, increasing the solidarity of community homeowners."

In his candidate profile, Mr. Lu tried to link his environmental company back to Community Marigold, framing it as helping Marigold residents achieve a celebrity trash-separation status (reflective of his experience rising to fame through his government designation as the anti-incinerator representative). This characterization may have been an overstatement of the company's interest in Marigold's success, yet at its core, an environmental company is a durable organizational form and was a consequence of Mr. Lu's participation in Marigold's anti-incinerator protests.

Mr. Lu followed through with his promise to focus on Marigold's trash-separation efforts. Through the HOA, he and other homeowners created

CONSEQUENCES OF COMMUNITY ENVIRONMENTAL ORGANIZING

a trash-separation committee to help implement the practice in the community. When we last spoke in 2012, he said that he planned to mobilize more homeowners to join the effort, including by creating and distributing an instructional handbook to residents in the area, including those beyond Marigold's gates.

Although homeowners' environmental protests across all communities had subsided by 2010, Mr. Bo, the environmental organization staff member, told me he believed that homeowners were continuing to spread environmental awareness across the city on topics such as trash separation and trash management. He further acknowledged that, across the three community sites, citizen specialists had emerged from anti-incinerator organizing. These individuals had educated themselves on environmental issues during the process and were still learning about environmental issues after protests had ended. Recognizing the importance of these citizen scientists, several environmental organizations ran workshops inviting homeowners to attend to share their organizing experiences and trash-management expertise. Their perspectives allowed the staff of environmental organizations and government experts in attendance to hear firsthand accounts of Beijing citizens confronting pollution and to learn more about these issues in the contexts of communities and neighborhoods.

Becoming Part of Environmental Civil Society

Although most homeowners did not succeed in reversing decisions about incinerator construction or achieving breakthroughs in government policies, an important unintended consequence of their community organizing was the incorporation of citizen voices into environmental civil society, which comprises a constellation of nongovernmental organizations (NGOs), groups, and actors who address environmental issues. This process was set in motion with homeowners' increased presence at the events and on the forums of environmental nonprofit organizations, along with media coverage of their work.

Initially, I was surprised to learn that the homeowners involved in the three anti-incinerator organizing efforts had not known much about one another until meeting at an event in 2010. The lack of community interaction across the city can be attributed to general government restrictions in media coverage of protest events and information. In the early 2000s, this type of information suppression was common across Chinese protests. Censorship contributed to the cellularization of protests even when residents fought for similar issues and were located in the same city. Local press rarely focused on citizen resistance because of censorship concerns. As mentioned in the introduction, the reporting of news in China is often delayed, and local media may hide information about protests in their region, not reporting on them until more remote news sources cover the story first.[25] When journalists do cover news involving criticism of the government, they may distort or choose not to present certain information in their stories to avoid being censored. Because of the lack of intercommunity knowledge, environmental NGOs—which do not participate in contentious protests—played a critical role in bringing together disparate and far-flung communities that were fighting incinerator construction.

Community leaders from Meadow, Rose, and Marigold met for the first time at a 2010 environmental salon in Beijing hosted by the environmental organization for which Mr. Bo worked. Gathered in a small conference room, Huang *laoshi*, Ms. Hua, and Mr. Lu were finally able to share personal experiences in conversation with one another in front of an audience, and in private afterward, marking the convergence of these three anti-incinerator movements that had occurred in Beijing. Ms. Hua shared stories of her pollution-triggered illnesses, Mr. Lu talked about his new company, and Huang *laoshi* asked about the current state of the incinerators near Rose and Marigold. Huang *laoshi* learned about Mr. Lu's plans for trash separation and found them incredibly innovative, he later told me. Overcoming fragmented urban associational spaces remains a challenge in an authoritarian setting, yet here, equipped with citizen-science expertise, these homeowners were given a public platform to share their stories with many people—an opportunity for which the community representatives had long yearned.

Mr. Bo's organization became the setting for this convergence because of its gradual shift toward including homeowners' voices. During the anti-incineration struggles, the organization had been involved in some bottom-up grassroots efforts, particularly in the area of providing education about trash separation and running battery-recycling campaigns. Toward the end of 2010, the organization started drafting policy recommendations for environmental government agencies suggesting trash-sorting measures.[26] Simultaneously, organization staff who were seeking speakers with expertise in trash incineration and waste management began to invite not only academic specialists (some appointed by the government) but also the community activists who had come to be known as "citizen specialists." Huang *laoshi* and Mr. Lu, in particular, would go on to become frequent workshop speakers.

At the first salon—with an audience of representatives of environmental organizations, members of the public who held organization memberships, academics, and government specialists—Huang *laoshi* presented an elaborate PowerPoint presentation titled "Incinerator Case Study Analysis" based on the anti-incinerator organizing of Meadow, Willow, and Pine. In a recording provided by the nonprofit, I heard Huang *laoshi* provide an overview of dioxins and other health threats of incineration; present information on the incinerator project near the Meadow, Willow, and Pine communities; and describe the actions taken by homeowners. It was Huang *laoshi*'s first salon, yet he sounded as if he had been giving the talk for years. He mentioned the institutional channels pursued by homeowners but focused on presenting the data collected by the community, pointing out the problem they had found in the EIA regarding wind direction and describing how the gathering of public opinion had been absent before the incinerator project was authorized. He also incorporated the results of the community survey Mr. Wu had conducted on the number of cancer-related deaths in the community.

On the PowerPoint slides, Huang *laoshi* listed the consequences of environmental organizing for the Meadow, Willow, and Pine communities:

1) Learned environmental protection and environmental evaluation knowledge
2) Visited related specialists
3) Learned laws and regulations
4) Gained knowledge from lawyers and academics who knew about environmental protection
5) Actively communicated with environmental agencies
6) Learned how to exert pressure on government agencies (through administrative reconsiderations, letter-writing, [and] telephone complaints)
7) Allowed more of the public to understand the situation (through posters, banners, [and] online forums)
8) Used the internet comprehensively (for research, promotion, [and] communication)
9) Gained the attention and support of the media eventually[27]

This list reflected my conversations with Huang *laoshi* and other homeowners (although in the workshop setting, the role of academics and lawyers in helping their cause was emphasized more, likely for the benefit of the audience). Reflecting the journey of Meadow, Willow, and Pine homeowners, Huang *laoshi* heavily emphasized that learning—about environmental science, laws, and institutional channels—was critical in the communities' early mobilizing efforts, when every document and discovery was uploaded to the online forum for joint discussion and feedback (chapter 4).

Mr. Lu from Marigold was also a frequent favorite at such nonprofit workshops, another organization staff member told me, because he was a charismatic speaker with humorous analogies (for example, joking that he and the government are like husband and wife, always bickering but still loving each other at the end of the day). Mr. Lu was always the sole representative from Marigold in attendance, indicating that environmental organizations considered him the leading voice of his community. During workshops, Mr. Lu mostly spoke about his international incinerator tour and the formation of his new company, rather than his public resistance. Always aiming to engage the audience at these events, Mr. Lu told me, "You can see my character, my attitude. Environmental organizations remember me deeply. All the boring forums they hold, if I attend, it's different ... then it doesn't sound like a stuffy environmental speech. I want them to not view these issues as political. We should have a happy attitude, like we're acting out a comedy with government officials. We don't want a tragic ending, culminating in them knocking us down."

Here, Mr. Lu implies that politics can seem to be a heavy and serious topic, a reflection of his earlier struggles and interactions with the government. Later, as he embraced his civic duty to address the urban waste-management problem and his new passion for environmental causes—and clearly enjoyed the government's blessing of his efforts and the attention from the media and the public—he became much more lighthearted about trash and pollution issues. Mr. Lu never spoke of his detainment (chapter 4) at such events, focusing instead on his improved relationship with government officials over time and his experiences with sharing citizen-science suggestions.

Ms. Hua occasionally attended these workshops but only spoke at the first one, about her illness and her citizen-science photo collection: a "pollution diary," she called it. One environmental nonprofit, however,

CONSEQUENCES OF COMMUNITY ENVIRONMENTAL ORGANIZING

presented her with a "citizen journalist award" for her careful recording and documentation of Community Rose pollution. Ms. Hua explained the media's shift in attitude toward her because of the award:

> I received an award from the environmental nonprofit . . . it was an environmental reporting award. The award money was 10,000 yuan, and I had to pay 2,000 yuan in taxes. . . . Anyway, I went to receive the award. I was shocked [that] there were so many reporters there [at the award event], even [from] central news channels. So, after receiving the award, my contact information was displayed on the organization's website. The information was discovered by journalists. All the contact [with journalists] was through the environmental organization. Whoever wanted to talk about trash, they would get my number through the organization. . . . Ha! In the beginning [of community organizing], I was crying, begging for reporters to come cover our struggles. . . . Like when the *chengguan* abused us [during the protests], they wouldn't come; they wouldn't dare report that. So now I'm finally noticed by reporters; even if I don't feel like meeting with them, they still insist on doing interviews.

Ms. Hua's observations reflected journalists' hesitancy in covering protests at the time of occurrence. Often in China, only in the aftermath of struggles are protest activities covered, and, even then, the reports are typically spun in a positive light to avoid government censorship. In this case, Ms. Hua was now a citizen environmental journalist who collected data documenting her community's struggle with pollution rather than a community troublemaker showing up to argue with government officials. This progression also resembles Mr. Lu's experience with the media. Rather than being portrayed as the activist who was detained for protesting publicly, months later, he was primarily reported on as the official "citizen opposition to trash incineration" who was a lawyer and lived in a villa community.

Ms. Hua reflected on the transition to incorporating anti-incinerator voices and ideas into trash-management dialogue in various venues:

> You know, it's changed . . . workshops I knew used to be composed of incinerator or landfill management company leaders or government officials; now it's all these scholars, specialists, and citizens who come to participate. It's changed! The attitude has changed. . . . Now when people talk about the

issue... like on my text message threads, I get shared posts that say, "Our land has been used as landfills; we're running out of space; let's recycle and do trash separation!" Before, I would get messages that say, "We've only used three-quarters of the landfill; we need to build incinerators!"[28] So the atmosphere is different now. Specialists who attend [workshops] now talk about organic fertilizers and composting. I am so happy.

In a rare expression of pleasure, Ms. Hua marveled at seeing citizen representatives and environmental experts participating in environmental discussions. Even nonprofit organizational news had shifted from incineration as a solution to the promotion of recycling. Homeowners' newfound roles in environmental education—through salons, citizen science, and citizen journalism[29]—demonstrated the incorporation of their voices into environmental civil society. Within these roles, community representatives found further ways to engage in the events of environmental organizations. To be able to participate in more nonprofit-organized conferences, Ms. Hua became a member of the group that presented her with the award.[30]

Similarly, Meadow, Willow, and Pine experienced a notable change in their communities when a surge in online posts related to events and activities of environmental organizations occurred after the incinerator had been relocated. Information on public talks about environmental protection featuring environmental photographers, environmental film screenings, or scheduled nature outings was often posted by Mr. Zhao on all three community forums. This activity showed that interactions between environmental organizations and homeowners in these communities were likely increasing.

For example, a call for applications was released by Mr. Bo's organization in conjunction with a charity foundation, recruiting "model families" willing to experiment with trash separation in their homes. Mr. Zhao, who told me that he had become increasingly involved in the activities of this organization, circulated the post widely. The organization was looking to enter the community to work with families and educate them on composting. Participants would receive perks: free composting bags and a discount when attending organizational events.

On the forum, Mr. Zhao encouraged homeowners to participate: "Let's implement trash separation [and] decrease trash production for us and for others, for our country, for our people. Hoping more and more families join, sustainably, little by little. [One day] we won't have to smell the stench of trash . . . this is not a farfetched dream." Following Mr. Zhao's typical rhetoric around collective responsibility, he believed that the impact of trash separation would extend beyond Meadow, Willow, and Pine. Around fifty households signed up to be model families, and the organization made arrangements to enter the communities, particularly Meadow and Willow, to conduct promotional activities. At one of the first events, the organization set up a stage, provided pamphlets on trash separation and "green living," and encouraged more people to sign up as model families.

I tagged along with staff members in 2011 to observe the organization's role in Meadow. The staff was on its first return visit after starting the model-family trash-separation campaign the previous year. This type of revisiting was rare, Mr. Bo told me. It was hard for the organization to assess the concrete outcomes of their educational programs, mostly because of a lack of resources. He also told me that in the midst of their educational program, they had been barred from holding events in Community Meadow because the name of the community contained a sensitive term that was censored for a period of time in China.[31] Sure enough, we were denied entrance at the guard station at Meadow's gate, which I had easily passed through (after registering my name) during my initial visit to the community the year before. After some calls, a homeowner hurried out to receive us at the gate. This obstacle revealed one of the challenges faced by environmental organizations working in an authoritarian setting: an apolitical educational campaign about recycling could suddenly be restricted because of unrelated censorship rules.

With a list of names, phone numbers, and unit numbers of homeowners, two staff members and I walked from building to building, pressing buzzers. The first few buzzers went unanswered. "They said they'd be home," one staff member told me, puzzled. We tried several others, but no one answered. Finally, a staff member called Huang *laoshi* on his cell phone, prompting him to come dashing out of his building. He had been watching his grandson and missed the buzzer. Huang *laoshi* presented a little cardboard booklet with the words "Green Passport" on the cover to the staff member, who proceeded to stamp the booklet to indicate that Huang *laoshi* was following the trash-separation rules (although the staff member did not verify that this was actually the case).

I asked Huang *laoshi* what he was doing in terms of trash separation in the home, and he told me that he had a tiny countertop waste bin for kitchen compost. Even his young grandson was learning what to put in the bin, he told me. That conversation reminded him that he had left the child alone at home, so he hurried home, cutting the conversation short.

We were unable to find anyone else in the community wishing to get their passport stamped. Considering that this campaign was conducted in a community that was self-motivated to practice trash separation because of their environmental organizing experiences, the lack of engagement was discouraging. One possibility could be that trash separation was being actively practiced at home, but residents were avoiding public interactions with the organization due to the government restrictions and censorship mentioned above. Still, our experience at Meadow highlighted not only the uphill battle nonprofits face when designing and implementing community campaigns, but also when collecting community feedback or measuring program outcomes.

Inspiring Environmental Participation?

During the span of organizing for all three community sites (from about 2005 to 2010), I could find only three instances of a forum post mentioning one of the other communities, and none mentioned Marigold. These posts were (1) Mr. Zhao of Willow sharing a news article on waste incineration on Rose's forum following Meadow, Willow, and Pine's first wave of organizing; (2) Ms. Hua of Rose sharing a link on the Rose forum about Meadow's success in relocating the incinerator; and (3) a resident of Meadow posting a link to a news article on Meadow's forum about Ms. Hua's environmental journalism award, after residents of the communities had already met in person at the environmental salon.

These efforts may not have been so isolated had they occurred a few years later. The environmental organizing of these communities occurred at a historic juncture, right before the popularized ascent of social media in China, which included online forums, blogs, and platforms for citizen journalism. However, even when homeowners in Meadow, Willow, and Pine did hear about other homeowners' incinerator struggles, the representatives said they had not had the capacity to help farther-flung communities. When Rose began its resistance, Meadow, Willow and Pine were preparing to launch their second wave of organizing (after their citizen-science efforts). Showing frustration with the limits of their ability to help, Ms. Yu said,

> We care about other incinerators, but there is not much we can do . . . they're being built everywhere! We had a very active homeowner; he was originally one of the mobilizers in our community [in the first wave]. I called him [during the second wave], [but] he didn't pick up . . . so I asked another homeowner, [and] they told me he sold his house! I asked, "Where did he buy?" It turned out that he bought his new place near Marigold, the incinerator construction site! He was so angry. He really cared about our community environment issue, but in the end he felt that there was no hope so he sold it . . . but he can't hide [from other incinerators]![32]

As this example of homeowner relocation shows, even though middle-class homeowners gained civic skills, a sense of civic responsibility, and environmental knowledge from their organizing experiences, incinerators continued to be built across the country. Despite community leaders' many talks at environmental conferences, very little knowledge appeared to be carried from one community's protest to another's.

I was able to find only one example of an anti-incinerator effort that drew on the successes of Meadow, Willow, and Pine. It was a rural anti-incinerator protest in Zhejiang, a province nearly 1,500 kilometers from Beijing. Local farmers had discovered plans to build an incinerator in 2009 but at the time were warned by local officials not to cause trouble. After seeing a news feature on incineration in early 2010, some farmers became worried about the harmful effects. Simultaneously, increasing news coverage of environmental experts opposing incineration (spurred by community resistance in Beijing) reached the Zhejiang villagers.[33] Younger villagers with access to the internet found the citizen-science booklet produced by Meadow, Willow, and Pine homeowners online and available for download.

According to Bondes and Johnson, the farmers viewed the booklet as a critical part of their own resistance effort. The farmers distributed printed copies of the booklet for everyone in the village to read and then collected signatures opposing the incinerator construction. One farmer said that, had he not come across the booklet, no villager would have believed him when he explained the dangers of incinerator pollution.[34] After reading the booklet, which documented the health effects of pollution, villagers came together to oppose the project. In other words, Meadow, Willow, and Pine's citizen-science booklet contained the information villagers needed to persuade more people to mobilize. However, unlike middle-class homeowners, the farmers did not seem to have the capacity to launch their own citizen-science effort with regard to their specific incinerator threat; for example, they had no professionals within their communities, and they lacked the time needed to conduct research and implement surveys. Instead, they relied on the information provided in the booklet.

However, the farmers eventually attracted the attention of environmental scholars in Beijing (whose names and ideas were mentioned in Meadow, Willow, and Pine's booklet). One in particular helped them understand the EIA for their incinerator project and pointed out flaws that provided the basis of the villagers' subsequent environmental litigation, with which they were aided by a legal scholar. These scholars also helped the farmers reframe the focus of their environmental resistance from issues of land and local corruption (which some locals perceived to be part of the problem) to issues of pollution and environmental hazards, following Meadow, Willow, and Pine's rhetoric. However, Bondes and Johnson note that the scholars had something to gain from their collaboration with the Zhejiang villagers, whereas Beijing's incinerator resistance had been relatively successful on its own, without scholar collaboration. They argue that these scholars were, to some extent, "embedded" within the Party and that one of their goals was to use the case of the farmers' resistance as "a precedent for advancing better environmental governance practices within the existing one-party system." With the help of the scholars, the incinerator project was postponed and remained so as of the latest news update in 2018.[35]

The case of the farmers' anti-incinerator resistance shows that middle-class organizing and its corresponding citizen-science efforts can have far-reaching effects. A farmer who was interviewed for Bondes and Johnson's case study of Zhejiang commented on Meadow, Willow, and Pine: "We drew a lesson from them; we learned from them. We used their strong points to mend our shortcomings. Because they understand everything. So we also drew a lesson from their methods to do this. . . . If it hadn't been for [them], we really wouldn't have known . . . from where to start."[36]

Having now charted the anti-incinerator journey of the Meadow, Willow, and Pine homeowners, it is interesting to note that this farmer referred to the homeowners as "understanding everything." The process of moving from bewilderment to "understanding everything" was a long one and full of informational uncertainty, framing and reframing, strategy development through trial and error, and long-term organizing and community engagement. Further, to gather evidence for the booklet through citizen-science efforts and determine which methods would be successful, middle-class homeowners had to leverage their professional and social networks, the civic skills they had developed through informal organizing, and the technical knowledge they had gained from their own educational and professional backgrounds, as well as their research efforts.

The consequences of community organizing are reflected in the newly cultivated civic life of middle-class homeowners. Community leaders in urban Beijing's gated housing communities perceived that their organizing efforts had made a difference. Their collective efforts demonstrated that protesting was possible and that they could bring environmental issues to government attention. More importantly, even though engagement varied across communities, homeowners' efforts left behind a legacy of increased environmental awareness, deeper understanding of environmental laws and rights, insights into how the government operated, civic skills, and leadership abilities. The citizen science that occurred in these communities also deepened middle-class environmental participation, requiring homeowners to research and interpret complex information. In this way, citizen science promoted meaningful participation and a sense of civic duty. Although the three community sites were unable to converge during their collective action, this large group of urban middle-class homeowners cultivated sets of skills and the capacity for organizing locally. These skills, accompanied by a sense of civic responsibility as Beijing citizens, are reflected in many homeowners' continued environmental efforts—whether in the form of an environmental company, a community organization, or recycling and composting at home.

CONCLUSION

Environmental organizing emerged in an unlikely place in the early 2000s: new urban gated residential communities in authoritarian China. This book traces the beginnings of the associational lives of the residents of these communities, middle-class homeowners, after significant shifts in housing policy dissolved prior work-unit living arrangements. With the privatization of housing, new urban residential communities came to offer an important space for the cultivation of everyday civic participation in China. Whether in the form of homeowners' associations (HOAs), local sports clubs, or, increasingly, environmental organizations, middle-class homeowners became meaningfully engaged in shaping community affairs.

The book centers on a set of questions about how government forces intersect with evolving ideas of citizenship in newly middle-class spaces: How does middle-class home ownership lead to the formation of associational life in an authoritarian setting, and what does associational life rooted in these new housing communities look like? How might urban homeownership cultivate civic skills and capacity for organizing under authoritarianism? In what ways and to what extent does the state shape homeowners' sense of civic duty and engagement as urban citizens?

To address these questions, the book compares three case studies in which environmental threats from landfills and incinerator construction projects plagued middle-class, first-time homeowners in Beijing. Initially, few homeowners moving into these communities spoke up or took action against the creeping landfill stench experienced at each location. Over time, however, as residents learned to organize informal community activities, file letters of complaint against property developers about housing construction issues, and form HOAs to address community problems overlooked by property management, they developed the skills and capacities needed for collective action and organizing. Middle-class homeowners across residential communities in Beijing not only formed networks of trust and information but also cultivated community leadership and experience that readied them to take later action against incinerator construction projects. Although the degree and effectiveness of associational life and subsequent environmental organizing varied among communities, a collective identity of "homeowner" was developed at each site, along with a sense of community belonging.

All the communities featured in this book—identified by the pseudonyms Meadow, Willow, Pine, Rose, and Marigold—engaged in varying forms of collective action, from petitioning to street demonstrations to citizen science, yet they experienced divergent outcomes. Careful readers may have picked up on the color-coding symbolism of the names chosen to represent the communities. Neighboring communities Meadow, Willow, and Pine were the "green-light" communities in which environmental organizing moved steadily forward and achieved the most success. Within and among these three co-located communities, community representatives and leaders were more inclusive and more effective in engaging the majority of homeowners to make sense of environmental problems, strategize protest actions, and collect citizen-science data. Because of their approach, collective organizing against incinerator construction was sustained over a period of several years, resulting not only in the relocation of the planned incinerator but also in the establishment of a durable environmental organization that continued to tackle other pollution issues in the neighborhood. In contrast, Community Rose was the "red-light" case study in which progress stopped short because of a lack of community cohesion and a high degree of government repression. Results in "yellow-light" Community Marigold were harder to classify as either thriving or failing: the most active community leader was co-opted by the government to publicly represent community environmental interests. He continued to advocate for improved environmental practices but did so primarily as an individual

CONCLUSION

government partner and business owner rather than as a community leader bringing together fellow homeowners.

Homeowners are the protagonists in this story, yet government officials also played key roles. Whether Beijing homeowners were able to effectively use their skills beyond their gates to address environmental issues was conditioned by the actions of the authoritarian state. The legitimacy of petitioning, protest, and citizen science—though all are legal in China—is contingent upon government response. Government response also influences the degree of homeowners' participation and engagement in political processes and institutional channels, ultimately shaping their perceptions of civic duty. In the process of organizing, homeowners learned that public displays such as banners and demonstrations led to government intervention. Government officials and police also intervened in both online and off-line private community spaces during periods of organizing, exercising repression ranging from online information control and censorship to police visits to people's homes. In contrast, homeowners discovered that citizen science was an effective tool for establishing dialogue with local government officials, if used in conjunction with institutional channels. Communities that successfully navigated these government systems created more robust and enduring associations, whereas those that experienced stronger repression became less involved in collective organizing. In short, although these new middle-class communities were able to build capacity to organize, the Chinese state determined the degree to which citizen civic engagement was possible for them.

These three contrasting community examples demonstrate how newly emerging Beijing housing spaces have served as schools of democracy for resident participation in community affairs. Their "training exercise" took the form of attempting to establish HOAs to monitor property developers, which prepared homeowners not only to organize collectively against incinerator construction in their neighborhoods but also to engage in larger political processes.

This book carves a new channel of inquiry by emphasizing the building of *civic capacity* in new communities that organized against incinerator construction, rather than the specific *events* of collective action. Prior studies of Chinese social movements have recounted similar homeowners' struggles, but most have focused on protest events, rather than on why and how homeowners were able to organize effectively. For example, homeowners in the southern city of Guangzhou organized against road construction in their neighborhood, filing petitions and lawsuits and protesting, ultimately bringing the construction company to the table for dialogue.[1] Studies of such cases examine who took what actions in the actual confrontation, yet it is important to recognize that these homeowners did not build their community networks overnight. Living together in the same spatial setting, sharing an online homeowners' forum or chat group, and jointly shaping their collective identity as homeowners enabled the residents studied in this book to move toward large-scale mobilization. The idea of capacity centers on the informational networks homeowners establish, the formation of community membership, and the cultivation of community leadership and representation, along with the experiences and civic skills gained from everyday community participation such as by planning group purchases or engaging in social activities. By examining these factors, the case studies in this book go beyond the short-lived spectacle of protest events to investigate how and when homeowners succeed or fail in overcoming obstacles to longer-term organizing.

Additionally, this book aims to shed light on middle-class associational life in authoritarian settings and the unexpected durability of civic life in the face of constant government intervention. The persistence of urban homeowners in engaging with political processes shows that, even with the continuous presence of government and police in their online and offline private community spaces, most residents actively looked for ways to overcome soft repression of their dissent. Counterintuitively, many homeowners did not fear intervention; instead, they made jokes, sometimes even sympathizing with police, and shared strategies for circumventing government monitoring.

Political scientists studying civil society in the Chinese setting provide in-depth explanations of authoritarian stability[2] and argue that even with the current "threat" of an open internet, increased public dissent, and contentious protest activities, the authoritarian state has maintained control.[3] This book adds nuance to their argument by highlighting how civil society can be actively created in restrictive contexts and how urban homeowners play important and proactive roles in reinforcing the resiliency of civic spaces. The durability of authoritarian influence is in some sense mirrored by the persistence of citizen organizing. Citizen-science efforts in these communities also show the unique capacity of the middle class to challenge and resist the government's informational authority: Beijing homeowners gathered their own data to contest government conclusions on the environmental health impact of trash incinerators.

THE CIVIC CAPACITY OF BEIJING HOMEOWNERS

Urbanization can shape how and where new civic spaces arise. In rapidly urbanizing areas of developing nations, the spatial distribution of citizens' living arrangements can transform in a short span of time. And these new urban housing communities can become stable spaces for civic participation in a dynamic urban environment.

As described in chapter 1, the work-unit system formed the structure of social organization in China for more than four decades. Within this system, most urban residents' homes and family lives were intrinsically tied to their work status, with their local community composed of their fellow workers. Beginning in the 1990s, as authorities became concerned that urban housing shortages and substandard living conditions would motivate social unrest, the state began to privatize housing, newly allowing urban residents to purchase homes. In less than two decades, China shifted from predominantly public housing to having one of the highest rates of homeownership in the world.[4] This shift was explicitly encouraged by the central government: Chinese cities were instructed to speed up the monetization of housing and embrace private homeownership.[5] New commercial housing was built at an unprecedented pace; scholars have described the rapid proliferation of middle-class and upper-middle-class gated enclaves in Chinese cities from the mid-1990s onward.[6]

The explosion of privatized housing was part of a landmark change in the spatial composition of urban China. What was until that time rural land abruptly transformed not only into expansive housing developments but also key economic and high-tech development zones, shopping centers, and university campuses. In the early 2000s, new gated and semigated communities, often consisting of many thousands of households, were constructed across Beijing to attract middle-class homebuyers engaged in the urbanizing economy.

For the first time, these residents had agency in choosing their housing. New homeowners also began to understand property rights and learn how to protect these rights—not only as individuals but also collectively with other first-time homeowners in their new communities. As part of this process,

CONCLUSION

informal housing associations began to form (chapter 2). The gated nature of the communities facilitated this formation through the development of homeowners' collective identities and neighborly associational life. Within community walls, homeowners could interact in shared spaces such as courtyards and parking lots, plan community events, and compare notes on property management.

In addition to these in-person interactions, homeowners engaged in frequent and active discussions on online forums specific to their housing communities. In Communities Meadow and Willow, homeowners were setting up meetings to discuss property development and management issues even before construction had been completed. The formation of a shared "homeowner" identity had begun prior to moving in, catalyzed by the common challenges homebuyers faced in securing the facilities, amenities, and services promised in their purchase agreements. In all the case-study communities, residents took pride in being homeowners—specifically in owning homes in their respective communities—and actively looked for ways to contribute to their communities, whether through organizing group purchases, documenting homeowners' meeting minutes, or drafting letters of complaint against property management. Through these group activities, residents' homeowner identities were tied to one another and to the spaces they collectively occupied.

These observations contrast with some of the prior scholarship on middle-class homeownership. Li Zhang, an anthropologist studying Chinese middle-class housing, described middle-class homeowners as shying away from public participation, indicating that this retreat was facilitated by the privacy newly afforded by gated condominium complexes.[7] Studies of middle-class suburban communities in the United States have recounted similar "withdrawal" from the surrounding social structure.[8] In juxtaposition to these studies, this book expands on the notion of participation, arguing that even the most mundane interactions can lay foundations and establish networks (i.e., capacity) for future collective organizing. Putting together a community sports club, for example, requires networks to be formed, documents to be produced, and group decision-making processes to be clarified. In this way, associational life builds and reinforces community networks, skills, and experiences on which residents may later draw in larger-scale mobilization. Civic capacity is thereby fostered in these residential community spaces through seemingly inward-facing actions.

CONCLUSION

One explanation for the departure from Zhang's conclusions may be found in this book's focus on activity at the level of the residential community and its examination of the processes of community building that necessarily precede, but do not always ensure, effective mobilization. Researching the case-study communities by attending community meetings, talking to community leaders, and tracking more than a decade's worth of activity on online homeowners' forums allowed for observations of both successful and failed instances of mobilization. Within scholarship, failed attempts at collective action are often overlooked, in part because they may not be documented, leaving the impression of a lack of participation. Drilling into the online and off-line communal discussions that took place not only in the successfully mobilized communities of Meadow, Willow, and Pine but also in the more challenged contexts of Rose and Marigold reveals the collective organizing that occurred behind the scenes in all communities, even those that did not achieve broader influence. Although Rose and Marigold did not meet their goals of preventing incinerator construction, these communities nevertheless demonstrate the potential to become schools of democracy that teach civic skills, as many homeowners in these Beijing enclaves proved consistently eager to contribute to community organizing and still more remained attuned to receiving pertinent information and following discussions.

The issue that motivated a turn outward, beyond the gates, at first appeared to be a residential problem. When homeowners experienced a rotting smell, they were faced with uncertainty regarding its source and began searching for information (chapter 3). Some communities—Meadow, Willow, and Pine—were able to collectively make sense of the problem through the work of leaders who linked resident discussions across community boundaries and articulated the issue in ways that highlighted the need for collective action. These key figures bridged off-line conversation with online forum activity, incorporating information on the landfill and incinerator construction, homeowners' experiences of the growing stench, and an analysis of the likely environmental and health outcomes of incineration. In facilitating and participating in this collective sensemaking process, homeowners in Meadow, Willow, and Pine came to view addressing the landfill problem as a collective responsibility, holding one another accountable when it came time to mobilize.

CONCLUSION

In contrast, neither Rose homeowners nor those in Marigold achieved collective sensemaking, despite the large number of individuals complaining to one another about the stench. In Community Marigold, homeowners learned of the plans for incinerator construction, yet no community representative stepped up to guide a response. The Marigold online forum could have supported the sharing and interpretation of this common grievance in the same manner as those of Meadow, Willow, and Pine, but Marigold's looser social network (which mirrored its more dispersed physical layout) appeared to preclude this type of online mobilization. In Rose, though civic life was vibrant among its younger homeowners, leaders focused on encouraging individual actions, such as calling government complaint hotlines, rather than providing a common framing to seek collective redress. In Meadow, Willow, and Pine, the focus of community leadership on knitting together individuals' efforts was pivotal in shaping the strategic direction of their anti-incinerator organizing—and prompting government responses to their demands. Through these activities, community leaders helped develop homeowners' civic skills and their civic capacity, laying the groundwork for more durable community-based organizations to be established.

Similar to movement leaders in a democratic context, these Chinese community representatives played important roles in organizing collective efforts, articulating community grievances, and engaging with government officials. In this authoritarian context, however, representatives also took on the challenge of directly confronting repression. Leaders in Meadow, Willow, and Pine emphasized their diplomatic relationships with government officials and their in-depth knowledge of government structure and function as critical aspects of their successful campaign. In contrast, the leader of Rose, Ms. Hua, described herself as being in open conflict with local government officials, and the leader of Marigold, Mr. Lu, appeared to shift allegiance such that he became at least as tied to the municipal government as to his residential community.

The attitudes of homeowners toward government actors can in some ways be seen as extensions of their communities' earlier approaches to property developers and management. During anti-incinerator organizing, collective petitions were often worded similarly to letters of complaint sent to property developers (chapter 4). This evolution demonstrates how letter-writing skills cultivated at the level of the residential community

CONCLUSION

were applied to larger issues. Similarly, using the networks they had developed through residential communal life, homeowners were able to quickly organize emergency meetings to discuss incinerator construction, collect funding to create posters and banners, and mobilize for demonstrations. Again, these case studies demonstrate the groundwork that an exclusive focus on protest events does not capture. Communication networks and cooperative relationships were in place *before* residents were faced with an external environmental threat. The social cohesion and mutual trust established among neighbors shaped their willingness to intervene on behalf of the common good. Thus, new housing communities are places where collective efficacy is nurtured.

Middle-class housing communities in Beijing serve as civic training schools, cultivating skills by which the growing middle class can become more politically engaged. To be sure, its level of involvement is conditioned by state responses to community organizing, which itself is shaped by organizing strategies, framing, and rhetoric, as well as leaders' understandings of their roles in relation to the state. However, even in the digital era, organizing arises from and is tied to physical space. While much mobilization takes place online, meaningful online interactions are built on trust established off-line.

Some communities were able to build durable environmental organizations that survived beyond anti-incinerator mobilization (chapter 6). Regardless of the government's ultimate decisions on incinerator construction, most communities continued to work on trash-related issues such as trash separation and recycling or expanded their efforts to monitoring pollution issues in the larger neighborhood. In Meadow, Willow, and Pine, community representatives—having already organized events and protests together for several years—were able to form a durable organization that met regularly to discuss environmental issues in the neighborhood such as polluting emissions from an old brick factory and waterway pollution. Willow also successfully established an HOA, which committed to continuing to monitor trash-related concerns. In Community Marigold, rather than forming a community-based organization, leader Mr. Lu decided to establish his own environmental company serving a number of Beijing residential communities to promote trash classification and separation, including processing kitchen waste.

CONCLUSION

COMMUNITY AND ENVIRONMENTAL ORGANIZING IN CONTEMPORARY CHINA

The case studies featured in this book are not anomalies; they reflect broader trends of community and environmental organizing in China. In 2009, toward the end of the featured communities' anti-incinerator organizing efforts, a community organization registration (i.e., reporting) system was officially established. Based on government registration data, from 2010 to 2018, registration reached its highest monthly level following the announcement of reporting requirements and surged again when registration procedures were simplified. Looking exclusively at the registration of community environmental organizations reveals similar growth trends, with the highest peak seen following a relaxation of reporting requirements. These data reflect community organizations that specifically register as "environmental" or have "environmental protection" or "environmentalism" in their names. The data likely underestimate the number of environmentally focused efforts, as this accounting does not capture, for example, community organizations that might be registered as book clubs but read environmental texts or outdoor adventure clubs that also participate in trash cleanup. Additionally, "general-topic" community organizations—typically those established by and named after housing communities—often address environmental issues (such as community sanitation or environmental upkeep of the community).

The communities featured in this book therefore represent the birth, but by no means the full life, of these types of community-based organizing (and organizations) in new residential complexes in China. The data seen in the years subsequent to the organizing efforts of these communities provide a picture of the consistent growth of community-based organizations over time, with new organizations regularly being established.

In addition to an increase in community organizations focused on environmental issues, this time period also saw an increase in environmentally focused nonprofit organizations (which in China comprise private nonenterprise organizations, social groups, and foundations). While the growth in both types of organizations indicates a broad surge in environmental activity, community-based environmental organizations outpaced nonprofits, particularly after 2012 (figure C.1). Additionally, at that critical juncture, the total number of registered community

CONCLUSION

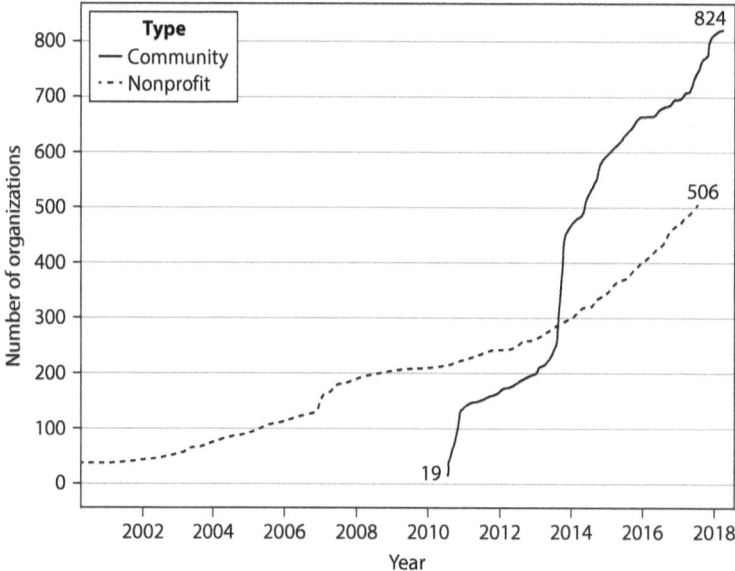

FIGURE C.1. The cumulative number of registered community and nonprofit environmental organizations. Source: Beijing Municipal Civil Affairs Bureau Social Organization Registry, 2018.

environmental organizations began to surpass that of registered environmental nonprofits.

Clearly, Meadow, Willow, Pine, Rose, and Marigold were part of a broader trend of urban residents' increasing social awareness of environmental problems. The growing number of community environmental organizations also reflects the need of urban residents like those in the featured communities to take environmental education and protection into their own hands. Although environmental nonprofits are also growing in number, they often do not have the capacity to engage in community-oriented programs, instead focusing on promoting and implementing environmental policy.

It is important to point out, however, that at the citizen level the legal differences between "community" and "noncommunity" organizations may not be especially meaningful. Participants of a community organization may also be participants of other urban associations. Gated housing community residents may become members of environmental nonprofits or participate in the activities of environmental organizations, in addition to engaging in community associational life, as several leaders from the featured communities did. In residential communities, those who establish community organizations may create organizational statutes adapted from local environmental organizations or replicate the activities of environmental nonprofits in which they have taken part. The environmental civil society is therefore composed of both community-based organizations that address issues at the community level and nonprofit organizations that address issues at the city level.

The rise of nonprofit social organizations in China has been the focus of many studies, but these formal organizations are rarely considered in the context of the larger social world of a city and its residents. This book paints an intimate portrait of emerging self-organization at the level of the residential community in China, providing a piece of the puzzle of contemporary social action that has not been well researched or understood.

MIDDLE-CLASS ORGANIZING IN CHINA AND BEYOND

In Sian Lazar's anthropological study of the political activism of unions in Argentina, she calls for a return to studying organized class-based movements.[9] Studies of social movements have shifted toward a focus on movement identity, but class, according to Lazar, is an explicit category of identity and a strong foundation for protest mobilization. Unions, she argues, have been sites of active citizenship and political activism held together by personal and kinship ties. While her focus is on working-class identities, her observation is relevant to the middle class as well. New middle-class identities are being constructed all over the world, at the same time that citizens of developing countries are becoming more active in protecting their political, economic, and civil rights. Whereas working-class identity is often associated with professional occupation, collective middle-class identities shaped specifically by *homeownership* have arisen in Beijing.

In China, with an increasing number of middle-class urban residents, the continuing construction of commercial housing in growing cities, and state plans to initiate residential property taxation in the near future,[10] environmental pollution threatening middle-class communities will inevitably lead to more instances of resistance.[11] Based on media coverage alone, there were at least nineteen reported cases of anti-incinerator resistance across China from 2006 to 2016.[12] Of these, thirteen were described as urban, and all reportedly involved homeowners. Some of the most successful protests—like those of Meadow, Willow, and Pine—leveraged citizen science to achieve incinerator relocation or cancellation, whereas several others led to the temporary suspension of incinerator construction.

Environmental organizing demonstrates middle-class homeowners' capacity to mobilize, pursue institutional channels like petitioning, and stage public demonstrations to pressure and shape discussions with the government, environmental experts, and environmental nonprofits (chapters 4, 5, and 6). Chapter 5 depicts how homeowners across the featured Beijing communities were all able to launch initiatives to collect citizen-science data on the environmental and health impact of landfills and planned incinerators. Citizen science became an alternative to disruptive protesting for these communities, and the reports produced by homeowners based on their citizen-science efforts conferred legitimacy on their actions taken through legal institutional channels including petitioning and lawsuits. Although homeowners' citizen science varied both in the type of information they captured and in the accuracy of their findings, the process allowed residents to more thoroughly comprehend the incineration issue, understand environmental laws and case studies, and produce and present scientific evidence to government officials and environmental nonprofits.

Citizen science is certainly a middle- and upper-middle-class strategy, as it requires professional connections (e.g., having worked in government, knowing which government expert to call), specialized leadership (a central person or team with the capacity to oversee and organize data collection), and an understanding of how to present and frame data in a way that is acceptable to government agencies or similar to governmental presentations of environmental reports. Therefore, citizen science—producing new community-based knowledge and evidence that may run counter to government information and authority—is a form of middle-class environmental resistance. Regardless of the success of their efforts, this resistance-via-data points to a larger process of the middle class increasingly providing feedback on policies and incorporating their voices into the decision-making process regarding environmental policies. Through these processes, not only does the collective homeowner identity support mobilization within residential communities, but also, increasingly, civic engagement is becoming associated with a new urban middle-class identity.

China is not the only site of civic activity via citizen science. For example, in Nigeria, residents of Ibadan are organizing to protect the biodiversity of birds, which is suffering from rapid urbanization. These citizens are exchanging knowledge about birds in their area on Facebook, meeting once a month, and sharing strategies for becoming active in conservation. In Taiwan, urban citizens are pursuing conservation by monitoring roadkill: photographing animals killed on roadways and even sending specimens to a research institute that uses the samples to investigate patterns of movement and possible strategies to reduce these incidents.[13]

While environmental organizing is a clear trend globally, middle-class resistance in developing countries can also be seen in response to broader issues. In Brazil, a new middle class that has expanded tremendously during the country's economic boom protested in Rio De Janeiro and São Paulo in June 2018, demanding greater accountability from politicians in the face of rising prices, corruption, and police repression.[14] Middle-class protests have also emerged in urban Niger because of economic grievances.[15] These protests are both middle class *and* urban. In urban studies, scholars have also begun to discuss the role of residential settlements and gated communities in the rapidly urbanizing contexts of Asia and Latin America.[16] As housing settings shift in cities, residents' interactions with one another also change and adapt, paving the way for new forms of civic organizing.

HOUSING STABILITY AND CIVIC CAPACITY

The focus of this book on the emergence of newly stable spaces for middle-class homeowners to cultivate civic skills departs from the contemporary narrative of breakdowns in social cohesion. In the field of urban sociology, scholars often examine housing as a source of inequality and the impact of housing instability, reflecting current urban housing challenges in the United States, such as increasing rents and housing prices and gentrification. But elsewhere in the world, rates of homeownership are increasing rapidly and are already much higher than in the United States. China has a homeownership rate of around 90 percent, whereas that of the United States is about 65.8 percent, according to recent data.[17] If housing stability is actually *increasing* in urban areas in many parts of the world, then some positive and empowering changes may be in store for the middle class and, relatedly, their civic lives.

CONCLUSION

This book's spotlight on stable housing arrangements allows sociological inquiry to bring place and community back into studies of collective organizing, even as we move into a digital age in which online communication has become the focus of mobilization. As the examples from Beijing illustrate, online networks are made meaningful by an off-line, in-person community infrastructure, networks, and shared spaces. More broadly, the COVID-19 pandemic has also demonstrated that the schools and community organizations that were able to pivot their activities and services to online spaces were largely able to do so because of preexisting in-person relationships. The off-line community reinforces the online space; the online facilitates the off-line.

Housing is a major part of the urban environment. Yet sociologists, who study social organizations of all types that provide resources for urban residents, seldom consider housing to be a source of capacity building.[18] Housing instability is a pressing social problem, but housing can also represent stability. Even the United States has seen a resurgence of community organizing involving the middle class. In long-term battles against gentrification and housing displacement—such as in the Chinatown or Mission communities of San Francisco—neighborhood identity is central to organizing efforts. The residents of these communities have lived together in the same neighborhood space for decades and have thus developed the capacity to organize against city development plans when the need arises. As newly stable housing arrangements continue to emerge in cities around the world, we can expect to witness further identity formation and civic action in support of community health and well-being. Importantly, incorporating case studies of residential organizing *outside the United States* can provide an opportunity for sociologists to understand how urban housing and environmental issues are interpreted in a broader variety of localities and how democratic forms of participation may manifest, not only in liberal contexts but even in authoritarian and oppressive regimes.

A CONSCIOUS SHIFT

As part of my attempt to connect personally with homeowners in China, I recently conversed with Mr. Mou, who lives in China's historical capital city, Nanjing. Like many other Chinese cities, Nanjing has experienced patterns of urban residential growth similar to those of Beijing, including two recent reported cases of anti-incinerator resistance (one in 2009 and one in 2016). Mr. Mou, in his late fifties, works for an agency of the provincial government in a position similar to those held by Meadow's Huang *laoshi* and Pine's Mr. Wu before their retirements. Experiencing the housing reforms firsthand as a government employee, Mr. Mou described to me his housing history, which serves to illustrate the rapid changes that took place over thirty years.

As a young, single worker in the 1980s, he lived in a dorm-like accommodation with others in his work unit. In the early 1990s, he had his own room. Toward the end of that decade, when he started a family, he moved to a newly built housing complex subsidized by his work unit. Finally, in 2013, he purchased his own home ("complete with property rights!") in a gated housing community: a newly constructed residential complex with a layout similar to those of Meadow, Willow, Pine, and Rose. On a WeChat call, without particular knowledge of my research interests, he told me,

> You know, [in our family] we're just traditional, salaried-class folks who wanted to live in a better environment. I wasn't trying to flip new homes to make money, even though I do hear that's the "hot" thing to do now.... This is the biggest reflection I've had: with all the places I've lived at, my housing environment is really continuously getting better—from wanting a room to myself, to wanting a better home, to wanting a home of my own with a good environment. The living environment is always improving. That is the biggest change, and it's not just the broad environment; it's wanting a green community environment. I feel like, nowadays, the ecological environment has become really important to homeowners.

In describing his family as "salaried class," Mr. Mou identified his middle-class position, emphasizing that they worked hard to save money to own a home—what he called a "traditional" aspiration—not to buy and sell property to make money on the real estate market. In finally locating a home to purchase, he considered the "ecological environment" to be centrally important, seeking a "green" environment.

In addition to valuing environmental health, Mr. Mou also spoke of the importance of civic participation in his community, paralleling how the

CONCLUSION

Beijing communities featured in this book experienced engagement on homeowners' forums:

> We get community information from our WeChat homeowners' forum and chat group. Property management sends information via the group. People talk about community and communal affairs in the group. They share their opinions in the group so we know what's going on in the community, what problems there are, what residents think of those problems. Sometimes property management puts up notices at the community gates, but we're busy most of the time, so we don't really see the flyers. But when we go home, we remember to check the WeChat group, to see what's going on in the chat, what issues people care about or are talking about.

The online forum and chat group play a key role in keeping Mr. Mou and his wife updated on community affairs, but the shared physical space of the community foregrounds what issues are discussed. Messages from property management are less important than what other community members have to say.

Most recently, Mr. Mou told me that the residents are talking about installing security cameras in the community. He is interested but admits that he did not participate in the recent HOA elections. Chuckling a little sheepishly, he explained that he worked during the day and so missed the elections but knew that they were occurring. He also demonstrated considerable knowledge of community affairs, providing me with details about community leadership: half the HOA members are retired; some are former government employees, whereas others are former businesspeople. The other half are younger residents still working but passionate about the community. As we were casually talking about the HOA, he commented thoughtfully, "I would say in the recent ten years, people's rights protection consciousness is becoming so much stronger. This is especially seen in residential community management and attention to the civic good . . . this type of awareness is pretty strong now. Civic consciousness is strengthening, based on the changes I see happening around me [in the community]. I think we'll see the changes pick up pace, with people's sense of civic responsibility only becoming stronger."

I was pleasantly surprised that he referred to the idea of civic consciousness and responsibility without my prompting or inquiry and that he had observed that involvement in community affairs had expanded in recent years.

This conversation showed me that something truly empowering is happening in middle-class homeowners' communities, even outside Beijing. The process and progression are evident not only to scholars like me who are studying these changes but also to those experiencing them, like the "traditional, salaried-class" Mr. Mou. Demonstrating his hardworking nature, he wrapped up our conversation as his lunch hour concluded and he returned to work, even though we were speaking during the Mid-Autumn Festival holiday. I wondered how many other middle-class homeowners across China found themselves occasionally pausing in their work to reflect on the growing promise of neighborhood collaboration and environmental stewardship in their new communities.

NOTES

INTRODUCTION

1. See Yongshun Cai, "China's Moderate Middle Class: The Case of Homeowners' Resistance," *Asian Survey* 45, no. 5 (2005): 777–99; Choon-Piew Pow, *Gated Communities in China: Class, Privilege, and the Moral Politics of the Good Life* (New York: Routledge, 2009); Li Zhang, *In Search of Paradise: Middle-Class Living in a Chinese Metropolis* (Ithaca, NY: Cornell University Press, 2010).
2. See Rick Grannis, "The Importance of Trivial Streets: Residential Streets and Residential Segregation," *American Journal of Sociology* 103, no. 6 (1998): 1530–64.
3. In this book, when speaking of physical spaces, "communities" refers to gated housing communities, whereas "neighborhood" refers to the larger geographical area where public and commercial amenities are shared. This denotation differs from the classic urban sociological definition of "neighborhood," which refers to a *subsection of a larger community* that constitutes both people and institutions occupying a spatially defined area influenced by various cultural and political forces. See Robert E. Park, "The City: Suggestions for the Investigation of Human Behavior in the City Environment," *American Journal of Sociology* 20, no. 5 (March 1915): 577–612.
4. Huang *laoshi* is not actually a teacher. He was often referred to as "teacher" out of respect for his organizing efforts against the incinerator and his knowledge of related issues.
5. The brick factory dates back to the era of the Second Sino-Japanese War or Japanese occupation period, roughly 1937–1945.
6. From 1993 to 2005, official reports saw contentious political action (across all types of issues) jump from 8,700 to 87,000 cases. The number of events defined as "mass protests" was not mentioned, only that over half were related to environmental issues. See Lin Li and He Tian, *Zhongguo fazhi fazhan baogao* (Annual report on China's rule of law) (Beijing: Academy of Social Sciences Press, 2014); Fen Lin and

INTRODUCTION

Xinzhi Zhang, "Movement–Press Dynamics and News Diffusion: A Typology of Activism in Digital China," *China Review* 18, no. 2 (2018): 33–64.

7. Zhifeng Tong, "Reflections on Environmental Mass Incidents in China," in *The China Environment Yearbook*, vol. 3, ed. International Advisory Board Chinese Research Perspectives Online (Leiden: Brill, 2017), 235–48.
8. Peter Ho, "Greening Without Conflict? Environmentalism, NGOs and Civil Society in China," *Development and Change* 32, no. 5 (2001): 893–921; Elizabeth C. Economy, *The River Runs Black: The Environmental Challenge to China's Future*, 2nd. ed. (Ithaca, NY: Cornell University Press, 2010).
9. See Lin and Zhang, "Movement–Press Dynamics."
10. Economy argues that environmental nongovernmental organizations (NGOs) are skilled at pushing the boundaries of what is permitted by the government while avoiding censorship. Ho depicts environmental NGOs as courting government approval and seeking to influence policy, rather than targeting the state. Regardless of the explanation, environmental protests tend to be accepted by central-government officials in China. Economy, *The River Runs Black*; Ho, "Greening Without Conflict."
11. Chaohua Tu. "Xiamen PX Xiangmu Shijian Shimo," [The case of Xiamen PX incident]. *China Youth Daily*, December 27, 2007.
12. Kingsyhon Lee and Ming-Sho Ho, "The Maoming Anti-PX Protest of 2014: An Environmental Movement in Contemporary China," *China Perspectives* 2014, no. 3 (2014): 33–39.
13. Patrick Devine-Wright, "Rethinking NIMBYism: The Role of Place Attachment and Place Identity in Explaining Place-Protective Action," *Journal of Community & Applied Social Psychology* 19, no. 6 (2009): 426–41.
14. Bray argues that the *danwei* provides its members with a social identity and a sense of personal belonging because it is composed of collective groups and social relationships centered on work and the workplace. David Bray, *Social Space and Governance in Urban China: The Danwei System from Origins to Reform* (Stanford, CA: Stanford University Press, 2005).
15. Privately owned housing existed before 1949, but many such homes were later appropriated by housing bureaus. According to Read, some of these properties were returned to their original owners during the housing reforms. Benjamin L. Read, "Democratizing the Neighbourhood? New Private Housing and Home-Owner Self-Organization in Urban China," *China Journal* 49 (January 2003): 31–59.
16. The work-unit housing system was officially abolished in 1998, and the ownership of these housing units was privatized.
17. Read, "Democratizing the Neighbourhood?"
18. Ying Miao, "Middle Class Identity in China: Subjectivity and Stratification," *Asian Studies Review* 41, no. 4 (October 2, 2017): 629–46.
19. Feng Wang, "The Social Functions of Private Neighborhood Associations: The Case of Homeowner Associations in Urban China" (PhD dissertation, University of Southern California, 2008). Homeownership includes the ownership of previously state-owned work-unit housing (now privatized), government-subsidized housing (commercial housing bought by the state and resold to residents at a subsidized rate), or new commodified housing.
20. Humna Bint-e-Waheed and Obaidullah Nadeem, "Perception of Security Risk in Gated and Non-gated Communities in Lahore, Pakistan," *Journal of Housing and the*

INTRODUCTION

Built Environment 35, no. 3 (September 1, 2020): 897–915; Olusola Oladapo Makinde, "The Correlates of Residents' Perception of Safety in Gated Communities in Nigeria," *Social Sciences & Humanities Open* 2, no. 1 (January 1, 2020): 100018; Ming Cai et al., "Evaluation of External Costs in Road Transport Under the Openness of a Gated Community," *Frontiers of Earth Science* 14, no. 1 (March 1, 2020): 140–51.

21. Edward J. Blakely and Mary Gail Snyder, *Fortress America: Gated Communities in the United States* (Washington, DC: Brookings Institution Press, 1997).
22. Pow, *Gated Communities in China*, 2.
23. Teresa P. R. Caldeira, *City of Walls: Crime, Segregation, and Citizenship in São Paulo* (Berkeley: University of California Press, 2000).
24. Zhang, *In Search of Paradise*.
25. Robert J. Sampson et al., "Civil Society Reconsidered: The Durable Nature and Community Structure of Collective Civic Action," *American Journal of Sociology* 111, no. 3 (November 2005): 673–714.
26. Robert D. Putnam, "Bowling Alone: America's Declining Social Capital," *Journal of Democracy* 6, no. 1 (1995): 65–78.
27. Mario Luis Small, *Unanticipated Gains: Origins of Network Inequality in Everyday Life* (New York: Oxford University Press, 2010).
28. Extremely popular in China, "group purchasing" refers to groups of people organizing to buy items in bulk to take advantage of cheaper prices. Purchases are organized both online and off-line. Homeowners' communities often organize group purchases to buy items like construction materials, appliances, or home decor items shortly after moving in.
29. Eric Klinenberg, *Heat Wave: A Social Autopsy of Disaster in Chicago*, 2nd ed. (Chicago: University of Chicago Press, 2015).
30. Sampson et al., "Civil Society Reconsidered."
31. Michael Edwards, *Civil Society* (Cambridge: Polity, 2009), 405.
32. David Horton Smith, *Grassroots Associations* (Thousand Oaks, CA: Sage, 2000); Jie Chen and Chunlong Lu, "Social Capital in Urban China: Attitudinal and Behavioral Effects on Grassroots Self-Government," *Social Science Quarterly* 88, no. 2 (2007): 422–42; Edwards, *Civil Society*.
33. Sidney Verba, Kay Lehman Schlozman, and Henry E. Brady, *Voice and Equality: Civic Voluntarism in American Politics* (Cambridge, MA: Harvard University Press, 1995).
34. Doug McAdam and Hilary Boudet, *Putting Social Movements in Their Place: Explaining Opposition to Energy Projects in the United States, 2000–2005* (Cambridge: Cambridge University Press, 2012).
35. Elisabeth S. Clemens, *The People's Lobby: Organizational Innovation and the Rise of Interest Group Politics in the United States, 1890–1925* (Chicago: University of Chicago Press, 1997); Sampson et al., "Civil Society Reconsidered"; Edward T. Walker, "Contingent Pathways from Joiner to Activist: The Indirect Effect of Participation in Voluntary Associations on Civic Engagement," *Sociological Forum* 23, no. 1 (2008): 116–43.
36. Ted Robert Gurr, *Why Men Rebel* (Princeton, NJ: Princeton University Press, 1970); Ted Robert Gurr, *Why Men Rebel*, 40th anniversary ed. (New York: Paradigm, 2010); Ralph H. Turner and Lewis M. Killian, *Collective Behavior* (Englewood Cliffs, NJ: Prentice-Hall, 1972); John D. McCarthy and Mayer N. Zald, "Resource Mobilization and Social Movements: A Partial Theory," *American Journal of Sociology* 82,

no. 6 (1977): 1212–41; Doug McAdam, John D. McCarthy, and Mayer N. Zald, eds., *Comparative Perspectives on Social Movements: Political Opportunities, Mobilizing Structures, and Cultural Framings* (Cambridge: Cambridge University Press, 1996).
37. Edwards, *Civil Society*.
38. Jennifer Earl, "Introduction: Repression and the Social Control of Protest," *Mobilization: An International Quarterly* 11, no. 2 (August 4, 2006): 129–43; Zeynep Tufekci, *Twitter and Tear Gas: The Power and Fragility of Networked Protest* (New Haven, CT: Yale University Press, 2018).
39. Xin Chen, *Yezhu Zizhi: Yi Jianzhuwu Qufen Suoyouquan Wei Jichu* [Homeowners' self-governance: On the basis of proportional property rights] (Beijing: Peking University Press, 2007); Yongshun Cai, "Civil Resistance and Rule of Law in China: The Defense of Homeowners' Rights," *Harvard Contemporary China Series* 14 (2007):174–95; Sarah Blandy and Feng Wang, "Curbing the Power of Developers? Law and Power in Chinese and English Gated Urban Enclaves," *Geoforum* 47 (June 1, 2013): 199–208; Limei Li and Si-ming Li, "Becoming Homeowners: The Emergence and Use of Online Neighborhood Forums in Transitional Urban China," *Habitat International* 38 (April 1, 2013): 232–39; Feng Wang, "Regulations and the Imbalance of Power Relationships in Newly Developed Residential Neighbourhoods in Urban China," in *Multi-owned Housing: Law, Power, and Practice*, ed. Sarah Blandy, Ann Dupuis, and Jennifer Dixon (London: Routledge, 2016).
40. Tufekci, *Twitter and Tear Gas*.
41. Archon Fung, "Associations and Democracy: Between Theories, Hopes, and Realities," *Annual Review of Sociology* 29, no. 1 (2003): 515–39; Putnam, "Bowing Alone"; Mark E. Warren, *Democracy and Association* (Princeton, NJ: Princeton University Press, 2001).
42. Margaret R. Somers, "Citizenship and the Place of the Public Sphere: Law, Community, and Political Culture in the Transition to Democracy," *American Sociological Review* 58, no. 5 (1993): 587–620.
43. Somers, "Citizenship," 587.
44. Dingxin Zhao, *The Power of Tiananmen: State-Society Relations and the 1989 Beijing Student Movement* (Chicago: University of Chicago Press, 2004).
45. Roger V. Gould, "Trade Cohesion, Class Unity, and Urban Insurrection: Artisanal Activism in the Paris Commune," *American Journal of Sociology* 98, no. 4 (January 1993): 721–54; Roger V. Gould, *Insurgent Identities: Class, Community, and Protest in Paris from 1848 to the Commune* (Chicago: University of Chicago Press, 1995).
46. There is a broad range of GONGOs. Typically, they receive some sort of financial support or sponsorship from the government, and they often serve as a government tool to repress civil society. The environmental GONGOs I visited operated fairly independently but had government officials posted within some of their departments. They were also responsible for promoting government-issued environmental regulations and policies.
47. I recorded some interviews but more often took notes by hand to avoid appearing too forward or intrusive. I have translated quotations from their original Mandarin.
48. To set up a forum, all homeowners need to do is submit a request with the web platform company. Aside from forums, the website also offers housing and rental information and runs real estate advertisements.

49. Guobin Yang, "The Internet and the Rise of a Transnational Chinese Cultural Sphere," *Media, Culture & Society* 25, no. 4 (July 1, 2003): 469–90. For an in-depth discussion of virtual communities in China, see Guobin Yang, "The Internet and Civil Society in China: A Preliminary Assessment," *Journal of Contemporary China* 12, no. 36 (August 1, 2003): 453–75.
50. This amounted to 17,860 registered community-based organizations and 11,598 registered nonprofits, each providing their organization's name, date of establishment, address, and goals. In 2016, the social organization registry was made public, and in January 2018, the community-based organization registration data were released. Beijing Municipal Civil Affairs Bureau, "Beijing Shehui Zuzhi Gonggong Fuwu Pingtai" [Social organization service platform/registry], https://ggfw.mzj.beijing.gov.cn/, accessed 2017–2018.

1. A STENCH ON SUCCESS: URBAN MIDDLE-CLASS HOMEOWNERS AND RISING ENVIRONMENTAL CHALLENGES

1. Andrew G. Walder, *Communist Neo-Traditionalism: Work and Authority in Chinese Industry* (Berkeley: University of California Press, 1988); Xiaobo Lu and Elizabeth J. Perry, *The Danwei: Changing Chinese Workplace in Historical and Comparative Perspective* (New York: Routledge, 2015).
2. The *danwei* is similar to the "microregion" initiated in the Soviet Union in the late 1950s. The microregion "comprised a neighborhood unit of living spaces in the form of blocks or flats, along with associated services, for perhaps five thousand to fifteen thousand people." Graham Smith, *The Nationalities Question in the Post-Soviet States* (London: Longman, 1996), 75. According to Zhang, the main difference between the Soviet microregion and the Chinese *danwei* is that the *danwei* is sometimes gated, with the workplace providing all services. Li Zhang, *In Search of Paradise: Middle-Class Living in a Chinese Metropolis* (Ithaca, NY: Cornell University Press, 2010). See also David Bray, *Social Space and Governance in Urban China: The Danwei System from Origins to Reform* (Stanford, CA: Stanford University Press, 2005).
3. Rent was low and fixed (i.e., it did not increase as a household's income increased), averaging about 0.3 yuan per square meter for public housing. On average, about 1 percent of a worker's annual income went toward rent in the mid-1950s. Xing Quan Zhang, "Privatization and the Chinese Housing Model," *International Planning Studies* 5, no. 2 (June 2000): 191–204. For a deeper discussion of living conditions and housing shortages, see Ya Ping Wang and Alan Murie, "The Process of Commercialisation of Urban Housing in China," *Urban Studies* 33, no. 6 (1996): 971–89; Ya Ping Wang and Alan Murie, "Commercial Housing Development in Urban China," *Urban Studies* 36, no. 9 (1999): 1475–94; Xing Quan Zhang, *Privatisation: A Study of Housing Policy in Urban China* (Hauppauge, NY: Nova Science, 1998); Kenneth T. Rosen and Madelyn C. Ross, "Increasing Home Ownership in Urban China: Notes on the Problem of Affordability," *Housing Studies* 15, no. 1 (January 1, 2000): 77–88; Youqin Huang, "The Road to Homeownership: A Longitudinal Analysis of Tenure Transition in Urban China (1949–94)," *International Journal of Urban and Regional Research* 28 (2004): 774–95.

1. A STENCH ON SUCCESS

4. Wang and Murie, "The Process of Commercialisation."
5. Zhang, "Privatization." A government official with whom I spoke told me that high-ranking government employees often had multiple homes.
6. Wang and Murie, "Commercial Housing Development."
7. The main supplier of housing in China from the 1950s through the 1990s was the state (and relatedly, the *danwei*). During the reform, the supplier gradually became the market, with housing becoming commercialized and its distribution monetized. First, public housing was "propertized": the property rights of *danwei* homes were transferred from the state to workers' families through housing transactions. Housing was then "commercialized," allowing private (nonstate) housing construction and even encouraging foreign businesses and real estate enterprises to participate in commercial housing developments. Wang and Murie, "The Process of Commercialisation"; Hongming Zhang, *Housing Economics* (Shanghai: Shanghai University of Finance and Economics Press, 1998); Youqin Huang and William A. V. Clark, "Housing Tenure Choice in Transitional Urban China: A Multilevel Analysis," *Urban Studies* 39, no. 1 (2002): 7–32; Yapeng Zhu, *Zhufang zhidu gaige: zhengce chuangxin yu zhufang gongping* [Housing reform in China: Policy innovation and equality] (Guangzhou: Sun Yat-sen University Press, 2007); Kaize Wu, "Housing Reform, Life Course, and Urban Housing Acquisition (1980–2010)," *Journal of Chinese Sociology* 6, no. 15 (July 25, 2019).
8. Zhang, *Privatisation*; Zhang, "Privatization."
9. Zhang, *In Search of Paradise*, 36.
10. Zhang, *In Search of Paradise*, 36.
11. This new system was also exploited. For example, some work unit leaders would purchase large apartments at cheap prices, then sell public housing to unqualified family members or friends. Though the work unit was no longer the direct provider of housing, some work units played an important role in the emerging privatization process as purchasers of new construction. Zhang, *In Search of Paradise*.
12. Choon-Piew Pow, *Gated Communities in China: Class, Privilege, and the Moral Politics of the Good Life* (New York: Routledge, 2009).
13. The economic reforms included policies such as opening up to foreign investments and the privatization of businesses, which led to the growth of the private sector (even though many industries remained state owned).
14. World Bank, "World Urbanization Prospects: 2018 Revision," World Bank Open Data, 2018, https://data.worldbank.org/indicator/SP.URB.TOTL.IN.ZS?locations=CN.
15. Disposable income is income available to spend or save after taxes and other mandatory expenses are deducted.
16. Average annual housing expenditures refer to private and public housing rent. From 2008 to 2009, the gap between disposable income and annual housing expenditures widened, which means that while disposable income increased for Beijing residents, their expenditures on housing dropped for a period of two years, picking up again in 2010.
17. Joyce Y. Man, ed., *China's Housing Reform and Outcomes* (Cambridge, MA: Lincoln Institute of Land Policy, 2011).
18. Rising housing prices led to government efforts to contain these prices in 2013.

1. A STENCH ON SUCCESS

19. Kevin J. O'Brien and Lianjiang Li, *Rightful Resistance in Rural China* (Cambridge: Cambridge University Press, 2006).
20. Wang et al. describe the rise of homeowners' associations in China as a way for homeowners to combat unjust treatment from property management, which frequently occurs in gated communities. Zhengxu Wang et al., "Leadership in China's Urban Middle Class Protest: The Movement to Protect Homeowners' Rights in Beijing," *China Quarterly* 214 (2013): 411–31.
21. Zhang, *In Search of Paradise*; Wang et al., "Leadership in China"; Feng Wang, "Determinants of the Effectiveness of Chinese Homeowner Associations in Solving Neighborhood Issues," *Urban Affairs Review* 50, no. 3 (May 1, 2014): 311–39.
22. Yongshun Cai, "Civil Resistance and Rule of Law in China: The Defense of Homeowners' Rights," *Harvard Contemporary China Series* 14 (2007): 174–95; Zhang, *In Search of Paradise*; Wang, "Determinants."
23. Zan Yang and Jie Chen, *Housing Affordability and Housing Policy in Urban China* (Berlin: Springer, 2014).
24. Ya Ping Wang, "Recent Housing Reform Practice in Chinese Cities: Social and Spatial Implications," in *China's Housing Reform and Outcomes*, ed. Joyce Y. Man (Cambridge, MA: Lincoln Institute of Land Policy, 2011), 19–44.
25. Pow, *Gated Communities in China*.
26. David Fraser, "Inventing Oasis: Luxury Housing Advertisements and Reconfiguring Domestic Space in Shanghai," in *The Consumer Revolution in Urban China*, ed. Deborah Davis (Berkeley: University of California Press, 2000), 25–53; Helen Siu, "The Cultural Landscape of Luxury Housing in South China: A Regional History," in *Locating China: Space, Place, and Popular Culture*, ed. Jing Wang (London: Routledge, 2005), 72–93; Mike Davis, "Fortress Los Angeles: The Militarization of Urban Space," in *Cultural Criminology*, ed. Keith Hayward (New York: Routledge, 2011).
27. Blakely and Snyder found that new homes in over 40 percent of planned developments in the United States are gated in the West, the South, and southeastern parts of the country. Edward J. Blakely and Mary Gail Snyder, *Fortress America: Gated Communities in the United States* (Washington, DC: Brookings Institution Press, 1997).
28. Mike Davis, "Fortress Los Angeles: The Militarization of Urban Space," in *Variations on a Theme Park: The New American City and the End of Public Space*, ed. Michael Sorkin (New York: Noonday, 1992), 154–80; David Ley, *The New Middle Class and the Remaking of the Central City* (Oxford: Oxford University Press, 1996); Neil Smith, *The New Urban Frontier: Gentrification and the Revanchist City* (London: Routledge, 1996); Setha Low, *Behind the Gates: Life, Security, and the Pursuit of Happiness in Fortress America* (New York: Routledge, 2003).
29. Mark Liechty, *Suitably Modern* (Princeton, NJ: Princeton University Press, 2003); Leela Fernandes, *India's New Middle Class: Democratic Politics in an Era of Economic Reform* (Minneapolis: University of Minnesota Press, 2006); David S. G. Goodman, ed., *The New Rich in China: Future Rulers, Present Lives* (London: Routledge, 2008).
30. See Ezra F. Vogel, *Japan's New Middle Class: The Salary Man and His Family in a Tokyo Suburb* (Berkeley: University of California Press, 1963).
31. C. Wright Mills, *White Collar: The American Middle Classes* (New York: Oxford University Press, 1951).

1. A STENCH ON SUCCESS

32. Cheng Li, "Introduction: The Rise of the Middle Class in the Middle Kingdom," in *China's Emerging Middle Class: Beyond Economic Transformation*, ed. Cheng Li (Washington, DC: Brookings Institution Press, 2010), 3–31; David S. G. Goodman, "Middle Class China: Dreams and Aspirations," *Journal of Chinese Political Science* 19, no. 1 (March 1, 2014): 49–67.
33. Ying Miao, "Middle Class Identity in China: Subjectivity and Stratification," *Asian Studies Review* 41, no. 4 (October 2, 2017): 629–46.
34. Li, "Introduction"; Minglu Chen and David S. G. Goodman, eds., *Middle Class China* (Cheltenham: Edward Elgar, 2013).
35. Miao, "Middle Class."
36. Zhang, *In Search of Paradise*.
37. Beng-Huat Chua, "Consuming Asians: Ideas and Issues," in *Consumption in Asia: Lifestyle and Identities*, ed. Beng-Huat Chua (London: Routledge, 2000), 1–34; Fernandes, *India's New Middle Class*; Zhang, *In Search of Paradise*.
38. In her study of middle-class communities in the southern city of Kunming, Zhang found that homeowners sometimes talked about themselves as being "middle stratum" (*jieceng*) but not "middle class." Zhang, *In Search of Paradise*.
39. Zhang, *In Search of Paradise*.
40. Martin King Whyte and William L. Parish, *Urban Life in Contemporary China* (Chicago: University of Chicago Press, 1984).
41. Nowadays, typical RC responsibilities include promoting laws and government policies, mediating civil disputes, helping maintain social order and security, assisting local governments in implementing policies, and providing community services to residents. However, service provision to neighborhood residents is not always realized. Additionally, unlike HOAs, which are based in gated communities or property-management areas, RCs fall under the administrative division of the "community" (*shequ*), which, in terms of size and area, most closely translates to "neighborhood" as I have defined it. The administrative division of an RC is often composed of several gated communities or properties, similar to the ones discussed in this book. For a discussion of RCs, see Benjamin L. Read, "Revitalizing the State's Urban 'Nerve Tips,'" *China Quarterly* 163 (September 2000): 806–20.
42. Qiang Fu and Nan Lin, "The Weaknesses of Civic Territorial Organizations: Civic Engagement and Homeowners Associations in Urban China," *International Journal of Urban and Regional Research* 38, no. 6 (2014): 2309–27; Shenjing He, "Homeowner Associations and Neighborhood Governance in Guangzhou, China," *Eurasian Geography and Economics* 56, no. 3 (May 4, 2015): 260–84.
43. Cai, "Civil Resistance"; Zhang, *In Search of Paradise*; Feng Wang, Haitao Yin, and Zhiren Zhou, "The Adoption of Bottom-Up Governance in China's Homeowner Associations," *Management and Organization Review* 8, no. 3 (2012): 559–83.
44. In this book, only one of the HOAs (Community Marigold's) functioned similarly to what we would expect of an American HOA: setting internal community rules and guidelines rather than organizing for collective action against property management and developers.
45. The guiding framework for the establishment and governance of China's HOAs is based on two central governmental rules issued in 2003. One is the "Regulations on Real Property" adopted by the State Council. The other is Executive Order No. 131, "The Notice of the Ministry of Construction on Distributing Rules and Procedures

1. A STENCH ON SUCCESS

of Homeowner Associations," issued by the Ministry of Construction. For more details, see Wang, Yin, and Zhou, "The Adoption of Bottom-Up Governance"; Feng Wang, "Regulations and the Imbalance of Power Relationships in Newly Developed Residential Neighbourhoods in Urban China," in *Multi-owned Housing: Law, Power, and Practice*, ed. Sarah Blandy, Ann Dupuis, and Jennifer Dixon (London: Routledge, 2016), 125–44.
46. Some gated communities consist of as many as one hundred thousand people; however, according to a recent news article, the regulations stipulate that a gated community can have only one HOA. Li Li, "Yige Xiaoqu Zhineng Chengli Yige Yeweihui Nandao Jin Shiwan Jumin Chaoji Xiaoqu" [One community can only have one HOA, puts tens of thousands of residents in a 'super community' in a tough spot], *Sanxiang Dushi Bao*, July 19, 2020, https://hn.rednet.cn/content/2020/07/19/7681625.html.
47. Zhang, *In Search of Paradise*.
48. Based on available city data, as of 2007, only an estimated 500 out of 3,000 communities (or 16.6 percent) in the city of Beijing had formed HOAs. Aurore Merle, "Homeowners of Beijing, Unite! The Construction of a Collective Mobilisation," trans. Will Thornely, *China Perspectives* 2014, no. 2 (June 1, 2014): 7–15.
49. Shenjing He, "Homeowner Associations and Neighborhood Governance in Guangzhou, China," *Eurasian Geography and Economics* 56, no. 3 (May 4, 2015): 260–84.
50. Blakely and Snyder, *Fortress America*; James Holston, *The Modernist City: An Anthropological Critique of Brasilia* (Chicago: University of Chicago Press, 1989); Teresa P. R. Caldeira, *City of Walls: Crime, Segregation, and Citizenship in São Paulo* (Berkeley: University of California Press, 2000); Low, *Behind the Gates*.
51. Edward J. Walsh, Rex Warland, and Douglas Clayton Smith, *Don't Burn It Here: Grassroots Challenges to Trash Incinerators* (University Park, PA: Penn State University Press, 1997).
52. Benjamin L. Read, "Democratizing the Neighbourhood? New Private Housing and Home-Owner Self-Organization in Urban China," *China Journal* 49 (2003): 31–59; Luigi Tomba, "Residential Space and Collective Interest Formation in Beijing's Housing Disputes," *China Quarterly* 184 (December 2005): 934–51; Cai (Vera) Zuo, "Attitudes and Actions of Homeowner Activist Leaders in Contemporary China," *China Review* 16, no. 1 (2016): 151–67.
53. Yongshun Cai, *Collective Resistance in China: Why Popular Protests Succeed or Fail* (Stanford, CA: Stanford University Press, 2010).
54. Though Cai did not describe the Guangzhou residents as middle class, that social stratum is implied. Homeowner self-organizing in China is also uneven across localities. For example, residents of Beijing, Shanghai, and Guangzhou are more organized and active than those of smaller cities and inland areas. Cai, *Collective Resistance*; Zhang, *In Search of Paradise*.
55. Qiangyu Fang, "Shequ Shehui Zuzhi Beian, NGO Zhunbei Haole Ma" [Community social organization registrations: Are NGOs prepared?], *China Development Brief*, April 28, 2009, http://www.chinadevelopmentbrief.org.cn/customer/details.html?id=13278&type=.
56. Fang, "Shequ Shehui Zuzhi Beian."
57. In Shandong and Yunnan provinces, community organizations are required to have names that include their administrative unit (city, county, or district), street

or subdistrict, service area, and organizational form. Community organizations in some cities like Guangzhou are required to have at least twenty members, a set community space within the community, and an activity fund of more than 10,000 yuan ($1,590 in U.S. dollars).

58. Additional costs associated with pollution-related resource depletion and ecological damage could not be calculated because of a lack of data. State Environmental Protection Administration of China, "Green GDP Accounting Study Report Press Release," 2006, http://www.gov.cn/english/2006-09/11/content_384596.htm.
59. According to a 2007 report, plans were in place to limit approval of new development projects in regions with excessive environmental pollution, including provinces such as Hebei, Henan, and Shangdong. Ministry of Environmental Protection, "Report on the State of the Environment in China," 2007.
60. For example, vehicles with license plates ending in odd or even numbers took turns being on the road on specified days.
61. As of 2009, there was one reported incidence of a "cancer village" in Beijing. Cancer villages, towns or cities where the rates of cancer deaths related to air or water pollution are above the national average, have been documented across the country. The media have reported that by 2010, there were 459 cancer villages in twenty-nine of thirty-one provinces. Although no additional details for Beijing were available, a suspected cancer village linked to waste incineration near Guangzhou received national attention in 2008 when Guangzhou Panyu residents protested against the construction of a new incinerator in the city. Lee Liu, "Made in China: Cancer Villages," *Environment: Science and Policy for Sustainable Development* 52, no. 2 (February 26, 2010): 8–21.
62. Judith Shapiro, *China's Environmental Challenges* (Cambridge: Polity, 2012), 59.
63. To further understand the competing perspectives on development and the environment within the state, see Elizabeth C. Economy, *The River Runs Black: The Environmental Challenge to China's Future*, 2nd ed. (Ithaca, NY: Cornell University Press, 2010); Shapiro, *China's Environmental Challenges*.
64. Economy, *The River Runs Black*.
65. Typically, laws leave room for interpretation by local officials, and implementation is often negotiated on a case-by-case basis. Laws are vaguely worded and difficult to enforce because of the gap that remains between the legal standards that are set and the feasibility of implementation. For example, the Law on the Prevention of Environmental Pollution Caused by Solid Waste requires that measures be taken for the "safe disposal" of waste. However, many locations have no treatment facilities for solid or hazardous waste. Stockholm Environment Institute and United Nations Development Programme, *China Human Development Report 2002: Making Green Development a Choice* (Oxford: Oxford University Press, 2022), https://www.undp.org/china/publications/china-human-development-report-2002.
66. Shapiro, *China's Environmental Challenges*.
67. Xi Chen, *Social Protest and Contentious Authoritarianism in China* (Cambridge: Cambridge University Press, 2011).
68. Ministry of Environmental Protection, *China Environmental Evaluation 2008* (Beijing: Ministry of Environmental Protection, 2008).
69. Dawei Yu, "Chinese Waste: The Burning Issue," *China Dialogue*, January 26, 2012, https://chinadialogue.net/en/business/4739-chinese-waste-the-burning-issue/.

2. GATED COMMUNITIES AS SCHOOLS OF DEMOCRACY

China Dialogue is a nonprofit organization that produces reports and news articles related to China's environmental challenges. It was established in 2006, and its headquarters are in London.

70. Jing Meng, "To Burn or Not to Burn: A Hot Topic," *China Daily*, June 25, 2010, http://www.chinadaily.com.cn/cndy/2010-06/22/content_10000256.htm. *China Daily* is a government-owned English newspaper.
71. Yu, "Chinese Waste."

2. GATED COMMUNITIES AS SCHOOLS OF DEMOCRACY

1. Michael Edwards, *Civil Society* (Cambridge: Polity, 2009).
2. Teresa P. R. Caldeira, *City of Walls: Crime, Segregation, and Citizenship in São Paulo* (Berkeley: University of California Press, 2000); Li Zhang, *In Search of Paradise: Middle-Class Living in a Chinese Metropolis* (Ithaca, NY: Cornell University Press, 2010).
3. Similar gated community designs are prevalent in urban areas in developing countries such as Brazil, Malaysia, Turkey, South Africa, India, Indonesia, and Pakistan. See Caldeira, *City of Walls*; Karina Landman and Martin Schönteich, "Urban Fortresses: Gated Communities as a Reaction to Crime," *African Security Review* 11, no. 4 (2002): 71–85; Harald Leisch, "Gated Communities in Indonesia," *Cities* 19, no. 5 (October 2002): 341–50; Mark-Anthony Falzon, "Paragons of Lifestyle: Gated Communities and the Politics of Space in Bombay," *City & Society* 16, no. 2 (2004): 145–67; Anis Rahmaan and Anis Bushra, "Dynamics of Gated Communities, Their Impact, and Challenges for Sustainable Development: A Case Study of Lahore, Pakistan," *Archnet-IJAR: International Journal of Architectural Research* 3, no. 1 (March 1, 2009): 57–70; Siti Rasidah Md Sakip, Noraini Johari, and Mohd Najib Mohd Salleh, "Perception of Safety in Gated and Non-gated Neighborhoods," *Procedia—Social and Behavioral Sciences* 85 (2013): 383–91; Basak Tanulku, "Gated Communities: Ideal Packages or Processual Spaces of Conflict?," *Housing Studies* 28, no. 7 (2013): 937–59.
4. In reality, we would not expect all members of a community to be activists. Small describes this well in his Villa Victoria study: even in periods of high participation, only a small proportion of residents were true "community activists." He explains, "When many people think of a highly engaged neighborhood they imagine large numbers of residents knocking on doors, leading neighborhood clean-up drives, and passing out leaflets for upcoming events. Yet community participation might well be what business economists have termed an 80/20 phenomenon, where a large portion of the activity (say, 80 percent) is undertaken by a small proportion of the population (20 percent)." Therefore, understanding participation as an 80/20 phenomenon—or even a 95/5 phenomenon—helps us understand why the rate of participation may appear high in some communities. If even 20 percent of households participated in an anti-incinerator movement, we would see protest groups of more than one thousand people. Mario Luis Small, *Villa Victoria: The Transformation of Social Capital in a Boston Barrio* (Chicago: University of Chicago Press, 2004).
5. In the case of Rose, the fourth phase of construction was completed in 2008, when discussions of landfill stench were already taking place. Based on online forum posts, some later-phase homeowners did read about environmental problems on

online forums before moving in, but many asked about the problem only *after* making a down payment. For these homeowners, timing contributed to their willingness to join in collective action efforts immediately after moving in: they had made their payments, and refunds were not possible.
6. Sohu runs a web platform that hosts homeowners' forums and provides housing and rental information. The forums are free to create; homeowners simply need to put in a request (one per community). Real estate advertisements generate revenue for the platform.
7. Xin Chen, *Yezhu Zizhi: Yi Jianzhuwu Qufen Suoyouquan Wei Jichu* [Homeowners' self-governance: On the basis of proportional property rights] (Beijing: Peking University Press, 2007); Yongshun Cai, "Civil Resistance and Rule of Law in China: The Defense of Homeowners' Rights," *Harvard Contemporary China Series* 14 (2007): 174–95; Feng Wang, Haitao Yin, and Zhiren Zhou, "The Adoption of Bottom-Up Governance in China's Homeowner Associations," *Management and Organization Review* 8, no. 3 (2012): 559–83; Sarah Blandy and Feng Wang, "Curbing the Power of Developers? Law and Power in Chinese and English Gated Urban Enclaves," *Geoforum* 47 (June 1, 2013): 199–208; Feng Wang, "Determinants of the Effectiveness of Chinese Homeowner Associations in Solving Neighborhood Issues," *Urban Affairs Review* 50, no. 3 (May 1, 2014): 311–39.
8. Most posts are generated by homeowners, with the exception of Community Marigold, whose property managers used the community's forum to post information for residents, though infrequently.
9. Sampson et al., "Civil Society Reconsidered: The Durable Nature and Community Structure of Collective Civic Action," *American Journal of Sociology* 111, no. 3 (November 2005): 673–714. See discussion of "blended social action."
10. It is possible that the number views includes those from people outside the communities (e.g., me). However, based on my observations of recognized homeowners' accounts and the history of posts, responses were posted by Meadow, Willow, and Pine homeowners.
11. A note on Community Pine: This community was completed a year before the Sohu platform for homeowners' forums was created in 1999, so there are no online records of homeowners' interactions before residents moved in. However, some Pine homeowners recalled anxiety around dealing with property management early on. Although lacking online interaction, some Pine residents later joined in anti-incinerator mobilization with residents of Communities Meadow and Willow (chapters 3, 4, and 5). Because of Pine's more limited data on informal associations, I hold off on telling its story until chapter 3.
12. Zeynep Tufekci, *Twitter and Tear Gas: The Power and Fragility of Networked Protest*, reprint ed. (New Haven, CT: Yale University Press, 2018).
13. Denise DiPasquale and Edward L. Glaeser, "Incentives and Social Capital: Are Homeowners Better Citizens?," *Journal of Urban Economics* 45, no. 2 (March 1, 1999): 354–84; Zhonghua Huang, Xuejun Du, and Xiaofen Yu, "Home Ownership and Residential Satisfaction: Evidence from Hangzhou, China," *Habitat International* 49 (October 2015): 74–83.
14. Cai, "Civil Resistance"; Choon-Piew Pow, *Gated Communities in China: Class, Privilege, and the Moral Politics of the Good Life* (New York: Routledge, 2009); Zhang, *In Search of Paradise*.

2. GATED COMMUNITIES AS SCHOOLS OF DEMOCRACY

15. One plaque was from the Beijing Municipal Commission of Planning, and the other was from the tech company Sina.
16. Chinese hot pot is a popular meal for gatherings in which a communal pot of seasoned soup is simmered at the table, with each diner putting in a variety of raw ingredients.
17. It is not uncommon for homeowners moving into newly built communities to organize information sessions around housing inspection and the logistics of closing.
18. This practice involves organizing a group of homeowners to go through the process of closing, or signing the final contract before getting their keys, with the goal of more effectively pressuring developers to fix issues noted during their final inspection. Homeowners collectively inspect the final product—the constructed home—including all appliances, construction materials, and related legal documents. The housing inspection (*yanfang*) is a key element of the closing process (which many people do individually), allowing homeowners a final opportunity to discover problems and address them with the developer before signing their contract. Collective closing is becoming a frequent practice of new middle-class homeowners in China to protect new homeowners' rights. A number of collective closings in middle-class communities have been conducted, but many do not come together as planned, often because the homeowners lack organization, have no unified demands or goals, or experience internal conflict (e.g., regarding which problems to focus on).
19. These forty-seven households constituted more than half the registered homeowners on the forum at the time.
20. Zhang, *In Search of Paradise*.
21. After closing, Mr. Zhao reposted his experience on neighboring Community Meadow's forum, advising new homeowners in that community on what to look out for during the process.
22. It is difficult to estimate how many gated communities had forums on the Sohu platform (and therefore were in the competition) in the middle of the first decade of the 2000s. However, based on my estimate, as of 2015, in Beijing alone, around five hundred residential communities used Sohu to host their forums.
23. Robert J. Sampson, "What 'Community' Supplies," in *Urban Problems and Community Development*, ed. William T. Dickens and Ronald F. Ferguson (Washington, DC: Brookings Institution Press, 1999), 241–92; Bruce H. Rankin and James M. Quane, "Neighborhood Poverty and the Social Isolation of Inner-City African American Families," *Social Forces* 79, no. 1 (2000): 139–64.
24. Hanging laundry on balconies is a culturally common practice yet banned by property management in some gated communities because of the perception that it is an eyesore.
25. See Sidney Verba, Kay Lehman Schlozman, and Henry E. Brady, *Voice and Equality: Civic Voluntarism in American Politics* (Cambridge, MA: Harvard University Press, 1995).
26. This is a quote from Mao Tse-tung, found in the book *Quotations from Chairman Mao Tse-tung* (commonly known as the *Little Red Book*). It is not uncommon for Mao's sayings to be quoted, especially among those who grew up during the era of the Cultural Revolution—many axioms are taught in history classes and shared through mass media and popular culture. Contextually, in this instance, the writer

is invoking a sense of revolutionary spirit not as an oppositional political stance but as an inspiration and motivation to join their badminton club.
27. This is a traditional saying originating from the Yuan dynasty. Its meaning is similar to that of the Bible verse "Better is a neighbor that is near than a brother far off," which refers to neighborly bonds being stronger than those of blood relations who are distant, physically and emotionally.
28. As noted in chapter 1, the concept of *weiquan* refers to protecting one's rights, with the implication that citizens engaged in *weiquan* are rightfully resisting and invoking their legal rights.
29. Regulations require that an HOA preparatory group be established under the direction of the District Housing Administrative Department and Street Office. The preparatory group also needs to include representatives from the developer, as well as homeowners. These requirements pose serious obstacles to establishing an HOA. Shenjing He, "Homeowner Associations and Neighborhood Governance in Guangzhou, China," *Eurasian Geography and Economics* 56, no. 3 (May 4, 2015): 260–84.
30. *Shangbanzu* ("working or salaried group") refers to white-collar workers.
31. Most members of the preparatory committee were sixty-three years of age or older. Ms. Hua was a homeowner in building 10.
32. Though Ms. Hua was previously in support of an HOA, she later told me that conflicts which had surfaced between older and younger homeowners in the community made it increasingly difficult to work together cohesively as a single organization (HOA).
33. According to the 2003 HOA regulations, the number of votes required to establish an HOA needed to reach two-thirds of housing occupancy at the time of formation (see chapter 1 for details of the HOA regulations). Because many Marigold houses were unoccupied at the time (about 50 percent), homeowners were able to garner enough votes to create an HOA, even with only a small group of active participants on the committee. The total number of homes in Marigold is 610, so at the time, about three hundred households were living there. Two-thirds of the final number of households would be about two hundred, a number much easier to mobilize than that of a community like Rose, which has thousands of households.
34. Between 2005 and 2009, homeowners occasionally posted online, mostly asking about renovation materials, discussing the opening of their new community spa, or soliciting furniture recommendations.
35. In 2013, the developers agreed to buy back the family's villa at full market price and provide an additional 2 million yuan in compensation. The compensation was not to influence the outcome of the investigation of the developer's role in the accident, which may have resulted in further compensation and legal responsibility. However, I was unable to find information regarding the outcome of the investigation.
36. Robert J. Sampson et al., "Civil Society Reconsidered: The Durable Nature and Community Structure of Collective Civic Action," *American Journal of Sociology* 111, no. 3 (November 2005): 673–714.
37. Verba, Lehman Schlozman, and Brady, *Voice and Equality*; John J. Patrick, "Introduction to Education for Civic Engagement in Democracy," in *Education for Civic Engagement in Democracy: Service Learning and Other Promising Practices*, ed. Sheilah Mann and John J. Patrick (Bloomington: ERIC Clearinghouse for Social Studies/Social Science Education, Indiana University, 2000), 1–8.

3. MAKING SENSE OF EXTERNAL THREATS: INDIVIDUAL, COLLECTIVE, AND REPRESENTATIVE RESPONSES

1. See Karl E. Weick, *The Social Psychology of Organizing* (New York: McGraw-Hill, 1979).
2. For a discussion of movement leaders, see Joseph R. Gusfield, "Functional Areas of Leadership in Social Movements," *Sociological Quarterly* 7, no. 2 (1966): 137–56.
3. The post followed the meticulous style of Mr. Zhao (recall his community polls and letters to property management described in chapter 2), seeking community opinion and input.
4. Based on the timeline, these disagreements were likely those over balcony redesign discussed in chapter 2.
5. Note 22 in chapter 2 describes Mr. Zhao posting about his experience of closing on his new home on Meadow's forum. Generally, however, before and while moving in, homeowners across communities typically did not engage with cross-community posts, being more focused on associational activities within their own gates. Mr. Ru's willingness to consider the needs of other communities thus represents an expansion in perspective.
6. There are two reasons why the landfill stench may have been worse at night: (1) garbage trucks collected garbage and unloaded it at the landfill overnight; and (2) a weather inversion phenomenon may have been occurring—at night, when the air cooled down, it may have drifted from the landfill toward the community, and during the day, as the air warmed, it may have drifted in the opposite direction.
7. After the three communities came together to mobilize against the incinerator, participating homeowners also viewed Mr. Zhao as the "representative" of the movement when "people from the outside" (e.g., journalists) asked questions about the landfill or incinerator.
8. On the difference between mobilizers and organizers, see Hahrie Han, *How Organizations Develop Activists: Civic Associations and Leadership in the 21st Century* (New York: Oxford University Press, 2014).
9. "Chloramine" is my best guess as a translation; the original Chinese term used did not correspond to any actual gas compounds.
10. This comment was translated to preserve Mr. Zhao's ambiguous description of a government agency without a specific name.
11. See Weick, *The Social Psychology*.
12. My emphasis.
13. I use the term "anti-incinerator" rather than "anti-incineration" because at this point, homeowners across all communities were opposed to the incinerator being built near their communities, rather than to incineration itself (i.e., the environmental and health consequences of incineration).
14. The list of homeowners on the committee was not released until later, but the committee consisted of fifteen residents (seven from Meadow and eight from Willow). Pine homeowners also responded to the letter, even though the community was not addressed in the letter directly.
15. Effective trash-separation policies meant that less trash would need to be incinerated. Recycling is a fairly new concept in China. For example, during the 2008 Olympics, recycling bins installed in public parks created confusion because many did not understand what they were for.

3. MAKING SENSE OF EXTERNAL THREATS

16. The *Jiusan* (September 3) Society is one of eight legally recognized political parties in China. Its members are members of the Chinese People's Political Consultative Conference (a political advisory body). The party's name refers to the date of Chinese victory in the Second Sino-Japanese War (September 3, 1945). The party's mission is to "lead the nation to power and the people to prosperity." However, this mission is subordinate to the Chinese Community Party's interests. As of 2016, the party had 167,000 members and was composed mostly of intellectuals in the fields of science and technology. See Lu Yan, "Heading in One Direction," *Beijing Review*, September 27, 2018, https://www.bjreview.com/China_Focus/Time/201809/t20180927_800142644.html.
17. During my time with community homeowners, they frequently cited international examples or case studies of incinerator use as a "problematic" practice, but when I spoke with municipal government officials, the same cases were often described as "best practices." This discrepancy demonstrates how case studies can be interpreted in very different ways. For example, incineration technology can be the most advanced and efficient trash solution (important for government officials) but at the same time have a negative impact on citizens who are exposed to air pollution (important to citizens).
18. The "harmonious society" is an ideal socioeconomic vision in China. Particularly when President Hu Jintao was in office (2003–2013), the concept was frequently used to reflect the goal of maintaining political and social stability. Therefore, citizens and grassroots organizations at the time often used the term "harmonious" (strategically) to signal that they were following Party ideals. In the threads, only two comments opined that the language was "too polite" and that it should be more aggressive. This comment did not seem to have an impact on later community documents.
19. "To wave flags and yell" is a popular saying used to show team spirit.
20. Even with this warning, some homeowners claimed that their emails did not go through when they tried to send them and instead posted their personal information openly on the forum. Though collective action was presented and largely understood as risky, many still treated the online forum as a trusted community space.
21. The analogy implies that the company may have been given special treatment but should not be allowed to get away with illegal actions, such as nighttime construction.
22. Community Rose residents often described themselves as "quality homeowners." When I interviewed Ms. Hua in 2009, she often used the term to describe herself and other homeowners in relation to the "stupid" or "uncivilized" government officials who lacked "quality."
23. While there was documentation of homeowners who called hotlines, it is unclear whether any resident was able to reach a reporter.
24. In 2008, with Beijing about to host the Olympics, environmental protection became a frequently discussed topic. For example, the city limited the number of cars on the streets to reduce air pollution before the Games began.
25. This is an environmental protection hotline that citizens can call to file complaints. The popularity of the hotline has soared in more recent years with the rise of pollution problems in China. Common reasons for calling include to provide tip-offs about polluting factories and to lodge personal grievances about air pollution.
26. Even though there are national exams for police officers and government officials, this homeowner's comment demonstrates the belief that civil servant appointments are still based on a person's family background and personal connections.

27. It was unclear to whom the letter was addressed and whether it was ultimately sent.
28. Chinese income is taxed in a similar manner to that in the United States.
29. The word "PARTY" was written in English and capitalized. Chinese words are sometimes substituted with English words or pinyin acronyms to avoid censorship. However, when the party was mentioned again two sentences later, it was written in Chinese. Therefore, the peculiar use of the word "PARTY" in this instance was probably not to avoid censorship.
30. Communities Dandelion and Daffodil were nearby villa communities. Their forums remained rather silent on the topics of the landfill and incinerator. The topics of other posts on their forums were similar to Marigold's, such as home renovation and furniture recommendations.
31. A collective action in China is often vaguely referred to as a "mass incident," which is viewed as a less sensitive term than "collective protest," "social movement," or "contentious protest."
32. Some of Marigold's upper-middle-class homeowners had professions that likely required them to maintain good relations with central government officials, such as those who worked at research institutes and those who were lawyers, businesspeople, or doctors working for state hospitals. This necessity may explain the more careful and positive rhetoric around the Party on their forum compared with the other communities.
33. The homeowner inserted a question mark after "township government" to indicate that the writer of the original post was uncertain whether the person who tore down the banner was indeed from the township government.
34. In both Rose's and Marigold's forums, these types of rhetorical outbursts vanished after off-line anti-incinerator demonstrations occurred. When coupled with publicly disruptive actions in the streets, such posts were much more likely to be censored.
35. Compared with Meadow, Willow, Pine, and Rose, Marigold was farther from central Beijing. Therefore, the landfill was not taking in as much urban trash as were landfills closer to the city center. It could also be that the wind direction favored Marigold, with the stench drifting away from the community rather than toward it.
36. Meadow and Willow were the first to face problems with the landfill and plans for incinerator construction (2006), followed by Rose (2008) and then Marigold (2009). The timelines of their experiences overlapped, with organizing in Meadow and Willow continuing into 2010 (chapter 4). However, the framing and tactics of the communities' organizing efforts remained distinct, and community leaders noted that they did not learn about one another's struggles until much later. This delay is likely related to the lack of transparent news reporting and distribution characteristic of authoritarian settings, resulting in homeowners in the early 2000s having to seek information in other ways (chapter 6).

4. MOBILIZING AND ORGANIZING FOR ENVIRONMENTAL COLLECTIVE ACTION

1. Hahrie Han, *Moved to Action: Motivation, Participation, and Inequality in American Politics* (Stanford, CA: Stanford University Press, 2009).
2. Xi Chen, "Collective Petitioning and Institutional Conversion," in *Popular Protest in China*, ed. Kevin J. O'Brien (Cambridge, MA: Harvard University Press, 2008),

4. MOBILIZING AND ORGANIZING FOR ENVIRONMENTAL

54–70; Yongshun Cai, "Disruptive Collective Action in the Reform Era," in *Popular Protest in China*, ed. Kevin J. O'Brien (Cambridge, MA: Harvard University Press, 2008), 163–78; Yongshun Cai, *Collective Resistance in China: Why Popular Protests Succeed or Fail* (Stanford, CA: Stanford University Press, 2010); Lianjiang Li, Mingxing Liu, and Kevin J. O'Brien, "Petitioning Beijing: The High Tide of 2003–2006," *China Quarterly* 210 (June 2012): 313–34.

3. While lawsuits and media outreach are becoming more common as protest tactics in China, appealing to government agencies was the dominant form of action in the early 2000s. See Cai, "Disruptive Collective Action." However, only a small number of people found responses to their petitions satisfactory. In recent years, collective petitioning has been increasingly used to address grievances and in many instances has been used in conjunction with disruptive action. See Xi Chen, *Social Protest and Contentious Authoritarianism in China* (Cambridge: Cambridge University Press, 2011).
4. Chen, "Collective Petitioning."
5. Officials often refer to disruptive actions that accompany petitioning as "abnormal petitioning" or "nonnormal petitioning." See Li, Liu, and O'Brien, "Petitioning Beijing."
6. Cai, "Disruptive Collective Action."
7. Yanhua Deng and Kevin J. O'Brien, "Relational Repression in China: Using Social Ties to Demobilize Protesters," *China Quarterly* 215 (September 2013): 533–52.
8. At the end of July 2006, a Willow homeowner named Ms. Liao became concerned about the management of community tap water after receiving conflicting information from property management about whether their water service was provided by a state-run or private utility company. Typically, urban water supply is a public service provided by the city, yet property management would not produce evidence of Community Willow's water source. Dissatisfied with the response from property management, Ms. Liao contacted several private water utility companies in Beijing, but none had records of supplying Willow's water. Worried about unregulated water quality, she launched a three-day fundraiser for water quality testing by a state-owned water inspection center, successfully mobilizing more than thirty neighbors to contribute funds. Although the inspection was only 2,300 yuan (about $359 in U.S. dollars), homeowners contributed more than 3,000 yuan, and this accounting was posted transparently on the homeowners' forum. One month later, Ms. Liao reported that the inspection center said that municipal pipes were located close to Willow, but it was "unclear" whether the pipes supplied the community's water. According to the center, municipal water would have residual chlorine levels that complied with state standards, whereas water provided by a private utility company might not, as such companies were not always compliant with state standards. However, the water quality testing that homeowners paid for did *not* include testing for residual chlorine levels. Therefore, Ms. Liao "pestered" the center into giving her a chlorine test reagent (for free) to conduct water quality tests on her own.
9. A forum post the following month finally provided some clarity regarding the attitude of Willow property management toward the trash issue. As the Lunar New Year approached, property management wanted to put up festive decorations and banners in each Willow building. However, they noticed that meeting flyers for the second homeowners' meeting on January 27 were still posted in each building. Even though the date of the meeting had passed, property management contacted

4. MOBILIZING AND ORGANIZING FOR ENVIRONMENTAL

Mr. Zhao to ask whether they could remove the flyers. This interaction indicated that property management did not want homeowners to interpret the flyer removal as being motivated by "other reasons"; that is, disapproval of environmental organizing. This gesture of goodwill seemed to indicate that property managers hoped to maintain good relations with homeowners, even after conflicts over housing renovations, and were not seeking to discourage the community's organizing efforts.

10. The National Environmental Inspection Office was originally overseen by the State Environmental Protection Administration (SEPA), the highest-ranking environmental agency at the time. In 2008, SEPA was superseded by the Ministry of Environmental Protection (MEP) (which in 2018 became the Ministry of Ecology and Environment). The promotion from SEPA to MEP, making the office a ministry-level institution, indicated that the state was beginning to devote more resources to addressing environmental issues.
11. This saying comes from a common proverb: "Just as a fence needs the support of three stakes, an able fellow needs the help of three other people."
12. This is a common proverb used to describe strength in numbers.
13. Two scientific articles featuring case studies from Japan circulating on the forum described the harms of incineration. However, the articles' original sources were not cited. Homeowners incorporated much of the articles' content into their letters and, later, into their administrative reconsideration filing (discussed later in the chapter).
14. Mr. Ru is the homeowner who worked on the issue of bus lines in the community (chapter 3). His presence at the EPB demonstrated his continued participation in community affairs.
15. "Parent officials" was used historically as a term of respect for officials, signifying that these authorities love their people as parents love their children. The term is used here ironically.
16. The Political Consultative Conference (PCC), established in 1949, was intended to be a platform for democratic participation in state affairs. The PCC includes legally recognized minority parties such as the China Democratic League and the *Jiusan* (September 3) Society, and members serve as advisers of legislation. Definitionally, China has a multiparty political system, although it is still effectively a one-party state because of the Chinese Communist Party's dominance at the national level.
17. It was unclear who the "experts" were or for whom they worked. Many questions on this topic circulated on the forum. One homeowner replied to the question aptly, reflecting the confusion: "some expert from some institute related to the Ministry of Housing and Urban–Rural Development." It is not uncommon in China for those presented as objective experts to be contracted by or affiliated with government agencies.
18. The Administrative Reconsideration Law, passed in 1999, allows a citizen or group who perceive their rights to be impinged upon by an administrative decision to seek reconsideration from the relevant superior administrative agency for review. This law was established to protect the rights of citizens and provide a check on administrative institutions' exercise of power. However, responses to ARs are often delayed or inadequate. For more information on the Administrative Reconsideration Law, see Weidong Yang, "Can the Introduction of Administrative Reconsideration Committees Help Reform China's System of Administrative Reconsideration?" *University of Pennsylvania Asian Law Review* 13 (January 1, 2018): 107–34.

4. MOBILIZING AND ORGANIZING FOR ENVIRONMENTAL

19. In addition to filing with the EPB, one homeowner recommended filing the AR with other relevant agencies, such as the urban management bureau that played a role in site selection. The group did not implement this suggestion, most likely because it took months to receive a response to the AR from the EPB and SEPA. Reframing the AR for each agency would have required a large amount of work and various fields of expertise.
20. The *chengguan* have a notorious reputation for using heavy-handed techniques (e.g., bullying, physical force) in cracking down on illegal street vendors and businesses. Some severe incidents have resulted in injuries and deaths, resulting in news headlines and discussions on social media forums. For an example, see BBC News, "Killing Sparks Protests in China," January 9, 2008, http://news.bbc.co.uk/2/hi/asia-pacific/7178382.stm. Technically, *chengguan* officers can fine violators of city sanitation and order but do not have the authority to detain citizens or use force.
21. For example, Mr. Zhao told forum users to swap the Chinese character for "burn" (烧, *shao*) for a homonym character (稍, *shao*)—pronounced the same but meaning "a little bit." Substituting a sensitive Chinese character with a homonym or with pinyin (a romanized spelling, such as "*fenshao*") is a common practice online to avoid censorship.
22. These quotes reflect Ms. Hua's account of the situation a year and a half later. It is unclear exactly how homeowners "heard" about the government meetings being held. I could not confirm whether these reports were just rumors or whether someone really had connections to the district government and had learned that meetings had taken place. It is likely that homeowners saw the cars of government officials parked in the community and, having read her account of her landfill excursion, were prompted to alert Ms. Hua.
23. The homeowner is referring to the methane released by decomposing trash.
24. Ms. Hua preserved the post as an electronic text file. To my knowledge, after it was removed, it was circulated privately through chats and text messages.
25. "Take a stroll" is a common phrase in China used to refer to protesting, as it is less incendiary than "street demonstration" or "protest." One notable example is the citywide resistance in Xiamen against the paraxylene factory in 2007 in which both protesters (led by grassroots environmental NGOs) and the media referred to the protest as a "stroll." Regarding the use of "tomorrow," the homeowners' protest did not actually occur the next day, which was a weekday. Rather, it took residents until a Saturday, a day off from work, to hit the streets.
26. Ms. Hua told me that local officials tried to pin responsibility for the protest on her and pressure her to admit guilt. It appeared to me that her motivation for describing the mobilization process as occurring in this spontaneous and collective way was to emphasize joint responsibility for the actions.
27. Some homeowners reported seeing an urban planning commission official and others that *chengguan* officials had arrived. It is likely that homeowners did not know who the urban planning official was at the time of the protest and only learned to recognize him later as conflicts with government officials increased. Government bureaucrats are often identifiable because of their professional clothing (dark polo shirts with dark dress slacks).
28. The article, titled "Worried About the Environment, Beijing Citizens Protest Peacefully," was not published until three days after the protest. This delay is typical;

4. MOBILIZING AND ORGANIZING FOR ENVIRONMENTAL

as discussed in the introduction, stories of protests often do not emerge immediately. See Fen Lin and Xinzhi Zhang, "Movement–Press Dynamics and News Diffusion: A Typology of Activism in Digital China," *China Review* 18, no. 2 (2018): 33–64; Kevin J. O'Brien, ed., *Popular Protest in China* (Cambridge, MA: Harvard University Press, 2008).
29. A subdistrict is typically composed of several neighborhoods. Its main administrative agency is the subdistrict office.
30. Here, Ms. Hua uses the word "baiting" to describe officials attempting to trick her into using rhetoric that may be interpreted as subversive to the state. In China, inciting subversion of the state—and, relatedly, being seen as anti-Party or anti-socialism—is a criminal offense that can result in imprisonment.
31. The term *fenqing*, literally "angry youths," historically referred to young people who were dissatisfied with the state of affairs in China and sought social reform. In the 1970s, it was a positive term used to describe youths who cared deeply about their country. Currently, on social media, "angry youths" has become a derogatory slang term for young people who comment fervently and often aggressively on social topics but do not always follow up with action. Comparably, the term "woke" used in many Western countries—meaning to be aware of injustices and often associated with young people—is used both positively and negatively depending on the context and speaker.
32. Mr. Lu was most likely referring to district officials here. Unlike representatives of Meadow, Willow, Pine, and Rose, Mr. Lu typically did not discern between levels of officials, possibly because his interactions with the government were mostly at the municipal level (chapter 5).
33. While I initially wondered about the role of censorship in the lack of posts, homeowners never directly mentioned censorship to me. Additionally, Marigold homeowners were always less active on their forum compared with other communities, primarily relying on phone calls to communicate.
34. The forum of Community Dandelion, a similar villa community (mentioned in chapter 3), featured more frequent discussions about the incinerator. There as well, however, there was no account of mobilization, other than one homeowner providing a design for an anti-incinerator sticker reading "Resist waste incineration; we have only one Beijing!" A few homeowners made suggestions about font size, but no other comments were posted.
35. In a 2011 media interview, Mr. Lu told a reporter that he had actually voted against demonstrating and that he was opposed to such methods because negotiations could be achieved in many other ways. Much as Ms. Hua denied her role in mobilizing protesters in Rose, Mr. Lu likely changed his public account of his role in the Marigold protest because of the outcome of the protest and based on the comments made in the media interview .
36. While Mr. Lu recalled seeing residents of two other villa communities at the protest, it was not evident from the forums of these communities that they had done their own mobilizing. As discussed in chapter 3, Dandelion and Daffodil were mentioned by a homeowner who sought to create cross-community unity in resisting construction of a new road. However, no multicommunity effort was evident in the planning of the anti-incinerator demonstration. Most likely some homeowners had informal ties with one another—for example, having met at a nearby golf course or store or through schools their children attended—and extended personal invitations.

37. While demographic information for the protesters is not readily available, a local Beijing professor, Xing Ying, who studies rural protests, told me in 2011 that male protesters outnumber females in rural protests because many women lack the familial support to participate in collective action. Class differences may explain the greater proportion of women involved in the protest held by Marigold and its neighbors compared with those typical of rural areas.
38. Of the seven individuals detained, three were women.
39. Unlike Rose homeowners, who continued protesting and even pushing back online against repression, Marigold homeowners immediately stopped participating in disruptive actions and pivoted to citizen science. To my knowledge, the detained Marigold residents experienced no further monitoring or other types of repression. However, as will be described, some residents suspected that their homes were being targeted because of their participation in the protest, although it was unclear who the perpetrators were.
40. An example of differential treatment in repressing those from the educated middle class versus those of a lower socioeconomic status is provided by a well-known incident from 1988. When a college student attending a rock concert was beaten by police, Jiang Zemin (then the mayor of Shanghai) publicly offered an explanation, saying that police "had mistaken the young concert-goer for a worker; had they only realized he was an intellectual, such heavy-handed treatment would never have been applied." According to Jones, few citizens took issue with that reasoning. See Andrew F. Jones, "The Politics of Popular Music in Post-Tiananmen China," in *Popular Protest and Political Culture in Modern China*, ed. Jeffrey N. Wasserstrom and Elizabeth J. Perry (New York: Routledge, 1994), 291–310. Additionally, in my conversations with a Beijing police officer, I was told that police "know better than to be violent to urban protesters since everyone will be watching," implying that actions toward rural citizens are less closely observed. The officer went on to outline techniques for surrounding urban middle-class protesters from all sides without escalating the demonstration, suggesting that police are trained to respond in a measured way to wealthier citizens.

5. TRAJECTORIES OF CITIZEN SCIENCE

1. An example of citizen science in action is Erin Brockovich, a legal clerk who, without much knowledge of environmental law or science, played a central role in building a case against the Pacific Gas and Electric Company in California for water contamination in 1993.
2. Bruce Lewenstein, "Can We Understand Citizen Science?," in "Citizen Science, Part I, 2016," special issue, *Journal of Science Communication* 15, no. 1 (January 21, 2016).
3. Interviews with two local social sciences scholars, Beijing, 2010 and 2011.
4. National People's Congress of the People's Republic of China, "Law of the People's Republic of China on Evaluation of Environmental Effects," Meeting of the Standing Committee of the Ninth National People's Congress, October 28, 2002, http://www.npc.gov.cn/englishnpc/Law/2007-12/06/content_1382122.htm.
5. Alex Wang, "Environmental Protection in China: The Role of Law," *China Dialogue*, February 5, 2007, https://chinadialogue.net/en/pollution/745-environmental-protection-in-china-the-role-of-law/.

5. TRAJECTORIES OF CITIZEN SCIENCE

6. "Environmental information" refers to both government and enterprise (business) environmental information. "Government environmental information" refers to information generated or obtained by environmental protection departments when carrying out their responsibilities, which is then recorded and stored. "Enterprise environmental information" refers to environmental impact information recorded and stored by businesses during operational activities and other forms of enterprise environmental behavior. State Environmental Protection Administration of China, "Open Government Information Regulations Act and the Measures on Environmental Information Disclosure," February 8, 2007, https://www.cecc.gov/resources/legal-provisions/measures-on-open-environmental-information-trial-cecc-full-translation. See also Alex Wang, "Explaining Environmental Information Disclosure in China," *Ecology Law Quarterly* 44 (2018): 865–921.
7. A Ministry of Environmental Protection report found that common EPB responses to applications for information disclosure regarding environmental pollution (caused by corporate emissions) included "information does not exist," "outright rejection," and "no response." Or partial information might be given; for example, "information provided but no detailed list of polluters provided." Ministry of Environmental Protection, *Annual Report on Open Government Information* (Beijing: Ministry of Environmental Protection, 2010).
8. In May 2007, some homeowners read in a media report that the construction of the incinerator had "stopped," even though they had not been made aware that construction had officially started.
9. A partial EIA for the incinerator project planned near Meadow, Willow, and Pine was published by the Beijing EPB the previous year, but homeowners wanted the full report. The measures regarding the provision of "open information" about environmental issues were not officially implemented until 2008, but residents still attempted to request the EIA from the EPB in 2007, given the promulgation of the measures.
10. The term "environmental capacity" is based on the concept of "assimilative capacity" (though this term was not used by Huang *laoshi*), which refers to the "maximum emission an area can take without violating the permissible pollutant standards." Prima Goyal and T. V. B. P. S. Rama Krishna, "Dispersion of Pollutants in Convective Low Wind: A Case Study of Delhi," *Atmospheric Environment* 36, no. 12 (2003): 2071–79. Improper calculations of emission loads, poor handling of pollution control mechanisms, and lack of technical expertise on the carrying capacity of a region can impact evaluations of environmental capacity. Amit Garg et al., "Large Point Source (LPS) Emissions from India: Regional and Sectoral Analysis," *Atmospheric Environment* 36, no. 2 (January 1, 2002): 213–24; S. K. Goyal and C. V. Chalapati Rao, "Air Assimilative Capacity-Based Environment Friendly Siting of New Industries—A Case Study of Kochi Region, India," *Journal of Environmental Management* 84, no. 4 (September 2007): 473–83.
11. The district is in the northwest of the city, with northwest winds and water that flows toward the city center. According to homeowners, since water and wind both come from the direction of the district, pollution in the area would also end up in the city center.
12. The officials present denied the content of the EIA, likely because they were not in charge of the project and had not been informed of the details of the assessment.

13. None of the Meadow, Willow, or Pine homeowners I spoke to mentioned any negative interactions with police. In photos of the protest, police are seen walking among homeowners. Several photos depict protest signs reading "Protect water canals" stuck to the windshield of a public security van. However, one homeowner posted on the forum that she had heard "an old man" say that a "youngster from the community" was taken away by the police, but she specified that she had not witnessed the event directly. Responses to the post provided no further details or acknowledgment of the incident.
14. I could not verify Mr. Wu's numbers, but his key point was the impact of pollution on mortality. Together, the Meadow, Willow, and Pine communities consist of more than 5,500 households. Estimating a minimum of two people per household, 100 deaths would be 0.9 percent of all residents in the time span to which he was referring.
15. This statement is drawn from a document that compiled a timeline of important events, written by homeowners from Meadow, Willow, and Pine.
16. Researcher's note: Because it was known that I was an American researcher of Taiwanese origins, the homeowners would sometimes refer to the United States and Taiwan when providing examples. I preserved this reference to Taiwan, as it is an example of political campaigning in a democracy. During local elections in Taiwan, it is common for candidates to conduct door-to-door canvassing themselves, visiting the residents of their voting districts.
17. I have translated the Chinese content as closely as possible to convey homeowner intent, perceptions, and phrasing, which alternated between formal and informal language.
18. About $187 million U.S. dollars in 2005.
19. Further examples of how Meadow, Willow, and Pine homeowners cultivated civic responsibility in the public sphere are provided in chapter 6, which describes how some community representatives began giving talks at citywide environmental salons organized by nonprofit organizations.
20. There was some ambiguity around when construction for the incinerator actually started. Several local Beijing media reports suggested early 2009, whereas another stated that the incinerator would undergo a test run in 2009 (which would require it to be completed). A government document in Ms. Hua's files showed that the construction had begun in July 2008. When Ms. Hua snuck into the landfill area at the end of August 2008 (chapter 3), she suspected that the "foundation" of a building she had seen was evidence of the beginning of incinerator construction.
21. To my knowledge, unlike Meadow, Willow, and Pine homeowners, Ms. Hua and other Rose residents did not appear in person to request EIA documents. Therefore, it is unclear whether they experienced the same types of obstacles to obtaining documents that Mr. Wu did. Many Rose homeowners faxed requests for the EIAs, but not all received responses.
22. The medical incinerator was planned in 2003, construction began in 2005 (right after Rose homeowners moved in), and the incinerator was fully functioning in 2007. The medical incinerator was separate from the pharmaceutical factory that residents suspected was emitting smoke and stench (chapter 3).
23. At the time the incinerator was not yet constructed, so this "stench" was likely thought to come from the landfill or more generally from the local area, including both the landfill and the smoke from the medical incinerator.

6. CONSEQUENCES OF COMMUNITY ENVIRONMENTAL ORGANIZING

24. Ms. Hua suspected that environmental organizations did not want to be involved in any citizen-led efforts of collective action. Staff members of environmental organizations I interviewed explained that they would participate in environmental protests only as individuals, never using the names of their organizations, in order to avoid being shut down by the government. One staffer said that he was careful never to use a work-issued phone when discussing environmental protest issues.
25. CEMPRE refers to the Compromisso Empresarial para Reciclagem (Brazilian Business Commitment for Recycling), a nonprofit organization established by private companies in 1992 to promote recycling and better management of urban waste. See CEMPRE, *CEMPRE Review 2019* (São Paolo: CEMPRE, 2019), https://cempre.org.br/wp-content/uploads/2020/11/CEMPRE-Review2019.pdf.
26. "MBT" stands for "mechanical biological treatment," which is a type of solid-waste treatment system. These systems allow the recovery of materials contained within mixed waste, such as glass, plastic, or metals. "RDF" stands for "refuse-derived fuel," which can be produced during the MBT process and used to generate power.
27. Similarly, during my field work, I was able to access certain government officials through academic connections and introductions, rather than having to resort to the cold-calling approach taken by Rose homeowners.
28. Presumably introduced by the engineer, who was part of the Urban Management Commission, a municipal government agency.
29. At the time Mr. Lu made the comment in 2010, the outcome of the incinerator construction was still unclear. "Too early" meant that the government had decided to postpone the construction but that homeowners were still waiting for the final decision. The incinerator was eventually constructed and officially activated in 2019, according to media reports.
30. Presumably here the anticipated "stench" refers to the odor that would be caused by the incinerator rather than the landfill. In chapter 2, I noted that Marigold residents did not experience landfill stench, unlike the Meadow, Willow, Pine, and Rose homeowners. Mr. Lu wrote this poem before incinerator construction began, so he could be referring to a possible future occurrence, or he could be using hyperbole.
31. Yanfei Sun and Dingxin Zhao, "Explaining Dynamics and Outcomes of Environmental Campaigns in China: Multi-Actor State and Diverse Civil Society," in *Popular Protest in China* (Cambridge, MA: Harvard University Press, 2008), 144–62.

6. CONSEQUENCES OF COMMUNITY ENVIRONMENTAL ORGANIZING

1. When I visited in 2010 and 2011, the events were already over. What my time allowed me to observe was how much was *still* occurring beyond the protests and beyond the decisions about incinerator construction.
2. Although we initially spoke in Chicago, this interview, like all others for this book, was conducted in Mandarin.
3. Mr. Chen oversaw government-appointed academics and specialists who conducted EIAs.
4. Mr. Chen did not visit the site as a government representative. Rather, he visited out of personal interest in the issue. Though sympathetic, he did not seem to play a direct role in advocating for citizens or for incinerator construction. However, he

6. CONSEQUENCES OF COMMUNITY ENVIRONMENTAL ORGANIZING

followed discussions about incinerator construction closely and was able to tell me about relocation plans in detail (mentioned later in this chapter).
5. The Beijing EPB refused my numerous interview requests, even when I gave Mr. Chen's name as a reference.
6. I believe that Mr. Bo's commentary that incinerator relocation was in part due to homeowner pressure was fair here, given that in our conversations he did not attribute the success of every middle-class environmental protest to "government officials responding to pressure from citizens." Because his nonprofit had been collaborating with some homeowners' communities on education about trash separation, I wondered whether its staff would attribute too much of the anti-incinerator success to homeowners. However, when I asked about an anti-factory pollution case in a southern Chinese city occurring at around the same time that had reportedly been successful, Mr. Bo's explanation was very different. In that city, citizens, mostly middle-class professionals, had blocked a large highway to protest the factory. According to news reports, the polluting plant was shut down soon after. Several staff members of Mr. Bo's organization were quick to tell me with respect to that case, "Don't do it [as a case study].... There were 'internal [governmental] reasons' behind the success of that case." They explained that they had been advised by local officials not to divulge the reasons. These conversations demonstrated to me that the staff of environmental organizations maintain relationships with local officials and are able to differentiate between an outcome related to "internal government arrangements" and one influenced by "homeowner pressure."
7. However, Ms. Hua said that nearby residents reported that the area was smelly again soon after the tour; the "fragrant water" was not being sprayed regularly.
8. During this time, Ms. Hua was less active on the forum because of her ongoing lawsuits. Her lawyer had advised her to be wary of posting publicly, she told me. Likely because of this advice, no posts related to the tour were uploaded, even though several other homeowners had been present.
9. After Marigold's incinerator resistance, the topic of incineration gradually disappeared from the homeowners' forum. When relevant posts did appear, they were reposts of news articles on incineration or incinerator technology. Of all the communities, Marigold's forum had always been the least interactive. When homeowners did post, the predominant topic was home decor and renovation. The silence around the incinerator may also have been caused by the repression experienced by Marigold homeowners. In 2016, all posting dwindled significantly, likely because many residents switched over to WeChat discussion groups, which is now the preferred method of communication in most communities. I was not able to access WeChat groups.
10. Researcher's note: Taiwan was again used as an example here because of the speaker's knowledge of my Taiwanese origins. Taiwan has a progressive and efficient recycling program. To reduce waste, Taiwanese citizens are required to purchase government-mandated trash bags for their mixed waste, incentivizing them to separate waste from recyclable materials (which can be placed in any type of bag).
11. This notion of recycling is deeply shaped by social context. It reflects the prevalence of traditional rubbish scavengers (*shihuangzhe*) who hunt for plastic bottles or waste scraps to sell in order to make a living. In recent years, as trash separation and sorting have been implemented by the government, some scavengers have

6. CONSEQUENCES OF COMMUNITY ENVIRONMENTAL ORGANIZING

been officially hired to work in municipal sorting plants. Traditionally, scavengers often operated in a legal gray area. Local officials often let individual scavengers exist because they informally helped with urban trash management (e.g., recycling). However, many scavengers still try to stay out of sight when local officials show up to do routine neighborhood patrols or inspections. Although government officials often use catchphrases such as "reduce, reuse, recycle," their definitions of recycling still revolve around these local and traditional notions of environmentalism.

12. The terms "uncivilized" and "uneducated" in this context do not mean that government employees had no higher education. These terms are translated from the term "*jiaoyang*," which refers to education in terms of manners.
13. Selznik's influential study of the Tennessee Valley Authority (TVA), a federally owned corporation, demonstrates how co-optation happens: the TVA targeted and eventually absorbed local elites and community activists into its administrative structure to transform local opposition to TVA policies into support for those policies. Philip Selznick, *TVA and the Grass Roots: A Study in the Sociology of Formal Organization* (Berkeley: University of California Press, 1949).
14. The incorporation of scholarly expert and social-sector voices has recently been demonstrated in laws governing nonprofits and charities in China, but the incorporation of middle-class *citizen* opinions has not been as marked.
15. "Wet and dry separation" refers to separating kitchen compost from mixed waste.
16. In China, internal migration and household registration (*hukou*) status is tightly controlled by the government. A *hukou* refers to the registration of an individual in the system, which includes a person's name, date of birth, parental or spousal information, and establishes a person's permanent residency status. A person's permanent residency status is based on the residency location and categorization (i.e., urban or rural) of one's parent(s). This urban/rural classification was set up as a means to control population mobility and determine location-based eligibility for state-provided services and welfare. For example, there tend to be higher quality social services and more job opportunities in cities. In order to prevent an influx of rural migrants moving to cities for services and opportunities, the government has strict regulations limiting mobility. Switching the location and categorization of one's *hukou* is extremely difficult and requires government authorization. Because of this policy, rural workers who come to an urban area from another province (e.g., outside Beijing) cannot settle legally in cities, leading them to be without basic welfare and state-provided social services.
17. Examples of international media reports referring specifically to the "middle class" in China include features by Radio Free Asia (a nonprofit organization based in the United States that broadcasts radio programs and publishes online articles for audiences in Asia), *Week in China* (an independent publication based in Hong Kong), and Reuters. The term "middle class" is not typically used in Chinese media publications, however.
18. H. Christoph Steinhardt and Fengshi Wu, "In the Name of the Public: Environmental Protest and the Changing Landscape of Popular Contention in China," *China Journal* 75 (January 2016).
19. "Playing lute to the cow" is a Chinese proverb with the same meaning as the English saying "preaching to deaf ears." It can also be interpreted as implying stupidity in an audience.

6. CONSEQUENCES OF COMMUNITY ENVIRONMENTAL ORGANIZING

20. Contaminated communities are frequently located in impoverished areas, typically affecting people living in poverty and people from underrepresented groups. For example, see Robert D. Bullard, *Dumping In Dixie: Race, Class, and Environmental Quality* (New York: Routledge, 2000); Javier Auyero and Débora Alejandra Swistun, *Flammable: Environmental Suffering in an Argentine Shantytown* (New York: Oxford University Press, 2009).
21. The *People's Daily* is the official newspaper of the Central Committee of the Chinese Communist Party. Although government run, it occasionally publishes opinion pieces that express the views of authors (though generally not those that strongly oppose government views or behavior). In the case of Ms. Hua's father, criticism of train schedules was likely considered minor enough to be acceptable.
22. Meanwhile, the Rose forum continued to be active, even without Ms. Hua. Sports clubs resumed, and complaints about property management appeared frequently.
23. Mr. Lu started the company after investing 140,000 yuan (about $22,000 in U.S. dollars) of his own money. He never discussed profits with me, other than in reference to his intention to sell fertilizer later on. I expect that the initial investment was used to set up and run the trial sites. Because he often spoke about establishing this company as a model for community trash separation and processing *for* the municipal government and seemed to consult the government frequently regarding establishing and scaling up the sites, it appeared that he was moving toward a government-contractor model that would enable his company to provide government services.
24. This statement refers to Mr. Lu using his own money (140,000 yuan) to start his company, covering the costs of the sheds and equipment. He uses "we" to refer to his company.
25. Fen Lin and Xinzhi Zhang, "Movement–Press Dynamics and News Diffusion: A Typology of Activism in Digital China," *China Review* 18, no. 2 (2018): 33–64.
26. It is common and less risky in terms of attracting negative government attention for environmental NGOs to make policy recommendations rather than acting as social movement organizations.
27. Once resistance in Meadow, Willow, and Pine became more successful (i.e., peaceful dialogues with the government began to occur, a large World Environment Day march was not repressed, and the planned incinerator location was changed), the press covered the aspect of citizen resistance with regard to the incinerator issue much more thoroughly. Huang *laoshi* refers to this progress by characterizing the media as "eventually" providing coverage.
28. Ms. Hua subscribed to environmental text messaging threads (similar to mailing lists).
29. A citizen journalist, much like a citizen scientist, is a person who is not a member of the press and who writes new stories based on their own investigative work, especially when they suspect that an event or incident is not being covered by the media or a topic is being censored in the mainstream media. Articles written by citizen journalists often circulate on blogs or social media platforms.
30. To be a member of an environmental organization, individuals pay membership fees, thereby obtaining access to the organization's conferences.
31. Meadow's real community name included a Chinese term that overlapped with the name of an international revolutionary movement active at the time. Nearly

everything that included the term was placed under censorship—from children's songs to movies to the name of a community.
32. Based on interviews and online forum accounts, the decision to move in response to incinerator plans was rare.
33. See the introduction for explanations of media reporting. For examples of media framing and coverage strategies to avoid censorship, see Lin and Zhang, "Movement-Press Dynamics."
34. According to Bondes and Johnson, villagers did not establish contact with Meadow, Willow, and Pine residents, claiming that they had learned enough from the online materials, and instead contacted the experts and lawyers mentioned in the booklet. The homeowners never mentioned the farmers' protests to me. Maria Bondes and Thomas Johnson, "Beyond Localized Environmental Contention: Horizontal and Vertical Diffusion in a Chinese Anti-incinerator Campaign," *Journal of Contemporary China* 26, no. 106 (July 4, 2017): 504–20.
35. Bondes and Johnson, "Beyond Localized Environmental Contention," 518.
36. Bondes and Johnson, "Beyond Localized Environmental Contention," 516.

CONCLUSION

1. Yongshun Cai, *Collective Resistance in China: Why Popular Protests Succeed or Fail* (Stanford, CA: Stanford University Press, 2010).
2. Xi Chen, *Social Protest and Contentious Authoritarianism in China* (Cambridge: Cambridge University Press, 2011).
3. Rongbin Han, *Contesting Cyberspace in China: Online Expression and Authoritarian Resilience* (New York: Columbia University Press, 2018).
4. Joyce Y. Man, ed., *China's Housing Reform and Outcomes* (Cambridge, MA: Lincoln Institute of Land Policy, 2011).
5. Li Zhang, *In Search of Paradise: Middle-Class Living in a Chinese Metropolis* (Ithaca, NY: Cornell University Press, 2010).
6. Choon-Piew Pow, *Gated Communities in China: Class, Privilege and the Moral Politics of the Good Life* (New York: Routledge, 2009).
7. Zhang, *In Search of Paradise*.
8. Edward J. Blakely and Mary Gail Snyder, *Fortress America: Gated Communities in the United States* (Washington, DC: Brookings Institution Press, 1997).
9. Sian Lazar, *The Social Life of Politics: Ethics, Kinship, and Union Activism in Argentina* (Stanford, CA: Stanford University Press, 2017).
10. China has considered a property tax for more than a decade. The Chinese government announced in 2019 that it would draft a property tax deter real estate speculators. However, the property tax issue was omitted in both the 2020 and 2021 legislative plans, likely because of concerns around boosting the economy and consumption in the wake of the COVID-19 pandemic. However, the government plans to implement the tax within the next five years. Reuters, "China Omits Property Tax from 2021 Legislative Agenda," March 8, 2021, https://www.reuters.com/article/us-china-property-tax/china-omits-property-tax-from-2021-legislative-agenda-idUSKBN2B01GD. Currently, property fees are collected primarily during the process of property development, and few costs fall to residential homeowners.

Frank Tang, "China Urged to Push Ahead with Controversial Property Tax as 'Inevitable' Solution to Local Debt Crisis," *South China Morning Post*, May 16, 2021, https://www.scmp.com/economy/china-economy/article/3133531/china-urged-push-ahead-controversial-property-tax-inevitable?module=perpetual_scroll_0&pgtype=article&campaign=3133531.

11. For example, in October 2018, homeowners in several cities in China, including Shanghai, Xiamen, and Guiyang, hit the streets to protest, demanding refunds after property developers cut new property prices to stimulate sales. Tom Hancock, "China Homeowners Stage Protests Over Falling Prices," *Financial Times*, October 16, 2018, https://www.ft.com/content/fcb5af7c-d0fc-11e8-a9f2-7574db66bcd5.

12. I conducted this search using the CNKI China Core Newspapers Full-Text Database, a database of Chinese newspapers, with the broad keywords "*fenshao*" ("incineration"), "*fenhua*" (also "incineration"), and "*laji*" ("trash") to account for news coverage that may not have directly mentioned terms related to protesting.

13. Abubakar S Ringim et al., "How Citizen Scientists Are Rapidly Generating Big Distribution Data: Lessons from the Arewa Atlas Team, Nigerian Bird Atlas Project," *Ostrich* 93, no. 1 (January 2, 2022): 24–33, https://doi.org/10.2989/00306525.2022.2058105; Chia-Hsuan Hsu et al., "Taiwan Roadkill Observation Network: An Example of a Community of Practice Contributing to Taiwanese Environmental Literacy for Sustainability," *Sustainability* 10, no. 10 (October 2018): 3610, https://doi.org/10.3390/su10103610.

14. John Lyons and Paul Kiernan, "Middle-Class Brazil Finds Its Voice in Protests," *Wall Street Journal*, June 19, 2013, https://www.wsj.com/articles/SB10001424127887324021104578553491848777544.

15. Lisa Mueller, *Political Protest in Contemporary Africa* (Cambridge: Cambridge University Press, 2018).

16. Samer Bagaeen and Ola Uduku, eds., *Gated Communities: Social Sustainability in Contemporary and Historical Gated Developments* (New York: Routledge, 2010); Zaire Zenit Dinzey-Flores, "Gated Communities for the Rich and the Poor," *Contexts* 12, no. 4 (November 1, 2013): 24–29.

17. William A. V. Clark, Youqin Huang, and Diachun Yi, "Can Millennials Access Homeownership in Urban China?," *Journal of Housing and the Built Environment* 36, no. 1 (March 1, 2021): 69–87; Youqin Huang, Shenjing He, and Li Gan, "Introduction to SI: Homeownership and Housing Divide in China," *Cities* 108 (January 2021): 102967; United States Census Bureau, "Housing Vacancies and Homeownership," 2020, https://www.census.gov/housing/hvs/index.html.

18. Historians such as Rhonda Williams have studied the role of public housing in fostering political participation and civic engagement. Rhonda Y. Williams, *The Politics of Public Housing: Black Women's Struggles Against Urban Inequality* (New York: Oxford University Press, 2005).

BIBLIOGRAPHY

Auyero, Javier, and Débora Alejandra Swistun. *Flammable: Environmental Suffering in an Argentine Shantytown*. New York: Oxford University Press, 2009.

Bagaeen, Samer, and Ola Uduku, eds. *Gated Communities: Social Sustainability in Contemporary and Historical Gated Developments*. New York: Routledge, 2010.

BBC News. "Killing Sparks Protests in China," January 9, 2008. http://news.bbc.co.uk/2/hi/asia-pacific/7178382.stm.

Beijing Municipal Civil Affairs Bureau. "Beijing Shehui Zuzhi Gonggong Fuwu Pingtai" [Social organization service platform/registry]. Accessed 2017–2018. https://ggfw.mzj.beijing.gov.cn.

Bint-e-Waheed, Humna, and Obaidullah Nadeem. "Perception of Security Risk in Gated and Non-gated Communities in Lahore, Pakistan." *Journal of Housing and the Built Environment* 35, no. 3 (September 1, 2020): 897–915. https://doi.org/10.1007/s10901-019-09719-2.

Blakely, Edward J., and Mary Gail Snyder. *Fortress America: Gated Communities in the United States*. Washington, DC: Brookings Institution Press, 1997.

Blandy, Sarah, and Feng Wang. "Curbing the Power of Developers? Law and Power in Chinese and English Gated Urban Enclaves." *Geoforum* 47 (June 1, 2013): 199–208. https://doi.org/10.1016/j.geoforum.2013.01.011.

Bondes, Maria, and Thomas Johnson. "Beyond Localized Environmental Contention: Horizontal and Vertical Diffusion in a Chinese Anti-incinerator Campaign." *Journal of Contemporary China* 26, no. 106 (July 4, 2017): 504–20. https://doi.org/10.1080/10670564.2017.1275079.

Bray, David. *Social Space and Governance in Urban China: The Danwei System from Origins to Reform*. Stanford, CA: Stanford University Press, 2005.

Bullard, Robert D. *Dumping in Dixie: Race, Class, and Environmental Quality*. New York: Routledge, 2000.

BIBLIOGRAPHY

Cai, Ming, Jing Li, Zhanyong Wang, and Haibo Wang. "Evaluation of External Costs in Road Transport Under the Openness of a Gated Community." *Frontiers of Earth Science* 14, no. 1 (March 1, 2020): 140–51. https://doi.org/10.1007/s11707-019-0762-z.

Cai, Yongshun. "China's Moderate Middle Class: The Case of Homeowners' Resistance." *Asian Survey* 45, no. 5 (2005): 777–99. https://doi.org/10.1525/as.2005.45.5.777.

———. "Civil Resistance and Rule of Law in China: The Defense of Homeowners' Rights." *Harvard Contemporary China Series* 14 (2007): 174–95.

———. *Collective Resistance in China: Why Popular Protests Succeed or Fail* (Stanford, CA: Stanford University Press, 2010).

———. "Disruptive Collective Action in the Reform Era." In *Popular Protest in China*, ed. Kevin J. O'Brien, 163–78. Cambridge, MA: Harvard University Press, 2008.

Caldeira, Teresa P. R. *City of Walls: Crime, Segregation, and Citizenship in São Paulo.* Berkeley: University of California Press, 2000.

CEMPRE (Compromisso Empresarial para Reciclagem [Brazilian Business Commitment for Recycling]). *CEMPRE Review 2019.* São Paulo: CEMPRE, 2019. https://cempre.org.br/wp-content/uploads/2020/11/CEMPRE-Review2019.pdf.

Chen, Jie, and Chunlong Lu. "Social Capital in Urban China: Attitudinal and Behavioral Effects on Grassroots Self-Government." *Social Science Quarterly* 88, no. 2 (2007): 422–42. https://doi.org/10.1111/j.1540-6237.2007.00465.x.

Chen, Minglu, and David S. G. Goodman, eds. *Middle Class China.* Cheltenham: Edward Elgar, 2013.

Chen, Xi. "Collective Petitioning and Institutional Conversion." In *Popular Protest in China*, ed. Kevin J. O'Brien, 54–70. Cambridge, MA: Harvard University Press, 2008.

———. *Social Protest and Contentious Authoritarianism in China.* Cambridge: Cambridge University Press, 2011.

Chen, Xin. *Yezhu Zizhi: Yi Jianzhuwu Qufen Suoyouquan Wei Jichu* [Homeowners' self-governance: On the basis of proportional property rights]. Beijing: Peking University Press, 2007.

Chua, Beng-Huat. "Consuming Asians: Ideas and Issues." In *Consumption in Asia: Lifestyle and Identities*, ed. Beng-Huat Chua, 1–34. London: Routledge, 2000.

———, ed. *Consumption in Asia: Lifestyle and Identities.* London: Routledge, 2000.

Clark, William A. V., Youqin Huang, and Diachun Yi. "Can Millennials Access Homeownership in Urban China?" *Journal of Housing and the Built Environment* 36, no. 1 (March 1, 2021): 69–87. https://doi.org/10.1007/s10901-019-09672-0.

Clemens, Elisabeth S. *The People's Lobby: Organizational Innovation and the Rise of Interest Group Politics in the United States, 1890–1925.* Chicago: University of Chicago Press, 1997.

CNKI Zhongguo Zhiwang. *China Core Newspapers Full-Text Database.* Accessed 2016. https://gongjushu.oversea.cnki.net/oversea/.

Davis, Deborah, ed. *The Consumer Revolution in Urban China.* Berkeley: University of California Press, 2000.

Davis, Mike. "Fortress Los Angeles: The Militarization of Urban Space." In *Cultural Criminology: Theories of Crime*, ed. Jeff Ferrell and Keith Hayward, 287–314. New York: Routledge, 2011.

———. "Fortress Los Angeles: The Militarization of Urban Space." In *Variations on a Theme Park: The New American City and the End of Public Space*, ed. Michael Sorkin, 154–80. New York: Noonday, 1992.

BIBLIOGRAPHY

Deng, Yanhua, and Kevin J. O'Brien. "Relational Repression in China: Using Social Ties to Demobilize Protesters." *China Quarterly* 215 (September 2013): 533–52. https://doi.org/10.1017/S0305741013000714.

Devine-Wright, Patrick. "Rethinking NIMBYism: The Role of Place Attachment and Place Identity in Explaining Place-Protective Action." *Journal of Community & Applied Social Psychology* 19, no. 6 (2009): 426–41. https://doi.org/10.1002/casp.1004.

Dinzey-Flores, Zaire Zenit. "Gated Communities for the Rich and the Poor." *Contexts* 12, no. 4 (November 1, 2013): 24–29. https://doi.org/10.1177/1536504213511212.

DiPasquale, Denise, and Edward L. Glaeser. "Incentives and Social Capital: Are Homeowners Better Citizens?" *Journal of Urban Economics* 45, no. 2 (March 1, 1999): 354–84. https://doi.org/10.1006/juec.1998.2098.

Dupuis, Anna, Sarah Blandy, and Jennifer Dixon, eds. *Multi-owned Housing: Law, Power, and Practice.* London: Routledge, 2016.

Earl, Jennifer. "Introduction: Repression and the Social Control of Protest." *Mobilization: An International Quarterly* 11, no. 2 (August 4, 2006): 129–43. https://doi.org/10.17813/maiq.11.2.b55gm84032815278.

Economy, Elizabeth C. *The River Runs Black: The Environmental Challenge to China's Future,* 2nd ed. Ithaca, NY: Cornell University Press, 2010.

Edwards, Michael. *Civil Society.* Cambridge: Polity, 2009.

Falzon, Mark-Anthony. "Paragons of Lifestyle: Gated Communities and the Politics of Space in Bombay." *City & Society* 16, no. 2 (2004): 145–67. https://doi.org/10.1525/city.2004.16.2.145.

Fang, Qiangyu. "Shequ Shehui Zuzhi Beian, NGO Zhunbei Haole Ma" [Community social organization registrations: Are NGOs prepared?]. *China Development Brief,* April 28, 2009. http://www.chinadevelopmentbrief.org.cn/customer/details.html?id=13278&type=.

Fernandes, Leela. *India's New Middle Class: Democratic Politics in an Era of Economic Reform.* Minneapolis: University of Minnesota Press, 2006.

Fraser, David. "Inventing Oasis: Luxury Housing Advertisements and Reconfiguring Domestic Space in Shanghai." In *The Consumer Revolution in Urban China,* ed. Deborah Davis, 25–53. Berkeley: University of California Press, 2000.

Fu, Qiang, and Nan Lin. "The Weaknesses of Civic Territorial Organizations: Civic Engagement and Homeowners Associations in Urban China." *International Journal of Urban and Regional Research* 38, no. 6 (2014): 2309–27. https://doi.org/10.1111/1468-2427.12080.

Fung, Archon. "Associations and Democracy: Between Theories, Hopes, and Realities." *Annual Review of Sociology* 29, no. 1 (2003): 515–39. https://doi.org/10.1146/annurev.soc.29.010202.100134.

Garg, Amit, Manmohan Kapshe, Priyadarshi Shukla, and Debyani Ghosh. "Large Point Source (LPS) Emissions from India: Regional and Sectoral Analysis." *Atmospheric Environment* 36, no. 2 (January 1, 2002): 213–24. https://doi.org/10.1016/S1352-2310(01)00439-3.

Goodman, David S. G. "Middle Class China: Dreams and Aspirations." *Journal of Chinese Political Science* 19, no. 1 (March 1, 2014): 49–67. https://doi.org/10.1007/s11366-013-9275-x.

——, ed. *The New Rich in China: Future Rulers, Present Lives.* London: Routledge, 2008.

Gould, Roger V. *Insurgent Identities: Class, Community, and Protest in Paris from 1848 to the Commune.* Chicago: University of Chicago Press, 1995.

―. "Trade Cohesion, Class Unity, and Urban Insurrection: Artisanal Activism in the Paris Commune." *American Journal of Sociology* 98, no. 4 (January 1993): 721–54. https://doi.org/10.1086/230088.

Goyal, Prima, and T. V. B. P. S. Rama Krishna. "Dispersion of Pollutants in Convective Low Wind: A Case Study of Delhi." *Atmospheric Environment* 36, no. 12 (2003): 2071–79. https://doi.org/10.1016/S1352-2310(01)00458-7.

Goyal, S. K., and C. V. Chalapati Rao. "Air Assimilative Capacity-Based Environment Friendly Siting of New Industries—A Case Study of Kochi Region, India." *Journal of Environmental Management* 84, no. 4 (September 2007): 473–83. https://doi.org/10.1016/j.jenvman.2006.06.020.

Grannis, Rick. "T-Communities: Pedestrian Street Networks and Residential Segregation in Chicago, Los Angeles, and New York." *City & Community* 4, no. 3 (September 1, 2005): 295–321. https://doi.org/10.1111/j.1540-6040.2005.00118.x.

―. "The Importance of Trivial Streets: Residential Streets and Residential Segregation." *American Journal of Sociology* 103, no. 6 (1998): 1530–64. https://doi.org/10.1086/231400.

Gurr, Ted Robert. *Why Men Rebel*. Princeton, NJ: Princeton University Press, 1970.

―. *Why Men Rebel*, 40th anniversary ed. New York: Paradigm, 2010.

Gusfield, Joseph R. "Functional Areas of Leadership in Social Movements." *Sociological Quarterly* 7, no. 2 (1966): 137–56.

Han, Hahrie. *How Organizations Develop Activists: Civic Associations and Leadership in the 21st Century*. New York: Oxford University Press, 2014.

―. *Moved to Action: Motivation, Participation, and Inequality in American Politics*. Stanford, CA: Stanford University Press, 2009.

Han, Rongbin. *Contesting Cyberspace in China: Online Expression and Authoritarian Resilience*. New York: Columbia University Press, 2018.

Hancock, Tom. "China Homeowners Stage Protests Over Falling Prices." *Financial Times*, October 16, 2018. https://www.ft.com/content/fcb5af7c-d0fc-11e8-a9f2-7574db66bcd5.

He, Shenjing. "Homeowner Associations and Neighborhood Governance in Guangzhou, China." *Eurasian Geography and Economics* 56, no. 3 (May 4, 2015): 260–84. https://doi.org/10.1080/15387216.2015.1095108.

Ho, Peter. "Greening Without Conflict? Environmentalism, NGOs and Civil Society in China." *Development and Change* 32, no. 5 (2001): 893–921.

Holston, James. *The Modernist City: An Anthropological Critique of Brasilia*. Chicago: University of Chicago Press, 1989.

Hsu, Chia-Hsuan, Te-En Lin, Wei-Ta Fang, and Chi-Chang Liu. "Taiwan Roadkill Observation Network: An Example of a Community of Practice Contributing to Taiwanese Environmental Literacy for Sustainability." *Sustainability* 10, no. 10 (October 2018): 3610. https://doi.org/10.3390/su10103610.

Huang, Youqin. "The Road to Homeownership: A Longitudinal Analysis of Tenure Transition in Urban China (1949–94)." *International Journal of Urban and Regional Research* 28 (2004): 774–95. https://doi.org/10.1111/j.0309-1317.2004.00551.x.

Huang, Youqin, and William A. V. Clark. "Housing Tenure Choice in Transitional Urban China: A Multilevel Analysis." *Urban Studies* 39, no. 1 (2002): 7–32. https://doi.org/10.1080/00420980220099041.

Huang, Youqin, Shenjing He, and Li Gan. "Introduction to SI: Homeownership and Housing Divide in China." *Cities* 108 (January 2021): 102967.

BIBLIOGRAPHY

Huang, Zhonghua, Xuejun Du, and Xiaofen Yu. "Home Ownership and Residential Satisfaction: Evidence from Hangzhou, China." *Habitat International* 49 (October 2015): 74–83. https://doi.org/10.1016/j.habitatint.2015.05.008.
Jones, Andrew F. "The Politics of Popular Music in Post-Tiananmen China." In *Popular Protest and Political Culture in Modern China*, ed. Jeffrey N. Wasserstrom and Elizabeth J. Perry, 291–310. New York: Routledge, 1994.
Klinenberg, Eric. *Heat Wave: A Social Autopsy of Disaster in Chicago*, 2nd ed. Chicago: University of Chicago Press, 2015.
Landman, Karina, and Martin Schönteich. "Urban Fortresses: Gated Communities as a Reaction to Crime." *African Security Review* 11, no. 4 (2002): 71–85. https://doi.org/10.1080/10246029.2002.9628147.
Lazar, Sian. *The Social Life of Politics: Ethics, Kinship, and Union Activism in Argentina*. Stanford, CA: Stanford University Press, 2017.
Lee, Kingsyhon, and Ming-Sho Ho. "The Maoming Anti-PX Protest of 2014: An Environmental Movement in Contemporary China." *China Perspectives* 2014, no. 3 (2014): 33–39. https://doi.org/10.4000/chinaperspectives.6537.
Leisch, Harald. "Gated Communities in Indonesia." *Cities* 19, no. 5 (October 2002): 341–50. https://doi.org/10.1016/S0264-2751(02)00042-2.
Lewenstein, Bruce. "Can We Understand Citizen Science?" In "Citizen Science, Part I, 2016," special issue. *Journal of Science Communication* 15, no. 1 (January 21, 2016). https://doi.org/10.22323/2.15010501.
Ley, David. *The New Middle Class and the Remaking of the Central City*. Oxford: Oxford University Press, 1996.
Li, Cheng. "Introduction: The Rise of the Middle Class in the Middle Kingdom." In *China's Emerging Middle Class: Beyond Economic Transformation*, ed. Cheng Li, 3–31. Washington, DC: Brookings Institution Press, 2010.
Li, Li. "Yige Xiaoqu Zhineng Chengli Yige Yeweihui Nandao Jin Shiwan Jumin Chaoji Xiaoqu" [One community can only have one HOA, puts tens of thousands of residents in a 'super community' in a tough spot]. *Sanxiang Dushi Bao*, July 19, 2020. https://hn.rednet.cn/content/2020/07/19/7681625.html.
Li, Lianjiang, Mingxing Liu, and Kevin J. O'Brien. "Petitioning Beijing: The High Tide of 2003–2006." *China Quarterly* 210 (June 2012): 313–34. https://doi.org/10.1017/S0305741012000227.
Li, Limei, and Si-ming Li. "Becoming Homeowners: The Emergence and Use of Online Neighborhood Forums in Transitional Urban China." *Habitat International* 38 (April 1, 2013): 232–39. https://doi.org/10.1016/j.habitatint.2012.07.003.
———. "Living the Networked Life in the Commodity Housing Estates: Everyday Use of Online Neighborhood Forums and Community Participation in Urban China." In *Housing Inequality in Chinese Cities*, ed. Youqin Huang and Si-ming Li, 181–98. London: Routledge, 2014.
Li, Lin, and He Tian. *Zhongguo fazhi fazhan baogao* [Annual report on China's rule of law]. Beijing: Academy of Social Sciences Press, 2014.
Liechty, Mark. *Suitably Modern*. Princeton, NJ: Princeton University Press, 2003.
Lin, Fen, and Xinzhi Zhang. "Movement-Press Dynamics and News Diffusion: A Typology of Activism in Digital China." *China Review* 18, no. 2 (2018): 33–64.
Liu, Lee. "Made in China: Cancer Villages." *Environment: Science and Policy for Sustainable Development* 52, no. 2 (February 26, 2010): 8–21. https://doi.org/10.1080/00139151003618118.

BIBLIOGRAPHY

Low, Setha. *Behind the Gates: Life, Security, and the Pursuit of Happiness in Fortress America*. New York: Routledge, 2003. https://doi.org/10.4324/9780203491256.

Lu, Xiaobo, and Elizabeth J. Perry. *The Danwei: Changing Chinese Workplace in Historical and Comparative Perspective*. New York: Routledge, 2015. https://doi.org/10.4324/9781315700014.

Lyons, John, and Paul Kiernan. "Middle-Class Brazil Finds Its Voice in Protests." *Wall Street Journal*, June 19, 2013. https://www.wsj.com/articles/SB10001424127887324021104578553491848777544.

Makinde, Olusola Oladapo. "The Correlates of Residents' Perception of Safety in Gated Communities in Nigeria." *Social Sciences & Humanities Open* 2, no. 1 (January 1, 2020): 100018. https://doi.org/10.1016/j.ssaho.2020.100018.

Man, Joyce Y., ed. *China's Housing Reform and Outcomes*. Cambridge, MA: Lincoln Institute of Land Policy, 2011.

Mann, Sheilah, and John J. Patrick, eds. *Education for Civic Engagement in Democracy: Service Learning and Other Promising Practices*. Bloomington: ERIC Clearinghouse for Social Studies/Social Science Education, Indiana University, 2000.

McAdam, Doug, and Hilary Boudet. *Putting Social Movements in Their Place: Explaining Opposition to Energy Projects in the United States, 2000–2005*. Cambridge: Cambridge University Press, 2012. https://doi.org/10.1017/CBO9781139105811.

McAdam, Doug, John D. McCarthy, and Mayer N. Zald, eds. *Comparative Perspectives on Social Movements: Political Opportunities, Mobilizing Structures, and Cultural Framings*. Cambridge: Cambridge University Press, 1996.

McCarthy, John D., and Mayer N. Zald. "Resource Mobilization and Social Movements: A Partial Theory." *American Journal of Sociology* 82, no. 6 (1977): 1212–41.

Meng, Jing. "To Burn or Not to Burn: A Hot Topic." *China Daily*, June 25, 2010. http://www.chinadaily.com.cn/cndy/2010-06/22/content_10000256.htm.

Merle, Aurore. "Homeowners of Beijing, Unite! The Construction of a Collective Mobilisation." Translated by Will Thornely. *China Perspectives* 2014, no. 2 (June 1, 2014): 7–15. https://doi.org/10.4000/chinaperspectives.6441.

Miao, Ying. "Middle Class Identity in China: Subjectivity and Stratification." *Asian Studies Review* 41, no. 4 (October 2, 2017): 629–46. https://doi.org/10.1080/10357823.2017.1372360.

Mills, C. Wright. *White Collar: The American Middle Classes*. New York: Oxford University Press, 1951.

Ministry of Environmental Protection. *Annual Report on Open Government Information*. Beijing: Ministry of Environmental Protection, 2010.

——. *China Environmental Evaluation 2008*. Beijing: Ministry of Environmental Protection, 2008.

——. *Report on the State of the Environment in* China, 2007.

Mueller, Lisa. *Political Protest in Contemporary Africa*. Cambridge: Cambridge University Press, 2018.

National Bureau of Statistics of China. *Beijing Statistical Yearbooks*. Beijing: China Statistics, 2003–2014.

——. *China 2010 County Population Census Data*. Beijing: China Statistics, 2011.

——. *China Statistical Yearbooks*. . Beijing: China Statistics, 1998-2013.

National People's Congress of the People's Republic of China. "Law of the People's Republic of China on Evaluation of Environmental Effects." Meeting of the Standing Committee

BIBLIOGRAPHY

of the Ninth National People's Congress, October 28, 2002. http://www.npc.gov.cn /englishnpc/Law/2007-12/06/content_1382122.htm.

O'Brien, Kevin J., ed. *Popular Protest in China*. Cambridge, MA: Harvard University Press, 2008.

O'Brien, Kevin J., and Lianjiang Li. *Rightful Resistance in Rural China*. Cambridge: Cambridge University Press, 2006.

Park, Robert E. "The City: Suggestions for the Investigation of Human Behavior in the City Environment." *American Journal of Sociology* 20, no. 5 (March 1915): 577–612. https://doi.org/10.1086/212433.

Patrick, John J. "Introduction to Education for Civic Engagement in Democracy." In *Education for Civic Engagement in Democracy: Service Learning and Other Promising Practices*, ed. Sheilah Mann and John J. Patrick, 1–8. Bloomington: ERIC Clearinghouse for Social Studies/Social Science Education, Indiana University, 2000.

Pow, Choon-Piew. *Gated Communities in China: Class, Privilege, and the Moral Politics of the Good Life*. New York: Routledge, 2009.

Putnam, Robert D. "Bowling Alone: America's Declining Social Capital." *Journal of Democracy* 6, no. 1 (1995): 65–78. https://doi.org/10.1353/jod.1995.0002.

Rahmaan, Anis, and Anis Bushra. "Dynamics of Gated Communities, Their Impact and Challenges for Sustainable Development: A Case Study of Lahore, Pakistan." *Archnet-IJAR: International Journal of Architectural Research* 3, no. 1 (March 1, 2009): 57–70. https://doi.org/10.26687/archnet-ijar.v3i1.253.

Rankin, Bruce H., and James M. Quane. "Neighborhood Poverty and the Social Isolation of Inner-City African American Families." *Social Forces* 79, no. 1 (2000): 139–64. https://doi.org/10.2307/2675567.

Read, Benjamin L. "Democratizing the Neighbourhood? New Private Housing and Home-Owner Self-Organization in Urban China." *China Journal* 49 (January 2003): 31–59. https://doi.org/10.2307/3182194.

———. "Revitalizing the State's Urban 'Nerve Tips.'" *China Quarterly* 163 (September 2000): 806–20. https://doi.org/10.1017/S0305741000014673.

Reuters. "China Omits Property Tax from 2021 Legislative Agenda," March 8, 2021. https://www.reuters.com/article/us-china-property-tax/china-omits-property -tax-from-2021-legislative-agenda-idUSKBN2B01GD.

Ringim, Abubakar S, Sulaiman I Muhammad, Longji A Bako, Haruna M Abubakar, Sulaiman M Isa, Doofan J Nelly, Aliyu A Bajoga, et al. "How Citizen Scientists Are Rapidly Generating Big Distribution Data: Lessons from the Arewa Atlas Team, Nigerian Bird Atlas Project." *Ostrich* 93, no. 1 (January 2, 2022): 24–33. https://doi.org /10.2989/00306525.2022.2058105.

Rosen, Kenneth T., and Madelyn C. Ross. "Increasing Home Ownership in Urban China: Notes on the Problem of Affordability." *Housing Studies* 15, no. 1 (January 1, 2000): 77–88. https://doi.org/10.1080/02673030082487.

Sakip, Siti Rasidah Md, Noraini Johari, and Mohd Najib Mohd Salleh. "Perception of Safety in Gated and Non-gated Neighborhoods." *Procedia—Social and Behavioral Sciences* 85 (2013): 383–91.

Sampson, Robert J. "What 'Community' Supplies." In *Urban Problems and Community Development*, ed. William T. Dickens and Ronald F. Ferguson, 241–92. Washington, DC: Brookings Institution Press, 1999.

Sampson, Robert J., Doug McAdam, Heather MacIndoe, and Simón Weffer-Elizondo. "Civil Society Reconsidered: The Durable Nature and Community Structure of Collective Civic Action." *American Journal of Sociology* 111, no. 3 (November 2005): 673–714. https://doi.org/10.1086/497351.

Selznick, Philip. *TVA and the Grass Roots: A Study in the Sociology of Formal Organization*. Berkeley: University of California Press, 1949.

Shapiro, Judith. *China's Environmental Challenges*. Cambridge: Polity, 2012.

Siu, Helen. "The Cultural Landscape of Luxury Housing in South China: A Regional History." In *Locating China: Space, Place, and Popular Culture*, ed. Jing Wang, 72–93. London: Routledge, 2005.

Small, Mario Luis. *Unanticipated Gains: Origins of Network Inequality in Everyday Life*. New York: Oxford University Press, 2010.

———. *Villa Victoria: The Transformation of Social Capital in a Boston Barrio*. Chicago: University of Chicago Press, 2004.

Smith, David Horton. *Grassroots Associations*. Thousand Oaks, CA: Sage, 2000.

Smith, Graham. *The Nationalities Question in the Post-Soviet States*. London: Longman, 1996.

Smith, Neil. *The New Urban Frontier: Gentrification and the Revanchist City*. London: Routledge, 1996.

Somers, Margaret R. "Citizenship and the Place of the Public Sphere: Law, Community, and Political Culture in the Transition to Democracy." *American Sociological Review* 58, no. 5 (1993): 587–620. https://doi.org/10.2307/2096277.

State Environmental Protection Administration of China. "Green GDP Accounting Study Report Press Release." 2006. http://www.gov.cn/english/2006-09/11/content_384596.htm.

———. "Open Government Information Regulations Act and the Measures on Environmental Information Disclosure." February 8, 2007. https://www.cecc.gov/resources/legal-provisions/measures-on-open-environmental-information-trial-cecc-full-translation.

Steinhardt, H. Christoph, and Fengshi Wu. "In the Name of the Public: Environmental Protest and the Changing Landscape of Popular Contention in China." *China Journal* 75 (January 2016). https://doi.org/10.1086/684010.

Stockholm Environment Institute and United Nations Development Programme. *China Human Development Report 2002: Making Green Development a Choice*. Oxford: Oxford University Press, 2002. https://www.undp.org/china/publications/china-human-development-report-2002.

Sun, Yanfei, and Dingxin Zhao. "Explaining Dynamics and Outcomes of Environmental Campaigns in China: Multi-Actor State and Diverse Civil Society." In *Popular Protest in China*, 144–62. Cambridge, Mass: Harvard University Press, 2008.

Tang, Frank. "China Urged to Push Ahead with Controversial Property Tax as 'Inevitable' Solution to Local Debt Crisis." *South China Morning Post*, May 16, 2021. https://www.scmp.com/economy/china-economy/article/3133531/china-urged-push-ahead-controversial-property-tax-inevitable?module=perpetual_scroll_0&pgtype=article&campaign=3133531.

Tanulku, Basak. "Gated Communities: Ideal Packages or Processual Spaces of Conflict?" *Housing Studies* 28, no. 7 (2013): 937–59. https://doi.org/10.1080/02673037.2013.803042.

BIBLIOGRAPHY

Tomba, Luigi. "Residential Space and Collective Interest Formation in Beijing's Housing Disputes." *China Quarterly* 184 (December 2005): 934–51. https://doi.org/10.1017/S0305741005000573.

Tong, Zhifeng. "Reflections on Environmental Mass Incidents in China." In *The China Environment Yearbook*, vol. 3, ed. International Advisory Board Chinese Research Perspectives Online, 235–48. Leiden: Brill, 2017. https://referenceworks.brillonline.com/entries/chinese-research-perspectives-online/reflections-on-environmental-mass-incidents-in-china-C9789004173491_021.

Tu, Chaohua. "Xiamen PX Xiangmu Shijian Shimo." [The case of Xiamen PX incident]. *China Youth Daily*, December 27, 2007.

Tufekci, Zeynep. *Twitter and Tear Gas: The Power and Fragility of Networked Protest*, reprint ed. New Haven, CT: Yale University Press, 2018.

Turner, Ralph H., and Lewis M. Killian. *Collective Behavior*. Englewood Cliffs, NJ: Prentice-Hall, 1972.

United States Census Bureau. "Housing Vacancies and Homeownership," 2020. https://www.census.gov/housing/hvs/index.html.

Verba, Sidney, Kay Lehman Schlozman, and Henry E. Brady. *Voice and Equality: Civic Voluntarism in American Politics*. Cambridge, MA: Harvard University Press, 1995.

Vogel, Ezra F. *Japan's New Middle Class: The Salary Man and His Family in a Tokyo Suburb*. Berkeley: University of California Press, 1963.

Walder, Andrew G. *Communist Neo-Traditionalism: Work and Authority in Chinese Industry*. Berkeley: University of California Press, 1988.

Walker, Edward T. "Contingent Pathways from Joiner to Activist: The Indirect Effect of Participation in Voluntary Associations on Civic Engagement." *Sociological Forum* 23, no. 1 (2008): 116–43.

Walsh, Edward J., Rex Warland, and Douglas Clayton Smith. *Don't Burn It Here: Grassroots Challenges to Trash Incinerators*. University Park, PA: Penn State University Press, 1997.

Wan fang shu ju (Firm). *China Real Estate Statistics, 2007–2016*. EPS shu ju ping tai [EPS China Data Platform]. Accessed 2016 to 2018. http://www.epschinadata.com/index.html.

Wang, Alex. "Environmental Protection in China: The Role of Law." *China Dialogue*, February 5, 2007. https://chinadialogue.net/en/pollution/745-environmental-protection-in-china-the-role-of-law/.

———. "Explaining Environmental Information Disclosure in China." *Ecology Law Quarterly* 44 (2018): 865–921.

Wang, Feng. "Determinants of the Effectiveness of Chinese Homeowner Associations in Solving Neighborhood Issues." *Urban Affairs Review* 50, no. 3 (May 1, 2014): 311–39. https://doi.org/10.1177/1078087413501641.

———. "Regulations and the Imbalance of Power Relationships in Newly Developed Residential Neighbourhoods in Urban China." In *Multi-owned Housing: Law, Power, and Practice*, ed. Sarah Blandy, Anna Dupuis, and Jennifer Dixon, 125–44. London: Routledge, 2016.

———. "The Social Functions of Private Neighborhood Associations: The Case of Homeowner Associations in Urban China." PhD diss., University of Southern California, 2008. https://doi.org/10.25549/usctheses-m1588.

BIBLIOGRAPHY

Wang, Feng, Haitao Yin, and Zhiren Zhou. "The Adoption of Bottom-Up Governance in China's Homeowner Associations." *Management and Organization Review* 8, no. 3 (2012): 559–83. https://doi.org/10.1111/j.1740-8784.2011.00277.x.

Wang, Ya Ping. "Recent Housing Reform Practice in Chinese Cities: Social and Spatial Implications." In *China's Housing Reform and Outcomes*, ed. Joyce Y. Man, 19–44. Cambridge, MA: Lincoln Institute of Land Policy, 2011.

Wang, Ya Ping, and Alan Murie. "Commercial Housing Development in Urban China." *Urban Studies* 36, no. 9 (1999): 1475–94.

———. "The Process of Commercialisation of Urban Housing in China." *Urban Studies* 33, no. 6 (1996): 971–89.

Wang, Zhengxu, Long Sun, Liuqing Xu, and Dragan Pavlićević. "Leadership in China's Urban Middle Class Protest: The Movement to Protect Homeowners' Rights in Beijing." *China Quarterly* 214 (2013): 411–31.

Warren, Mark E. *Democracy and Association*. Princeton, NJ: Princeton University Press, 2001.

Weick, Karl E. *The Social Psychology of Organizing*. New York: McGraw-Hill, 1979.

Whyte, Martin King, and William L. Parish. *Urban Life in Contemporary China*. Chicago: University of Chicago Press, 1984.

Williams, Rhonda Y. *The Politics of Public Housing: Black Women's Struggles Against Urban Inequality*. New York: Oxford University Press, 2005.

World Bank. "Urban Development Overview." Last updated October 6, 2022. https://www.worldbank.org/en/topic/urbandevelopment/overview

———. "World Urbanization Prospects: 2018 Revision." World Bank Open Data, 2018. https://data.worldbank.org/indicator/SP.URB.TOTL.IN.ZS?locations=CN.

Wu, Kaize. "Housing Reform, Life Course, and Urban Housing Acquisition (1980–2010)." *Journal of Chinese Sociology* 6, no. 15 (July 25, 2019). https://doi.org/10.1186/s40711-019-0101-5.

Yan, Lu. "Heading in One Direction." *Beijing Review*, September 27, 2018. https://www.bjreview.com/China_Focus/Time/201809/t20180927_800142644.html.

Yang, Guobin. "The Internet and Civil Society in China: A Preliminary Assessment." *Journal of Contemporary China* 12, no. 36 (August 1, 2003): 453–75. https://doi.org/10.1080/10670560305471.

———. "The Internet and the Rise of a Transnational Chinese Cultural Sphere." *Media, Culture & Society* 25, no. 4 (July 1, 2003): 469–90. https://doi.org/10.1177/01634437030254003.

Yang, Weidong. "Can the Introduction of Administrative Reconsideration Committees Help Reform China's System of Administrative Reconsideration?" *University of Pennsylvania Asian Law Review* 13 (January 1, 2018): 107–34.

Yang, Zan, and Jie Chen. *Housing Affordability and Housing Policy in Urban China*. Berlin: Springer, 2014.

Yu, Dawei. "Chinese Waste: The Burning Issue." *China Dialogue*, January 26, 2012. https://chinadialogue.net/en/business/4739-chinese-waste-the-burning-issue/.

Zhang, Hongming. *Housing Economics*. Shanghai: Shanghai University of Finance and Economics Press, 1998.

Zhang, Li. *In Search of Paradise: Middle-Class Living in a Chinese Metropolis*. Ithaca, NY: Cornell University Press, 2010.

Zhang, Xing Quan. *Privatisation: A Study of Housing Policy in Urban China*. Hauppauge, NY: Nova Science, 1998.

BIBLIOGRAPHY

———. "Privatization and the Chinese Housing Model." *International Planning Studies* 5, no. 2 (June 2000): 191–204.
Zhao, Dingxin. *The Power of Tiananmen: State-Society Relations and the 1989 Beijing Student Movement*. Chicago: University of Chicago Press, 2004.
Zhu, Yapeng. *Zhufang zhidu gaige: zhengce chuangxin yu zhufang gongping* [Housing reform in China: Policy innovation and equality]. Guangzhou: Sun Yat-sen University Press, 2007.
Zuo, Cai (Vera). "Attitudes and Actions of Homeowner Activist Leaders in Contemporary China." *China Review* 16, no. 1 (2016): 151–67.

INDEX

Page numbers in *italics* indicate figures or tables.

activism: homeowners influenced by, 209; Ms. Hua reflecting on, 221; participation in, 281n4. *See also* citizen science; collective action; protests
administrative reconsideration (AR), 172, 289n18, 290n19; core action committee filing, 139; EPBs receiving, 142–43, 168; SEPA rejecting, 195–96
Administrative Reconsideration Law (1999), 289n18
air quality, 6, 43
anger, homeowners motivated by, 156–57
angry youths (*fenqing*): collective action lacked by, 235; Ms. Hua describing, 144, 153, 161, 235; "woke" compared with, 291n31
Anjuke (website), 54
anti-incinerator action: by communities, 126; in Community Marigold, 154–60; in Community Rose, 143–44; environmental awareness expanded through, 240; identity fostered through, 208–9; NIMBY movements compared with, 10–11
anti-incinerator banners, hanging from balconies, 140, *141*
anti-paraxylene protests, in Xiamen, 9–10
AR. *See* administrative reconsideration
associational life, 58–68; under authoritarianism, 256; civic skills developed through, 83; collective action and, 23, 84; in gated communities, 28, 253; identity formed through, 54; of middle-class, 18–19; of Rose homeowners, 106–7; shared space facilitating, 47; sports clubs catalyzing, 70–71; urban residents experiencing, 26. *See also* informal associational life
auntie (*dama*), 93
authoritarian government, middle-class and citizen science and, 205–7
authoritarianism, 15; associational life under, 256; civil society and, 256–57; collective action under, 27–28; convening publicly opposed under, 55; democracy contrasted with, 62–63; environmental organizing under, 253; informal associational life under, 48; middle-class homeowners under, 1; movement data restricted in, 20

INDEX

badminton club, 71
balconies, of homes: anti-incinerator banners hung from, 140, *141*; Meadow homeowners disliking, 75–76; property management monitoring, 283n24
banners, anti-incinerator, 140, *141*
BBC China, 149
Beijing, China, 1, 33, *34*, *50*, 280n61; air quality in, 43; area of homes built in, *32*; disposable income in, 31, *33*; garbage generated in, 45; gated communities transforming, 11; home prices in, *35*; incinerator construction in, 253–54; middle-class homeowners considering, 179; Municipal Administration Commission for, 134; Municipal and City Appearance Management Committee for, 210; Municipal Commission of Planning for, 283n15; Olympics in, 43, 110–11, 175, 285n15, 286n24. *See also* Community Marigold; Community Meadow; Community Pine; Community Rose; Community Willow
Mr. Bo (nonprofit staff member), 212, 241–42, 246–47, 295n6
Bondes, Maria, 249–50
booklet, on incinerator construction, 176–79
Boudet, Hilary, 15
Brady, Henry E., 15
Brazil, 266, 295n25
brick factory, 6, 170, 174, 233–34, 271n5
Brockovich, Erin, 292n1
burn (*shao*), 290n21
Business Commitment for Recycling, Brazil (*Compromisso Empresarial para Reciclagem*) (CEMPRE), 295n25
businesses, nonprofits contrasted with, 238

cancers, upper-respiratory, 174
cancer village, pollution causing, 280n61
capacity, civic. *See* civic capacity
car march, by Marigold homeowners, 119, 155
CEMPRE. *See* Business Commitment for Recycling

censorship, 298n31; homonyms used in avoiding, 290n21; of online forums, 141–42, 146–47, 287n34; protests and, 9–10, 242, 245; self-, 106
Central Committee of the Chinese Communist Party, 298n21
central government, Chinese: citizens served by, 218; environmental efforts of, 10; upper-middle-class in relation to, 287n32. *See also* Chinese Communist Party
Mr. Chen (environmental official), 210–11, 295n4
chengguan. *See* Urban Administrative and Law Enforcement Bureau
childcare centers, Small studying, 13–14
China, 8–9, 149, 198–200, 297n17; collective action repressed in, 15; Environmental Impact Assessment Law of, 166; environmental organizing in, 262–64, *263*; Guangzhou in, 40, 231, 256, 279n54; land ownership nationalized in, 28; Likeng in, 231; Nanjing in, 268; private residences transforming, 36; property tax considering, 299n10; Public Security Bureau in, 22, 56; quality of life in, 42; United States contrasted with, 20, 37, 266–67; urban population growing in, 31, *31*; Xiamen in, 9, 10, 290n25; Zhejiang in, 249. *See also* Beijing; central government; media; Urban Administrative and Law Enforcement Bureau
China Democratic League, 289n16
Chinese Academy of Sciences, 168
Chinese Academy of Social Sciences, 93
Chinese Communist Party, 286n16, 286n18, 289n16; Central Committee of, 298n21; local officials contrasted with, 115–16, *117*; residents disappointed in, 152–53; science elevated by, 164
Chinese People's Political Consultative Conference, 286n16
citizen journalists, 245, 298n27
citizen representatives, Ms. Hua praising, 246

INDEX

citizens: central government serving, 218; common contrasted with wealthy, 230–31; environmental awareness demonstrated by, 235; government contrasted with, 203–4
citizen science, 167–68, 177–78, 250, 266; authoritarian government and middle-class and, 205–7; Brockovich exemplifying, 292n1; in Community Marigold, 197–98; in Community Rose, 181–82; co-optation of, 201–5; core action committee focusing on, 143–44; data collection through, 162, 163–64; environmental organizations recognizing, 241; government officials responding to, 192–93; by homeowners, 25–26; by Ms. Hua, 186, 236; incinerator construction postponed by, 172–73; institutional channels contrasted with, 180; Mr. Lu prioritizing, 160, 222–23, 225, 237–38; Marigold homeowners shifting to, 292n39; by Meadow, Willow, and Pine homeowners, 249; protests contrasted by, 265; trash separation influenced by, 223–24; by upper-middle-class homeowners, 204–5; waste management influenced by, 219. *See also* data collection
citizenship, middle-class reconsidering, 37–38
civic capacity, 266–70; civic skills building, 14–15; of communities, 83–84; of gated communities, 12–14; of homeowners, 257–61; incinerator construction and, 255–56
civic duty: Mr. Lu embracing, 244; middle-class homeowners expanding, 84; state truncating, 17
civic education, in middle-class spaces, 49–50
civic life, organizing cultivating, 251
civic participation, Mr. Mou emphasizing, 268–69
civic responsibility: collective action fostering, 207; durable organizing and, 232–40; Ms. Hua demonstrating, 236–37; Meadow, Willow, and Pine

homeowners cultivating, 294n19; state shaping, 15, 18; urban residents and, 17; Mr. Zhao exemplifying, 226
civic skills, 28, 69, 249, 266; associational life developing, 83; civic capacity built through, 14–15; communities cultivating, 1; middle-class homeowners cultivating, 266; residents developing, 49. *See also* letter writing; petitioning
civil servants, 286n26
civil skills, informal associational life fostering, 69
civil society: authoritarianism and, 256–57; environmental, 241–48; formal organizations engaging with, 14
class, identity influenced by, 264
closing, collective, 65, 283n18
collective action: angry youths lacking, 235; associational life and, 23, 84; under authoritarianism, 27–28; China repressing, 15; civic responsibility fostered through, 207; communities differentiated by, 254–55; community leaders catalyzing, 25, 103; community representatives fostering, 124–25, 160; Community Rose lacking, 79, 121, 235–36; core action committee signifying, 129; environmental organizations avoiding, 295n24; government officials influenced by, 219–20; HOAs and, 74–83; Huang *laoshi* engaging in, 136; individual action contrasted with, 107, 121, 146; informal associational life fostering, 68; law and science and, 168–74; letter of mobilization demonstrating, 99–103; "mass incident" referring to, 287n31; Meadow and Willow homeowners planning, 127; by middle-class homeowners, 101, 197; mobilizing for, 99; against municipal environmental bureau, 16; in online spaces, 55–56; physical spaces influencing, 19; property management influenced by, 76; repression suppressing, 159; Rose homeowners lacking, 113–14, 154, 227; state tolerating, 9

collective closing, 65, 283n18
collective identity: gated communities forming, 11–13; of middle-class, 26; online forums developing, 22, 49
collective responsibility: accountability demonstrated through, 101; inclusiveness and, 99–103; individual action contrasted with, 105–6; landfills as, 121
collective sensemaking: community representatives influencing, 84–85; by homeowners, 96–97; of incinerator construction, 90–92; of landfill stench, 90–92; within middle-class spaces, 24–25; Rose homeowners lacking, 260; Mr. Zhao facilitating, 94–95
commodity apartments (*shangping fang*), 3
commodity residences, average prices of, 34
Communist Party. *See* Chinese Communist Party
communities, 24; anti-incinerator action by, 126; civic capacity of, 83–84; civic skills cultivated through, 1; collective action differentiating, 254–55; community leaders representing, 120–22; contamination in impoverished, 298n20; environmental organizing sustained by, 261; government and relationship to, 218–25; grievances shared within, 84; homeowners investing in, 99; identity cultivated by, 47; incinerator construction opposed by, 163; incinerators protested by, 8; institutional channels navigated by, 225; interaction lacked between, 241–42; letter-writing learned by, 260–61; meetings connecting, 129; neighborhoods contrasted with, 271n3; online forums connecting, 16, 57–58, 248–49; surveillance of, 3; Urban Administrative and Law Enforcement Bureau visiting, 150. *See also* gated communities
community (*shequ*), 41, 278n41

community-based organizations, government regulating, 41
Community Daffodil (pseudonym), 287n30, 291n36
Community Dandelion (pseudonym), 157, 158, 287n30, 291n34, 291n36, 292n37
community leaders, 84; collective action catalyzed by, 25, 103; communities represented by, 120–22; environmental organizations hosting, 242; government described by, 218; government officials influenced by, 122; Mr. Lu as, 119; perceptions of, 26; on policy implementation, 225
Community Marigold, in Beijing (pseudonym), 17, 21, 53–55, 54, 117–18; anti-incinerator action in, 154–60; citizen science in, 197–98; group purchases lacked in, 74; HOA of, 81–82, 240, 284n33; informal associational life lacked by, 114, 161; landfill stench lacked in, 121–22, 287n35; meetings lacked at, 73, 121–22; online forums of, 66–67, 115–16, 119, 260; protests by, 155–61; tragedy connecting, 81–82; upper-middle-class homeowners differentiating, 230. *See also* Marigold homeowners
Community Meadow, in Beijing (pseudonym), 4, 5, 21, 54, 298n31; community spaces within, 51–52; Community Willow connecting with, 57–58; informal community activities within, 87; online forums of, 98; trash separation at, 247–48. *See also* Meadow, Willow, and Pine homeowners; Meadow and Willow homeowners; Meadow homeowners
community networks, 106–7, 121, 126, 161
"Community Organization Reporting Trial Regulations," 41
community organizations, 40–41, 264, 279n57; nonprofits contrasted with, 262–63, 263; registration of, 262, 275n50; Ms. Yu on, 233. *See also* homeowners' associations

INDEX

Community Pine, in Beijing (pseudonym), 17, 21, 52, 54, 87, 282n11
community representatives, 94–99, 102–3, 110–14, 161–62, 232; collective action fostered by, 124–25, 160; collective sensemaking influenced by, 84–85; external concerns investigated by, 86; government officials engaging with, 260; homeowners engaged by, 87; Ms. Hua as, 143–44; Mr. Lu as, 157; physical spaces prioritized by, 93; volunteers managed by, 232; Mr. Zhao as, 285n7. *See also* community leaders
Community Rose, in Beijing (pseudonym), 1, 21, 52–53, 54, 103–6, 213; anti-incinerator action in, 143–44; citizen science in, 181–82; collective action lacked in, 79, 121, 235–36; community network benefiting, 161; government officials in conflict with, 197, 221; HOA sought by, 79–80; incinerator near, 214, 215; landfill not known to, 281n5; online forums for, 66, 71–73, 221–22; repression in, 193; scientific information not shared within, 109. *See also* Rose homeowners
community social organizations (*shequ shehui zuzhi*), 40–41
Community Willow, in Beijing (pseudonym), 5, 17, 21, 52, 54, 87; Community Meadow connecting with, 57–58; homeowners connecting in, 63; online forums for, 62, 64–65; organizing efforts lacked at, 65; property management of, 288n9; tap water at, 288n8. *See also* Willow homeowners
Compromisso Empresarial para Reciclagem. *See* Business Commitment for Recycling
core action committee, by Meadow and Willow homeowners, 131–32; AR filed by, 139; citizen science focused on by, 143–44; collective action signified by, 129; community networks drawn on by, 126; letters writing by, 133–34

dama. *See* auntie
danwei. *See* "work unit"
data collection, 180; homeowners empowered by, 165; by Ms. Hua, 153–54; through citizen science, 162, 163–64
democracy, authoritarianism contrasted with, 62–63
Deng Xiaoping, 29–30
detainment, of Marigold homeowners, 158–59
Ms. Ding (homeowner), 69, 93–94, 127–28, 132–33
Dingxin Zhao, 19
dioxins (pollutant), 174, 177, 183, 191, 194–95
disposable income, of homeowners: in Beijing, 31, 33; housing expenditures contrasted with, 276n16; in urban households, 32
district government: EIAs contradicting, 170; homeowners disappointed in, 135–36; Ms. Hua suing, 194–95; State Bureau for Letters and Visits contrasted with, 137
District Housing Administrative Department and Street Office, 284n29
durable organizing, civic responsibility and, 232–40

Earl, Jennifer, 16
Edwards, Michael, 15–16
EIAs. *See* environmental impact assessments
emigration, 152, 159–60
environmental awareness: anti-incinerator action expanding, 240; citizens demonstrating, 235; homeowners spread by, 241; of urban residents, 263
environmental capacity, 293n10
environmental degradation, middle-class homeowners impacted by, 42–43
environmental education, by homeowners, 209
Environmental Impact Assessment Law, China, 166

environmental impact assessments (EIAs): district government contradicted by, 170; Environmental Impact Assessment Law requiring, 166; homeowners questioning, 170; for incinerator construction, 139, 169, 195, 250, 293n9; of road-construction, 116; Rose homeowners requesting, 294n21; Mr. Wu obtaining, 168
Environmental Impact Evaluation Department, MEP, 210
environmental information, 166–67, 293n6
Environmental Information Disclosure, 166
environmental organizations: citizen science recognized by, 241; collective action avoided by, 295n24; community leaders hosted by, 242; homeowners interacting with, 246; SEPA sympathizing with, 206; trash separation experimented with by, 246–48
environmental organizing: under authoritarianism, 253; in China, 262–64, 263; communities sustaining, 261; Ms. Ding planning, 132–33; by homeowners, 21; by Meadow, Willow, and Pine homeowners, 243; by middle-class, 232, 266; by middle-class homeowners, 265; before social media, 248–49
Environmental Protection Bureaus (EPBs), 134–36, 139, 195, 290n19, 293n6, 293n9; AR received by, 142–43, 168; homeowners and, 145–46, 171–72; local officials controlling, 43–44; MEP contrasted with, 211–12; open-information measures contradicted by, 167; petitioning of, 170–71; SEPA confused for, 168; Ms. Yang suing, 196
environmental scholars, farmers helped by, 250
EPBs. *See* Environmental Protection Bureau

Fang (website), 54
farmers, 206; environmental scholars helping, 250; Meadow, Willow, and Pine homeowners contrasted with, 249–51, 299n34; middle-class contrasted with, 231; middle-class homeowners contrasted with, 227; public housing of, 212–13
fenhua. *See* incineration
fenqing. *See* angry youths
fenshao. *See* incineration
formal organizations, civil society engaged with by, 14
forums, online. *See* online forums
fuel, refuse-derived, 295n26
fundraising, homeowners embracing, 129–30

garbage, generated by Beijing, 45
gated communities, 4, 54, 281n3; associational life in, 28, 253; Beijing transformed by, 11; civic capacity of, 12–14; collective identity formed through, 11–13; HOAs of, 279n46, 279n48; layout of, 50; middle-class segregated by, 36–37; middle-class spaces created by, 12; property management opposed by, 82–83; residents privileged by, 12; as schools of democracy, 1, 13–14, 74–75, 225; in United States, 277n27
"Glue Gate" (tragedy), 82
GONGOs. *See* government-organized nongovernmental organizations
Gould, Roger V., 19
government, Chinese: authoritarian, 205–7; citizens contrasted with, 203–4; communities and relationship to, 218–25; community-based organizations regulated by, 41; community leaders describing, 218; environmental information provided by, 166–67; hotlines for complaints concerning, 182; incinerator construction finalized by, 208–9; migration controlled by, 297n16; science

influencing, 198; trash separation enforced by, 239. *See also* central government; Chinese Communist Party; district government; local officials; municipal government; state; State Environmental Protection Administration

government agencies, 147; homeowners impacted by, 136–37; institutional channels ignoring, 145; at meetings, 128; middle-class homeowners conceded to by, 164; petitioning of, 288n3; symposium held by, 138

government officials: citizen science responded to by, 192–93; collective action influencing, 219–20; community leaders influencing, 122; community representative engaging with, 260; Community Rose in conflict with, 197, 221; homeowners contrasted with, 109–10, 166, 185–86, 255, 286n17; Ms. Hua visited by, 153; institutional channels disregarded by, 142–43; local contrasted with central, 218–19; online forums repressed by, 151; protests accepted by, 272n10. *See also* local officials; police

government-organized nongovernmental organizations (GONGOs), 19, 224–25, 274n46

group purchases, 69, 74, 273n28

Guangzhou, China, 40, 231, 256, 279n54

Han, Hahrie, 124

HOAs. *See* homeowners' associations

homeowner research committee, municipal government influenced by, 223

homeowners, 24, 229, 272n19; activism influencing, 209; anger motivating, 156–57; associational life of, 38–40; citizen science by, 25–26; civic capacity of, 257–61; collective sensemaking by, 96–97; communities invested in by, 99; community representatives engaging, 87; Community Willow connecting, 63; connection between, 48–49; coordination among, 68; core action committee formed by, 126; data collection empowering, 165; district government disappointing, 135–36; educational campaigns by, 133–34; EIAs questioned by, 170; environmental awareness spread by, 241; environmental education by, 209; environmental organizations interacting with, 246; environmental organizing by, 21; EPBs and, 145–46, 171–72; fundraising embraced by, 129–30; government agencies impacting, 136–37; government officials contrasted with, 109–10, 166, 185–86, 255, 286n17; housing reforms influencing, 33; identity as, 46–47, 202; incinerator construction opposed by, 46, 98, 100–101, 123, 138, 296n6; incinerators investigated by, 155–56; institutional channels pursued by, 182; landfills not known to, 8, 97; Municipal and City Appearance Management Committee influenced by, 210; older contrasted with younger, 79–80; online forums trusted by, 286n20; perception of policy impact of, 218–25; police visiting, 150–51; pollution opposed by, 104–5; property management considered by, 128; property rights protected by, 58–59, 257–58; real estate developers monitored by, 35; scientific articles incorporated by, 289n13; self-organizing by, 40–42; self-perception of, 209; socioeconomic status and, 229; State Bureau for Letters and Visits considering, 137; strategies shared amongst, 75; tenants *versus*, 34; Urban Administrative and Law Enforcement Bureau visiting, 140–41; urban management bureau meeting with, 176; urban residents as, 30, 33. *See also* disposable income; middle-class homeowners; online forums

INDEX

homeowners' associations (HOAs), 28, 269, 278nn44–45; collective action and, 74–83; of Community Marigold, 81–82, 240, 284n33; of Community Rose, 79–80; of gated communities, 279n46, 279n48; Ms. Hua on, 284n32; landfill stench eclipsing, 77; Meadow homeowners seeking, 76–77; preparatory group of, 284n29; property management motivating, 277n20; RCs compared with, 278n41; registration struggled with by, 83; Regulations on Real Property Management permitting, 39; residents helped by, 39; Mr. Zhao prioritizing, 234

homonyms, censorship avoided by using, 290n21

hotlines, government complaint, 44–45, 145, 182, 184–85, 286n25

household registration (*hukou*), 228, 297n16

housing expenditures, disposable income contrasted with, 276n16

housing policy, middle-class homeowners created through, 28–30

housing reforms, 276n7; homeowners influenced by, 33; middle-class created by, 12, 27; property rights expanded by, 30

housing stability, 266–70

Ms. Hua (homeowner), 66, 72–73, 79–80, 104, 110, 227; activism reflected on by, 221; angry youths described by, 144, 153, 161, 235; citizen representatives praised by, 246; citizen science by, 186, 236; civic responsibility demonstrated by, 236–37; as community representative, 143–44; data collection by, 153–54; dioxins researched by, 191; district government sued by, 194–95; evidence collection by, 181–82; government officials visiting, 153; on HOAs, 284n32; incinerator construction suspected by, 294n20; incinerator toured by, 213–16, *214*, *215*; landfill photographed by, 111–12; lawsuit by, 196–97, 222, 296n8; medical incinerator concerning, 183–84; municipal planning office questioning, 113; online forums moderated by, 107–8; photographic documentation by, *187–91*; police questioning, 144–45; pollution photographed by, 244–45; protests distanced from by, 290n26; on socioeconomic status, 231; Urban Administrative and Law Enforcement Bureau negotiating with, 149; working-class excluded by, 230

Huang *laoshi* (homeowner), 138, 157, 167, 171, 218, 271n4; collective action engaged in by, 136; "Incinerator Case Study Analysis" presented by, 243; incinerators explained by, 178; on media, 298n27; pollution explained by, 168, 170; on recycling, 3–4, 220, 224–25; trash separation emphasized by, 219; Mr. Wu described by, 169

Hu Jintao, 286n18

hukou. *See* household registration

Ibadan, Nigeria, 266

identity: anti-incinerator action fostering, 208–9; associational life forming, 54; class influencing, 264; communities cultivating, 47; as homeowners, 46–47, 202; of middle-class, 225–32; as Willow homeowners, 64; work unit providing, 272n14. *See also* collective identity

incineration (*fenshao* or *fenhua*), 141, 300n12

"Incinerator Case Study Analysis" (PowerPoint presentation), 243

incinerator construction, 97, 287n36; in Beijing, 253–54; booklet on, 176–79; citizen science postponing, 172–73; civic capacity and, 255–56; collective sensemaking of, 90–92; communities opposing, 163; EIAs for, 139, 169, 195, 250, 293n9; government finalizing, 208–9; homeowners opposing, 46, 98, 100–101, 123, 138, 296n6; Ms. Hua suspecting, 294n20; landfill stench compared with, 120–21, 138;

INDEX

lawsuit against, 181–82; Mr. Lu on, 217, 295n29; Marigold homeowners opposing, 118, 122, 157, 200; Meadow, Willow, and Pine homeowners impacting, 212; Meadow homeowners discussing, *134*; outcomes of, 209–18; petitioning against, 175; public hearings proceeding, 216–17; socioeconomic status and, 206; trash separation reducing, 285n15; Ms. Yu frustrated by, 249
incinerators, 20; communities protesting, 8; Community Dandelion opposing, 291n34; homeowners investigating, 155–56; Huang *laoshi* explaining, 178; Ms. Hua touring, 213–16, *214*, *215*; Mr. Lu touring, 197–98, 201–2; Meadow homeowners protesting, 2; municipal government relocating, 179–80; near Community Rose, *214*, *215*; state planning, 45. *See also* anti-incinerator action; medical incinerator
income, disposable. *See* disposable income
individual action, collective action contrasted with, 105–7, 121, 146
infection, upper-respiratory, 194
informal associational life: under authoritarianism, 48; civil skills fostered through, 69; collective action fostered through, 68; Community Marigold lacking, 114, 161
informal associations, 12–15, 41
informal community activities, within Community Meadow, 87
institutional channels: citizen science contrasted with, 180; communities navigating, 225; government agencies ignoring, 145; government officials disregarding, 142–43; homeowners pursing, 182; Meadow and Willow homeowners utilizing, 139–40, 161–62. *See also* letter writing; petitioning

Jiang Zemin, 292n40
jieceng. *See* middle stratum
Jiusan Society. *See* September 3 Society
Johnson, Thomas, 249–50

kaifashang. *See* property developers

laji. *See* trash
landfills, 7, 227, 287n36; Mr. Chen investigating, 211; as collective responsibility, 121; expansion of, 118–19; homeowners not knowing about, 8, 97; Ms. Hua photographing, 111–12; middle-class homeowners plagued by, 253–54; migrant workers at, 228; Rose homeowners and, *148*, 148–49, 281n5; worker housing at, 6
landfill stench, 5–7, 45–46, 107, 285n6; collective sensemaking of, 90–92; Community Marigold lacking, 121–22, 287n35; HOAs eclipsed by, 77; incinerator construction compared with, 120–21, 138; Meadow, Willow, and Pine homeowners impacted by, 213, 259; online forums discussed by, 91–92, 94–95; pharmaceutical factory confusing, 106, 109–10, 113–14; pollution compared with, 101
land ownership, China nationalizing, 28
laoshi. *See* teacher
law, science and collective action and, 168–74
Law on the Prevention of Environmental Pollution Caused by Solid Waste, 280n65
lawsuit, by Ms. Hua, 196–97, 222, 296n8
Lazar, Sian, 264
leaders, community. *See* community leaders
letter writing, 115, 125; communities learning, 260–61; by core action committee, 133–34; at meetings, 61, 64
Ms. Liao, 288n8
"Life-and-Death Decisions of China's Urban Environment, The" (report), 198–200
Likeng, China, 231
"a little bit" (*shao*), 290n21
local officials: central government officials contrasted with, 218–19; Chinese Communist Party contrasted with, 115–16, 117; EPBs controlled by, 43–44; laws interpreted by, 280n65

INDEX

Mr. Lu (homeowner), 155–56, 158, 230–31, 291n35, 295n30; citizen science prioritized by, 160, 222–23, 225, 237–38; civic duty embraced by, 244; as community leader, 119; as community representative, 157; environmental company began by, 238–40, 298nn23–24; on incinerator construction, 217, 295n29; incinerators toured by, 197–98, 201–2; Meadow, Willow, and Pine homeowners contrasted with, 239; municipal government portraying, 202–3; on trash management, 203–4, 216–17, 223; urban management engineer contacted by, 200–201

Mao Tse-tung, 283n26
Marigold homeowners, 216–17, 296n9; car march by, 119, 155; citizen science shifted to by, 292n39; detainment of, 158–59; incinerator construction opposed by, 118, 122, 157, 200; layout influencing, 83; private space requested by, 67; property developers addressed by, 67–68; report by, 204; research committee formed by, 198–99; trash management influenced by, 204
mass demonstration, by Meadow, Willow, and Pine homeowners, 172
MBT. *See* mechanical biological treatment
McAdam, Doug, 15
Meadow, Willow, and Pine homeowners, 205, 211, 232–33; citizen science by, 249; civic responsibility cultivated by, 294n19; environmental organizing by, 243; farmers contrasted with, 249–51, 299n34; housing variation acknowledged by, 228–29; incinerator construction impacted by, 212; landfill stench impacting, 213, 259; Mr. Lu contrasted with, 239; mass demonstration by, 172; as middle-class, 226; police and, 294n13; policy meetings attended by, 220; political system understood by, 219

Meadow and Willow homeowners, 99–100, 102–3; collective action planned for by, 127; institutional channels utilized by, 139–40, 161–62; online forums connecting, 57–58; repression influencing, 143–44; "Supplementary Suggestions for the AR" by, 172; transportation projects discussed by, 88–89; working together exemplified by, 135. *See also* core action committee, by Meadow and Willow homeowners
Meadow homeowners, 89–90, 99–103; balconies disliked by, 75–76; group purchases by, 69; HOA sought by, 76–77; hot-pot gathering connecting, 60–61, 70; incinerator construction discussed by, *134*; incinerators opposed by, 2; Pine homeowners connecting through, 91–92; Willow homeowners consulting, 61
mechanical biological treatment (MBT), 295n26
media, Chinese, 297n17; Huang *laoshi* on, 298n27; protests covered by, 9; urban waste covered by, 202
medical incinerator, 182; Ms. Hua concerned by, 183–84; Ms. Yang investigating, 196; pharmaceutical factory differentiated from, 294n22; smoke emitted from, 186
meetings, of homeowners, 67–68, 120, 139; communities connecting through, 129; Community Marigold lacking, 73, 121–22; documentation of, 63, 131; government agencies at, 128; letter writing at, 61, 64; property management addressed at, 64; Mr. Zhao planning, 62, 78, 127–28
Ms. Meng, 158–59
MEP. *See* Ministry of Environmental Protection
microregion, work unit contrasted with, 274n2
middle-class, 4, *50*, 279n54; associational life of, 18–19; authoritarian government and citizen science and,

INDEX

205–7; citizenship reconsidering by, 37–38; collective identity of, 26; emigration considered by, 152; environmental organizing by, 232, 266; farmers contrasted with, 231; gated communities segregating, 36–37; housing reforms creating, 12, 27; identity of, 225–32; informal associations formed among, 13; Meadow, Willow, and Pine homeowners as, 226; middle stratum contrasted with, 278n38; organizing by, 264–66; rising, 36–38; socioeconomic status and, 292n40; working class contrasted with, 213

middle-class homeowners, 27, 37–40, 229, 270; under authoritarianism, 1; Beijing considered by, 179; civic duty expanded by, 84; civic skills cultivated by, 266; collective action by, 101, 197; collective closing by, 283n18; environmental degradation impacting, 42–43; environmental organizing by, 265; farmers contrasted with, 227; government agencies conceding to, 164; housing policy creating, 28–30; landfills plaguing, 253–54; property developers monitored by, 59; property rights exercised by, 35–36; public participation by, 65, 258; residential data on, *31*, 31–35, *32*, *33*, *34*; urban trash impacting, 45–46. *See also* upper-middle-class homeowners

middle-class spaces: civic education in, 49–50; collective sensemaking within, 24–25; gated communities creating, 12

middle stratum (*jieceng*), 278n38

migrant workers, at landfills, 228

migration, internal, 297n16

Ministry of Environmental Protection (MEP), 210–12, 289n10

mobilizing: for collective action, 99; community building contrasted with, 259; organizing contrasted with, 123–24, 144, 155–56, 285n8

Mr. Mou (homeowner), 267–70

Municipal Administration Commission, Beijing, 134

Municipal and City Appearance Management Committee, Beijing, 210

Municipal Commission of Planning, Beijing, 283n15

municipal environmental bureau, collective action against, 16

municipal government: homeowner research committee influencing, 223; incinerators relocated by, 179–80, 209–10; Mr. Lu portrayed by, 202–3; trash separation promoted by, 3–4

municipal planning office, Ms. Hua questioned by, 113

Nanjing, China, 268

National Environmental Inspection Office, MEP, 289n10

neighborhoods, communities contrasted with, 271n3

NGOs. *See* nongovernmental organizations

Nigeria, 266

NIMBY movements. *See* not in my back yard movements

nongovernmental organizations (NGOs), 19–20, 272n10, 298n26

nonprofits, 297n17; businesses contrasted with, 238; community organizations contrasted with, 262–63, *263*; workshops held by, 244

"Notice of the Ministry of Construction on Distributing Rules and Procedures of Homeowner Associations, The" (executive order), 278n45

not in my back yard (NIMBY) movements, 10–11, 40

officials. *See* government officials; local officials

Olympics, Beijing (2008), 43, 110–11, 175, 285n15, 286n24

online forums, of homeowners (*yezhu luntan*), 60, 258, 269, 274n48, 285n5, 296n9; censorship of, 141–42, 146–47, 287n34; collective identity developed

online forums (*continued*)
in, 22, 49; communities connected by, 16, 57–58, 248–49; of Community Marigold, 66–67, 115–16, 119, 260; of Community Meadow, 98; for Community Pine, 87, 282n11; for Community Rose, 66, 71–73, 221–22; for Community Willow, 62, 64–65; content categories structuring, 56–57; government officials repressing, 151; homeowners trusting, 286n20; Ms. Hua moderating, 107–8; landfill stench discussing, 91–92, 94–95; Meadow and Willow homeowners connecting through, 57–58; Olympics impacting, 110; property management not addressed by, 104; "small windows" included in, 56; Sohu running, 282n6, 283n22; without self-censorship, 106; Mr. Zhao facilitating, 88, 92–93, 129–30

Open Government Information Regulations Act, 166

open-information measures, EPBs contradicting, 167

organizing: civic life cultivated through, 251; durable, 232–40; by middle-class, 264–66; mobilizing contrasted with, 123–24, 144, 155–56, 285n8; Ms. Yu describing, 175; by Mr. Zhao, 70. *See also* environmental organizing

Pacific Gas and Electric Company, 292n1
Panyu, Guangzhou, China, 231
paraxylene, protests against, 9, 10
paraxylene factory, 290n25
parking, residents lacking, 51, 55
PCC. *See* Political Consultative Conference
People's Daily (newspaper), 298n21
petitioning, 125, 288n5; of EPBs, 170–71; of government agencies, 288n3; against incinerator construction, 175; by Mr. Wu, 234
petitioning (*xinfang*) system, 44
pharmaceutical factory, 111; landfill stench confused for, 106, 109–10, 113–14; medical incinerator differentiated from, 294n22; smoke emitted from, 187–91

physical spaces: collective action influenced by, 19; community representatives prioritizing, 93; online community spaces contrasted with, 58

Pine homeowners, Meadow homeowners connecting with, 91–92

police, *148*; homeowners visited by, 150–51; Ms. Hua questioned by, 144–45; Meadow, Willow, and Pine homeowners and, 294n13

policy implementation, community leaders on, 225

policy meetings, governmental, 220

political action, increase in reports of, 271n6

Political Consultative Conference (PCC), 135, 289n16

pollution, 233–34, 280n65, 293n11; air quality impacted by, 6; cancer village caused by, 280n61; costs associated with, 280n58; health effects of, 174; homeowners opposed to, 104–5; Huang *laoshi* explaining, 168, 170; Ms. Hua photographing, 244–45; landfill stench compared with, 101; mortality impacted by, 294n14; upper-respiratory infection and, 194; urban residents concerned by, 42

posters, Urban Administrative and Law Enforcement Bureau destroying, 191–92

privately owned housing, 272n15

private residences, China transformed by, 36

private space, Marigold homeowners requesting, 67

privatized housing, public housing replaced by, 257

property developers (*kaifashang*), 59, 67–68, 284n35

property management, 39, 74; balconies monitored by, 283n24; collective action influencing, 76; of Community Willow, 288n9; gated communities

INDEX

opposing, 82–83; HOAs motivated by, 277n20; homeowners considering, 128; meeting addressing, 64; online forums not addressing, 104
property-management companies (*wuyei* or *wuguan*), 50–51
property rights: homeowners protecting, 58–59, 257–58; housing reforms expanding, 30; middle-class homeowners exercising, 35–36
Property Rights Law (2007), 36
property tax, China considering, 299n10
protesters, demographics of, 292n37
protests: censorship and, 9–10, 242, 245; citizen science contrasted with, 265; by Community Marigold, 155–61; government officials accepting, 272n10; Ms. Hua distancing from, 290n26; media covering, 9; Olympics pausing, 175; repression of, 125–26, 149–50; residents continuing, 40; by Rose homeowners, *148*, 149–50; "take a stroll" referring to, 290n25. *See also* anti-incinerator action
public hearings, 166, 216–17
public housing, 300n18; of farmers, 212–13; privatized housing replacing, 257; rent at, 275n3
Public Security Bureau, China, 22, 56

Radio Free Asia (nonprofit organization), 297n17
RCs. *See* Residents' committees
RDT. *See* refuse-derived fuel
real estate developers, homeowners monitoring, 35
recycling, 242–43, 285n15; Huang *laoshi* on, 3–4, 220, 224–25; rubbish scavengers facilitating, 235, 296n11; in Taiwan, 296n10; urban residents participating in, 5
reforms, housing. *See* housing reforms
refuse-derived fuel (RDT), 295n26
registration: of community organizations, 262, 275n50; of community social organizations, 41; HOAs struggling with, 83; for households, 228, 297n16

"Regulations on Real Property" (governmental rule), 278n45
Regulations on Real Property Management (2003), 39
rent, at public housing, 275n3
representatives, community. *See* community representatives
repression, government, 158, 160; collective action suppressed by, 159; in Community Rose, 193; Meadow and Willow homeowners influenced by, 143–44; of protests, 125–26, 149–50; residents challenging, 151. *See also* censorship
research committee, Marigold homeowners forming, 198–99
residential community spaces, 3
residential complexes, property-management companies supplying, 50–51
residents, 46, 179; Chinese Communist Party disappointing, 152–53; civic skills developed by, 49; gated communities privileging, 12; HOAs helping, 39; parking lacked by, 51, 55; protests continued by, 40; RCs complained about by, 39; repression challenged by, 151; in shared community spaces, 51–52. *See also* homeowners; urban residents
Residents' committees (RCs): HOAs compared with, 278n41; residential spaces managed by, 38; residents complaining about, 39
responsibility, collective. *See* collective responsibility
Reuters (news agency), 297n17
rights-protection (*weiquan*), 35, 284n28
road-construction, 115–16
Rose homeowners, 205, 286n22; associational life of, 106–7; collective action lacked by, 113–14, 154, 227; collective sensemaking lacked by, 260; EIAs requested by, 294n21; landfills and, *148*, 148–49, 281n5; protests by, *148*, 148–49; working-class not considered by, 229

Mr. Ru (homeowner), 88–89, 135, 285n5, 289n14
rubbish scavengers (*shihuangzhe*), recycling facilitated by, 235, 296n11

Sampson, Robert J., 82
Schlozman, Kay Lehman, 15
schools of democracy, gated communities as, 1, 13–14, 74–75, 225, 255
science: Chinese Communist Party elevating, 164; government influenced by, 198; law and collective action and, 168–74. *See also* citizen science
Second Sino-Japanese War, 286n16
self-organizing, by homeowners, 40–42
sensemaking, collective. *See* collective sensemaking
SEPA. *See* State Environmental Protection Administration
September 3 Society (*Jiusan* Society), 286n16, 289n16
shangping fang (commodity apartments), 3
shao. *See* burn; "a little bit"
shared community spaces, 51–52
shequ. *See* community
shequ shehui zuzhi. *See* community social organization
skills, civic. *See* civic skills
Small, Mario Luis, 13–14, 281n4
"small windows" (*xiaochuang*), online forums including, 56
smoke, emissions of, 186, 187–91
social media, 22, 248–49
socioeconomic status: homeowners and, 229; Ms. Hua on, 231; incinerator construction and, 206; middle-class and, 292n40. *See also* middle-class; upper-middle-class homeowners
Sohu (internet company), 282n6, 283n22
Somers, Margaret R., 18
spaces: Marigold homeowners requesting private, 67; residential community, 3; shared community, 51–52. *See also* middle-class spaces; physical spaces

sports clubs, associational life catalyzed by, 70–71
state, Chinese: civic duty truncated by, 17; civic responsibility shaped by, 15, 18; collective action tolerated by, 9; environmental problems governed by, 43–45; housing privatized by, 29–30; incinerators planned by, 45. *See also* Chinese Communist Party; government, Chinese
State Bureau for Letters and Visits, 137
State Environmental Protection Administration (SEPA), 134, 172, 177, 289n10, 290n19; AR rejected by, 195–96; environmental organizations sympathized with by, 206; EPB confused for, 168. *See also* Ministry of Environmental Protection
stench, landfill. *See* landfill stench
Mr. Sui (homeowner), 193
"Supplementary Suggestions for the AR," by Willow and Meadow homeowners, 172
surveillance, of communities, 3

Taiwan, 294n16, 296n10
tap water, at Community Willow, 288n8
teacher (*laoshi*), 3
tenants, homeowners *versus*, 34
Tennessee Valley Authority (TVA), 297n13
Tiananmen student movement, 19
Tocqueville, Alexis de, 13
transportation projects, Meadow and Willow homeowners discussing, 88–89
trash (*laji*), 45–46, 296n11, 300n12
trash management: anti-incinerator voices incorporated by, 245–46; Mr. Lu on, 203–4, 216–17, 223; Marigold homeowners influencing, 204; specialists in, 201–2
trash processing, 178
trash separation, 220, 238, 240–43; citizen science influencing, 223–24;

at Community Meadow, 247–48;
environmental organizations
experimenting with, 246–48;
GONGOs promoting, 224–25;
government enforcing, 239; Huang
laoshi emphasizing, 219; incinerator
construction reduced by, 285n15;
municipal government promoting,
3–4
Tufekci, Zeynep, 16
TVA. *See* Tennessee Valley Authority

United States, 20, 37, 266–67, 277n27,
294n16
upper-middle-class homeowners: citizen
science by, 204–5; Community
Marigold differentiated by, 230;
emigration considered by, 160
upper-middle-class officials, central
government in relation to, 287n32
upper-respiratory cancers, Mr. Wu
tracking, 174
upper-respiratory infection, pollution
and, 194
Urban Administrative and Law
Enforcement Bureau (*chengguan*),
China, 21–22, 105, 221, 290n20,
290n27; communities visited by, 150;
homeowners visited by, 140–41; Ms.
Hua negotiating with, 149; posters
destroyed by, 191–92
urban households, disposable income
in, 32
urban management bureau, homeowners
meeting with, 176
urban population, increasing in China,
31, *31*
urban residents, 12, 264–65; associational
life experienced by, 26; civic
responsibility and, 17; environmental
awareness of, 263; as homeowners, 30,
33; pollution concerning, 42; recycling
not participated in by, 5; work unit
influencing, 11, 257
urban trash, 45–46, 296n11
urban waste, 20, 202

Verba, Sidney, 15
Villa Victoria, Small studying, 281n4

Ms. Wang (homeowner), 119
waste, urban, 20, 202
waste management, citizen science
influencing, 219
WeChat, 296n9
Week in China (publication), 297n17
weiquan. *See* rights-protection
Williams, Rhonda, 300n18
Willow homeowners, 70–71, 89–90,
99–103; identity as, 64; Meadow
homeowners consulting, 61; Mr. Zhao
polling, 77–78. *See also* Meadow,
Willow, and Pine homeowners;
Meadow and Willow homeowners
"woke" (term), "angry youths" compared
with, 291n31
working-class: Ms. Hua excluding,
230; middle-class contrasted with,
213; Rose homeowners considering,
229
work unit (*danwei*), 30, 268, 276n7;
allocation problems within, 29;
identity provided through, 272n14;
microregion contrasted with, 274n2;
privatization and, 276n11; social
organization structured by, 257; urban
residents influenced by, 11, 257
Mr. Wu (homeowner), 5–6, 58, 167,
219–20, 225; brick factory opposed by,
233–34; EIAs obtained by, 168; Huang
laoshi describing, 169; petitioning by,
234; upper-respiratory cancers tracked
by, 174
wuguan. *See* property-management
companies
wuyei. *See* property-management
companies

Ms. Xi (homeowner), 184–85
Xiamen, China, 9, 10, 290n25
xiaochuang. *See* "small windows"
xinfang. *See* petitioning
Xing Ying, 292n37

Yang, Guobin, 23
Ms. Yang (homeowner), 112–13, 194–96
yezhu luntan. See online forums
youths, angry. *See* angry youths
Ms. Yu (homeowner), 5, 60–61, 93–94, 98, 167–68, 232; on community organizations, 233; Ms. Ding befriended by, 69; incinerator construction frustrating, 249; organizing described by, 175; Mr. Zhao inspiring, 97
Yuan dynasty, 284n27

Zhang, Li, 37–38, 65, 258–59
Mr. Zhao (homeowner), 64, 120, 141–42, 246–47, 285n2; civic responsibility exemplified by, 226; collective closing proposed by, 65; collective sensemaking facilitated by, 94–95; as community representative, 285n7; HOAs prioritized by, 234; meetings planned by, 62, 78, 127–28; online forums facilitated by, 88, 92–93, 129–30; organizing by, 70; Willow homeowners polled by, 77–78; Ms. Yu inspired by, 97
Zhejiang, China, 249

GPSR Authorized Representative: Easy Access System Europe, Mustamäe tee 50, 10621 Tallinn, Estonia, gpsr.requests@easproject.com

www.ingramcontent.com/pod-product-compliance
Lightning Source LLC
Chambersburg PA
CBHW031232290426
44109CB00012B/258